ANGLISTISCHE FORSCHUNGEN
Band 428

Begründet von
Johannes Hoops

Herausgegeben von
Rüdiger Ahrens
Heinz Antor
Klaus Stierstorfer

NORA TUNKEL

Transcultural Imaginaries

History and Globalization in Contemporary Canadian Literature

Universitätsverlag
WINTER
Heidelberg

Bibliografische Information der Deutschen Nationalbibliothek
Die Deutsche Nationalbibliothek verzeichnet diese Publikation in der Deutschen Nationalbibliografie; detaillierte bibliografische Daten sind im Internet über *http://dnb.d-nb.de* abrufbar.

Gefördert durch die Österreichische Forschungsgemeinschaft

UMSCHLAGBILD
Philipp Kruder, *Untitled (peeling images)*, 2011.
Combine painting: acrylic, paper, magazine cutouts, crayon, and pencil on canvas, 80 x 60 cm.
Mit freundlicher Genehmigung des Künstlers.

ISBN 978-3-8253-6035-1

Imprimé en Allemagne · Printed in Germany
Druck: Memminger MedienCentrum, 87700 Memmingen
Gedruckt auf umweltfreundlichem, chlorfrei gebleichtem und alterungsbeständigem Papier

Den Verlag erreichen Sie im Internet unter:
www.winter-verlag.de

For my parents

And yet, if everything is moving where is here?
(Doreen Massey, *For Space*)

Contents

Preface

Many studies have been published on the postmodern historical novel. Probably an even greater number of works has dealt with Canada's postcolonial literary and cultural pluralities, as well as with the problem of the coordination of these pluralities in the ever-complex processes of identity construction. Literature that rewrites history is not only one of the most popular and diversified literary forms in Canadian literature, it is also a genre in which many other current issues seem to have found their culmination and possibly even a turning point at the turn of the twenty-first century. The English-language historical novel, in its contemporary form, and especially in the context of the plurilingual and multicultural Canadian literary scene, thus represents a genre difficult to map. It should not come as a great surprise that the means for the discussion and theorization of these developments, too, have become increasingly divergent, while at the same time older approaches no longer suffice to grasp the incredible variety of these recent literary expressions.

This study presents a reading of Canadian historical fictions written in English. Contemporary Canadian writers and critics alike can look back on what might today already be referred to as a 'tradition' of postmodern rewritings of the past. At the same time, voices have been calling for a newly revised vision of postnational Canadian identities – literary voices that, in the process, have also probed established forms of historical fiction. The popularity and academic interest in the genre over the past decades is rooted in its generic diversity, and, in the Canadian case, in its potential to unite so many issues that lie at the center of Canadian society, culture, and literature. These "kaleidoscopic histories," as they are called in the introduction to this work (with reference to an early essay by Canadian author-critic Janice Kulyk-Keefer), is analyzed via the concept of *transcultural imaginaries*, which is explicated in the middle section of this study. Hereby, an attempt is made to explore interdisciplinary theoretical approaches and alternative possibilities to a contemporaneous literary analysis. Increasingly, in the light of globalizing forces that have had an impact on so many spheres of life, it has become insufficient to talk about present-day literature in terms of postmodernism or postcolonialism only – at least not in the same way it was practiced in theoretical discussions between approximately the 1970s and 1990s. Global transformations have not only had influence on our economies, but also on how we conceive and struggle to understand our existence in the fast-paced, seemingly open-ended spaces of modernity. The following pages suggest some tentative reflections and observations on developments within Canadian literature as well as possible new modes of approaching them, in the hope that they might resonate with future interdisciplinary, critical innovations of the twenty-first century.

The years spent on the development of this study have led through various stages of thought and frustration regarding the overwhelming amount of ideas, issues, arguments, and problems related to this field of inquiry. And then, too, some time has passed between the writing and the publication of this work – a period of time long enough for the highly productive academia to develop new insights, which could not all be incorporated in time. I have tried to come as close as possible to a representative discussion of contemporary anglophone historical fiction in Canada; however, the result is still only an incomplete fraction due to the obvious spatial and academic limits of this work. In my attempt to find new ways to read and situate recent historical fiction, it must be emphasized that all the topics discussed, and especially the introduction of the concept of transcultural imaginaries, must be seen as approximations that do not strive for ultimate interpretations, a final solution, nor a one-way argumentation, insofar as many of the discussed themes – and, more importantly, the analyzed texts themselves – defy clear-cut categorizations and single-perspective analyses.

There are ways to cross a minefield, but they are hard to detect and will never lead straight across. I would like to express my sincere gratefulness to those who accompanied me during my quest.

Introduction: Kaleidoscopic Histories

In January 2007, CBC launched a TV-series entitled *Little Mosque On the Prairie* – a series set in a small town in Saskatchewan, in which a Muslim and non-Muslim community live together, peacefully, in spite of the expected comical misunderstandings and caricatured disputes. The series, which attracted an unanticipated average of 1.23 million viewers in the initial weeks of its first season (MacDonald, "The Battle of the Small Town," *online resource*, n.pag.)[1], attempted to comically deconstruct prejudices fostered in the aftermath of 9/11. The reactions to its launch were diverse[2], however, as a commercialized expression of Canada's multicultural policy for respectful treatment across racial, religious, and ethnic divides, it also spurred some reviewers' optimism and nationalist pride:

> Right. But this is Canada and we pride ourselves on being more tolerant here. We roll our eyes at the paranoia and ignorance of Americans, and believe it's legitimate to strengthen our tolerance by poking gentle fun at those who are intolerant, and even by poking fun at Muslims. After all, they are kinda wacky, like the rest of us. [...]
>
> And the important thing is this – popular, consequential Canadian TV is a vigorous demonstration of our difference from the United States in our attitudes and national character. Trailer Park Boys celebrates lowlifes, dope-smoking and all manner of vulgarity. Da Vinci's Inquest and Intelligence deal with the reality of a dope economy and the thin line between cops and criminals. Corner Gas asserts that there's wonderful entertainment in the most gentle, never-nasty humour.
>
> The topics and the substance of these shows stand as rejections of the U.S. network style and preoccupations. Little Mosque on the Prairie is nobly in that Canadian tradition. The U.S. media can huff and puff in wonder, but this is who we are, and we're fine with it, thanks. And thanks to CBC for doing its job. (Doyle, "Little Mosque is gloriously Canadian," *online resource*, n.pag.)

One may ask, what does this TV series have to do with the analysis of historical fiction? To understand the approaches brought forward in the following chapters, we ought to ask instead: does the mere existence of this series have anything to do with contemporary Canadian literature? Or rather: might the fact that this inter- or even

[1] Gayle MacDonald, "The battle of the small-town, high-stakes, big-network sitcoms just got a whole lot hotter, with two pivotal writers deciding to abandon CTV's Corner for CBC's Prairie." For a further review cf. Carter "Muslim Sitcom debuts in Canada." Both *online resources*, n.pag.

[2] Several reviews are available on the producer's homepage (Westwind Pictures): http://home.westwind pictures.com/index.html; the writer and creator of the series, Zarqa Nawaz, also at one occasion answered the questions posed by readers of the *Globe and Mail* online – the reactions and questions of the readership ranged from high praise to racist comments. Rebecca Dube, "Little Mosque on the Prairie: Globe and Mail Update," *online resource*, n.pag.

trans-cultural, culturally dialogic series was so popular in Canada and embraced by its society, be related to developments in Canadian postmodern, postcolonial, and postnational fictions, many of which negotiate the complex processes of cultural identifications (and constructions of identities) through the re-interpretations of histories and memories? This study, which is not a work in media studies but rather an interdisciplinary literary analysis, argues that they are related and, in the process of doing so, searches for ways to conceptualize such a reading from various angles.

In the introduction to her anthology of multicultural Canadian literature, *Making a Difference*, Smaro Kamboureli notes in 1996 that what led her to the compilation of the collection was the desire for a "questioning of representation" ("Introduction" 3). As she explains,

> I believe that we reside forever within the realm of representation: we represent ourselves through language and through our bodies, but we also see ourselves represented by others. No image, no story, no anthology can represent us or others without bringing into play—serious play—differing contexts, places, or people. (3)

Historical fiction, and its major constituents, history and memory, which according to the renowned Canadian critic Linda Hutcheon "[are] the defining feature of Canadian postmodernism" ("Multicultural Furor" 13), are all about representation. Fictions that rewrite history, create a web of images of "contexts, places, or people" of the past, which we use to identify, not only ourselves and others, but also others within ourselves, or the self in the other, and so on. However, if throughout the second half of the twentieth century it seemed essential to emphasize the necessity to continuously question representations, this insistence no longer appears to be a primary concern in contemporary fictions (especially those dealing with the past). The constructed nature of the mimetic act and the awareness of its continuing flux and temporality has become a literary commonplace in post-postmodern times.

This book builds upon the, by now established, insight that histories, identities, and cultures are both intricately interwoven constructs and continuous processes:

> Identities are seen to be instituted in particular social and historical contexts, to be strategic fictions, having to react to changing circumstances, and therefore subject to continuous change and reconfiguration. [...] identities cannot be self-sufficient: they are in fact instituted through the play of differences, constituted in and through their multiple relations to other identities. (Bennett, Grossberg, and Morris 173)

The present-day expression of these socio-identitary complexities in a multicultural nation under the impact of globalization and migration stand in a challenging relation and are echoed in the works of Canadian authors of historical fictions, which devise multiple ways of dealing with cultural differences – varying from resistance to the acceptance of cultural dialogue and exchange. This study primarily focuses on English-language Canadian literature, while Québécois and other French-language literature in Canada are alluded to only on occasion. Within this realm it works toward an understanding of these current expressions by studying developments in critical approaches to identities and the interpretation of fictionalized histories in Canada, considering theories on globalization, cultural memories, and the triad of multi-, inter, and trans-culturalism. Most importantly, the herein-developed concept of transcultural imaginaries tries to link all these theoretical concerns and, by connecting the dots, negotiates a new reading of contemporary literature. The idea of a transcultural imaginary thereby assumes that societies might have developed a realm within their identitary consciences (and sub-consciences) that – more than before – allows for an exchange of cultural images and representations across socially constructed fields of difference. It is against the same backdrop that Janice Kulyk Keefer proposed the revision of the long-time popular image of the 'Canadian Mosaic,' which is until today frequently used to refer to Canada's multicultural society. Her alternative, the kaleidoscope, indeed suggests a more fitting representation of contemporary identitary and literary complexities.

> The problem with our much vaunted "mosaic" is not that it insists upon fragmentation, but rather that it privileges separation and rigidity over interconnection, mobility, and transformation. Furthermore, the notion of mosaic demands that someone – Artist or Authority – decree which figures are accorded more or less power and importance in the overall design. Perhaps a better model would be that of a kaleidoscope, which suggest ongoing process rather than fixed and finished product. The user of the kaleidoscope can make out of separate pieces, none of which is more privileged than any other, a changing and infinitely variable pattern precisely because the shifts parts are held together by the cylinder that contains them. And that cylinder, passed from hand to hand, we may liken to Canada itself, with its wilderness and farms, its towns and cities, its people, and the values enshrined in our Charter of Rights. (16)

In order to trace the development of this specific kaleidoscopic nature in Candian literature the first part of this study attempts to come to terms with the two major related contextual issues at stake: the socio-historical and theoretical foil against which the fictional rewritings of history became popular in English-speaking Canada in the twentieth century and the consequently diversified (and therefore in some regards complicated) development of this form of literature and its generic features. The first chapter (Chapter 1, "Construction Identities – Fictionalizing Histories") connects the highly diffuse emergence of a self-reformed, twentieth-century Canadian identity with the equally meandering evolvement of historical fiction in Canada. It does so by taking into consideration various, increasingly influential, critical approaches to the construction of identities, the role of memory and past in identity formation, especially in relation to Canadian multiculturalism and postcolonialism. The study of the variety of critical and contextual influences on the development of the genre and its critical reception in Canada leads to a filtering of various evolutionary 'phases' or rather sets of discourses that dominantly marked the genre in the past fifty years – as becomes obvious from the numerous examples given. This overview of developments, though in some instances rather general, is imperative in order to understand contemporary anglophone Canadian historical fiction and the later reflections on the transcultural; this becomes even more obvious in the investigation of more recent ruptures and problems with critical theories on historical fictions and the reception of the genre in Canadian literature.

In the next section of the first part (Chapter 2, "Past – Memory – Fictions") I turn toward a more specific discussion of diverse approaches to the genre of historical fiction. After scanning some less-recently developed, however fairly well-established, theories, I eventually focus on current, and in some cases, highly-innovative perspectives. One of the main issues concerns how to deal with the genre in general and more particularly within Canadian literature, today – a question not easily answered due to the immense variety of texts produced in this genre. I will distance myself from definitions and long established discourses on the traditional (romantic) historical novel, and concentrate on a critical reading of Linda Hutcheon's postmodern, 'historiographic metafiction,' as well as the studies that followed. I will then direct my attention to recent scholarly attempts to deal with Canadian historical fiction. It is the aim of not only this part, but this study as a whole, to highlight the diversification and fluidity of this genre and the difficulties that therefore exist to grasp it in its wholeness. In response to this situation, I propose the introduction of the transitory generic category 'fictions of the past' in the final section of Part 1. This contemporary expression of historical fiction, which will be richly exemplified, stands under the influence of novel sets of the already mentioned critical as well as contextual discourses, thereby producing new specificities, all of which resonate with a reading of transcultural imaginaries.

The second part of this study turns to a rather different, though equally relevant critical realm: it introduces a number of recent interdisciplinary perspectives on literary and cultural developments that lay bare the potential for innovative insights into Canadian 'fictions of the past.' One crucial step in my movement of arguments, brought together in the assessment of diverse approaches in Chapter 3, consists of an attempt to explore the impact of globalization on literature. At the same time it is an attempt to adopt an interdisciplinary perspective on the forces at work in literature and literary theory today. The insight gained by these socio-, cultural-anthropological, and philosophical investigations, as purported by the contemporary thinkers Ulf Hannerz, Arjun Appadurai, Homi Bhabha, and others, will be complemented in the chapter that follows – entitled "From Multi to Trans: the Rise of Transcultural Studies" – by an overview of and critical inquiry into transcultural theories. This rather young field of research has been highly popularized yet not unanimously abstracted in recent years. Here, my perspective is one that is strongly informed by the Cuban heritage of the term and its later emergence in the Québecois intellectual scene, as well as by more recent European scholarly approaches; for example, the approach brought forward by Frank Schulze-Engler. Due to the increasing confusion that has accompanied the growing popularity of this term, it will be necessary to retrace its origins and to dissect recent diverging strands within and across disciplines. In this chapter, I also attempt to clarify the relationship of transculturalism as a socio-literary approach to the political concept and cultural manifestations of multiculturalism. These discussions will ultimately lead to my major theoretical suggestions, which are introduced in Chapter 5: the 'concept' of *transcultural imaginary*. It is here that I venture to explicate the relevance of this concept for literary analyses within various theoretical contexts.

Part 3, "Case Studies," represents the crucial, analytical part of this book. The corpus of analyzed texts is comprised of Canadian historical fictions written in English that were published approximately in or after 2000[3] and includes fictional texts of all lengths and inclinations. The choice of works analyzed in Chapter 6, 7, and 8 reflects a far more liberal understanding of the genre of historical fiction in comparison to that firmly rooted in the popular mind as well as that conventionally promoted by literary scholars; the case studies include readings of works spanning one-and-a-half centuries, several generations and at least three continents, such as Dionne Brand's *At the Full and Change of the Moon* that represents a view of the African Diaspora; novels that combine present and historical settings, as in Jane Urquhart's *A Map of Glass*; the linguistically experimental and highly poetic novel of George Elliott Clarke, *George and Rue*, as well as one collection of short stories that rewrites (partially pre-) 'Canadian' history from Native perspectives. As it is my intention to carry out a broad examination of English Canadian fictions of the past, I have included a variety of works grouped into three literary 'spheres' – the selection and distribution of which is obvious, though never conclusive. Within each of the first two groups (migrant writers, non-migrant writers), I selected works by three representative authors, the analysis of which should provide a well-balanced insight. This mode of selection is slightly altered in the final analytical chapter, in which the reading of one book, the above-mentioned collection of contributions by nine Aboriginal authors, stands at the center of our interest.

The conclusion ("The Necessity and Ethics of Trans") finally recapitulates the major observations made throughout the first three parts of this study. Here, I will return to some of the initial questions asked and consider unresolved aspects in order to evaluate possible further developments and new directions for the writing and study of these "kaleidoscopic histories" and the many issues involved.

> All my life I have loved travelling at night, with a companion, each of us discussing and sharing the known and the familiar behaviour of the other. It's like a villanelle, this inclination of going back to events in our past, the way the villanelle's form refuses to move forward in a linear development, circling instead at those familiar moments of emotion. Only the rereading counts, Nabokov said. So the strange form of that belfry, turning onto itself again and again, felt familiar to me. For we live with those retrievals from childhood that coalesce and echo throughout our lives, the way shattered pieces of glass in a kaleidoscope reappear in new forms and are songlike in their refrains and rhymes, making up a single monologue. We live permanently in the recurrence of our own stories, whatever story we tell. (Ondaatje, *Divisadero* 136)

[3] There is only one work included that was published before 2000, Dionne Brand's *At the Full and Change of the Moon* (1999).

Part 1 – Socio-historical, Theoretical, and Generic Layers

In 1971, in the introduction to a collection of essays on the Canadian imagination, Northrop Frye spoke of the already then "famous Canadian problem of identity" (i). Many scholars have been concerned with the issue[1]; Frye was the most prominent of them, the one whose comments would resonate in the criticism of decades to come. One of the most fascinating aspects of Frye's critical work, as Branko Gorjup has noted, is the discrepancy between the broad scale and internationality of his major criticism and the nationalist, environmental-regional determinism of his less-extensive Canadian content studies ("Introduction" 9-10).

Despite the limits that have long been discerned in Frye's cultural criticism, considering the time it was written in, which was an important period in Canada's national cultural development, it appears perspicuous and justified that Frye would observe that "the creative instinct has a great deal to do with the assertion of territorial rights" (*Bush Garden* i) and that he grew aware of the fact that "the question of identity is primarily a cultural and imaginative question" (i).[2] During the decades in which Frye published his essays, this very expression of a Canadian imagination found itself at a crossroads – as if between two states of aggregation. On one side, Canada's imperial past as a settler-invader colony devoted to the British Crown, can be accepted as a fact, but the question that has remained unresolved to the present concerns the other side: what is it that the Canadian nation developed into in the twentieth and twenty-first centuries? Is Canada, its culture, and imagination, postmodern, postcolonial or postnational? Or has Canada even reached a further new phase of socio-cultural development? These questions stand at the center of the following chapters. I will first explore them from a more general historical perspective, considering them as the context in which the genre of historical fiction developed and then subsequently relate them to this particular literary development. In doing so, this section intends to capture the expansion and blasting of former limits attributed to the Canadian (historical and literary) imagination, thus questioning the regionalist perspective expressed in the second half of Frye's above-quoted observation: "The question of identity is primarily a cultural and imaginative question, and there is always something vegetable about imagination, something sharply limited in range" (*Bush Garden* i).

[1] Some of these scholars will be discussed on the following pages: George Woodcock, E.K. Brown, Marshall McLuhan, George Grant, Margaret Atwood, Eli Mandel, W.H. New, E.D. Blodgett, David Staines, Jonathan Kertzer, just to name a few. Cf. also Redekop, "Canadian literary criticism and the idea of a national literature"; Rosenthal "English-Canadian Literary Theory and Literary Criticism"; and, more specifically on N. Frye, M. McLuhan and H.A. Innis: Staines, "The Pillars of Canadian Non-Fiction."

[2] The essays in *The Bush Garden* date from 1940 to 1969; though of course Frye also published essays on the Canadian imagination in later periods, cf. Frye, *Mythologyzing Canada*. A recent publication – Vol. 12 of Frye's collected works – edited by David Staines and Jean O'Grady unites Frye's writing on Canada in one volume. See O'Grady and Staines; cf. also Zacharasiewicz, "Rereading Frye."

1 Constructing Identities – Fictionalizing Histories

When speaking of Canadian identity and discussing its evolution, where might one begin? Should one set off in the 1950s and 60s, when the search for a unified Canadian national consciousness was becoming increasingly pressing and Canadians were becoming more self-aware (even if this awareness might have been ambiguous in the light of the influence exerted by the presence of its strong Southern neighbor)?[1] Should one focus on the period of the two World Wars – in the course of which Canadian battalions played decisive roles in several battles and Canadian nationalism was cemented by the many lives lost? Or should one move even further back in time and take the Confederation in 1867 or even the Battle of the Plains of Abraham in 1759 as point of departure? Already this listing of specific historical moments points to two crucial considerations: on one hand, it calls to mind the fact that we must differentiate between definitions of nation, as geographical region, political entity, or unifying culture as determinants for a national consciousness.[2] On the other hand, it recalls the obvious importance of history for the construction and discussion of any identity – no matter the social scope.[3] This history, which is so essential for our understanding of who we are, obviously changes according to the context and perspective, as does our judgment of what aspects should be considered as viable information for the construction of our identity. It is necessary to go back in time to satisfy our need to understand the present via the parameters of cause and effect, as an outcome of a linear development – one of the reasons that already made historical fiction a popular genre in the nineteenth century in Canada that fostered the emergence of a – then still colonial – national consciousness.

Thus the question of where to begin the discussion of Canadian identity, in my case, results in the following limitation: my interest circles around the evolution of an 'independent' (i.e. non-colonial) Canadian cultural imagination toward its contemporary, transcultural ramifications, a focus on some influential, socio-cultural and literary critical publications of the twentieth century will and must suffice as point of departure. The fact that Canada went through one of its most decisive periods of formation and transgression from one form or context of identity to another somewhere in the middle of the twentieth century, as mentioned above, marks this limitation. Yet when I speak of these two configurations, by which I refer to what might be called colonial on the one hand, and postmodern, multicultural Canada on the other, I am of course reducing a highly complex and multi-leveled process, one that might not even be fully completed today, to its two basic components.

[1] As already noted elsewhere, the observations of the following chapters (and in the whole book) are primarily based on the criticism of developments in *anglophone* Canadian cultures, identities and literatures.

[2] Cf. Donna Bennett, "Nation and its Discontents" 15.

[3] Thus, this claim refers to individual, communal, and national forms of identity alike.

"Disunity as Unity" – The Emergence of the Canadian Mosaic

In many ways, the impression one gets from the study of Canada's most significant decade in the twentieth century, from 1960 to 1970, is a conflicting one. It was the decade of the Centennial Celebrations, marking the 100th anniversary of the Canadian confederation as well as the decade of the '67 Expo – both representative of an open and optimistic Canadian nation.[4] It was however also the decade in which George Grant's *Lament for a Nation* was published and in which Northrop Frye famously concluded the nation's first substantial and comprehensive literary history, the *Literary History of Canada* edited by Carl Klinck, with an evaluation of Canada's closed-minded, fearsome 'garrison mentality' as a consequence of the "bewilderment of a neglected child" ("Conclusion" 70).
Both published in 1965, Grant's much discussed *Lament* as well as Carl Klinck's collection of studies on "Canadian Literature in English," as the subtitle was formulated, were highly influential for the intellectual discourse on, and the engagement in, the emergence of a Canadian national consciousness. While George Grant was troubled by the disappearance of a Canadian nationalism (strongly based on former colonial values), due to the increasing impact of modernization, or if one wants, Americanization, many Canadian critics (and Quebecois, in their own right) were in fact only beginning to establish a 'modern' and independent national consciousness, as reflected in the search for a distinctly 'Canadian' literature (or littérature quebecoise, in the other case). However, both were still, in a way, very far from realizing and acknowledging the dimensions of what was later to be included into a reformed and postmodern understanding of Canadian identity or rather, identit*ies*, such as Indigenous cultures and other disregarded literatures and histories of marginalized groups.

As Andrew Potter observes in his detailed introduction to the 40th Anniversary edition of George Grant's *Lament for a Nation*, it is important to keep in mind that the study was written in a very specific period of Canadian development (Potter ix-xvi, xxvii-xxxii) – one might even argue, in a pivotal moment, which in my eyes makes it a still very acute document for the understanding of Canadian (national) identity. Much has changed since the time in which Grant lamented the death of the Canadian nation – however, in certain aspects, Grant proved to be a clever and foresighted observer: even though his focus was on Canada's political situation, he also indirectly commented on general global developments that were only taking their beginning at the time of publication.

> To lament is to cry out at the death or at the dying of something loved. This lament mourns the end of Canada as a sovereign state. Political laments are not usual in the age of progress, because most people think that society always moves forward to better

[4] Cp. also Grace, "Sociopolitical and Cultural Developments from 1967 to the Present." The Expo was the highlight of the Centennial Celebrations; see "Expo 67," *online resource,* n.pag., and "Centennial Celebrations, 1967," *online resource,* n.pag.

> things. Lamentation is not an indulgence in despair or cynicism. In a lament for a child's death, there is not only pain and regret, but also celebration of passed good. (Grant 4)

After World War II, Canada was finally beginning to let go of its former colonial dependency[5] but was still struggling to find its hold in a "period of somewhat desultory soul-searching, and the country approached its centennial in a mood of growing collective self-doubt" (Potter xii); only shortly after freeing itself from the colonial embrace, Canada let a new one-sided economic and military alliance take a firm grip: this time with the rising superpower south of its border. The political and economic self-doubt and uncertainty of the Canadian post-World War nation is echoed in the dramatic political figure of John Diefenbaker, whose political failure, as Grant argued, was not Diefenbaker's fault, as a person (as suggested in the dominant public discourse) but lay in his too conservative, pro-British nationalist policies that displeased the (pro-American) liberalism of the elites, which as Grant feared would endanger Canada's further evolvement as a nation: "Not only did Diefenbaker lose political support in industrial Canada; he did not accomplish the work of economic nationalism. The "northern vision" was a pleasant extra, but no substitute for national survival. During his years in office, American control grew at a quickening rate" (Grant 16).
As Andrew Potter points out, Grant's work must also be seen in relation to his background. Both his grandfathers were upper middle class representatives of British-colonial descent, hard-working, conservative, nationalist servants to the crown. One of his maternal aunts was married to the first Canadian-born governor general of the twentieth century, Vincent Massey – like him, most of Grant's close family can be linked to a conservative nationalism that was not opposed to the former – of course idealized – imperial rule. However, what lies at the heart of Grant's arguments is primarily a strongly anti-modernist sentiment. In his study, Grant argues – in four thematic steps, as Potter describes (xxiii-xxiv) – that Canada would for various reasons disappear as a regional culture in the age of progress[6], mainly due to its 'problematic' geographical location and history (67-95).

> Canada has ceased to be a nation, but its formal political existence will not end quickly. Our social and economic blending into the empire will continue apace, but political union will probably be delayed. Some international catastrophe or great shift of power might speed up this process. (85)

[5] In 1931 the Statute of Westminster separated legislation of the dominions from the mother country; from 1947 on the Governor General took over all representative authority (1 Oct 1947, George VI formally delegated to the Governor General all the sovereign's authority in Canada). In 1952 Vincent Massey became the first Canadian-born to be appointed Governor General. After him an alternating mode between anglophone and francophone governors was established. Cf. "Constitutional History," *online resource,* n.pag.: "The Federal System – Towards Constitutional Independence."

[6] "It is worth noting that the idea behind the first premise – that technology is a universal homogenizing force – was an almost uncriticized assumption in mainstream social sciences from the 1950s to the 1970s," Potter xxiv.

Obviously Canada has *not* disappeared but the effect that globalization (as a cultural phenomenon) has had on the nation is greater than one might have imagined, and certainly different – though not completely contrary – to what Grant had professed.[7] Grant lamented the take-over of modernity, of technological society, and of global (or in his case still continental) culture, thought, and politics at the cost of local culture and nation. In many ways Grant was right with his predictions, but what he could not foresee was the possibility of 'plurality' that would become the Canadian nation's political and constitutional trademark. Even if he was right to some degree in his fear of the homogenizing nature of globalization and the 'sameness' that comes along with the increasing networking and connectedness of the world, he did not and could not have predicted that the local and the global could very well exist side by side and would even become reciprocal forces.

Interestingly, one thing that George Grant believed John Diefenbaker's political career lacked was his failure to communicate with the nationalist intellectuals of his time – one of whom was Northrop Frye.[8] On the one hand one might be tempted to ask, how aware Grant himself was of cultural nationalists like Northrop Frye and his followers, who were, at the time of the *Lament*, already working hard on the project of defining Canadian distinctiveness, especially in contrast to the American cultural landscape. On the other hand, in the "Introduction to the Carleton Library Edition" written by George Grant and published in 1970, he does acknowledge, "indeed, nationalism has a clearer place" (lxxi), yet he still dreads the processes of homogenization, which accompagny modernity and, which would, according to him, falsify Canada's inherent sense of common good and public order, as opposed to U.S.-capitalist individualism.[9] In effect, Grant's fears were not justified, especially considering recent studies on the social, cultural, and political differences between the U.S. and Canada.[10] The step that Grant failed to make as an intellectual, even though he must not be blamed for doing otherwise in his time, was to overcome his personal incompatible, oppositional concepts of 'common good' versus 'individualism,' and in an expanded perspective, of nationalism versus liberalism.[11] It is in this very longing for a national unity that would distinguish Canada not only from its imperialist mother country but even more so from its strong southern neighbor, which stood at the core not only of Grant's but also of

[7] For a further contested alternative approach to the regional development of North America – an approach in which, too, Canada disappears from the map as separate cultural entity, cf. Joel Garreau, *The Nine Nations of North America* (1981, New York: Avon, 1982). Garreau writes, for instance: "Canada, which is little save moose, Aleuts, and energy wealth north of the allegedly temperate strip along its border with the United States, has migraines about losing its 'identity.' It shouldn't. Apart from French-speaking Québec, which is properly a nation unto itself, Canada shares five perfectly respectable and different identities with the Northern United States," 6.

[8] Potter also mentions W.L. Morton and Donald Creighton, "Introduction" xix.

[9] Cf. Potter's comments, lxxiii.

[10] For a recent example of popular criticism on this issue, cp. Michael Adams, *Fire & Ice: The United States, Canada, and the Myth of Converging Values* (Toronto: Penguin Canada, 2003).

[11] As Potter remarks, Grant was simply also a conservative thinker, closer to present day American right politicians than to any contemporary "post-modern" Canadian nationalists, "Introduction" lxii.

Northrop Frye's work and which would be drastically re-interpreted less than a decade later.

Two decades earlier, around the 1940s, two internationally acclaimed 'Canadian' literary critics and contemporaries of Northrop Frye, George Woodcock and E. K. Brown, had been publishing critical essays on the state of Canadian literature.[12] Both of them had independently underlined that Canada lacked not a literature but rather literary awareness as well as structures and institutions that would promote it. Such observations, together with the results collected in the famous Massey Report, led to the creation of the Canada Council in 1957 ("Massey Report," *online resource*, n.pag.). It is in this context, that one must position the publication of Carl Klinck's *Literary History of Canada*, which was generously subsidized by the Canada Council[13], as an integral element and turning point for the establishment of an early after-colonial (though still strongly Anglo-centric) Canadian literary identity.

Of the many high-profiled contributions to the *Literary History*, Frye's essay was to become the most legendary and most dominant critical treatise of Canadian (literary) identity in the decades that followed, in terms of the critical discourse that it provoked. Many of the concepts and thoughts that Frye presented in his conclusion were strongly influenced by his thorough "classical" literary education, and today, some are considered out-dated. Other aspects however are surprisingly insightful – in fact, from a present day perspective, some of Frye's ideas seem to be more relevant than some critics have realized. Frye has always been respected for his work within Canadian academia[14], however, the potential of some of his observations has remained unnoticed due to the wave of "thematic criticism" that was substantially influenced by his work[15], and which was received with considerable skepticism.[16]

One of the main arguments in Frye's Canadian criticism is that Canada's literature and the patterns that can be discerned within it can be directly related to the country's environment – thus the explanation of the "garrison mentality" as a result of the hostile wilderness of the Canadian North. In spite of the shortcomings of this argument, we must recall that Frye was well aware of the limitations of his critical perspective; but not only that, he also made by far more forward-looking observations than some of his critics ever acknowledged. In the renowned "Conclusion" he writes:

[12] Cf. Brown, *Responses and Evaluation: Essays On Canada*; herein especially "Our Neglect of Our Literature" 72-77; and Woodcock, *Odysseus Ever Returning: Essays on Canadian Writers and Writing*; especially "Away From Lost Worlds" 1-11: 2, and "Views of Canadian Criticism" 130-143.

[13] Cf. the comments in introduction to the Literary History, Klinck xii.

[14] Cp. Mandel, "Northrop Frye and the Canadian Literary Tradition" (despite its overall critical tone); Rosenthal 292-295; Staines, "The Pillars of Canadian Non-Fiction"; Toye mentions "the influence Frye wielded, not only on academic and public critics alike but also, in a much more direct way, on Canadian poets" ("Frye" 151-152), 152.

[15] Margaret Atwood, together with D.G.Jones and John Moss were regarded as the major representatives of Canadian thematic criticism; cf. Cameron 111-116.

[16] Cf. Bennett, "Nation and its Discontents"; Redekop, "Canadian Literary Criticism"; Cameron, "Theory and Criticsm"; for a critical essay written directly in response to this issue, cp. Mandel, "Northrop Frye and the Canadian Literary Tradition."

> This book is a collection of essays in cultural history, and of the general principles of cultural history we still know relatively little. It is, of course, closely related to political and to economic history, but it is a separate and definable subject in itself. Like other kinds of history, it has its own themes of exploration, settlement, and development, but these themes relate to a *social imagination that explores and settles and develops*, and the *imagination has its own rhythms of growth as well as its own modes of expression* [my emphasis]. (64)

If this perspective of an evolving and non-stable imagination is seen not in terms of one but of several sets of myths, narratives, symbols, histories, and similar textual systems of meaning, and is furthermore not limited to the national but expanded to all organizing units and differentiating principles of society, we arrive at the presently more acute concept of the cultural imaginary that is the basis of the present study.[17] Obviously, what Frye decoded as a garrison mentality in the 1960s, was just about to develop into the opposite extreme in precisely that period – the Canadian imagination was opening up. In contrast to some of his followers, however, Frye also recognized that changes would occur: "as the twentieth century advances and Canadian society takes a firmer grip of its environment, it becomes easier to assume the role of an individual separated in standards and attitudes from the community" ("Conclusion" 83). Finally, it is interesting to observe that despite the (danger of) stereotyping that many of his opponents accused him of, Northrop Frye was – certainly influenced by the work of Marshall McLuhan[18] – on his side sensing how modernity was changing the world and how, in time, new factors would come to determine the Canadian imaginary:

> The writers of the last decade, at least, have begun to write in a world which is post-Canadian, as it is post-American, post-British, and post everything except the world itself. There are no provinces in the empire of aeroplane and television, and no physical separation from the centres of culture, such as they are. Sensibility is no longer dependent on a specific environment or even on sense experience itself. […][contemporary writing] foreshadows the poetry of the future, when physical nature has retreated to outer space and only individual and society are left as effective factors in the imagination. ("Conclusion" 94-95)

The impact which certain aspects of Northrop Frye's criticism had on the following generations of Canadian critics was enormous – an impact that expressed itself in the two extremes of the critical romanticizing of his environmental determinism, as opposed to the complete renouncement of a generalizing thematic approach in favor of formal(istic) analyses of specific texts. Thematic criticism was strongly connected to the emergence of an extended form of nationalism throughout the 1970s, which sought to define Canada's (literary and cultural) postcolonial unity and uniqueness (in opposition to the U.S.) – however, in terms of its regional setting and colonial history.[19]

[17] At this point of my discussion, it should suffice to mention that – in very simplified terms – I regard *imaginary* as a sum of various levels and forms of *imagination*. A more detailed approximation to the term *imaginary* is attempted in Chapter 5.

[18] Cf. Staines, "Three Pillars of Canadian Non-Fiction" 21.

[19] Cp. also Potter's section entitled "Post-Modern Canada" in the Introduction to Grant, lvi-lxiv.

In 1972 the most renowned of this emerging generation of critics, Margaret Atwood, who is today a widely appreciated international author, published her literary study *Survival*. It was to become the 'representative' text of thematic criticism. Even if it was instantly criticized by up-and-coming, post-Saussurean scholars such as Eli Mandel, the one thing that Atwood's *Thematic Guide to Canadian Literature* did achieve was to bring Canadian Literature to the attention of the Canadian public, the 'masses.' As Donna Bennett puts it, "what is remarkable about *Survival* is that, despite that negative characterization of Canadians and of the central content of Canadian literature, the book became that rarest of commodities: a best-selling work of literary criticism" ("Nation and its Discontents" 20).

Similar to Frye's "mythologies," by which she was of course strongly influenced, Atwood advanced a view that presupposed the influence of (environmentally determined) constructs of the mind on literature: "I'm talking about Canada as a state of mind, as the space you inhabit not just with your body but with your head" (18). The problem about Atwood's *Survival* and the other thematic studies that appeared at the time was that they were attempting to define a single Canadian identity. The fact that they were taking for granted only one specific imaginary and thus forcing upon the country a constructed national unity, was increasingly being questioned in academic circles in terms of the ideological stances that this view purported and simply did not resonate with Canada's changing social and political reality.

This kind of cultural nationalism communicated in works such as *Survival* was not only criticized by post-Saussurean critics but also far earlier by an older generation of scholars, already mentioned before, notably George Woodcock. In 1964, he had already pointed out the partially naïve quality of Canada's earliest national(ist) writer, Hugh MacLennan, and his stereotyped literary visions[20] as opposed to the important, high-standard contributions of immigrant Canadians or Canadians having lived outside Canada:

> The most vital Canadian fiction of the post-war period has in fact been written by people who, for various regional or traditional reasons, belong outside the main stream of ordinary Canadian life which writers like MacLennan and Callaghan seek to represent. There are, first, the immigrants. ("Away from Lost Worlds" 5)[21]

The socio-cultural developments and the presence of strong alternative identities and imaginaries became an even more pressing reality in Canada of the 1970s. Of course, Canada has always been a nation of cultural diversity: the indigenous population, at first, had been subdued and altered through cultural contact not by one, but by two 'founding nations' – the French and the British. They were gradually but steadily joined by more immigrants with mostly European roots and, in the late nineteenth and at the

[20] In fact he writes: "He is preoccupied to the point of obsession with the fact of living in a time and in a country where a sense of separate identity as a nation is emerging; [...] Every novel MacLennan has written is marred by the didacticism which such preoccupations force upon him" ("Away From Lost Worlds" 4).

[21] Woodcock continues his enumeration of remarkable contributions to post-war Canadian literature by highlighting the works written by members of the Jewish literary community and by regional writers, 5-10.

beginning of the twentieth century, by immigrants from Asia. However, as the rigid (and racist) immigration restrictions of the early twentieth century were slowly being reformed, increasing social plurality led to 'diversity' becoming an acknowledged part of Canadian identity; in fact, it was seen as *the* possibility to differentiate Canadian from US-'melting-pot' identity – a development that was facilitated and furthered by political measures such as the Act on Bilingualism and the Multiculturalism Act between the 1970s and 80s.[22] Donna Bennett points out other long-time existing cultural dividing lines within the nation (regionalism, rural/urban divide), in addition to those growing out of socio-political fluctuations, which also contributed to what she calls "tensions" or, in Fryean manner, "centri-fugal forces" ("Nation and Its Discontents" 21) that made a unifying vision of Canadian imaginaries, at least when the time *Survival* was published, impossible to accept for many critics. In addition to these much discussed socio-cultural and political changes of context, the academia was flooded by new emerging leftist, post-structural and post-modern critical perspectives on issues such as minorities, the "commonwealth," and feminism, which shifted the emphasis to the particularities and alternative sides of culture, thus rejecting the sweeping master narratives implied in former theoretical analyses.

In one of his later essays, Northrop Frye claimed that Canada "ha[d] passed from a pre-national to a post-national phase without ever becoming a nation" ("Culture as Interpenetration" 137); in his introduction to Frye's essay-collection, Branko Gorjup picks up on this argument by suggesting that Frye's criticism in fact was representative of this very transitional phase ("Introduction" 13). As the discussion in this chapter has shown, one may claim that George Grant's *Lament for a Nation* and Margaret Atwood's *Survival*, too, must be seen as providing momentum to this intermediary moment. Though their criticism in many ways did not completely succeed in acknowledging the complexity and plurality of an emerging Canadian nationhood, it nonetheless represented the onset of certain basic cultural-theoretical ideas mirroring the awareness of the strong impact of modernity (Grant, Frye) and the importance of an imaginary or "mythology" (Frye, Atwood), ideas that would be neglected by Canadian studies criticism in the years to come. One major point that misled these transition-phase critics was the assumption that Canada could and was to be defined in terms of unity. Only slowly did those concerned with the issue become aware of the fact that disunity would be the more convenient and appropriate concept for Canadian identity, an idea most convincingly and famously expressed in Robert Kroetsch's essay, "Disunity as Unity: A Canadian Strategy": "To make a long story disunited, let me assert here that I'm suggesting that Canadians cannot agree on what their metanarrative is. I am suggesting that, in some perverse way, this very falling apart of our story is what holds our story – and us – together" (1).

[22] For an overview of these developments, cf. Cameron, "Introduction" xv-xxiv; for a study devoted to the issue of immigration policies in Canada, cf. Gerald E. Dirks, *Canada's Refugee Policy: Indifference or Opportunism?* (Montreal: McGill-Queen's UP, 1977).

Canada's Beautiful Losers? De/Construction-sites, Pasts and Posts

It is difficult to judge exactly how long Canada's transitory phase from colonial dependency and identitary insecurity to postcolonial national and literary self-confidence lasted. What we can say with some certainty is that well into the 1980s Canadian literature and identity remained somewhat of a de/construction site. The building of a 'nation' required the construction and later the postmodern deconstruction of cultural memories and histories: thus, stories of the past had to be told, and re-told to achieve a sense of unity, even if it eventually was to consist of disunity. In the earlier cited passage, Robert Kroetsch captures the complexity of Canadian identity by referring to it as a "story" – a uniting disunited story. To think about and speak of identities in terms of narratives is a convenient metaphor, as it conveys the basic presence of fictional elements in these constructs of self, for both the individual mind and social collective alike. These narratives of a past, which imply a causal relationship to particular (not necessarily chronological) points in time and justify the present existence, needed to be told in order for a Canadian cultural identity to be established.[23] Thus begins the story of historical fiction in Canada.

'Traditional' historical fictions of the nineteenth and early twentieth centuries in Canada were strongly inspired by the British and American models.[24] They were predominantly occupied with the myth of a non-existent Canadian past. The desire for a unique, identity-founding history grew, while the continuing impact of British and American literary trends generally remained and led to the popularity of romantic historical novels.[25] Thus, the genre offered a possibility to narrate and imagine a past that some feared did not exist and consequently became a forum for the construction of an emerging Canadian, albeit initially a rather colonial, identity: "Nation, history, narrative, and rhetoric confirm each other so forcefully that it is easy to forget how hard nineteenth-century writers worked to establish the connections" (Kertzer 12).

Despite the fact that the genre became highly popular in the form of romantic historical novels, interestingly, little worth mentioning happened in the genre in the early years of what I refer to as the nation's "transitory phase" of identity formation. The most important reason for this was that historical fiction was, around the turn of the century and into the early twentieth century, not regarded as a serious form of literary

[23] Cp. the most often cited quotation by Robert Kroetsch: "In as sense, we haven't got an identity until somebody tells our story. The fiction makes us real." Kroetsch, et al., *Creation* (Toronto: New Press, 1970), 63, qtd. in Pache 71. And as Margaret Atwood observes in her lecture on Canadian historical fictions: "And I think that's part of the interest for writers and readers of Canadian historical fiction, now: by taking a long hard look backwards, we place ourselves," *In Search of Alias Grace* 27.

[24] As, for example, the works of Sir Walter Scott in Britain and James Fenimore Cooper in the U.S.

[25] Cf. Duffy, *Sounding the Iceberg*; Hatch, "Change and the Concept of History in the Canadian Historical Novel"; and MacLulich, "Romances of the New World."

expression but rather as trivial and non-representative.[26] As Edward A. McCourt observed in the Dalhousie Review in 1946:

> But in Canada the historical novel has always been escapist, and except in one or two instances continues to be so. And so long as Canadian novelists continue in the traditional mode, established by Longfellow and his immediate successors so long will the Canadian historical novel be no more than an idle tale written to while away an idle hour. (36)

Critics were slow in raising their voices toward a more differentiated, less "escapist" understanding of Canada's colonial past, thereby insisting on an awareness of the constructedness and subjectivity of history and other (master-) narratives on a larger scale.[27] As Margaret Atwood put it in her renowned Bronfman Lecture in which she discussed Canadian historical fiction and her personal experiences in writing *Alias Grace* half a century later: "The lure of the Canadian past for the writers of my generation, has been partly the lure of the unmentionable—the mysterious, the buried, the forgotten, the discarded, the taboo" (19).

Though largely due to the historical circumstance of a developing Canadian national identity that led to the emergence of historical fiction as a means for *post*colonial "placement" (Atwood, *In Search* 27), there were also a fair amount of theoretical movements that exerted a considerable impact on the re-emerging genre of historical fiction. One of these movements was the narrative approach to historiography, heralded by its critically acclaimed, and influential pioneer, Hayden White, whose theories revolutionized the belief in the objectivity of historical research:[28]

> A more profound consequence of the current reconfiguration of historiography, however, is that not only might historical fiction be much more informative and much closer epistemologically to historical writing than most historians would be inclined to concede, but also history might be closer to fiction. In the wake of the work of Hayden White, Michel Foucault, Dominick LaCapra and other theorists, the distinction between history and fiction has increasingly been blurred, and the conception of history as a kind

[26] Additionally one might mention the fact that Canada is often said to have skipped the modern phase, thus moving directly from the romanticist and realist phase to postmodernism: "Canadian literature evolved directly from Victorian into postmodern. Morley Callaghan [Hemingway's contemporary and colleague] went to Paris and met the Modern writers; he, for Canada, experienced the real and symbolic encounter; he, heroically and successfully resisted. The country that invented Marshall McLuhan and Northrop Frye did so by not ever being Modern," Kroetsch, "A Canadian Issue," *Labyrinths of Voice: Conversations with Robert Kroetsch*, eds. Shirley Neuman and Robert Wilson (Edmonton: NeWest Press, 1982), 111-112; qtd. in Pache 75.

[27] Cf. Wyile, *Speculative Fictions* 13; Atwood, *In Search* 7-19.

[28] His most influential works were *Metahistory: The Historical Imagination in Nineteenth-Century Europe* (Baltimore: Johns Hopkins UP, 1973), and *Tropics of Discourse: Essays in Cultural Criticism* (Baltimore: Johns Hopkins UP, 1978). It is worth mentioning, as explained in the Penguin *Dictionary of Critical Theory*, that "White borrows the term 'metahistory' from an essay by Frye (1957) and his study of historiography is heavily influenced by the Canadian critic's archetypal theory of literary genre and the theory of pregeneric tropes that underpins it" ("White, Hayden V." 396).

> of mimesis of the past has been substantially questioned, if not quite staked through the heart. (Wyile, *Speaking* 13)

Canada's postmodern and postcolonial momentum of the 1960s to 1980s can well be linked to the emerging critical viewpoints of the twentieth century, such as the reform of scientific perspectives on the writing of history and the influence of discursive interpretations of the structures of society[29] as human constructs of the mind. Historical fiction suddenly represented the ideal medium to rewrite the former colonial dominant historical narratives and consequently to reinterpret the Canadian identity built upon them. The genre offered the possibility to open up perspectives on alternative histories and multicultural collective memories, the entirety of which would form part of the basis of the "new" Canadian identity.[30]

Due to the diverse strands of theoretical and contextual impacts, criticism of Canadian historical fiction, too, has been remarkably disunited, even if there have been obvious tendencies in approaches echoing developments in the genre itself, as well as general theoretical currents. Even if it appears almost impossible to produce a structured mapping of this criticism, the task is all the more necessary as potential insights into the more recent changes in the genre have also remained obscure. A closer look at the muddle of critical theories related to historical fiction does allow for the filtering of certain nuances in discourses that determined the genre in the twentieth century. Overall, interest of studies on historical fiction over the past thirty years, as well as the dispositions, especially of historical novels, published in the past forty years, reveal a pattern that can be broken down into three major "evolutionary" phases and five (or even more depending on the perspective) of what we might refer to as critical "discourses." The first two phases, which comprise the second half of the twentieth century, shall be discussed in the following part of this section; the subsequent phase toward the turn of the twentieth and beginning of the twenty-first centuries, reflecting the most recent developments, will mainly be discussed in Chapter 3 as well as in the second theoretical part of this study. Several literary examples illustrate the predominant influence of a specific discourse within the respective phases; nonetheless, most examples given do not fit into just one category, as all the mentioned critical forces – though possibly to varying degrees – operate simultaneously and continuously.

Discourses on Postmodern Aesthetics and on Historiography

The first phase of development in contemporary Canadian historical fiction, and from various perspectives its most dominant, even up to the present day, is characterized by two major discourses, which reflect the postmodern alteration in philosophical-political, mimetic, and aesthetic thought on the one hand, and post-structural, epistemological viewpoints on the other. The closeness and partial interdependence between these two discourses became most evident in relation to the prominent term of "historiographic

[29] This is meant to include everything from power relations, over political strategies and networks, and other social forces as well as memories and histories.

[30] Cf. Bölling, "Einleitung," *History in the Making* 9-24; Klooss, "Forms of Identity Construction," and Wyile, *Speculative Fictions* xi, 6.

metafiction," which has been used since the 1980s.[31] However, it makes sense to look at them separately, too, despite their natural interaction, in order to discern specific tendencies within Canadian historical novels. Thus, earlier examples of historical fiction, prototypically postmodern, primarily lean toward the challenge of mimetic practices and illusions through deconstructive narrative strategies and irony. One of the earliest examples of this, to a large degree, metafictional discourse in Canadian historical fiction is Leonard Cohen's *Beautiful Losers* (1966), even though – and here the interdependence of these to theoretic-discursive levels becomes obvious – it also has historiographic features, in that the protagonist of the novel re-visualizes the life of the Mohawk saint Kateri Tekakwitha.[32] Just as strongly representative and predominantly self-reflexive in a postmodern sense, particularly in its terms of deconstructive narrative strategy, is Timothy Findley's novel *Famous Last Words*, published in 1981. Again, strong emphasis is also placed on alternative historical perspectives (mainly on WWII) through personal memory and retelling. The major focus is nonetheless on the questioning of mimetic and epistemological experience.[33]

In novels situated within the historiographic discourse – and also already moving beyond, thus not only questioning historical mimesis as a mode of writing but in fact thematically focusing on repressed pasts[34] – which became more prominent from the late seventies onwards, the aesthetic issue is already less dominant; increasingly a stronger accent is put on the re-writing of history per se, the deconstruction of master narratives, and the challenge of collective memory through counter memory, as well as the questioning of historical documents. The most prominent of which is Michael Ondaatje's much discussed exemplary novel *In the Skin of A Lion* (1987), which – despite the fact that it also displays a challenging narrative structure – dominantly reflects the rewriting of history through the depiction of neglected social groups, immigrants, working class people, women, as essential protagonists in the history of one of Canada's most vibrant cities, Toronto.

Similarly, most of Rudy Wiebe's novels have, throughout his long and prolific writing career, been primarily concerned with the probing of marginalized histories, ranging

[31] The term "historiographic metafiction" (originally introduced by Linda Hutcheon) is problematic, as analyzed i.e. by Gordon Bölling, who proposes the term of meta-historical fiction, which as he argues, is more precise. Cf. Bölling, "Metafiktion im historischen Roman," *History in the Making* 31-57, especially 56.

[32] 1656-1680, "known as the Lily of the Mohawks, first North American native candidate for sainthood," "Tekakwitha, Kateri," *online resource,* n.pag.

[33] Cp. Bölling, *History in the Making* 123-172; Hatch, "Change and the Concept of History"; Sparling, "History and Identity"; Klooss "Forms of Identity Construction"; Lucking, *The Serpent's Part* 13-39; although I might emphasize again that in these critical studies, the two discourses are not treated separately.

[34] "Historiographic" is in criticism on historical fiction mostly used to refer to both fiction that rewrites *H*istory by situating (often marginal) historical settings and personae at the center of the work, as well as to fiction that has the writing (or research) of history as a self-reflexive theme. It is through this double usage that the expression is linked to the postmodern deconstructive aesthetics and politics, and that makes it difficult to distillate specific tendencies. Cp. Wyile, *Speculative Fictions* 5.

from Native perspectives on the past (in the *Temptations of Big Bear* (1973))[35] to alternative interpretations of Canadian history in *A Discovery of Strangers* (1994; on the first Franklin expedition) and readings of his own family's European heritage (*The Blue Mountains of China* (1970) and more recently *Sweeter Than All the World* (2001)). Finally, George Bowering's *Burning Water* (1980), another well-known novel of the early phase, can be classified as a novel that equally represents both discourses. On one hand, it is aesthetically quite deconstructive and self-reflexive, as is most clearly expressed in the famous prologue:

> We cannot tell a story that leaves us outside, and when I say we, I include you. But in order to include you, I feel that I cannot spend the pages saying *I* to a second person. Therefore let us say *he*, and stand together looking at them. We are making a story, after all, as we always have been, standing and speaking together to make up a history, a real historical fiction. (Bowering 10)

On the other hand, it focuses on the ironic re-imagining of Canadian history through the depiction of the voyages and relations of the prominent historical figure of George Vancouver. At the time of their publication, many of these novels were met with criticism and skepticism – a fact that is most significantly reflected in one of the few earlier detailed accounts of the development of Canadian historical fiction, Dennis Duffy's 1981 work *Sounding the Iceberg*, which only marginally discusses postmodern expressions of the genre. Despite this example of a more hesitant and doubtful reception, the discourses on postmodern aesthetics and historiography, as reflected in novels of the period, were increasingly becoming influential for the genre and for the re- and de-construction of Canadian literary and national identity. By the time Linda Hutcheon published her groundbreaking studies on this new generic expression[36], which would remain formative for literary studies over the following decades, other new discourses were already emerging and considerably altering Canada's historical fictions.

Postcolonial and Subaltern Discourses

In the second half of the twentieth century, major Canadian political innovations were beginning to change formerly one-(or two-)sided perspectives on the nation's cultural plurality: the Royal Commission on Bilingualism and Biculturalism (1963-69), which would eventually lead to the introduction of the Official Languages Act (1969 and 1988) and finally the Multiculturalism Act in 1988. Multiculturalism as a political and, later, identitary concept was developing into the new defining paradigm against former colonial identity and the emerging impact of Canada's southern neighbor, the United States. These socio-political strategies were the result of a post-World War II era that had seen the varying adaptations of policies of immigration and, consequently, of the Canadian demographic landscape.[37] This very transformation of Canada's society and

[35] In *Listening to Old Woman Speak*, Laura Smyth Groening criticizes Wiebe's historiographic metafiction, as it does not, according to her, deconstruct stereotypes of Aboriginal peoples; Groening 105-119.

[36] Cf., for example, Hutcheon, *The Canadian Postmodern*.

[37] Cp. Cameron, "Introduction" xv-xxiv; Berry and Laponce, *Ethnicity and Culture in Canada*.

politics, and the increasing awareness of this change, triggered the interest of writers, readers and critics alike in the stories, and even more so, the histories of primarily ethnically and racially othered, as well as generally repressed groups. Thus, the critical reception of literature within Canada was not only centering on innovative postmodern experimentalism, but was, by the 1980s, increasingly turning its attention toward authors and texts dealing with the subject of diverse ethnic and racial heritage, representing Canadian (multi)cultural realities other than that of the two founding nations.

Once again, despite the closeness of what I am referring to as postcolonial and subaltern discourses, especially in the literature that expresses these discourses, it makes sense to distinguish the two tendencies. Subaltern (or minority) discourse, in contrast to postcolonial discourse, not only touches upon issues of ethnicity and race[38], but also with the growing influence of feminist criticism on definitions and the subject of gender and other potential markers of difference and marginalization; the postcolonial tendency developed out of very specific historical contexts, which it therefore strongly reflects, and is thus more strongly linked to political and cultural circumstances as well as to a whole theoretical school.

Certainly, the emergence of "Commonwealth studies," later evolving into postcolonial studies, had a strengthening impact on the emergence of the general subaltern discourse – although it might just as well have been a mutual influence.[39] In any case, two aspects must be highlighted in this respect: postcolonial studies have developed, and constantly make use of, a specific terminology and theories which helped promote the theoretical perspectives in question; but, at the same time, they can only be used with certain limitations in the Canadian context. Here, the postcolonial discourse fit in well with the chorus of increasingly important critical voices calling for the deconstruction of colonial identity; thus, postcolonialism as a wide-scale theoretical approach had, and still has, a certain impact on the desire and methodological possibilities for the understanding of the immense diversity of authors from former colonies, whether East-Indian, Native Canadian or any other; on the level of the specific Canadian postcolonial situation, the discourse led most prominently to the overall questioning of nation and belonging, and to the institutionalization of general critical perspectives on dominant collective identities.[40]

If the postmodern and historiographic phase started in late 1960s, the postcolonial and subaltern discourses became dominant during the 1980s, as formal aesthetics seemed increasingly less pressing. Joy Kogawa's *Obasan* (1981) is often referred to as the most important and earliest "revisionist" historical novel in Canada.[41] Through the depiction

[38] This also includes Native voices; Aboriginal writing is often subsumed under the postcolonial discourse – much to the writers' discomfort; it is for this and several other reasons that I do not emphasize them here. Their contributions to the historical genre is more recent and very specific, therefore I discuss these features in a later chapter (Chapter 9).

[39] Cp. Hena Maes-Jelinek, "Postcolonial Criticism at the Crossroads: Subjective Questionings of an Old-Timer"; Rowland Smith, "Introduction."

[40] Cf., for example, Moss, *Is Canada Postcolonial?* and Verduyn, *Literary Pluralities*.

[41] "Writing as a Japanese Canadian, Kogawa with her first novel marks the entry of racial minority women's fiction into the Canadian mainstream, challenging the traditional white definitions of Canadianness and official history by transgressing the barrier of a forty-year silence

of the Canadian government's deportation and internment of Japanese-Canadians as enemy aliens during and after World War II, and discrimination against citizens of Japanese origin within society, it strongly stands for the postcolonial discourse of marginalized voice in the sense that it questions Canada's dominant collective memory and criticizes the amnesia of a whole ethnic group's history. The novel also displays several metafictional features and questions the value of historiographic sources and their interpretation;[42] however, the revelation of forgotten and repressed pasts remains the central focus throughout the novel. Gordon Bölling, in his study, rightly distinguishes between differing themes of revisionist historical fictions – as he notes, some novels insist on the communication of repressed histories, while others present parodic rewritings of existing, well-known moments and events of the past; from the perspective presented in this study, the latter form must be seen as a continuation of postmodern narrative modes.[43] It is even more intriguing to observe that, since the nineties, there have also been some historical fictions written by writers not necessarily belonging to repressed "minority" groups, which, in an equally compelling manner, thematize the deconstruction of colonial mindsets. Jane Urquhart's novels, for example *Away* (1993), re-imagine Canada's colonial pasts and thereby challenge imperialistic oppression in history.[44]

Urquhart's historical novels, as well as Kogawa's *Obasan* have also been widely discussed in the context of the re-writing of women's roles in history.[45] Their novels can also be seen in the light of the more general subaltern discourse that was influencing Canada's historical fictions from the 1980s onward. This critical discourse originates from more general issues and overall factors of minority discrimination, the most dominant of which is that defined by gender and touches upon socially marginalized ethnic groups and "non-ethnic," "majority" groups alike. Thus, in the wake of increasingly radical feminist discourses in the second half of the twentieth century, women writers have increasingly insisted on the fictional retellings of women in history, of which the earliest examples are represented by Susan Swan's *The Biggest Woman of the World* (1983) and Daphne Marlatt's *Ana Historic* (1988).[46]

Finally, the broader subaltern discourse also refers substantially to ethnic and racial issues, too – especially in terms of the theme of migration, which has assisted the appearance of fictions set in the past but not necessarily set in Canada, focusing instead on the histories of migrants' former home countries. Within the discourses of postmodern aesthetics and historiography, the link to the genre of historical fiction is natural, though not necessary; nonetheless, this connection was emphasized for a long

on internment and dispersal of Japanese Canadians after Pearl Harbour." Coral Ann Howells, "Writing by Women," 204.

[42] These two discourses are represented for example by a package of documents, letters, diaries, newspaper clippings and other materials documenting the past that the protagonist Naomi receives from her politically engaged aunt Emily, parts of which are integrated into the novel. Cp., i.e., *Obasan* 46-50, 200-208.

[43] Bölling 15-16.

[44] Further, very recent examples can be found in Guy Vanderhaeghe's *The Last Crossing* (2002) and Merilyn Simonds's *The Holding* (2004).

[45] Cp., for example, Mickey Pearlman, *Canadian Women Writing Fiction*.

[46] Cf. Marlene Goldman, *Paths of Desire*.

time and also remains strong in current writings and the respective criticism. The discourses discussed above, in contrast, are not necessarily only related to the historical genre; they have, in fact, encouraged the production of novels that express these concerns while simultaneously focusing on the present; novels that reflect the postcolonial and subaltern discourses need not deal with history, even though many examples do. Although this case can also be argued for some metafictional novels, I am suggesting that within metafictional and historiographic discourses the connection to history appears firmer.

It would be counterproductive to insist on the separation of the previously discussed discursive influences on Canadian historical fiction, as the boundaries between them are unstable and blurred. Nonetheless, these transitory categories help us to discern and understand specific thematic and formal characteristics within the bulk of Canadian historical fictions. Even more so, they facilitate our reading and situating of contemporary examples. Present day 'fictions of the past' represent a point at which all 'posts' meet at an angle – postmodernism, poststructuralism, and post-colonialism – and have thereby developed into an integral part of the de/construction site that is 'Canada.'

Literary Commodities and the Globalization of Histories

Heading into the 1990s, postmodern and postcolonial cultural processes – expressed in the genre of historical fiction – momentarily reached a certain peak and have since moved into several new directions. Even though the various basic formal and thematic concerns established within the previously discussed discourses have remained important prerequisites for the understanding of historical fiction in Canada in its contemporary form since the 1960s, as well as for Canadian culture in general, many of the fundamental ideas that nourished the genre since the mid-twentieth century are currently undergoing revisions. At the same time, new, innovative concerns are becoming more pressing and thus more influential.

1988 saw the coincidence of two inspirational key 'publications' in the broadest sense: the passing of the Multiculturalism Act, as has already been discussed, and in the very same year, the appearance of Linda Hutcheon's well-known study *The Canadian Postmodern: A Study of Contemporary English-Canadian Fiction*.[47] Both were essential for the development of the genre of historical fiction in Canada, but have been met with critical scrutiny in recent years.[48] Both were also immensely formative for the establishment of a reformed, self-confident Canadian national identity – each in its own

[47] In that year Hutcheon in fact published two important studies. Apart from the one mentioned, also *A Poetics of Postmodernism: History, Theory, Fiction* (London & New York: Routledge, 1988) appeared.

[48] Cf. the large number of critical publications on Canadian multicultural identity (and literature) in the past decades, as for example, Braun and Klooss, *Multiculturalism in North America and Europe;* Verduyn, *Literary Pluralities*; Heble, Palmateer Pennee, and Struthers, *New Contexts of Canadian Criticism*; Gunew, *Haunted Nations: The Colonial Dimensions of Multiculturalisms*.

right though to varying degrees on socio-political levels and in the academia.[49] However, since the time of their introduction and respective revolutionary impact, twenty years have past and critical perspectives as well as Canadian society have changed. Nonetheless both 'concepts' represent valuable reference points for the present study; I will repeatedly return to them in the course of my argumentation.[50] What is more important at this point is that, today, Canadian literatures and socio-political realities are characterized by the impact of globalization and a postnational turn, which effectively also engenders the questioning of the "borderlands" of postmodern, postcolonial, and Canadian multiculturalist ideas.[51]

The past twenty years have seen the emergence of voices that devise new approaches to issues of belonging, citizenship, and the construction of nation; voices that question the most obvious dichotomy that underlies the principle of multiculturalism and haunts most theories of the twentieth century: that of 'sameness' ideally leading to equality vs. 'difference,' more often than not, purporting othering and inequality. The difficulty that has been detected here lies in the danger of lapsing into essentialist positions; yet at the same time, both can be convincingly defended.[52] This very contradiction is equally reflected in discussions about the use of the terms 'ethnicity' versus 'race'[53] and has led to a certain instability between the intended practices of multiculturalism as a political concept and its perception by more critical observers. Critics such as Neil Bisoondath, Smaro Kamboureli and Fred Wah, have repeatedly emphasized the dangers of exotification of ethnic groups and of the simplification of cultural power and non-power structures and processes.[54] The development of Canada's multicultural visions of identification is an ongoing and highly controversial discourse that has yet to find its

[49] Cf. Kröller, "Introduction" 9-10; and Howells, "Writing by Women" 197-198; Rosenthal, "English-Canadian Literary Theory" 303-306.

[50] Linda Hutcheon's theories are briefly analyzed in 3.2.; the concept of Canadian multiculturalism is discussed in greater detail in Chapter 5, and especially in 5.1.

[51] New's *Borderlands: How We Talk About Canada* analyzes, in Rosenthal's words, "the location of Canadian identity on borders and in spaces-in-between" (307). The critical opening up of thought that the postnational turn (which is in some instances also related to Canadian globalized modernities) evokes, is in my eyes however linked to a redefinition or moving away from the idea of borders.

[52] The applicatory and fundamental nature of this basic dichotomy becomes obvious if we look at various terms used in contemporary critical approaches, each emphasizing a different aspect, but each built upon the same antagonism, for example, (cultural/economic/political) 'imperialism' vs. 'resistance' in Postcolonial Theory, 'race' vs. 'racial identity' (cf. Siemerling's discussion of Anthony Appiah's view on DuBois; Siemerling, *New North American Studies* 61-62). Or, in discussions on globalization the dichotomy is often reflected in the inappropriate usage of the terms 'global' vs. 'local.'

[53] See, for example, Enoch Padolsky's in depth analysis in "Ethnicity and Race: Canadian Minority Writing at the Crossroads," and in a different context, as quoted in footnote above, Siemerling 61-62.

[54] The most well-known publications of these authors, in which they convey critical approaches to multiculturalism and Canadian identity/ies, are Neil Bissoondath, *Selling Illusions: The Cult of Multiculturalism in Canada* (London: Penguin, 1994); Smaro Kamboureli, *Scandalous Bodies: Diasporic Literature in English Canada* (Don Mills (ON): Oxford, UP, 2000); Fred Wah, *Faking it: Poetics and Hybridity: Critical Writing 1984 – 1999* (Edmonton: NeWest Press, 2000).

mode of understanding, even if it were only a "consensual disagreement."[55] As Roy Miki suggests,

> The critical challenge for those of us who look towards more inclusive forms of cultural belonging is to make these relations [i.e. the contradictory and contradicted power networks between individual and national constructions of identities] visible through critical methods that can account for these different registers without resolving them into a foreordained unity. (Miki 14)

The fact that reflections on ethnicity, race, gender, and, especially since 9/11, religion[56] have become so prominent in contemporary socio-political discussions and cultural criticism alike, reaffirms an urge for a new sense of belonging that can no longer be satisfied by former visions of a unified nation-state. Multiculturalism, as the socio-political concept representative of a post-modern, increasingly self-assured and independent (i.e. postcolonial) Canadian nation and national identity, has been the defining and thus dominant "ideology" for Canada (and Canadian historical fictions) in the second half of the twentieth century. To a large degree, this political imagination prevails; at the same time, however, theories such as Benedict Anderson's on "imagined communities" have initiated discussions on the constructedness of nationalism and other "cultural artifacts,"[57] as well as how the growing impact of transnational power-, communication- and migration-flows has forcibly modified these once prevalent mindsets.

These very developments have led theorists to speak of a new era termed "post-national," which – as reflected in literature – encompasses revolutionary reactions to the increasing historical complexity, and the quantity and denseness of information available in variable degree to most contemporary individuals[58]:

> Because the cultural references of these newest writers are often larger than national, they are producing work that challenges the nationalist assumptions built into the earliest form of the postcolonial model, and they may be moving Canada a step beyond the postcolonial to a true postnationalism. (Bennett, "Nation and Its Discontents" 27)

In the process of these necessary and constant evaluations of identity-forming, cultural images and discourses, definitions of self and other have become more complicated and

[55] Cf. Imbert, *Consensual Disagreement: Canada and the Americas*, which partially conveys more positive outlooks on Canada's multicultural future.

[56] Cf., for example, Ann Keniston, and Jeanne F. Quinn, eds., *Literature after 9/11* (New York: Routledge, 2008).

[57] Cp. Anderson's "Introduction": "My point of departure is that nationality, or, as one might prefer to put it in view of that word's multiple significations, nation-ness, as well as nationalism, are cultural artifacts of a particular kind. [...] once created, they became 'modular,' capable of being transplanted, with varying degrees of self-consciousness, to a great variety of social terrains, to merge and be merged with a correspondingly wide variety of political and ideological constellations." 4. For an extended discussion on his concept from a postcolonial perspective, cf., for example, Loomba, *Colonialism/Postcolonialism* 156-59.

[58] For an in depth discussion of the issue from a critical sociological perspective, cf. Featherstone, "Postnational Flows, Identity Formation and Cultural Space."

harder to grasp. Despite the efforts of a whole generation of subaltern critics to theorize and essentialize repressed identities, separate identitary entities of ethnicity, race, gender and class are increasingly merged and eventually inform a transcultural expression of existence as one possible, and ethically more viable, solution to the crisis of deconstructed and dispersed global identities. In the words of Kalogeras, Arapoglou, and Manney:

> The invention of a transnational global sphere has not made the concepts of ethnic communities and bounded localities obsolete; rather, it has necessitated a reconceptualization of the politics of community, identity and cultural difference that sanctions new dynamics in a translocal world. (xiii)

Despite the specific, uneasy role Canada, as a settler-invader nation, has occupied within postcolonial criticism[59], the theoretical discrepancies of postcolonial criticism should challenge us, especially in relation to the analysis of fictions of the past, to consider reformed or new possible perspectives. Postcolonial theorists have, understandably so, been very reluctant to broach and integrate issues concerning the complex cultural processes in the light of globalization.[60] According to Frank Schulze-Engler, current postcolonial debates might "manoeuvre themselves into a dead end" ("From Postcolonial to Preglobal" 53) because "most participants assume that the conflicts between 'the West' and 'the Rest' or 'global capitalism' and the 'exploited margins' are of primary importance in any consideration of 'postcolonial' literatures and cultures" (55). As he explains in more detail:

> For a criticism interested in the political dimensions of contemporary literature, an exclusive focus on the resistance to globalization, on the subversion of Western master-discourse of cultural supremacy and on the reassertion of the local or the national will no longer suffice; instead, it will have to branch out to cover not only the new dynamics of global cultural ecumene and its significance for an emerging transnational public sphere, but also the politics of civil society and the micropolitics of modernity explored in literary works from all over the world. (Schulze-Engler, "From Postcolonial to Preglobal" 58-59)

Postcolonial criticism and the concepts of Eurocentric (cultural) imperialism have been highly relevant for the discussion of historical fiction in Canada because, as discussed in the former subchapter, they have influenced writers and critics in the inevitable process of re-writing Canadian history. Some critics argue that postmodernism, too, has been superceded by the idea of globalization: "As we've begun to see, since the nineties, globalization, a word with multiple meanings, has replaced 'postmodernism' as a master term used to name, interpret, and direct the social and technological transformations of the contemporary era" (During 81). As far as literature is concerned,

[59] For an insightful recent publication on this issue cf. Moss, *Is Canada Postcolonial?*.

[60] Postcolonial theory, originally intended and often still practiced as a highly political discourse, would by no means be able to sympathize with the 'merits' of globalization, as they represent the cultural and economic imperialism of 'the West.' Cp. Schulze-Engler, "From Postcolonial to Preglobal" 54-56; Ania Loomba, "Defining the Terms," Colonialism/Post-colonialism 7-22.

most critics will react with annoyance or skepticism toward suggestions, which insinuate that such an established mode of reading, as that represented by 'postmodernism,' might no longer be the adequate designation or framework for contemporary literature that it was twenty years ago. These reactions are engendered by two major, related problems: changes in literature reflecting the necessity to re-negotiate certain perspectives are still difficult to pinpoint; and, that it becomes even more difficult when set against a, by definition, 'open-ended' literary movement.

Earlier, I mentioned the idea that histories are fundamental for the definition of self and have to be told in order for an identity to be established – this assumption, which forms the basis of the 'success' of historical fiction, links the genre to a further issue: that of memory.[61] The field of research that deals with the processes and functions of cultural memories has contributed a number of innovative approaches that might unsettle older (postcolonial and postmodern) readings and engender new insights into contemporary complexities within the genre.

The observation that the past and the remembering of past events play a crucial role for the construction of identities can be found as early as in the seventeenth century in the works of the philosopher John Locke (Erll, Gymnich, and Nünning iii) – a fact already highlighted in recent years by scholars belonging to the various schools of memory theories, the work of which has led to a downright boom of 'memory research' in the fields of cultural studies and literary studies.[62] Since the beginning of the twentieth century, memory studies across the disciplines have emerged as a highly active field of research, in the area of cultural studies most dominantly influenced by the French philosopher and sociologist, Maurice Halbwachs (1877-1945), who worked on collective memory and the dependence of individual identity on communal remembering, and Pierre Nora (1931-), a French historian, who focused on national identity in France and developed the renowned concept of the "lieux de memoire."[63] As a separate young interdisciplinary realm, Holocaust studies (mostly in the Anglo-American academia), too, have contributed to the growing interest in the analysis of human re-constructions of the past, especially in relation to the understanding of trauma as well as amnesia; in more recent decades this field has also provoked discussions over the questions of (autobiographical) narrative, truth and the reliability of remembering.[64]

[61] For an insightful essay on the relation between memory, history and narrative, cf. Löschnigg, "Historical Perspectives on Migrant Communities." Here Löschnigg refers to two recent theorists of autobiography who "have paid due attention to the eminent importance of narrative in constructions of the self and of individual identity via memory," 184: Jerome Bruner, *Acts of Meaning* (Cambridge: Harvard UP, 1990), and Paul John Eakin, *Touching the World: Reference in Autobiography* (Princeton: Princeton UP 1992), and *How Our Lives Become Stories: Making Selves* (Ithaca, London: Cornell UP, 1999).

[62] Cf. Erll, Gymnich, and Nünning, *Literatur-Erinnerung-Identität*, "Einleitung"; Neumann, "Literatur, Erinnerung, Identität"; Rossington and Whitehead, "Introduction."

[63] Cf. Rimstead 4; Rossington and Whitehead 5; Patrick Schmidt, "Zwischen Medien und Topoi: Die *Lieux de mémoire* und die Medialität des kulturellen Gedächtnisses," Erll and Nünning, *Medien* 25-43.

[64] Rossington and Whitehead 6-7; Rimstead 6, 10; For an ambitious study on this issue also cf. Julia Stiebellehner, "The framing, reception, and effect of traumatic cultural memory in Joy

Finally, one should also mention the considerable amount of research undertaken in the other sciences, such as psychology, especially memory psychology ("Gedächtnispsychologie"), philosophy, and, most importantly, neurology, although the insights remain mostly remote and thus hardly integrated into literary or cultural analyses.[65]

As Aleida Assmann has observed, the term of 'cultural memory' has not only been turned into a trite expression in the past decades, it has also been prone to confusions in definition due to the contiguity of two particular independent scholarly discourses: the French school (P. Nora, M. Halbwachs), which initially focused its research on an analysis from the "center" of society with the impact of modernity on society as a backlash; while the other strand of research, the Anglo-American tradition, rooted its scientific perspective in and from the margins of society, thus initiating Holocaust studies and in later years strongly marking subaltern studies (Assmann 45).[66] The most influential insights of contemporary literary academia have been the cultural studies contributions to memory research represented primarily by Jan and Aleida Assmann, whose ideas on the historical-contextual development of collective remembering and the memory-dependent forms of culture(s) in general (Assmann 46) have been used and extended in the narratological school of Vera and Ansgar Nünning, the media approaches of Astrid Erll, and in the works of their academic followers.[67] What all of these approaches have in common is an acute awareness of, and an intention to solve, the complexity of human remembering – both in the collective and the individual; some try to simplify the processes and numerous elements involved, which is hardly possible; others, in an attempt to systematize the inscrutable, draft elaborate, in some cases disconcerting theoretical models.[68] Especially in recent years, there have been several studies that have extended their disciplinary perspectives, turning their interest toward

Kogawa's *Obasan* and Anne Michaels's *Fugitive Pieces*: Canadian fiction between autobiography and historiography in the light of the "Wilkomirski Affair"; a typological and didactic approach," Dipl.Thesis, Innsbruck University, 2008.

[65] For an account of the intersections between cultural and social theories, and psychology (in German, however), cf. G. Echterhoff, "Das Außen des Erinners: Was vermittelt individuelles und kollektives Gedächhtnis?"; Erll and Nünning, *Medien* 61-82; for a remarkable philosophical perspective on the relation of identity, memory and narrative, cf. the works of Paul Ricoeur, especially *Time and Narrative*, 1983, 1984, 1985, 3 vols. trans. Kathleen McLaughlin and David Pellauer (Chicago: University of Chicago Press, 1984, 1985, 1988), *Oneself as Another*, 1990, trans. Kathleen Blamey (Chicago: University of Chicago Press, 1992), and *Memory, History, Forgetting*, 2000, trans. Kathleen Blamey and David Pellauer (Chicago: University of Chicago Press, 2004); see also "Paul Ricoeur," *Stanford Encyclopedia of Philosophy*, *online resource*; also a stunning contribution is found in the work of the Viennese-born exile neuroscientist and psychiatrist Eric Kandel, see "Eric R. Kandel: The Nobel Prize in Physiology or Medicine 2000," *online resource*, and Erich R. Kandel, *In Search of Memory: The Emergence of a New Science of Mind* (W.W. Norton: New York, 2006).

[66] For a more detailed account on the relation of subaltern and memory studies, cf. Rossington and Whitehead 8-9.

[67] Cp. for example, Erll and Nünning; Erll, Gymnich and Nünning; Neumann, *Erinnerung–Identität –Narration*.

[68] Cp. the critical comments on the theories of P. Nora in Rossington and Whitehead 5.

the role of literature as a medium that constructs and reflects memories of diverse social configurations, thus taking into consideration the broad scope of processing levels.
As we thus commence to consider the analysis of fictions dealing with or set in the past – texts which can be termed as media of cultural memory[69] – several interesting questions arise in relation to the above discussed theoretical approaches: how do collective and individual memories interact in literature? How is memory expressed in specific texts?[70] How is, and should, memory be rated within the genre of historical fiction? How what exact features should a novel (or any other genre) display, to be referred to as memory-oriented or historical? How does memory, in terms of encoded texts and images, interact with the mind of the present? Is it justified to differentiate between cultural memory and the cultural imaginary?[71]
What should finally be highlighted at this stage, is that there is still much to be learned from memory studies for the analysis of the 'historical' genre in Canada. A short comparison of recent publications on theories of memory reveals that the genre of historical fiction and memory studies experienced similar theoretical influences. The recently published reader on Memory theory edited by Rossington and Whitehead, for example, divides its two final parts on recent theoretical approaches, "Positionings," and "Identities" into subchapters on collective memory, Jewish memory discourse, and trauma on one hand, and gender, race, nation, and diaspora on the other.[72] An *ECW* special edition on cultural memory and social identity edited by Roxanne Rimstead, in contrast, sets a stronger emphasis on the thematic organization of approaches ("counter-memory," "collective memory acts," "memory-maps," and "migrancy") and extends the sphere of remembering to include visual memory. One of the studies published by Ansgar Nünning (together with Astrid Erll and Marion Gymnich), to give a final example from the Central European literary and cultural studies school, is broken into a section on general interdisciplinary methodological propositions and three sections on in-depth case studies from narratological, generic, and (historical-)contextual analytical

[69] Cf. Erll, "Medium des kollektiven Gedächtnisses: Ein (erinnerungs)kulturwissenschaftlicher Kompakt-begriff," Erll and Nünning, *Medien* 3-22.
[70] A question most thoroughly discussed by Birgit Neumann.
[71] Many of these questions have already received considerable attention in publications focusing on the role of memory in literature, some of them I will return to myself in later parts of this study. As a methodology, these theories of the construction of memories, identities (via memories), and of literature as an active and passive medium of construction remain marginally discussed here despite their extreme significance for the contemporary (literary) academic community and despite the potential insights they open up for this present analysis. As will be demonstrated in chapters to come, the emphasis of my theoretical reflections and subsequent analyses will remain not upon the *processes and strategies* of memories, identity constructions and the media applied as well as the elements involved within (as in memory theories) but on their – both individual and collective – *results* (in the form of literary texts), which are additionally narrowed down by the attribute of *transcultural*. Cultural remembering is thus regarded here as *one* of the socio-mental forces exerting influence on the constantly renegotiated interspaces of the imaginary. In contrast to most predominant memory-oriented analyses, special attention is given to the impact of globalization in an age of modernity as reverberated in the instability and interplay of collective and individual identities.
[72] Note that this reader seems to pass over the work of Aleida and Jan Assmann, and other contemporary mainland European cultural studies scholars.

perspectives.[73] These examples make obvious the impact of specific, continentally varying critical developments and initiatives as well as the range of possible analytical viewpoints; these dividing lines and clear critical positionings are here far more obvious, a trait that is not usually found in studies specifically dealing with historical fiction, which has led to an increasing disarrangement (and flatness) in the reception of the genre.

As I am attempting to demonstrate, the kinship between the genre of historical fiction (and its analysis) and memory research can be traced not only in the shared interest in human interpretations of the past and its impact on identity-constructions, as well as in the relation of these elements to specific "historical" circumstances, but also in the possibilities of analytical approaches: critical theories on the genre of (Canadian) historical fiction, as a medium of a specific cultural memory[74], however, might still need to adjust to these new possibilities.

Canadian historical fictions of the recent decades are representative of a Canadian cultural identity that has moved beyond early postcolonial insecurities toward postnational mind-sets and of a literature that in present times is internationally acclaimed. Apart from the theoretical dilemmas discussed above, however, this evolution is accompanied by another set of discrepancies, which reverberate especially in fiction that deals with the past, that, in recent years, have witnessed another impressive wave of popularity: the extreme positions regarding the reception of this prolific genre oscillate between some critics' concern about the death of history due to the fast-living present-ness of contemporary society, on the one hand, and the immense popularity of, if not obsession with history as a subject matter on the other.[75] In fact, in the past twenty years, the interest of Canadian writers in the fictionalization of history and memory has risen to an extent that makes it difficult to keep track of the immense number and forms of rewritings of the past:

> While concern about the growing irrelevance of history is to a degree echoed in the field of Canadian literature, Canadian literature seems to be one forum in which there is undeniable evidence of a renewed interest in and revitalization of Canadian history. Indeed, for Canadian writers at the turn of the twenty-first century, history has undisputedly become a central preoccupation. [...] Of the current generation of novelists making a mark both nationally and internationally, a conspicuous proportion write about the past, whether those fictions are set in Canada or elsewhere: Joseph Boyden, George Elliott Clarke, Michael Crummey, Wayne Johnston, Sky Lee, Ann Marie MacDonald, Anne Michaels, Rohinton Mistry, Fred Stenson, Margaret Sweatman, Jane Urquhart, Guy Vanderhaeghe, Thomas Wharton, and others. (Wyile, *Speaking In the Past Tense* 2)

[73] Erll, Gymnich and Nünning, *Literatur – Erinnerung – Identität*.
[74] The notion of one specific "Canadian" cultural memory is more of temporary working concept: of course we have to be aware of the fact that this cultural "memory" is made up of many separate culturally diverse memories – this plurality will also be amply exposed (though in terms of transcultural imaginaries) in the analytical sections of this book.
[75] Cf. Wyile, *Speculative Fictions* 3, and ibid., *Speaking In the Past Tense* 1-2.

If critical discourses on historical fiction in the second half of the twentieth century centered on metafictional and historiographical concerns and then increasingly on postcolonial and subaltern perspectives, today the impact of these discourses on the genre has altered due to changing global concepts and perceptions. At the beginning of the twenty-first century these developments are calling for reformed and extended approaches in order to do the variety of expressions within the genre, as well as its kaleidoscopic nature justice.[76] Of course, many critics of historical fiction and writers alike have remained devoted to the predominant discourses of the past decades – however, others, as we will see in the chapters to follow, have moved on.

[76] Cp. Bölling, History in the Making 16.

2 Past – Memory – Fictions

In an extension to the already discussed postmodern and post-structural interpretations of the dialogic nature of contemporary texts, we must note the particular density of intertextuality, or, as it might be referred to on a larger scale, of 'intergenericity' as an identifiable transcultural characteristic of contemporary writings on the past.[1] Obviously, modernist and postmodernist modes of writing promoted in the twentieth century revolutionized the romanticizing aesthetics of traditional historical novels; in 'fictions of the past' written in the past decades we might, however, observe an even stronger layering of cultural references and blurring of boundaries between genres. The writers of these fictions use multiple strategies in order to grasp the potentialities of understanding histories and communicating narratives of the past from the perspective of an ever-densifying present. The spectrum of applied generic forms and cross-references in fictions of the past ranges from (auto-)biographies, oral tales, myths, and family histories to the use or re-imagination of historical documents, the inclusion of letters and travel notes, and so on. Additionally, as discussed above, individual recollection and personal interpretation have gained importance and have moved to the center of the genre – a feature that, too, accounts for a mounting generic plurality.
Thus, it is not surprising that contemporary historical fiction displays a particular kinship to alternative literary forms that have been emerging in recent decades – that, for example, which has been subsumed under the term of "life writing." This form of writing only differs from what is here referred to as "fictions of the past," in its even stronger leaning towards personal, individual narratives and, in its slightly less fictional intent, meaning that even if it might contain a considerable amount of fictional elements, it usually recounts or at least appears to recount actual events, lives, or personal memories. Reading the first paragraph of the section on "life writing" by Susanna Egan and Gabriele Helms included in Eva Maria Kröller's *Cambridge Companion to Canadian Literature*, one might observe that the passage could (with minor alterations) just as well apply to a description of present-day historical fiction:

> The last quarter of the twentieth century has been a profoundly autobiographical age with the personal narrative providing an important lens both on to history and on to the contemporary world. Narratives, productions and performances of identity have begun to permeate and transform Canadian culture in every medium. Furthermore, personal narratives no longer depend on speakers belonging to dominant social groups but emerge with pride from minority positions, cultivate the value of undervalued experiences, and risk distinctly intimate subject matter. Because the personal is also expressed as political, recent life writing contributes explicitly to changing cultures and to changing understanding of personal, communal, even national identities. In short,

[1] For a collection of essays on intertextuality and transcultural processes in postcolonial literatures, cp. Klooss, *Across the Lines: Intertextuality and Transcultural Communication in the New Literatures in English*.

> quite apart from the range and quality of life-writing production in Canada since the 1970s, and the rich archives that contribute to Canadian history, life-writing is now recognized as preeminent among the genres in which the evolving of character and concerns of the nation have been and continue to be written. (Egan and Helms 216)

The closeness of the two literary-generic siblings becomes even more obvious in works that can be assessed as borderline cases. Dionne Brand's *A Map to the Door of No Return*, for example, is clearly classified as life writing by Egan and Helms (219) but has alternately been referred to as autobiographic poetry (Gross et al. 318) and memoir (the subtitle of the book is *Notes to Belonging*) – as reflections and memories constitute the majority of the book; however, the work also contains several passages from historical books, and in some instances Brand critically re-imagines histories. Following a quote from Dürer, in which he rejoices the beauty of exotic artifacts sent to him, Brand muses:

> Katherina alt 20 jar: "I have drawn the portrait in charcoal of Faktor Brandao's Secretary. I drew a portrait of his negress with metal point." Kathernia was the servant of a Portuguese factor, Joao Brandao. The Portuguese at the time controlled the shipping routes to Asia and Africa. Katherina was African, enslaved. Durer was also a collector of exotica: parrots, tortoises, monkeys, Chinese porcelains, African ivories, coral, cane arrows, fish skins, buffalo horns, coconuts.
>
> All artists are involved in their time. (*Map to the Door* 30)

These similarities only partially highlight the broad spectrum of inter- and, as one might add here, *trans*generic variety found in the historical genre today, and they suggest that a more flexible understanding of historical fiction as *fictions of the past* should be considered. Thus, certain complexities within the genre might well be clarified through an in-depth approach to, what are today, common transgeneric narrative strategies and textual layers within fictions that rewrite the past.[2] It is obvious that the use of specific generic forms, in order to negotiate the past and collective or individual memories, vary across different cultures. Consequently, if we consider how authors today apply multiple traditions of rewriting and retelling the past in contemporary historical fictions and how the merging of varying forms of 'cultural remembering' influences the parameters of the genre, it seems valid to classify these as primarily and strategically transcultural fictions.

The complexity of textual form is just one of several predominant factors within historical fictions – discussed in more detail in the last part of this chapter and exemplified in Chapter 6 to 8 – that implies the necessity for a revision of our understanding of what makes up the genre nowadays. The development of this and other traits can best be grasped when related to the immense changes that the genre and

[2] I would like to emphasize once more that to a large degree, of course, this intertextual multiplicity was a feature introduced especially in postmodern aesthetics, yet it seems immensely relevant in a different sense nowadays, as it no longer necessarily disrupts the mimetic illusion and instead forces us to question the parameters of the genre as a whole. For recent discussions of these transgressions of genre, cf. Wyile, *Speculative Fictions*; Helms, and Neumann.

its criticism, especially in the English-language academia (which obviously originally focused on British and American literature), have undergone. One of the earlier well-established studies, apart from the seminal monograph on the genre by George Lukács,[3] was Avrom Fleishman's *The English Historical Novel: Walter Scott to Virginia Woolf.* Published in 1971, Fleishman's study, like Lukács's (though with less ideological implications), delineated the development of the genre from the nineteenth century to its modernist form. As his preface reveals, Fleishman felt uncertain about the future of this genre, which he estimated for its "principles of realist responsibilities, universality of vision, and the imaginative sympathy with the men (sic!) of the past" (xiii). Even though he acknowledged that the historical novel was "a parable of the present, if not a prophecy of the future" (xii), he also insisted that the fictional historical setting and action of the novel had to clearly be set apart from the present, at least by two generations.[4] His assertions, among them that "the symbolic truth of a historical novel may be an insight into the universal processes of history, a hypothetical explanation of an interstice in the historical knowledge (usual a personal motivation), or a vivification of a shadowy period or lost past" (xi), would be critically challenged only a few years later. In 1984, for example, Borgmeier and Reitz edited a two-volume collection of essays in German that, in comparison to Fleishman's, already suggests more case-sensitive categorizations and also includes the emerging postmodernist expressions of the genre (both in the theoretical introduction and in the included contributions).[5]
Arguing from the postmodernist perspective, Linda Hutcheon's studies of the early 1980s were surely ahead of their time – though once critics began to adopt and adapt Hutcheon's theoretical arguments towards the 1990s, they did so in great numbers: Susana Onega in *Telling Histories* and Elisabeth Wesseling in *Writing History as A Prophet* give detailed insights into the overall development of the genre from the Victorian historical novel towards postmodern innovations (the former a collection of essays, focusing on British authors; the latter a more general monograph)[6]; a collection by Bernd Engler and Kurt Müller published in 1994 presents, as the title promises, a

[3] I am in this discussion consciously excluding the highly influential work of the Hungarian Marxist critic Georg Lukács, *The Historical Novel* (1937, translation 1962, repr.1976); Lukács's criticism was occupied with an interpretation of the development of the "classical form" of the historical novel in the nineteenth and early twentieth century under the impact "[t]he inhumanity of capitalism, the chaos of competition, the destruction of the small by the big, the debasement of culture by the transformation of all things into commodities" (23). Although his study was crucial for literary criticism on the genre, a detailed discussion cannot be included here.
[4] Fleishman begins the first chapter of his study, "Towards a Theory of Historical Fiction," with the observation that "[e]veryone knows what a historical novel is; perhaps that is why few have volunteered to define it in print. [...] Most novels are set in the past—beyond an arbitrary number of years, say 40-60 (two generations)—are liable to be considered historical, while those of the present and preceding generations (of which the reader is more likely to have personal experience) have been called 'novels of the recent past'." Fleishman 3; cp. also the discussion in Borgmeier and Reitz on this issue (13-14).
[5] Cp. "Einleitung" 33-34; the second volume of the study, for example, features essays on John Barth's *The Sot-Weed Factor*, and E. L. Doctorow's *Ragtime*.
[6] Of course, as Elisabeth Wesseling notes, there were several critics before Hutcheon who studied the role of history in postmodern texts; however Hutcheon was among the first to argue that the historical genre represented a major subcategory of postmodernist literature; Wesseling 2-3.

variety of readings of "historiographic metafiction in modern American and Canadian literature."[7] Thus, while all of these studies reflect "the belief that true insight into the characteristics of this outstanding postmodernist phenomenon necessarily entails, firstly, going back to the origins of historical fiction and secondly, the establishment of the links between the development of this literary form and the evolution of the concept of history itself" (Onega 6) and that "[w]hat provides the impulse for the writing of historiographic metafiction is indeed the discovery of the ability of literature to reveal truths that cannot be grasped from traditional history" (ibid. 16), Engler and Müller place a greater emphasis on regional contexts that influence specific developments within the metafictional historiographic genre: "In fine, the intention of this collection is to illustrate the complexity, manifoldness, and diversity of historiographic literature, as well as the specifics of its national developments in the U.S. and in Canada" (Engler and Müller 12). Also, at the beginning of the twenty-first century, publications continue to interpret the explicit, postmodernist features of historical fiction. They do this by gradually integrating 'new literatures' or by becoming more focused; while Amy J. Elias's *Sublime Desire* acknowledges postcolonial writing (even if it is not included in the discussed corpus) (ix-x), David Lucking's *The Serpents Part* focuses on at least five influential Canadian postmodern historical fictions.[8]

As these studies began to appear, around the year 2000, other critics, for example Middleton and Woods, were already beginning to indicate alternative directions of development and critical study. However, a confrontation of the plurality of contemporary Canadian fictions of the past with the existing contemporary variety of theories on historical fiction – some single-edged or outdated, others innovative and challenging – might suggest the necessity for extended and even more flexible modes of analysis.

A Prolific Genre

In his extensive study on contemporary historical fiction in Canada, Herb Wyile dedicates a whole chapter to the discussion of a major ambivalence within postmodern representations of the past, the opposition between its skepticism toward history and historical representation and its embracing of history as a popular ingredient for marketable fiction (*Speculative Fictions* 214-254). This ambivalence, as he observes, is the result of a century marked by transnational power flows leading to postmodern, on the one hand popularized, on the other strictly aestheticized and politicized, cultural production; historical fiction, however, supposedly manages to bridge the gap and overcome internal tensions between the aesthetics of literary time and the politics of history: "They [historical fictions] cultivate a sense of history not as the passive consumption of a given past but as a more speculative and dialogic view of the past that takes in our modes of perception at the same time. They are simultaneously specular

[7] For detailed analyses of numerous critical works that deal with the metafictional mode in the historical genre, cf. Bölling 31-57.

[8] The other two works that Lucking discusses are earlier texts.

and speculative, like figures looking through a window whose view is obscured by the reflection of the interior in which they stand" (255).

Herb Wyile can be listed with Middleton and Woods as being among the first critics to include a discussion on the implications of the present cultural, economic, and political age of globalization for the genre of historical fiction; yet his thoughts on the oppositional stance within historical fiction concerning historicity, aesthetics, and politics could be extended, as contemporary fictions of the past reflect a polylogic, rather than merely dialogic, nature. As has already been indicated above, the parameters of the genre are calling for at least partial revision due to the complex layering of forms that reflect upon the past. However, as the formerly predominant discourses within postmodern, historiographical, postcolonial, and subaltern issues interact with the forces of globalization, further factors will complicate the understanding of productions in the genre even more.

Contemporary fictions of the past, especially those discussed in this study, which are termed 'transcultural,' do not only represent expressions of what has been heralded as new forms of imaginaries[9], they also negotiate the interdependent flux of global versus local forces and increasingly concern themselves with the plural representation of individual identities via histories, therein, also demanding more ethical solutions for conflicting imaginaries. In doing so, these fictions of the past neither completely reject globalization, despite its sweeping capitalist transnational 'dangers,' nor do they accept it uncritically with its idealistic cosmopolitan promises.

Even if certain transformations can be observed in contemporary Canadian literature, this does not mean that the critical discourses, which originally had an impact on historical fictions and led to their revival since the second half of the twentieth century, have ceased to exert a major influence on the genre. In fact, the continuing presence and persistence of some major earlier characteristics of postmodern and postcolonial historiographical metafiction are a prerequisite for the internal intertextual and transgeneric multiplicity found in the genre today. As underlined in Bölling's recent study, historical fiction has in many instances remained devoted to metafictional and metahistorical narrative strategies and themes.[10] In effect, the prolific amount and variety of texts that writers have produced in this genre over the past few decades, has established historical fiction as a major literary form in Canada – in the words of Sherrill Grace, who assesses the genre as "one sign of [the country's] confident cultural position" (288):

> Another sign of this productivity, and one of the most striking, is the rise to preeminence of the historical novel, which has become so important that almost all of Canada's major writers have experimented with the genre: Margaret Atwood, George Bowering, George Elliott Clarke, Jack Hodgins, Robert Kroetsch, Michael Ondaatje, Jane Urquhart, Guy Vanderhaeghe, and Rudy Wiebe are only a few examples of the most senior and prolific writers to have taken Canadian history as their domain. (ibid. 288)

[9] Appadurai 2-8, 53-56.

[10] Bölling's study is discussed in further detail in the next subsection of this chapter.

The works of Canada's most internationally acclaimed author, Margaret Atwood – to take the first example from Grace's alphabetical list – all display a major influence of postmodernist literary features. Her historical fictions, too, are strongly self-reflexive and communicate the subjective nature of historical recollections. *Alias Grace* (1996), a novel which rewrites the (hi)story of a young woman's unresolved involvement in a double murder in the nineteenth century, as analyzed by Gordon Bölling, offers a dense network of metafictional modes and themes. They range from the display of history's polyphonic nature through the integration of textual fragments from documents, of epigraphs, and intertextual cross-references over metanarrative comments to strong intermedial references (Bölling 59-122). Also the more recent *The Blind Assassin* (2000), set around the time of World War I, strongly questions the act of narration and its reception by juxtaposing simple narrative passages, newspaper clippings, a pulp fantasy and a novel within the novel.[11]

M.G. Vassanji's *The Book of Secrets* (1994), which is mainly set in East Africa, like almost all of Vassanji's work, presents the alternative perspectives of a postcolonial, immigrant Canadian author; however, in doing so it also does not fail to integrate metafictional and metahistorical elements. The novel centers around a diary ("the book of secrets") written by a colonial officer in what was then called "British East Africa"; it questions the relativity of history by mingling a variety of textual levels: diary entries, narrations about the lives of the officer Alfred Corbin at the beginning of the twentieth century and of the retired schoolteacher and amateur historian Pius Fernandes toward the end of the same century, as well as notes, letters, and other material collected by the latter who comes across the diary and wants to reveal its secrets.[12] As in all of his novels, Vassanji is additionally concerned with depicting the cultural interaction, positive and negative, of diverse ethnicities and classes, across communities – an interest fostered by his own cultural background.[13]

Guy Vanderhaeghe has published two historical fictions in the past decades, which in opposition to both Atwood's novels, as well as Vassanji's, are neither situated in Canada alone nor in remote countries of origin. Rather, they rework the historical conception of a North American continent, which includes territories which would later belong to either the U.S. or Canada. He does this by making use of strong metafictional and -historical modes and themes. In *The Englishman's Boy* (1996) he sheds light on the historical event of the Cypress Hill Massacre that is subjectively retold by a witness:

[11] To give an earlier example, already *Lady Oracle* published in 1976 (which however can not convincingly be classified as historical fiction) featured a woman working as the author of gothic romances; some passages from these novels are partially also integrated into the text.

[12] Cf. Cumyn, "Reconfiguring the Nation: Intercultural Textuality and M. G. Vassanji's *The Book of Secrets*," and Ball, "Locating M. G. Vassanji's *The Book of Secrets*: Postmodern, Postcolonial, or Other-Wise?".

[13] Cf. Ball, "Taboos"; in this interview Vassanji explains, for example, the "multiple cultural and racial ancestries" in his stories: "It was natural because people are syncretistic, and there are various kinds of Islam, various kinds of Hinduism. On the east coast of Africa, you have the Bantu culture and the Arab culture, and the Swahili culture that was a mixture of these two. You have stories from the Middle East, from China, which were spawned within the local context. Plus we had English-style education, and our influence from American films, Hindi films, and so on. For me, that is really a wealth of experience that I treasure" (203-204).

"the Englishman's boy." His narrative is re-interpreted by a Canadian protagonist and long-time U.S. resident (working as a copywriter for silent films in the 1920s) and then violently appropriated by a rich, xenophobic Hollywood filmmaker. Therefore, the novel also tackles the discussion of the influence of films and the film industry on the construction and reception of history.[14] Guy Vanderhaeghe's follow up, *The Last Crossing* (2001) – one of the novels that is discussed in detail later – less prominently operates on and around meta-levels by which it might be regarded as representative of certain trends within the genre as a whole. His second novel is just one of many more examples that again lean toward more traditional narratives and more realistic narrative strategies, possibly signaling less concern for the complete deconstruction of the discursive act and mimetic illusion, while, at the same time, still insisting on challenging our gridlocked perceptions of histories and memories.

Jack Hodgins's *Broken Ground* (1998) deals with one of the most prominent issues of Canadian historical fiction – that of Canada's involvement in the World Wars, especially WWI.[15] While in his early works Hodgins had strongly adhered to postmodern and magic realist traditions, as in *The Invention of the World* (1977), in this novel, which focuses on the marginal personal perspectives of the inhabitants of a small, multicultural community of settlers, the author applies modernist narrative strategies through the rendering of protagonists' internal perspectives. Thereby he, like Vanderhaeghe, suggests a slightly revised approach to postmodernist narrative trends.

One may in fact observe that, like Hodgins and Vanderhaeghe, many authors who once experienced success with historical themes, tend to return to the subject matter – one of the reasons for this surely being that historical fiction has become such a marketable genre in Canada. The same is true for the works of Wayne Johnston, who, renowned for his rewriting of the historical figure of Newfoundland's first premier, Joe Smallwood in *The Colony of Unrequited Dreams* (1998), has recently published highly popular historical fictions: *The Navigator of New York* (2003) and *The Custodian of Paradise* (2006) – the latter promoted as a sequel to his 1998 bestseller.[16]

Contemporary historical fictions have very often situated their stories within the past and geography of a specific Canadian region; however, fictions of the past are by no way restricted only to specific Canadian regions – there seem to be examples for all Canadian provinces. (However, again other examples, such as the works of M.G.

[14] Wyile, "Dances With Wolfers: Choreographing History in *The Englishman's Boy*"; Kuester, " 'A Mythic Act of Possession': Constructing the North American Frontier(s) in Guy Vanderhaeghe's *The Englishman's Boy*"; Linton, "Narrative Geography in Guy Vanderhaeghe's *The Englishman's Boy*"; Bölling, " 'You're Not the Indian I Had in Mind': Hollywood's Appropriation of the Native Other in Thomas King's *Green Grass, Running Water* and Guy Vanderhaeghe's *The Englishman's Boy*."

[15] Cp. Grace 288. Other novels that are situated during the World Wars are, for example, Timothy Findley's *The Wars*; Jane Urquhart's *The Underpainter* and *The Stone Carvers*; Frances Itani's *Deafening*; Joseph Boyden's *Three Day Road*.

[16] While *The Colony of Unrequited Dreams* has been vividly discussed in the academia since its publication, Johnston's two more recent novels have so far hardly received any attention. Cf. Bak, "Writing Newfoundland, Writing Canada: Wayne Johnston's *The Colony of Unrequited Dreams*"; Dragland, "*The Colony of Unrequited Dreams*: Romancing History?"; MacLeod, "History versus Geography in Wayne Johnston's *The Colony of Unrequited Dreams*."

Vassanji, disregard local histories and identities, or move across regional or national boundaries). Thus, if Wayne Johnston wrote about Newfoundland history, and Hodgins as well as Robert Kroetsch remained most dedicated to the Western regions, Fred Stenson's *The Trade* (2000) and *Lightening* (2003) are set in Alberta. Fred Stenson's *The Trade* also belongs to those examples of recent historical fictions that have been criticized for their return to slightly more superficial approaches to the past.[17] Even if they contribute to the demythologization of national or regional history, and also focus on marginal figures of the past, at the same time, they return to romanticized visions, sometimes applying heavily lyrical descriptions and stereotypical representations of protagonists.[18] Some – presumably with the initial intention of deconstructing historiographic objectivity – make excessive use of diverse forms of historical sources, (auto-)biographies, archival material (as for example Fred Stenson) or books on the period, which in some cases has provoked lively debate.[19] These novels thus run the risk of being classified as works which only superficially use history as a commodity – an issue that is discussed by Herb Wyile, who, while analyzing this conflict in postmodern fictions of the past, quotes Frederic Jameson's critical perspectives[20]:

> The sense of depthlessness is fortified by the intertextuality and self-consciousness of postmodern cultural productions, which amounts for Jameson to a "reshuffling of fragments of preexistent texts, the building blocks of older cultural and social production, in some new or heightened bricolage: metabooks which cannibalize other books, metatexts which collate bits of other texts – such is the logic of postmodern in general." (*Speculative Fictions* 215)

Consequently, the best-selling popular versions of historical fictions of the past years have, on one hand, remained dedicated to the rewriting of historical events and personalities, as well as to the reinterpretation of the evidence available; on the other hand, they have, in several instances, moved (back) toward more realist renderings of the past and a less radical inclusion of deconstructive approaches to both historiography and fictional aesthetics. Writers belonging to marginalized ethnic communities have also written such historical novels – for example, Eva Stachniak in *The Garden of Venus* (2005). However, not only are far fewer migrant authors interested in (local) Canadian *H*istory, they have also on a general level been more concerned with far more critical evaluations of racial and ethnic injustices and uneven power relations.

The influence of postcolonial and subaltern discourses has likewise remained very strong in contemporary historical fictions. The interest in the rewriting of history by focusing on those ignored and forgotten and on repressed marginal histories has in no way declined. Yet authors of such works initially focused more strongly on the fate of marginal groups in Canada and their elision from the master narrative of history (such

[17] Cp. Katherine Durnin's essay "Archives and truth in Fred Stenson's *The Trade*."
[18] Another example for such a text is Michael Crummey's *River Thieves* (2001); cp. Sugars, "Original Sin, or, The Last of the First Ancestors: Michael Crummey's *River Thieves*."
[19] Cp. the above mentioned essays by Durnin and Sugars.
[20] The passage quoted in Wyile is taken from Frederic Jameson, *Postmodernism, or, The Cultural Logic of Late Capitalism* (Durham: Duke UP, 1991), 96.

as Joy Kogawa in *Obasan*, or Daphne Marlatt's feminist rewriting in *Ana Historic*). Especially since the 1990s these renderings of the past – often written by migrant authors – have moved to settings outside Canada, in some cases situating the historical fiction completely elsewhere. This move, which is echoed in the altered Fryian riddle "Where is there?" suggested by David Staines ("Canadian Literature at the Millennium" 33) can be seen as the result of the growing interest of migrant (postcolonial) writers in the history of their countries of origin, and as a way to trace their own hybrid as well as Canada's multicultural identities.[21]

Michael Ondaatje is in many ways an exception; not only is he a remarkable poet, but his works have also always been ahead of their time. In his fictions, he has often integrated such a diverse assotment of historical settings and events that a clear-cut assessment remains hard to attain. Ondaatje's novels are set more or less in an alternating progression, either in Canada or elsewhere. From very early on in his career he contributed a semi-fictional memoir with *Running in the Family* (1976) set in his original homeland, Sri Lanka – and later in *The English Patient* (1992), his multicultural cast of characters meet in the pre- and post-Second World War locales of Africa and Italy. *In The Skin of A Lion* (1987), which explores the marginal history and role of immigrants in the emerging Toronto of the 1920s and 30s, primarily takes place in a Canadian setting, while his penultimate novel, *Anil's Ghost* (2000) returns again to the present civil war setting of his home country.[22]

The list of Canadian authors that contribute to a more large-scale, planetary vision of revised historics is long: Rohinton Mistry's *Such A Long Journey* (1991) and *A Fine Balance* (1995) are both set in India's more recent past (1970s) during Indira Gandhi's regime; M.G. Vassanji's novels, already mentioned above, are almost all set outside Canada reflecting the author's own heritage; Austin Clarke's *The Polished Hoe* (2002) is set on a Carribean Island in 1952; and A.R. Badami's *Can You Hear The Nightbird Call?* (2006) is set in Canada and India, weaving a complex narrative that spans from the 1940s to the 1980s – just to name a few. Some authors with a recent immigrant background prefer to remain within Canada and reflect former pasts and histories as part of memories of migration, thereby evoking personal narratives and family histories, such as Andre Alexis in *Childhood* (1998), Wayson Choy in *The Jade Peony* (1995) and *All That Matters* (2004), and Anita Rau Badami in *Tamarind Mem* (1996) (and partially also in *Can You Hear the Nightbird Call?*).

At the same time, authors whose families settled in Canada several generations earlier, have also become increasingly interested in the investigation of their family's (mostly European) roots. Mennonite author Rudy Wiebe in *Sweeter Than All the World* (2001) traces his ancestors' flight from Danzig in the sixteenth century, and Canada's favorite short story author Alice Munro, in a recent work – though history has not been a prominent subject in her literary career so far – investigates her family's Scottish

[21] Of course, there are also non-migrant Canadian writers who have been interested in historical settings outside Canada, as for example Peter Oliva in *The City of Yes* (1999).

[22] Ondaatje's transcultural layerings and aesthetics in his most recent novel are discussed in the first part of Chapter 6.

background in *The View From Castle Rock* (2006), as does G.E. Clarke his family's Nova-Scotian heritage in *George and Rue* (2005).[23]
Another issue that has by no means forfeited any of its topicality is the analysis of the subaltern role of women in history. Ann Marie MacDonald's *Fall On Your Knees* (1996), as well as Jane Urquhart's novels and Dionne Brand's *In Another Place, Not Here* (1996) and *At the Full and Change of the Moon* (1999), all engage in the rewriting of official and unofficial pasts from a female perspective.[24] The one marginalized group that is now only slowly becoming confident within the scene of historical fictions are Aboriginal authors; as some innovative rewritings of history in recent years have shown – for example, the highly praised *Green Grass, Running Water* (1993) by Thomas King – Native cultural backgrounds and story-telling traditions offer highly fertile ground for very complex, transgeneric histories.

Since the last decade of the twentieth century, the genre has not only reached a new peak in popularity, it also displays an increasing amount of plurality on thematic as well as formal levels. In the context of the above-exemplified multiplicity of the historical genre in Canada, the following sections present a re-reading of some of Linda Hutcheon's claims concerning historical fictions and a critical evaluation of more recent perspectives on the genre.

Historiographic Metafiction, and Other Histories

One of the greatest achievements, and at the same time the most negotiatable one in Canadian criticism today, in regard to the historical genre has been the work of Linda Hutcheon. The importance of her studies for the emergence of new historical fictions in Canada remains undisputed: when the Toronto-based scholar published her two groundbreaking works on postmodernism in the 1980s, especially *The Canadian Postmodern: A Study of Contemporary English-Canadian Fiction*, she hit the zeitgeist.[25] Her publications not only offered revolutionary insights, in comparison to older, more traditional approaches to the genre, they were also especially important for the coming-of-age of an increasingly self-assured Canadian literature that was neither British nor American but specifically Canadian.[26] Nonetheless, the discrepancy between Hutcheon's visions of the genre and the contemporary plurality of generic expressions calls for a critical investigation of some of her ideas and a confrontation with more recent insights.

[23] G.E. Clarke's *George and Rue* is discussed in detail in Chapter 7.
[24] Jane Urquhart's most recent novel, *A Map of Glass*, and Brand's *At the Full and Change of the Moon* are discussed in Chapter 7 and 6, respectively.
[25] Her most important publications next to *The Canadian Postmodern* were *A Poetics of Postmodernism: History, Theory, Fiction* (London: Routledge, 1988) and *The Politics of Postmodernism* (London: Routledge, 1989). For a detailed enumeration of her most important essays, cf. Bölling 89.
[26] Cp. Rosenthal 303-304.

The developments in the academia that led to Hutcheon's new perspectives started much earlier, approximately after WWII, but only reached their climax in the 1980s.[27] As already clarified earlier, two things happened in these decades that were of great importance and were reflected in Canadian postmodern literature: the deconstruction of the master-narrative in terms of what had been constructed in the preceding centuries as the dominant colonially-oriented history, a trend which went hand-in-hand with the reform of historiography initiated by Hayden White; secondly, directly related to this, the increasing integration of "other" voices, be they neglected Native or recently immigrated new voices, or other marginalized groups into the literary canon.[28] Linda Hutcheon's theoretical works on historiographical metafiction remain essential today for the understanding of contemporary historical fictions. However, I am also of the opinion that the term (and concept) of 'historiographical metafiction' is no longer as adequate as it used to be and – as already highlighted in the last two sections – needs considerable rethinking in relation to the multiplicity and complexity this genre shows in present-day Canadian literature.

For Linda Hutcheon, postmodernism, as the emerging representative literary form of the 1960s and after, was to represent the possibility of a Canadian answer to the increasingly prominent critical theories (related to poststructuralism and what was later to be referred to as postcolonialism) and Canada's chance to establish itself on the literary globe:

> Formed out of North and South American as well as European cultures, postmodernism both confronts and goes beyond the problematics of colonial dependency, offering a new context in which to view the specificities of Canadian writing. (*The Canadian Postmodern* viii)

Postmodernism was seen as the mode to express a breaking free from colonial mindsets – a desire, which no longer seems necessary nowadays, as at least this instance of hegemonic attitude seems overcome and the related identity constructions dismantled; in fact, Canada has not only acknowledged its own status as a postcolonial country (as a former settler-invader nation), its literature today appears to be moving beyond already: "Too much has been made of origins," Dionne Brand repeatedly claims in a postnational vein close to twenty years later (*Map to the Door* 64).

The issue of the deconstruction of master narratives, which obviously represents a prerequisite for the evolution of alternative, decentralized discourses is related to what Hutcheon sees as the establishment of a postcolonial and postmodern identity: "The postmodern 'different,' then, is starting to replace the humanist 'universal' as a prime cultural value" (*The Canadian Postmodern* ix). Considering Canadian literature today, also reflected on a more general level within University literary curricula, we will find that (postcolonial) "difference" has become – in a more positive sense – the new master

[27] Cp. Chapter 1. Cf. also Rosenthal 291-303, and Redekop 264-273.

[28] As already discussed, the most-frequently mentioned novel, which is often taken as a starting point for this development in terms of the genre of postmodern historiographic metafiction, is Joy Kogawa's *Obasan* (1981) which gave voice to the approximately 25.000 Japanese-Canadians interned during and after WWII.

narrative of the late twentieth and early twenty-first centuries. However, through the study of very recent texts, especially historical fictions, we can discern that the matter is far more complex today and that more flexible analytical strategies, which also integrate an extended ethics of similarities, need to be considered. As Gordon Bölling has noted, contemporary fictions are often increasingly engaged not with specific Canadian moments in history but with more universal issues[29] – a fact which, even if it sounds like a contradiction, can at the same time be related to an increased interest in local and individual histories in opposition to global realities.[30]

The deconstruction of master narratives particular to historiographic metafiction, has led to its major function as ideological fiction, as Hutcheon remarks: "To write either history or historical fiction is equally to raise the question of power and control" (*The Canadian Postmodern* 72). Nothing can be argued against this diagnosis – the disclosure and deconstruction of established "imaginary" power networks and related static, unequal socio-cultural conceptions of identity markers remains an equally pressing issue today (especially in fictions written within subaltern and postcolonial discourses). However, it seems equally compelling to note – as anthropologists have been pointing out in past years – that culture should no longer be understood as a container but rather as a system that is formed and influenced by every individual and for each one in their own right; apart from that, it also appears relevant to acknowledge that the power relations themselves, as well as the "questions" that ought to be asked, might have changed.[31]

At least as prominently as the arguments that postulate a break down of mimetic illusions and epistemological structures, Hutcheon's work displays other related, post-structural stances that emphasize the interrogative mode and the exposure of the constructed nature of meaning. In her view, the study of the postmodern, and the postmodern itself, "is suspicious of the very notion of final answers. The interrogative is the mode of the postmodern" (*The Canadian Postmodern* X). This questioning "mode" also includes critical self-questioning and thus reflects "the awareness that all our systems of understanding are deliberate and historically specific human constructs […], with all the limitations and strengths which that definition entails" (ibid. X). This awareness is still strongly felt today, but it is not reflected so much in deconstructive, discursive procedures, i.e. in the need to expose the act of writing and the reading processes. As a consequence, in Canadian historical fictions today, we find far fewer narrators who directly address the reader, while fragmentation and plurality of voices are still very frequently used devices – a fact, which shows that also contemporary authors are still very well aware of the subjective nature of history, identity, and writing. They might even be more strongly aware of it than before, due to the movement towards an increasing focus on the individual. The major aim of postmodernist fiction has been to dismantle and lay bare the very constructed nature of human existence as well as our representations of it – a strategy executed in postmodern

[29] "Eine steigende Zahl von Romanen setzt sich nicht mit Aspekten einer spezifisch kanadischen Vergangenheit auseinander, sondern wendet sich vielmehr universalen Themen zu" (16).

[30] Cp. Chapter 3.

[31] Cf. Schulze-Engler, "From Postcolonial to Preglobal" 56-58; "Theoretical Perspectives" 20-28; Cp. also Chapter 3.

historiographical metafiction in particular through self-reflexivity, intertextuality, irony, and parody. In recent literature, and especially fictions of the past, these creative and partially politically motivated deconstructions remain a casually practiced literary device yet – as narrative techniques – do not stand at the center of writing.

It is interesting to note that only one major monograph on historical fiction in Canada appeared before Hutcheon's groundbreaking publication: Dennis Duffy's *Sounding the Iceberg*. With very few minor exceptions, it was one of the first studies that gave a encompassing overview of the development and importance of the genre in Canada since the nineteenth century.[32] However, as Bölling has underlined, the work falls short once it arrives at the discussion of the innovative postmodern historical fictions of the time.[33]

The publications on historical fiction in Canada that followed Linda Hutcheon's work, published between the 1980s and the late 90s, were all informed by her understanding of what she had defined as historiographic metafiction.[34] These articles and fewer monographs often focus on giving a general overview of the rise of postmodern historical fiction especially in relation to the formation of a distinct Canadian national identity (specifically through an analysis of nineteenth century historical fictions and the development from then until the 1980s).[35] When we look at the progress of these contributions, it becomes clear that the development of the historical genre is very tightly entwined with the emancipation of Canadian postcolonial identities. Thus, as Ronald Hatch puts it, following the end of World War II, innovative writers turned to "nation itself as a source of values to free the individual from the forces of history" ("Narrative Development" 80); more than fifteen years later, Wolfgang Klooss somewhat closes the circle by claiming that "[i]dentity construction in Canadian historiographic (meta)fiction emerges as a discourse about the hiding and revealing of difference. The (imperial) master narrative of an all-encompassing Canadian identity is

[32] These minor exceptions were mainly articles appearing here and there; the genre was not taken seriously for a long period of time (until the publications of Duffy and Hutcheon), to such a degree that one article appeared in a Journal on Children's literature in 1981. See, for example, McCourt, "The Canadian Historical Novel," and Atkinson, "Canadian Historical Fiction: A Survey."

[33] Bölling 20.

[34] Cp. again my earlier discussion of some of these works, at the beginning of this chapter.

[35] Apart from the monographs mentioned earlier, one might here add Ronald Hatch, "Narrative Development in the Canadian Historical Novel" (1986); ibid., "Change and the Concept of History in the Canadian Historical Novel"; T.D. MacLulich, *Between Europe and America* (1988) – herein especially Chapter 2, "Romances of the New World"; after the 1990s, critics began to emphasize specific groups of (marginalized) writers, or certain aspects of the characteristics defined by Hutcheon, sometimes both. In *Framing Truths*, for example, Martin Kuester studied the parodic structure of historiographic metafiction); for more recent examples in which the analysis of historical fiction towards historiographic metafiction prevails: Wolfgang Klooss, "Forms of Identity Construction in English-Canadian Historical (Meta)Fiction" (2000); and Don Sparling, "History and Identity – The Case of Historical Fiction" (2002).

replaced by a post-colonial notion of an identity beyond nation" ("Forms of Identity Construction" 91).[36]

The first major, more recent, publication that considerably adapted and reworked former approaches to the genre was Herb Wyile's *Speculative Fictions: Contemporary Canadian Novelists and the Writing of History* published in 2001. I would like to highlight it in this discussion of the development of historical fiction as it represents a moment of climax and change in the evolving critical discourses on Canadian historical fiction since the 1980s. Wyile's study, which is extremely well-written and comprehensive, discusses at least twenty contemporary Anglo-Canadian novels and describes, in great detail, the bulk of critical theory that had an impact on and led to the forms of historical fictions that we read in Canada today. There are, however, as Wyile to a great extent notes himself, some weaknesses in his book. One example (and I am not sure there are many more), is the exclusion of a perspective on Native authors and the dominance of non-minority writers – a not completely tangible selective strategy, which he preserves in his most recent contribution, a collection of interviews with Canadian authors of historical fiction.

Many of the ideas that Wyile presents in his study, perpetuate the dominant perspective of 'historiographical metafiction' – yet, at the same time, his study, in many respects, offers a more accessible and inclusive approach. Thus, he also integrates a whole chapter that is dedicated to "the relation between the increasing interest in history on the part of English-Canadian historical novelists and our own historical moment [...] the ambivalent relationship between contemporary historical fiction and the commodity culture of which it is part"(xv).

In his analysis of contemporary Canadian metafictional historical novels, Gordon Bölling also acknowledges Wyile's valuable contribution that – contrary to other studies of the past decades – adequately attempts to deal with the multiplicity the genre has to offer. However, contrary to the reading suggested in this book, Bölling strongly objects to Wyile's comment that "Canadian historical novels have become less experimental rather than more" (Wyile, *Speculative Fictions* 162).[37] Bölling's reaction is, I would argue, just as valid as Wyile's statement: while Wyile rightly observes a certain tendency away from strictly postmodern historiographical metafiction, Gordon Bölling in his study focuses on metafictional narrative strategies in contemporary historical fiction, which admittedly still remains a prominent (though not the dominant) mode in present day literature. Bölling's *History in the Making*, published in 2007, represents a highly valuable resource as it opens up alternative perspectives on the understanding of the metafictional form of historical fiction. He regards it as a narrative genre, separate from postmodernism, which existed long before the 1960s and continues to do so.[38] Apart from this differing stance on the history and importance of metafiction,

[36] This essay by Klooss was also published in a longer version entitled "From Colonial Madness to Postcolonial Ex-Centricity."

[37] Quoted and discussed in Bölling 22.

[38] In this respect, Bölling also strongly criticizes Hutcheon, cp. *History in the Making* 39, and 46.

Bölling's analysis, which discusses five more recent contemporary texts in impressive detail, resonates with the dominant perspectives on the genre.[39]

In the introduction to their study, *Literatures of Memory*, which innovatively unites readings of drama, poetry and fiction in one book, Middleton and Woods highlight several critical developments and links between theoretical observations that – in their opinion were expressed in fiction through forms of memory – echo "the intensity of public literary debates centred upon the politics, ethics and epistemology of historical literature" (I). Most importantly, however, the two critics take conclusive first steps toward a newly reflected perspective on the postmodernist stance:

> Finally, as Bernstein and Ricoeur imply, existing critical recognition of history in literature has understandably been somewhat narrow – mostly confined to realist historical fiction. This is why the enormously influential periodising concept of postmodernism remains both useful and inadequate. Its rethinking of modernism, its rejection of foundationalism and its questioning of totalizing forms of history is crucial for the recognition of these new literatures; its epochal periodising and its coercive generality sometimes obscure the diversity of contemporary genres and their literary histories, as well as their different practices of memory, time and space. (Middleton and Woods 3)

Similarly to Peter Middleton and Tim Woods, Birgit Neumann in her recent study, *Erinnerung—Identität—Narration*, takes memory research as a starting point and the basis for her approach towards historical fictions.[40] However, while the analysis of *Literatures of Memory* remains strongly rooted in a theory-focused thematic perspective, Neumann's study eventually attempts (and succeeds in) the composition of an intricate narratological typology for contemporary fictions that rewrite the past.[41] Her study is theoretically well founded, as she explores the complex relations and interactions of memory, identity and narration via psychological and socio-cultural theories; furthermore, she manages to show how these very fictions, which despite the difference in the analytic emphasis and terminology, are also the subject of this study, in a reciprocal reaction, exert an influence on society's identity constructions and (communal) cultures of memory by taking Paul Ricoeur's mimetic model as a foundation. In her analytical section, which exemplifies her four-leveled typology of fictions of memory, Neumann discusses at least twenty contemporary Canadian novels, which include the works of writers with diverse cultural backgrounds. The result is a most-promising, first major interdisciplinary approach to the genre, which opens up new vistas and reveals the potential this many-facetted genre has come to offer.

[39] The novels he discusses are Margaret Atwood, *Alias Grace*; Timothy Findley, *Famous Last Words*; Anne Michaels, *Fugitive Pieces*; Michael Ondaatje, *In the Skin of a Lion*; and Carol Shields, *The Stone Diaries*.

[40] Birgit Neumann's work is related to the narratological and memory research school around Nünning and Erll, cp. also Chapter 1; I shortly discussed Middleton and Woods at the beginning of Chapter 2.

[41] In her typology Neumann differentiates especially between the following hard to translate categories: "Autobiographische Gedächtnisromane," "Autobiographische Erinnerungsromane," "Kommunale Gedächtnis-romane," and "Soziobiographische Erinnerungsromane."

In 2003, the spectrum of approaches to historical fiction was significantly broadened by Gabriele Helms's book-length study on Canadian texts that resist the hegemonic nature of history through the use of dialogic narrative techniques; the combination of an analysis in terms of modernist and postmodernist discursive strategies, as well as postcolonial fictional rewritings emphasizes the continued opening up of former generic boundaries, and thereby represents an exemplar for current approaches to the genre. The developments in English-language historical fiction in Canada, as well as the critical reactions of the past decades, are numerous and diversified. Yet the historical genre has to date hardly received attention in terms of interdisciplinary and transcultural readings, which take into account the impact of globalization. The following re-collects the major, more recent reactionary alterations within the genre and investigates why its parameters should be redefined in terms of *fictions of the past*.

'Tis Twenty Years Since. Or, 'Fictions of the Past'

The title of this subchapter refers to the title of Sir Walter Scott's widely read canonical historical novel *Waverley, Or, Tis Sixty Years Since* (1814). As Nathan Uglow observes in his article on the novel in the *Literary Encyclopedia*, it was the 'program' indicated in this very subtitle that largely contributed to its popularity:

> But its chief selling point was its detailed treatment of the customs and manners in Scotland (both Highland and Lowland) sixty years since – a phrase that acts as a leitmotif throughout the book. This evocation of patterns of life so recent yet so different from those of today was a fascinating reminder of the speed and thoroughness of modern development, and an appealing resource for a society that was beginning to treat lifestyles as fodder for commercial exploitation. (Uglow 2nd paragraph, *online resource*, n.pag.)

In the title of this chapter the reference to Sir Walter Scott points toward a twofold observation. On the one hand, it indicates a change in historical fictions today in comparison to the original romantic form on one specific level – namely in the perception of time. While the focus in the traditional novel, such as the novels written by Scott, used to be set on the alluring exoticism of older customs and the speed of their change over time, this separation in narrative time appears blurred in contemporary examples. On the other hand, the title points to the fact that, at the time of writing these pages, twenty years have passed since the revolutionary publication of Hutcheon's important studies on historiographic metafiction; a period long enough to suggest that several significant alterations may have occurred in the genre since.

There are two major innovations in contemporary fictions of the past, which are effective in several spheres, that justify a revision of analytical readings: the negotiation and loosening of the temporal boundaries between the past, present, and future within the genre (here suggestively termed trans-historicity), and the novel tendency toward the expression of a *trans*cultural imaginary – as a result of numerous socio-cultural, critical, and political developments. It is those present-day characteristics, represented on both formal and thematic levels of narration, which distinctly set them apart from earlier forms of the genre.

Already in modernist and postmodernist historical fiction, the relationship between past and present becomes an increasingly complex issue. Due to their skepticism toward historical knowledge and the accuracy of human representations of history, innovative writers after World War II have steadily called into question a sanctioned differentiation between past fact and present fiction. As David Lucking explains in regard to the construction of identities via narratives of the past:

> Since this is an essentially retrospective enterprise, taking as its real point of departure not some originating moment in the past but a state of affairs in the present, the narratives in both cases are subject to potentially limitless manipulation. It is not so much the present that is the product of the past, in other words, as it is the past that is a kind of backward projection of the present. In both the private and the public spheres the past is quarried for significance, and when the past fails to satisfy the exigencies of the present, it is more or less deliberately rewritten. An awareness of the dynamics of this process leads to a deep-seated ambivalence with respect both to the past in which identity is supposed to be rooted and to the memory which would seem to certify the stability and continuity of that identity. (Lucking 15)

Thus, especially in postmodern historiographic metafiction, the deconstruction of the discursive act and narrative illusion, which reveals the "potentially limitless manipulation" of "retrospective enterprises," leads to a stronger relationship and interaction between the temporal levels. Beginning in the late 1960s, postmodern authors developed a special interest in the integration of present perspectives (i.e. passages set in the present) into their historical fictions, which function as a means to disclose and question the historiographic epistemological as well as fictional mimetic strategies. The postmodern crossing of temporalities is often represented in fiction by a protagonist (for example, a historian) who does archival research on some past event or personality, and thereby contributes to the process of re-reading, re-narrating, and re-writing of history.[42] Additionally, intertextuality and the inclusion of other narrative forms such as myths and oral tales, as well as the role of the subjective interpretation of histories, lead to an abandonment of exotic, remote settings. In contemporary historical fictions, the breaking up of temporal limits, or rather the increasing connection between time-levels seems even more radical. What might have started out as a to some extent ideologically informed narrative strategy in postmodern fictions has undergone several extensions and alterations. Most importantly, however, the original aesthetic and deconstructive intent has gradually been superseded (though not completely replaced) by an attempt to understand the present 'sameness' in terms of past 'difference,' and by finding temporally unifying answers beyond the logics of politics and time, instead of primarily questioning the objectivity of present re-collections and interpretations of the past.

[42] Examples of such protagonists can be found in Daphne Marlatt's *Ana Historic*, Leonard Cohen's *Beautiful Losers*, Timothy Findley, *The Wars* and *Famous Last Words*, and Michael Ondaatje's *In the Skin of a Lion*.

In his final chapter on historical fiction in Canada, Herb Wyile argues – against widespread contemporary concerns that the presentness of postmodernity might eliminate our feeling for pastness – that in contemporary fictions of the past, this "temporal duality" (*Speculative Fictions* 214) is used dominantly in order to express critical perspectives on the impact of modern industries and technologies, transnational capitalism, and the possible loss of historical consciousness in the contemporary globalized age:

> While there is no doubt that contemporary Canadian historical novelists are exploiting the allure of history, the temporal duality of their work nonetheless provides for a very discriminating and critical stance toward postmodern society rather than simply a collusion with it. These novels quite obviously dramatize a consciousness of how perceptions of the past are necessarily infected by the present – especially the insistent present of a dehistoricizing postmodernity. Yet they resist the notion that such presentism amounts to a form of advanced glaucoma, a thorough obscuring of historical vision by contemporaneity, and instead strive to keep in view what might have preceded and shaped that present. (ibid. 255)

Yet there seems to be more to this dual temporality than one might assume from a reading of Wyile's comprehensive discussion of "Commodity Culture and Historicity." I would like to argue that this temporal dialogue, or rather polylogue, is a central feature of the genre in its contemporary form, in that it not only effectively bursts more rigid boundaries within the genre concerning temporal settings but also operates as a powerful source and starting point for several other major characteristics. It is at this point that we might come to speak of what might be called "trans-historicity" in contemporary historical fictions, which suggests that the past of 'fictions of the past' is not limited in scope to historical settings and interpretations of history only but rather has a profound impact on the present and in effect, also on the future. At the same time, this feature expresses a continued or even increased questioning of *H*istory as a master narrative and constitutive element of national identities, insofar as that an even stronger focus is set on individual and communal histories. The highest aim in historical novels of the late twentieth century has become the desire to value histories as anti-master-narratives in the postmodern anti-essentialist sense. However, in very recent contemporary fictions of the past, this aim does not ultimately result in a complete deconstruction of the epistemological meaning of history, but in a new desire to validate temporary stabilities in order to understand the pluralized complexities of human existence.

This development, which sheds relativism based on aesthetic considerations in favor of temporary ethical values, is also linked to a further important feature, the focus on individual narratives, identities, and memories. As Martin Löschnigg claims,

> there seems to have been a shift in contemporary Canadian literature from questions of 'Canadianness' to questions of individual or communal identity within larger national and international frames. Rather than commenting on the elusive concept of a collective 'Canadian' identity and its manifestations around the turn of the millennium, I propose to investigate the construction of individual identity in a Canadian context. ("Creating Lives" 95)

Within these individual identity explorations, the communal and postnational spheres become prominent, by which definitions of gender, ethnicity, race, class, and so on are revised in order to re-imagine them in and for the present via explorations of the past. This very feature – and here the extent of the increasingly pluri-hybrid nature of the genre is revealed – refers back to what was discussed at the beginning of the third chapter in terms of transgenericity. This focus on individual ramifications of identity also engenders the already mentioned movement towards an analysis of "literatures of memory" (Middleton and Woods) and "fictions of memory" (Neumann).

The memory-mode thus represents a further trait within the cluster of reconfigurations of the relation between past and present in present-day historical fictions. The connection here is twofold. On the one hand, the growing use of 'remembering' as a narrative strategy, as well as a thematic concern, has been a result of postcolonial, subaltern, and migrant authors' desires to include personal histories, family narratives, oral tales passed on between generations, and memories of places left behind or neglected in official history, into the network of "writing back" the past. The increased impact of postcolonial authors, as well as the actual experience and the rising number of immigrants, must be seen as resulting from the positive and negative effects of globalization. At the same time, on a more general level, the focus on memory, especially on individual memory, must be seen as a reaction – mainly of protest – to the confusing information-overload and superficiality of contemporary globalized existence. Thus, on the other hand, a focus on remembering, on the personal recollections and interpretation of pasts, offers the possibility to resist these global developments that pass over cultural individuality. At the same time, this form of resistance also makes use of the 'positive' effects of globalization by taking advantage of, rejecting, or incorporating cultural information flows and diversities: "Indeed, as Michael Watts has revealed, transnationalization has, on the one hand, contributed to local revitalization, while on the other it has triggered new modes of resistance" (Kalogeras et al. xiii).

The complex time travels which one finds in contemporary historical novels seem to have moved away from their focus on the national, not only by transgressing the national space in favor of places outside Canada that define planetary memories and histories of migration and cultural exchange.[43] In addition to this 'opening up,' they also display the opposite, a turning toward the personal, the individual self.[44] Absurdly, this contrasting combination of expanding and internalizing developments, to which the present-day globalized individual will easily and readily relate, makes contemporary fictions of the past more universal.[45] Both these characteristics, the closeness of past and present, and the predominance of memory (as opposed to either the complete historical immersion in or partial temporal separation of protagonists from historical settings)

[43] As in the works of so diverse authors as M.G.Vassanji, Rohinton Mistry, Sandra Birdsell, Michael Ondaatje, Peter Oliva, Dionne Brand, and many more.

[44] Cp. Schulze-Engler, "From Postcolonial to Preglobal," and Vautier, "Religion, Postcolonial Side-by-sideness, and *la transculture*." A good example for a Canadian text that displays many of the discussed complexities is Alistair MacLeod's *No Great Mischief*, also discussed by Birgit Neumann, *Erinnerung-Identität-Narration* 349-365.

[45] And as one might argue, also more popular and 'commercial.'

must then be regarded as catalysts for further dominant thematic dualities. These dichotomous concerns are not necessarily opposed but constantly interact, merge, and evolve, resulting in a complex web of pluralities, which challenge the most often antagonistically interpreted concepts of global versus local, and individual versus universal. Middleton and Woods describe these changing modes in similar terms:

> New genres of writing about the past have developed phenomenologies of spacetime that are not yet fully recognized and legitimised by either theory or the institutions of public history. Narrative, memory, performance and the production and circulation of texts are all implicated in the new spacetime and history, therefore, takes many forms in contemporary literature, some of them far from obvious. We argue that some of the most original investigations of historicity are taking place in literary practices that are especially aware of the changing conditions of life in space and time, and yet do not advertise themselves as historical literatures. (Middleton and Woods 9)

The second most apparent new tendency in contemporary fictions of the past concerns a major shift from postmodern aesthetic concerns and deconstructive modes to more ethical, postnational, and, to use Schulze-Engler's expression, "transmodern" retellings of the past ("Transnationale Kultur" 79). Contemporary fictions of the past must be regarded as reflecting cosmopolitan quests for identity on one hand, as well as the result and continuation of transnational migrant hybridities on the other; both have extended their potential to effect the emergence of transcultural imaginaries in literature, which defy both postcolonial essentialist politics and postmodern arbitrariness. As Vautier observes in regard to postcolonial fiction:

> In recent postcolonial novels, one can see a new direction. This new direction has less to do with resistance to forces of empire, less to do with land and territoriality and "nation," and perhaps less to do with belonging and non-belonging. It has more to do with *"l'imaginaire de l'identitaire,"* with the abstract, the mind, the spiritual, and even the soul. ("Religion, Postcolonial Side-by-Sidedness, and *la transculture*" 270)

Overall, the postmodern literary form offers a possibility to express liberation from imperialistic mindsets – a breaking free informed by poststructuralist thinking that insists on the relativization of meaning (which is always artificial and constructed), thus entailing the firmly established characteristics of historiographic metafiction.[46] However, we seem to have reached a period of increased questioning of the feasibility of everlasting fluidity and randomness of reality introduced and promoted in the postmodern form of the historical novel. The original skepticism toward master narratives appears to have taken a new route, displaying an increasing negotiation of the ever-deconstructive mode. Thus, contemporary fictions of the past express a growing yearning for what might be summarized as a renewed shift toward more stable forms of meaning. I am referring to what Werner Wolf several years ago defined as fiction that "turns postmodernist self-reflexivity against itself: instead of using it in order to illustrate once again the by now hackneyed thesis of the indifferent fictionality of all

[46] Characteristics such as parody, irony, self-reflexivity, and intertextuality. Cf. for example, Walter Pache, "'The Fiction Makes Us Real': Aspects of Postmodernism in Canada."

meaning, [it] employs self-reflexivity in order to show that both poetic and religious faith […] is still possible and can persuasively be linked to ethics" (Wolf 120).
Nowadays, an evolution of many of these formerly dominant (postmodern and postcolonial) notions seems to be in progress, a development which is expressed in contemporary Canadian literature. Canadian critics have not only questioned Canada's status as postcolonial country (as a former settler/invader nation), thus moving toward a realization of post-postcolonial responsibilities, which no longer focuses on the victimization of Canada.[47] There has also been, as displayed in a number of texts, a renewed yearning for the creation of temporary stable meaning. As Frank Schulze-Engler rightly observes in one of his essays, "the negotiation of intermediate truths, temporary frameworks of communication and provisionally shared ground may ultimately be an intellectually more pressing (and politically more rewarding) task than the incessant dismantling of universalist discourses or hegemonic master narratives ("From Postcolonial to Preglobal" 62). This very search for "intermediate truths" is in contemporary historical fictions echoed on formal-aesthetic, socio-political, and thematic levels. It would be misleading and presumptuous to claim that the postmodernist destabilizing aesthetics and narrative modes have disappeared from contemporary texts or are no longer regarded by authors as valid forms of writing, on the contrary, with few exceptions, most historical fictions written in the past decade manifest an awareness and willingness to openly display the discursive act, as well as the subjectivity of historical (re-) writing.[48] One might in fact argue that postmodernist aesthetics have been pushed closer to the margin of the genre – the postmodern awareness of constructed realities has nowadays become more commonplace – while at the same time, a less radical deconstruction of narrative form and theme also accommodates the new longing for temporary stability.

As all these developments show, a more flexible understanding of former traditional generic boundaries and a reformed, or extended, understanding of the postmodern strategies that deconstruct them is required in order for the works in question to be understood as contemporary *fictions of the past*. What makes these fictions 'historical,' from the perspective presented in this study, is their focus on the importance of past events in the construction of individual and collective cultural imaginaries. Due to the parallel development and mutual influence of contemporary literary theories and Canadian historical fiction, as well as the change in the contexts of realities on a planetary scale, the genre today displays an altered set of parameters. Contemporary fictions of the past prominently feature aspects of transgenericity, transhistoricity, and a transcultural ethics of identities – all of which contribute to the kaleidoscopic nature of these texts. The second theoretical part of this study develops this argument by "weighing the impact" of globalization on literature; it discusses the idea of multiculturalism in Canada in the context of emerging alternative critical interpretations of cultural plurality and expounds concrete suggestions towards an analysis of transcultural imaginaries.

[47] Cf. Moss, *Is Canada Postcolonial? Unsettling Canadian Literature*; as well as other critical approaches in Cynthia Sugar's anthology, such as Thomas King, "Godzilla vs. Post-colonial."
[48] Cf. the first section in Chapter 2.

Part 2 – Interdisciplinary Innovations and Reflections

In the past twenty years, postcolonial studies have been concerned with the development of theories that capture processes of cultural transfer in the context of forced interactions between former colonized and colonizing cultures. While Homi Bhabha, for example, introduced the concepts of "hybridity," "mimicry," and "third space" (*The Location of Culture* 158-166, 172, 121-131, 303-337), which are widely applied in discussions of New Literatures today, Mary L. Pratt in her study on imperial travel writing used the term "contact zones" to describe the actual and mental geographies of colonial encounter (Pratt 4-7). These critical conceptualizations attempt to theorize the intrinsic modes and the forces behind cultural constructions of the post-colonial and -colonized mind – constructions effected by imaginaries that have become many layered due to the imposed contact of originally disparate cultures. Notably, both Bhabha and Pratt succeed in explaining these processes and their effects through concepts that apply metaphors of 'space' as a dimension of the collective and individual mind.

Setting out from partially similar lines of thought, though from a very different angle, issues of space as well as discussions on local and global impact dimensions are also prominently disputed in sociological and cultural studies discourses on globalization. The obvious crossover of interests with regard to conceptualizations of space, culture, and identity has yet remained largely unattended to, and postcolonial scholars in particular have repeatedly expressed their reluctance to acknowledge the fact that globalizing forces have also had positive effects on cultures – though this reluctance is justified only to some extent.[1] Very few critics have attempted to develop further this most likely profitable collaboration between globalization research and postcolonial criticism, despite the very fact that the two parties share an interest and have both provided a fair amount of output on the analysis of hybrid cultural 'zones' and 'spaces.' Yet it is only at the crossroads of these theoretical realms that a discussion on transcultural imaginaries meets fertile ground.

The effects and quantity of cultural contact zones, as well as levels of contact that this world experiences, as we are all aware, by far exceed the limits of the postcolonial. Cultural transfer is as old as the cultures the Earth has seen; however, one must admit that the study of postcolonial cultures and literatures opened up new perspectives and paved the way for a set of key theories and terms that succeed in capturing major aspects of cultural exchange processes. Yet we must also concede that points of cultural contact were not only uniquely effected by imperial voyages and conquests but have in recent *post*colonial times additionally increased due to 'new imperialisms': developments in communication technology, transportation, and transnational cultural and economic exchange.[2] Thus, while these global developments might not be effectively evaluated to their greatest extent in Pratt's and Bhabha's postcolonial

[1] For a critical postcolonial perspective on globalization, cf. Brennan, "From Development to Globalization"; for essays that discuss this 'critical postcolonial perspective,' cf. Huggan, "Postcolonial Studies and the Anxiety of Interdisciplinarity"; Eckstein, "Introduction" and Schulze-Engler, "Theoretical Perspectives."

[2] Cf. Schulze-Engler, "Theoretical Perspectives" 23; Cp. also Kraidy, *Hybridity,* and Tomlinson, *Globalization and Culture*.

studies, they are still only one step away from the more general concepts of cultural space that have recently been developed in theories across the disciplines. My approach to transcultural imaginaries represents a similar attempt to study the many facets and levels of cultural mindscapes of the present, all of which are constituted by their multiple interactions with constructions of identities. They are reflected in literature and surface as mental 'spaces,' which are defined (and continuously redefined) by constantly negotiated contemporary – in our case Canadian – cultural images and imaginaries, transfers, and histories. These abstract spaces, which refer back to Kulyk Keefer's vision of a Canadian kaleidoscope, defy conventional, one-dimensional interpretations. As Henry LeFebvre has already knowingly questioned, "How many maps [...] might be needed to deal with a given space, to code and decode all its meanings and contents? It is doubtful whether a finite number can ever be given in answer to this sort of question" (LeFebvre qtd. in Yaeger 16: 86).[3] In a globalized age of technological modernity, migration, and postcolonial restitution, indeed some of the aspects that have come to determine Canadian identities cannot be adequately mapped. Dionne Brand insists on the very first page of her memoir-related book *A Map to the Door of No Return: Notes on Belonging* (2001), which includes memories from her childhood, reflections on the contemporary situation of the Black Diaspora, travel notes, as well as numerous literary and historical references (many on map-making):

> There are maps to the Door of No Return. The physical door. They are well worn, gone over by cartographer after cartographer [...] But to the Door of No Return which is illuminated in the consciousness of Blacks in the Diaspora there are no maps. This door is not mere physicality. It is a spiritual location. (Brand 1)[4]

Not only has the space extended in terms of specific places included in the mind-maps of Canadian imaginaries, but the amount of information and of possible defining spheres of difference and similarity has complicated constructions of cultural mindscapes. The realization of the amount and impact of mental processes at work behind constructions of self and other, necessitate new interdisciplinary collaborations, especially for the understanding of cultural productions, be it in literature or any other form of artistic or cultural expression.

The fictions of the past that are discussed later in this study, can be seen as literary examples for this new mode of complexity, which reflects the multiple impacts of global cultural forces, rethinks identities, and is not effectively narrowed down by deconstructive aesthetics and postcolonial politics (both of which have affected biased interpretations). An examination of postnational transcultural imaginaries as an extended vision of global hybridities and contact zones in cultural productions offers

[3] Yaeger quotes Henri LeFebvre, *The Production of Space* (trans. Donald Nicholson-Smith, Oxford: Blackwell 1991).

[4] The "Door of No Return" obviously refers to the Middle Passage.

itself as one possibility to approach the shifting nature of identities not only in fictions of the past, but also in other genres and literatures.[5]

[5] To give an example beyond the genre of fictions of the past, Dionne Brand's most recent novel *What We All Long For* (2005) would offer itself to an analysis of transcultural imaginaries. The novel depicts the interacting lives of multiethnic youths in contemporary Toronto. Cf. i.e. Johansen, "'Streets Are the Dwelling Place of the Collective'."

3 Globalization and Literature – Weighing the Impact

Globalization as well as theories on globalization are linked to a set of problems that need to be confronted in the present study. First, globalization theory is well developed within certain disciplines such as economic and political studies, and has received considerable attention in cultural studies, but few approaches exist in the field of literary studies. The second major problem concerning those approaches that refer to the effects of globalization on world structures and cultures is that many discussions are limited to two oppositional extremes. Either they focus on the negative effects of globalization as a (continued) form of imperialism in the name of capitalism, leading to worldwide cultural sameness;[1] or globalizing forces are heralded as the ultimate solution for humanity in that they foster a cosmopolitan cultural understanding and a new variety of cultural differences in the global community.[2] The one approach is solely critical, the other, most likely, too idealistic.[3] However, there are increasingly more theorists from various disciplines (some working on an interdisciplinary scale) that present more differentiated views on the details of the processes and effects of transnationalism, global cultural developments, and complexified identities. The academia still remains severely divided on how to approach the issue and whether it even should be approached – a situation which results in one group of scholars working extensively in this area of research, some producing remarkable thoughts and insights, and another group remaining ever skeptical and relentlessly focusing on the surely existent weaknesses of modernity. Thus, as Simon During sums up the critical perspective, in a comment on the recent wave of "contemporary cosmopolitan intellectualism," even if some approaches seem highly inspiring, they supposedly often lack "any analytic power to bear on the conceptual/political difficulties that beset the analysis of global culture," and he adds, "[w]e have yet to see what, if any, academic concepts and cultural maps will cover the various spheres of globalised culture as older terms such as postmodernism (and postcolonialism) fade" (During 92).

As will become obvious in the following pages, there are indeed several critical approaches that have produced highly useful "concepts and cultural maps" that can be integrated in interdisciplinary analytical approximations to literature, while at the same time allowing for a careful questioning of "older, fading terms." What can definitely be observed is that an increasing number of critical studies have overcome, and left behind, the possible extreme positions acknowledging the Janus-faced nature of globalization and weighing the results cautiously. Thus, in the preface to the second edition of the programmatic economic and political study *Globalization / Anti-globalization. Beyond the Great Divide*, to give an example, David Held and Anthony McGrew call attention

[1] These are most often theories with a Hegelian-Marxist background, such as the works of i.e. Immanuel Wallerstein, Francis Fukuyama, and Michael Hardt and Antonio Negri.

[2] Cf. for example, Arjun Appadurai, *Modernity at Large*.

[3] For an overview of the various approaches to globalization also cf. During 81-95.

to their "engaging with much more sophisticated critiques of globalization and responses to them, as well as with the blurring of the boundaries between these positions. In particular the distinction between globalizers and anti-globalizers has become less sharp as the political [and also cultural etc.] emphasis has shifted towards the shared ground of alternative forms of globalization – that of the 'alt-globalizers'" (xii).[4]

Approaches to Globalization

If we consider the significance of the matter in question – the relevance and effects of globalization in a plurality of fields, both in real life and in scientific theories –, the number of publications on the issue and the amount of controversies over how to classify and analyze it does not come as a surprise. The greatest potential for dispute and confusion might first be found in the differentiation made between modernity and globalization. Some critics like to see globalization as the recent (and possibly final) stage in the process of modernity, which is in certain fields often equated with industrialization and/or the technological revolution of the twentieth century as well as the development of societies from a small-scale, communal awareness to increasingly larger forms of social identification;[5] others insist on a strict division, thereby also communicating an understanding of 'postmodernity,' not as evolution or a new phase of modernity (as suggested in the former position), but as an "anti-modernism" and a temporary trend in capitalist society, and if one might carry further and dramatize this view, also as a whim of scholars in need of a new dashing epochal term.[6]

The vernacular use of the term "globalization," as discussed by Simon During, refers mainly to a process and condition of the twentieth century, however this perspective is opposed to the view of numerous scholars who have traced the long history of globalization(s).[7] Depending on the disciplinary perspective and emphasis[8], this approach discloses differing potential points of departure: the Peace of Westphalia 1648 (as the moment of introduction of the idea of sovereign states), the Enlightenment

[4] Held and McGrew's use of the terms of globalizers / anti- (/alt-) globalizers is slightly confusing, I am assuming it refers to the different forms of critics that believe in the existence of globalization as both condition and politics, respectively either viewing globalization positively and or negatively (or alternatively), all grouped as "globalists" (as opposed to the "skeptics," who question the viability of any analysis of globalization per se).

[5] Cp. Macey's entry on "modernity," 259-260.

[6] During 79-106; Roland Robertson, *Globalization* (modernity separated from globalization); Timothy Brennan, "From development to globalization" (globalization theory is counterproductive and imaginary, postmodernism as a variant of modernism/ty); Frederic Jameson, *Postmodernity, Or the Cultural Logic of Late Capitalism* (focus on negative effects of globalization).

[7] During 86; cf. MacGillivray, *A Brief History of Globalization* (typical approach and popular study on globalization as a century-long development).

[8] As highlighted earlier, it also depends on whether the critic quasi equates globalization to modernity, or not.

period of the sixteenth and seventeenth centuries (as the point of emergence of rationalism), and the beginning of Western expansionism and imperialism in 1492 (During 83), to name the most important.[9] Most approaches to globalization are often, and understandably, predominantly concerned with the economic situation[10], which is one of the factors at the core of the dispute; but attempts to grasp other major directions have often led to either greater confusion or involved radical simplifications and biased views; the cause of these problems can be found in the binaries and contradictions inherent in this very interdisciplinary phenomenon.

If we put aside all the negative implications in Timothy Brennan's article in *The Cambridge Companion to Postcolonialism*, "From Development to Globalization," and also ignore the one-sided, generalizing undertone in his list of five positions, which according to him regularly arise in the bulk of globalization theories, he does succeed in capturing some fundamental ambiguities (Brennan 122-128). First, he observes the opposition between globalization judged as a social, economic, and political process and progress, in short, a *general development* in the modern world, as opposed to it being seen as a *condition* and, in extension, a *policy* (designed by both "modern humans" – capitalists, neo-liberalist, western politicians, idealist cosmopolitans – and theoretical critics).[11] Secondly, he points toward a normative tension, between globalization nurturing new openness versus its limiting of heterogeneity leading to global sameness. The paradox of these ambiguities is echoed in approaches such as the one developed by Homi Bhabha, who simplifies the argument and also crosses the perspectives: on the one hand, he discerns a global form of cosmopolitanism, which summarizes all effects and positions of a world under the influence of neo-liberalist politicians, capitalist economists, booming technologies and other more or less optimistic agents: "A global cosmopolitanism of this sort readily celebrates a world of plural cultures and peoples located at the periphery, so long as they produce healthy profit margins within metropolitan societies" (Bhabha, *LC* xiv); on the other hand, he introduces the term 'vernacular cosmopolitanism,' which "measures global progress from a minoritarian perspective" (xvi). This brings in a more critical, though not completely negative view as it fosters cultural resistance, hybridity, and creativity of "unhomely" individuals in the "in-between spaces" of cultural difference.[12] What most scholars agree on undisputedly, however, is the shrinking of time and space, or as it is called, "time-space-compression." Questioning whether it is good or bad, leads to sameness or not, or is either a very recent trend or a long-time development appears to be the one certainty of globalization (Bennett, Grossberg, and Morris 150; During 82).

The starting point for this fundamental characteristic of globalization, just as for the whole original introduction of the theme into academic as well as political and popular

[9] Cf. also Macey 259-260; Brennan, "Postcolonial Studies and Globalization Theory" 131.

[10] Cp. Steger, *Globalization. A Very Short Introduction*, "Preface."

[11] This opposition, too, is of course a simplification. Manfred B. Steger, for example, lists the term globalization as having been used to refer to "a process, a condition, a system, a force and an age." (7) Though on the pages that follow he returns to the discussed ambiguity as well: he differentiates between *globality* (social condition) and *globalization* (set of social processes that lead to *globality*).

[12] Cf. Bhabha, *The Location of Culture*, "Introduction" 1-27.

debates, may be found in the economic and political theoretical realms, which often include social spheres in their discussion. These have in the past decade and a half focused on approximately four most apparent features of globalization that they see affected on a major scale by modern technologies and transportations: the increase of extensity (the field of influence and effects across the globe), a growing intensity (as it effects an increasing number of spheres), its velocity (of processes and interactions) concerning economic, political and social interrelations, and finally the deepening of interdependencies (mainly between the opposition of local versus global realms) (Held and McGrew 2-3).[13]
These points, which dominate the discussion in economic and political studies, can be seen as point of departure for a multitude of extended observations across the disciplines. However, due to global events and situations of the recent past[14], today, at the turn of the century the discussions have changed insofar as that in the field of politics, and hesitantly, also in other disciplines, voices, which observe either a reversal or the complexification and escalation of globalization, are getting louder expressed in pleas for either a "post-globalist turn" or a fear of the "clash of globalizations" respectively (Held and McGrew 1).

With regard to the concepts employed in this study, it is essential to differentiate between the expressions of transnationalism, on the one hand, and globalization, on the other. It has been one of the problems of the instable discourse between literary studies and globalization theory that these two 'perspectives' are often blurred[15]: while the first expresses one of the major effects of globalism (mainly economic and political) that is often related to its more negative effects such as the loss of national, communal and local power, the second, globalization – as it is used in this book – is a far larger term that bears more potential for far-reaching discussions of both positive and negative nature.[16] The differentiation between transnationalism and globalization must admittedly be seen as a relative one, as they are strongly related. However, the opposition highlights certain important issues; one of them is the partial deterritorialization and denationalization of power (Held and McGrew 4), both of which obviously also effect literary production and theories alike. Before moving on to the discussions developed in various disciplines in relation to these effects, I would like to emphasize once again the emerging focus on concepts of space (also expressed in terms

[13] Though Steger in his *Very Short Introduction* lists more or less the same features, he adds an important one not mentioned in Held and McGrew: the inequality or, to put it more neutral, the *unevenness* of globalization across the world, Steger 15-16. Cf. also Featherstone, who speaks of "multiple modernities," ("Postnational Flows" 487-489).
[14] Most prominently the events surrounding the 9/11-attacks and the Iraq War; I am certain, at the moment of writing, that the world financial crisis has also been triggering some rethinking in various fields.
[15] This observation is based first and foremost on reactions I received to papers presented on the subject of this study; however, most introductions to globalization also often emphasize the misunderstandings caused by the misinterpretation and misuse of the terms.
[16] Lechner and Boli under the subheading "*Is globalization harmful?*" 3; cf. also Ulrich Beck "What is Globalization?" 99-103, who calls for differentiation between globalism versus globality and globalization.

like "deterritorialization"). The idea of *space* and what we are to make of it is one of the pivotal points for present theories on globalization. It is in terms of space and cultural dynamics that these contemporary theories should be, and increasingly are, taking up the debate, especially as globalizing forces effect changes in the perception and construction of social and cultural space. In the past decades, sociologists, social anthropologists, and geographers have presented most intriguing results, thus laying the foundation for cultural and literary studies toward an inclusion of approaches related to the discipline of "cultural geography" (During 82).[17] The work of Saskia Sassen, which connects global economic forces with an analysis of the migration of people and changes in social space and the emergence of "global cities," and the theoretical studies of Doreen Massey represent valuable background sources towards the understanding of societies on the move and the altering of imaginaries.[18]

A shrinking world combined with the ever-existent political and economic causes for the migration of people, as well as the growing interconnectedness and the densification of space and place have engendered major re-conceptualizations of identities and the intensification of cultural interaction. These factors, which are crucial for an approach towards transcultural imaginaries, have also been a major concern in cultural studies theories. Both globalization theories and cultural studies in their own right owe some of their crucial insights to other disciplines such as the field of sociology and the younger field of media studies, which have inspired various contributions to the debate. The internationally acclaimed sociologists Roland Robertson and Anthony Giddens can be counted among the earliest influential thinkers of the social aspects on globalization, both arguing for a more differentiated understanding of the phenomenon and a revision of sociological thought. Anthony Giddens, who also understands globalization as a variant of modernity, has more recently challenged traditional sociological approaches through his theory on "global interconnectedness," which emphasizes human agency as an interdependent counterpart to the (social) structures in which this agency acts and which it creates.[19] Roland Robertson in his major work *Globalization. Social Theory and Global Culture,* for example, adapted the term of "glocalization" from Japanese economic theory in order to express the tension between local and global forces, which in his perspective effects plurality at least as much as it does 'global sameness':

> This inevitably raises again the much-discussed issue of global capitalism and the thesis of commodification and homogenization of culture across the contemporary world. Global capitalism both promotes and is conditioned by cultural homogeneity *and* cultural heterogeneity. The production and consolidation of difference and variety is an essential ingredient of contemporary capitalism, which is, in any case, increasingly involved with a growing variety of *micro*-markets [...] It must be emphasized, however,

[17] Cultural geography, a sub-field of human geography, developed in the U.S. in the first half of the twentieth century; in recent decades it has undergone significant changes, relating it more strongly to fields such as cultural studies; thus, critics now speak of "new cultural geography," Duncan, Johnson, and Schein 1-2.

[18] See Sassen, *Globalization and Its Discontents* and *The Global City*; Massey, *A Place in the World* and *For Space*.

[19] Cf. *Modernity and Self-Identity*. His most influential work is, however, *The Consequences of Modernity* (1990); cp. Elliott 137-138.

> that capitalism has to accommodate both to the *materiality* of the heliocentric global world, with its inherent space-time contingencies, and to the *culturality* of human life, including the 'making sense' – indeed the 'construction' – of the geosocial contingencies of in-group/out-group relations. (Robertson, *Globalization* 173)

His approach is valuable for cultural critics as he relates contemporary planet-wide systems such as global capitalism to the "culturality of human life" and discusses concepts that connect to issues of the construction of self and other. Robertson also attempts to theorize the emergence of a new global complexity by analyzing processes of relativization: he proposes to "take into account changes in each of the four major components (societies, individuals, international relations, and humankind) in tandem with shifts in the relations between them" (*Globalization* 26) – thus, globalization "involves *comparative interaction* of different forms of life" (ibid. 27). The German sociologist Ulrich Beck, though more cautious in the use of expressions such as 'world society' or "borderless world" (During 81), which for him implies "multiplicity without unity" (Beck 101), extends these observations by referring to the interaction between various social and cultural spheres. For him, the "*globalization process* [...] creates transnational social links and spaces, revalues local cultures, and promotes third cultures" (102) – cultures which develop within what Beck calls "regional-global relationship networks" and result from new "social spaces" that define themselves via increasing "image flows" (102).[20]

Socio-cultural anthropologist Arjun Appadurai achieved a fair amount of international, academic attention with his publication *Modernity at Large*, in which he brings forward similar arguments – some of which will be addressed in more detail below. As Appadurai, too, observes, globalization is a far more complex issue as diverse levels of existence must be taken into account – he distinguishes between five dimensions of global cultural flows also referred to as abstract "land*scapes,*" the interaction and layering of which account for the "disjunctures" of globalization[21]: "These landscapes thus are the building blocks of what (extending Benedict Anderson) I would like to call *imagined worlds*, that is, the multiple worlds that are constituted by the historically situated imagination of persons and groups spread around the globe" (33). Additionally, his approach goes one step further as it supposes the emergence of a new form of (communal) imagination, enforced by the two "m"-s, media and migration (Appadurai 3). Though his work has been criticized for its sweeping global idealism and alleged cosmopolitan naivety[22], his outlook on the interaction between individual, communal,

[20] The quotes from Beck that are used here are taken from Held and McGrew's *The Global Transformations Reader* 99-103; the section entitled "What is Globalization?" is a translation of *Was ist Globalisierung?* (1997): Ulrich Beck, "Introduction," *What is Globalization?* (trans. Patrick Camiller, Cambridge: Polity Press, 1999) n.pag.

[21] "The new global cultural economy has to be seen as a complex, overlapping, disjunctive order that cannot any longer be understood in terms of existing center-periphery models. [...] The complexity of the current global economy has to do with certain funadamental disjunctures between economy, culture, and politics that we have only begun to theorize," 32-33. The land*scapes* that he refers to are ethnoscapes, mediascapes, technoscapes, financescapes and ideoscapes; cf. Appadurai 27-43.

[22] Cf. During 94-95; Cp. also Featherstone's analysis of his work, "Postnational Flows" 501-506.

and global constructs and structures, could be an inspiration for new, innovative literary and cultural analyses; his approach definitely underscores the analysis of transcultural imaginaries developed in the present study, as he suggests that "the work of the imagination, viewed in this context, is neither purely emancipatory nor entirely disciplined but is a space of contestation in which individuals and groups seek to annex the global into their own practices of the modern" (Appadurai 4).

Thus, as these theorists of the late twentieth and early twenty-first centuries have led us to understand, the relation between local and global cultural social structures and cultures is in no way stable or one independent of the other, nor are the world's peripheries necessarily swallowed by the centers of culture by which we would arrive at global homogeneity. All these observations are, as we should note, invariably also linked to approaches that are committed to a more flexible and open understanding of cultures.[23] As Ulf Hannerz puts it,

> [I]t now must be more difficult than ever, or at least more unreasonable, to see the world [...] as a cultural mosaic, of separate pieces with hard, well-defined edges. Cultural interconnections increasingly reach across the world. More than ever, there is a global ecumene. The entities we routinely call cultures are becoming more like subcultures within this wider entity, with all that this suggests in terms of fuzzy boundaries and more or less arbitrary delimitation of analytical units. To grasp this fact of globalization, in its wide range of manifestations and implications, is the largest task at present confronting a macroanthropology of culture. (Hannerz 110)[24]

The vision and analysis of globalization as a complex network of connections nowadays extends to most levels of globalization, whether these are viewed from economic, political, social or cultural perspectives.[25] Sociologists and anthropologists have repeatedly pointed out the considerable influence of media within this development; correspondingly, media studies researchers have not only contributed parallel insights into the complex network structures of global media and media co-operations but also into the impact that media have had on the emergence of what internationally acclaimed Canadian media scholar Marshall McLuhan termed the "global village" (Featherstone 490).[26] Twenty years later, contemporary media scholars seem to tend more toward the position that the homogenizing effect of globalization has not been nearly as dramatic as feared by earlier theorists such as McLuhan.[27] Increasingly, scientists who have been studying the recent impact of media like to point to events such as those surrounding

[23] Approaches as those brought forward by Ulf Hannerz; his theories are also used and extended by Frank Schulze-Engler, i.e. "From Postcolonial to Preglobal" 57-59.

[24] This excerpt from a work by Hannerz is included in the reader compiled by Lechner and Boli; the original source is Ulf Hannerz, *Cultural Complexity: Studies in the Social Organization of Meaning* (Columbia UP, 1992), 217-222.

[25] Cp. John Tomlinson, *Globalization and Culture*.

[26] Cp. Castell, *The Information Age*; McChesney and Edward S. Herman, *The Global Media*; David Demers, *Global Media*. As Featherstone notes, McLuhan developed the term 'global village' in *Understanding Media* in 1960 (490), though the book was actually published in 1964; cf. Macey 246.

[27] Cp. Hepp und Löffelholz, *Grundlagentexte zur transkulturellen Kommunikation;* especially, "Transkulturelle Kommunikation. Einführung in die Grundlagentexte," 11-33.

9/11 as an example of not only the globalizing role that media play in our society today but also that their effects in spite of existing global (cultural) networks can be measured in terms of cultural differences or, in extremis, of the "clash of civilizations" (Huntington) rather than in that of homogeneity.[28] Parallel to this, the process of deterritorialization, too, is regarded as having a major impact on media and communication – and vice versa. The term, which expresses the decreasing importance of territorial boundaries represented by nations and states, is often found in recent media studies referring to the transportation and expansion of media and media texts across national borders and between cultural groups and individuals – this has led to the emergence of several theories that integrate concepts of transculturality and hybridization into their analysis of globalized media.[29] German media sociologist Andreas Hepp, for example, has strongly supported the perspective of "transcultural communication" and a "translocal analysis of media cultures" (Hepp und Löffelholz, "Transkulturelle Kommunikation" 16-17).[30] *Hybridity. Or the Cultural Logic of Globalization* by the American communications scholar, Marwan Kraidy, is a further example. The study provides an extensive analysis of the term and concept of hybridity, particularly in relation to international communication studies, though he eddorses a very broad and interdisciplinary view on the term. In *Hybridity* he

> propound[s] *critical transculturalism* as a new international communication framework with issues of hybridity at its core. The usage of the word "transculturalism," […] conveys a synthetic notion of culture and a dynamic understanding of relations between cultures. As I conceive it, critical transculturalism is at once an engagement with hybridity as a discursive formation, a framework for international communication theory, and an agenda for research. (vi-vii)

As shown by these two examples, the separation between these disciplines and cultural studies becomes porous, especially when the focus shifts to a specific perspective of culture as one of several main spheres within globalization processes. Considering cultural studies' occupation with popular culture and its strong links to postmodern, poststructural critical theories of the twentieth century, it does not come as a complete surprise that globalization – particularly in terms of media cultures and productions (During 109-110) – represents such a major issue within the discipline; conversely, the discipline's association with 'new left' readings of global developments explains the undeniable number of negative, criticizing voices on transnationalism and globalization. Cultural studies takes a very broad understanding of culture as the basis for their analyses – this not only means, as we know, that it includes and underscores popular forms of culture (as opposed to "high culture") but also that it increasingly fosters an understanding of the flexibility and porous nature of culture(s) (During 5-37; 193-213).

[28] Cf. Steger 1-7.
[29] These concepts differ considerably from my view of transcultural imaginaries, as they focus on the hybridity of media but often exclude extended discussions of the developed imaginaries in terms of the societies, individuals and contexts that form them.
[30] Cf. also Hepp, "Translokale Medienkulturen," and "Transkulturalität als Perspektive."

Again, many discussions here seem to revolve around concepts of space, which cultural studies has appropriated as a useful addition to its terminology;[31] however, some scholars observe the emergence of not only intricately interwoven networks of space and existence, but they also observe a cosmopolitan ethics, as argued for example by John Tomlinson in *Globalization and Culture*. With reference to a report on the development of the world published by the United Nations in 1995[32], at the end of his study, Tomlinson proposes "to explore the idea that the globally transformative action of individuals within their situated localities is dependent on the cultivation of a specific cultural disposition – a 'set towards the world.' This is a position that is proposed again by the authors of *Our Global Neighbourhood* in their stress on the development of a 'global ethics'" (183). In effect, Tomlinson's perspective on "the possibility of cosmopolitanism" attributes agency and responsibility to the world's individuals.[33] Jan Nederveen Pieterse is less concerned with ethics in his study, also entitled *Globalization and Culture*. Instead, he divides the positions concerning the effects of globalization on cultures into three general groups: he differentiates between those that assert that cultures are not influenced by homogenizing forces and that differences are maintained; those that insist on exactly the opposite; and a third group that believes that new forms of culture and identity will emerge from the process (41-55).[34] Pieterse who roots his own work in the third position, insists on "viewing globalization as hybridization, or the development of translocal mélange cultures," and adds that "hybridization refers to the closed concept of culture and to its opening up, in the process ushering in post-hybridity" (4).

One can only conclude that despite the varying positions, these studies on culture reveal that globalization, and the relation between globalization processes and culture in particular, are far more complex than initially thought. This complexity and the subsequent need for careful observations is also noted by Mike Featherstone, who draws our attention to the possibility of multiple modernities and plural forms of globalization; in his research, he also evaluates the interconnectedness and the tensions between economic, sociological, and cultural spheres of analysis; Featherstone calls for cautious new modes of reading global cultures and identities in the light of "a more

[31] During 82, 96-98, 105-106; Bennett, Grossberg, and Morris' *New Keywords: A Revised Vocabulary of Culture and Society* also includes an entry, "Space" 331-334. What has been termed the "spatial turn" is a much larger issue that has been discussed across the disciplines for several decades. Cf. publications such as Hubbard, Kitchin, and Valentine, *Key Thinkers on Space and Place*; Döring, *Spatial Turn: Das Raumparadigma in den Kultur- und Sozialwissenschaften*; Dünne, *Raumtheorie: Grundlagentexte aus Philosophie und Kulturwissenschaft;* Soja, *Postmodern Geographies: The Reassertion of Space in Critical Social Theory*. Of course, there is also Henry LeFebvre, whose study *The Production of Space*, was very influential, too; in fact he may be the starting point of the discussion – he also had some influence on the work of Frederic Jameson; cf. Bové, "Afterword" 372.

[32] He is referring to Commission of Global Governance, *Our Global Neighborhood*, Report of the Commission on Global Governance (Oxford: Oxford University Press, 1995).

[33] Cf. esp. the chapter on "The Possibility of Cosmopolitanism," Tomlinson 181-207.

[34] The three groups are reflected in the subdivisions of the third chapter in his publication inspired by three prominent more or less recent buzzwords/phrases respectively: "Clash of Civilizations" (Samuel Huntington) – "McDonaldization" (Benjamin Barber; George Ritzer) – "Hybridization: The Rhizome of Culture" (Bhabha; Deleuze and Guattari). See Pieterse 41-55.

flexible and mobile habitus which is periodically reconstituted" ("Postnational Flows" 523). Rob Wilson and Wimal Dissanayake summarize these difficulties that beset the analysis of globalized cultures:

> [p]ost-modern culture-workers, on the verge of becoming the "symbolic engineers" and critical self-consciousness of global capital, stand at the crossroads of an altered and more fractal terrain everywhere we gaze at century's end: a new world-space of cultural production and national representation which is simultaneously becoming more *globalized* (unified around dynamics of capitalogic moving across borders) and more *localized* (fragmented into contestatory enclaves of difference, coalition and resistance) in everyday texture and composition. (1)

Across the disciplines, scholars have been seeking ways to approach these complex developments, and many have succeeded in suggesting innovative critical theories; however, as Mike Featherstone has pointed out, "as yet the social sciences and humanities are in a very rudimentary stage for considering globalization" (488). In the following subsection I thus shift the focus toward the positioning of postmodern and postcolonial theories and literatures within these complex debates.

Globalizing Critical Theory and Literatures

The amount and complexity of discourses surrounding the phenomenon of globalization suggests that the assertion that "globalization [...] has replaced 'postmodernism' as master term" (During 81) might well bear a certain amount of truth. In the introduction to their collection of "global/local" positionings, Rob Wilson and Wimal Dissanayke acutely observe from a sociological and media oriented cultural studies perspective that the well established attributes "postmodern" and "postcolonial" no longer suffice to capture and theorize today's political, economic, and cultural realities:

> Regions and region-states increasingly override national borders and older territorial forms and create special economic zones of uneven development and transcultural hybridity. This global/local synergy within what we will track as the *transnational imaginary* enlivens and molests the textures of everyday life and spaces of subjectivity and reshapes those contemporary structures of feeling some cultural critics all too commonly banalize as "postmodern" or hypertextually consecrate as "postcolonial" resistance. (2)

As far as the assumed influence of globalization on the postmodern form of contemporary texts is concerned, we will have to delay our judgment in order to see how much and what has changed or what has become less or more experimental, in the past decades. Yet we should not hesitate to open up our conventionalized understanding of contemporary, postmodern literatures – as Neil Besner indicates, "by not allowing more latitude to the boundaries of our understanding of postmodernism – a category that is by its very nature inimical to notions of firm borders – we miss an opportunity to widen our understanding of how our writing has developed and where it might be going" (Besner 16-17). My argument for an analysis of transcultural imaginaries is based upon the assumption that the plurality of globalization processes has had an effect not only on our perceptions of time and space and on our construction of identities across borders of all sorts but also on our imaginaries, which are ultimately expressed in the literatures we read and write. Paul A. Bové, one of America's distinguished postmodern literary critics, in his critical after-thoughts added at the end of the above-mentioned study on global/local dynamics (Wilson and Dissanayake), has suggested not a solution but an explanation for this strange postmodern dilemma: "In other words, we are caught in a conundrum resulting from the fact that whatever is has not yet sprung itself fully upon us probably because, if we speak in Vichian terms, we are not yet done making it. But, we might ask, where would such notions lead us?" (Bové 375). The answer to this final question remains open in Bové's reflections and can certainly not be answered on the these pages; however, what should be attempted is to lay bare possible tendencies concerning which flexible, microcosmic differences and borders, and which temporary certainties are placed in opposition to postmodern, deconstructive aesthetics. If postmodern literature has been seen as the result of emerging capitalist and increasingly media-influenced twentieth century postmodernity[35], contemporary literature is beginning to show the effects of societies (and thus identities and cultures) in certain respects more complex, more evolved – if in many ways not for the better, then at least more transcultural, transhistorical, transgeneric and, in some cases, increasingly ethical. The processes that we are speaking of here, we have to admit, might yet well be too obscure and too indistinct and intricate for us to understand – as Paul Bové suggests, we might be at a far more crucial turning point of thought, criticism and reality than we can yet see:

> This means, I think, despite claims to the contrary which generally insist upon continuity and the persistent applicability of older notions like dialectic, base/superstructure, and mediation, that we may well be confronting a rupture in life forms and in knowledge more akin to those that mark the shifts from the medieval to modern than from modern to postmodern. Indeed, "postmodern theory" seems perfectly to obscure this shift, it blocks the development of the perceptual apparatus needed to theorize the emergent and to take action to modify its development. (Bové 383)

Similar claims can be made with regard to postcolonial theory.[36] Despite the postcolonial reluctance toward theories on reputedly imperializing forces such as globalization, several postcolonial critics – in fact, more than postmodern literary critics – have in the past decade begun to acknowledge the changing realities of postmodernity. Thereby, they have initiated a discussion on the globalized mode of postcolonial cultures and the "New Literatures in English," even though the deconstruction of binaries is still due in postcolonial criticism, as well as the rethinking

[35] The issue of the definition of postmodernity, and its separation from or inclusion in modernity remains too vast a discussion to be debated here in more detail.

[36] Cf. Schulze-Engler, "From Postcolonial to Preglobal"; some of Schulze-Engler's assertions regarding the problematic phase in which postcolonial criticism is finding itself currently are discussed at the end of Chapter 1.

of other large-scale considerations (also in postmodern criticism).[37] These reformulations have been far more successfully accomplished in other disciplines, where the necessity of this process has been anticipated for decades, such as by the earliest revisionist of space, Henry LeFebvre, in the 1970s.[38]
Since the 1990s, Homi Bhabha, whose concepts of 'hybridity' and 'third space' are definitely of relevance and ought to be discussed for the present approach, has been one of the most prominent representatives of postcolonial criticism to engage in the debates of globalized spaces and disseminated diasporic identities. Repeatedly, he has approached certain agendas related to globalization (and globalization theories) and has also to some effect argued towards the deconstruction of binaries: "In the wake of these [diasporic] voices, we are led to a philosophical and political responsibility for conceiving of minoritization and globalization as the quasi-colonial, a condition at once old and new, a dynamic, even dialectical relation that goes beyond the polarizations of the local and the global, the center and the periphery, or indeed, the 'citizen' and the 'stranger'" (*The Location* xxi). However, the very problem with Homi Bhabha's theories is that even if he acknowledges the new dynamics between what had been previously reduced to binary constructions, he does not completely escape these very binaries, as the larger part of his theoretical writings is built upon one major opposition: that of minorities and majorities. In this sense, Rob Wilson and Dissanayake might be right when they critique Bhabha's vision and rhetorics in the following passage:

> The ongoing process of disruption and manipulation of global discourses and technologies is all too uncritically being rearticulated as a process of *translating the transnational* structurations of nation, self, and community into "translational," *in-between* spaces of negotiated language, borderland being, and bi-cultural ambivalence. It is no longer adequate to map the globe into binary zones of center and periphery as an eternally Manichean space of colonial victimization nor even as Edward Said's rich culturescape of "contrapunctal" imperialism. (2)

Thus, even if Homi Bhabha's influential works deserve all our attention for its critical assessment of culture's location "in the realm of the *beyond*" (1) and of *post*-theories' transformation through the perspective of "an expanded and ex-centric site of experience and empowerment" (6), one has to keep in mind that his "in-between" spaces of "hybridity" are on the whole reserved to migrants and minorities. Thus, in order to avoid "dead ends" (Schulze Engler, "From Postcolonial to Preglobal" 53),

[37] Cf. for example, Eckstein; Kalogeras et al.; Achilles and Birkle; Antor and Stierstorfer.
[38] Rob Wilson and Wimal Dissanayake also refer to his influence: "Henri Lefebvre predicted, in the aftermath of '1968' experienced as a global/local crisis in social modernity, that the process of mass urbanization would be superseded (in David Harvey's overview of Lefebrvre's space-oriented poetics) by 'the production of [everyday] space, that was binding together the global and the local, the city and the country, the centre and the periphery, in new and quite unfamiliar ways.' According to Lefebvre's prescient analysis of situated possibility in *La production de l'espace*, the 'abstract space' of global capital would go on being fractured from within by enduring ties to religion, place, city, country, and above all, by amplified segregations of class" (3). The authors quote Lefebvre from David Harvey, "Afterword" to Henri Lefebvre, *The Production of Space*, trans. Donald Nicholson-Smith (Oxford: Blackwell, 1991), 431.

some postcolonial critics ought to reassess their relationship to globalization. They could do so by considering new insights into global cultural dynamics, by reevaluating former macro-political discourses and postcolonial categorizations of power and extending them with what Schulze-Engler calls "the micropolitics of modernity":

> the sometimes blatantly nostalgic politics of anticolonialism that have dominated much of postcolonialist critical discourse are hardly adequate for coming to terms with the complicated conflicts and constellations in many parts of the 'postcolonial' world that encompass the politics of multiculturalism, civil society and new democratic movements as well as a 'micropolitics of modernity.' All of these negotiate intimate questions of personal identity, gender relations and family life that turn out to be as decisive for the dynamics of modern societies as the macropolitics dominating public discourse, which focus on questions of economic policy, political systems and ideological conflicts. ("Theoretical Perspectives" 28)

I will return to Schulze-Engler's suggestions on the following pages. However, what must be stressed once again at this point, especially in respect to the passage above, is that there are several postcolonial critics who are already maneuvering into precisely this direction, or at least are re-considering certain critical aspects. Others remain stubbornly hostile to globalization theories, the insights of which they, more often than not, trivialize and cast off as superficial endeavors:

> globalization theory looks rather to a "new" dynamic forged by the happy chaos of an infinitely mobile citizenry, a constantly self-defined subjectivity, a terrain of virtual space consisting of multi-faceted niches of an always malleable and morphing freedom. [...] in the view of globalization theorists, their [historians and philosophers'] structures of understanding only impede their ability to recognize the future unfolding before their eyes, which is being created by investors, technologists, managers, and organizers, not – thankfully not – working according to plan, but swept along in a process that is anarchic and autopoetic. (Brennan 124)[39]

Graham Huggan, in contrast to Brennan's perspective, presents a more hopeful approach to new tendencies within the postcolonial discipline, and admits that "current theories of – and attitudes toward – globalization are shaping the field of postcolonial studies, helping both to isolate its immediate objects of analysis and to define its short- and long-term critical ambitions and research goals" (Huggan, "Postcolonialism, Gloalization, and the Rise of (Trans)cultural Studies" 33). Most of the optimistic analysts of the postcolonial-globalization relations agree on two basic assumptions: that on the one hand, globalization opens up opportunities for the postcolonial to define and exert a novel form of 'translocal' resistance[40]; on the other hand, the established

[39] Timothy Brennan's contribution to the *Cambridge Companion to Postcolonial Literary Studies* to a large degree presents a highly critical disposition towards globalization and globalization theory; however, it should be mentioned that in the last paragraph of the essay Brennan acknowledges some of globalization theories' accomplishments. Cf. Brennan 138.

[40] Graham Huggan also refers to other like-minded critics such as Neil Lazarus and Simon During, cf. "Postcolonialism, Globalization, and the Rise of (Trans)cultural Studies" 30; cf. also Kalogeras et al. "Introduction."

(political) agenda and "'postcolonial' (re)visions do still matter in our global systems of neo-colonial dependencies and are still seen as an essential task by many writers and critics" (Eckstein 17).[41] Even if Graham Huggan speaks of a "transcultural turn" in postcolonial studies ("Derailing" 56), he remains skeptical to some of the suppositions implied within this critical trend while Lars Eckstein, in his ambitious companion of *English Literature Across the Globe*, as well as Heinz Antor and Klaus Stierstorfer, in their collection of essays on *English Literatures in International Contexts* – to give two salient examples – already take a further, more confident step toward the recognition of multiple, new critical potentialities. From their perspective, this next step implies a new awareness of several complexities: that "the homogenizing and the diversifying impulses do not seem to exclude each other, but rather go hand in hand in the cultures of this world at the beginning of the new millennium" (Antor and Stierstorfer X), that contemporary processes of development from colonial over postcolonial towards transcultural writing and criticism are not linear but represent simultaneous, "discursive" modes (Eckstein 16)[42], and that cultures and identities have become far too complex, "international" and "multicultural" than to be read "along purely postcolonial lines" (Antor and Stierstorfer X). As Lars Eckstein summarizes this transcultural-postcolonial awareness:

> Imperial power itself has increasingly become a decentred and elusive phenomenon, and it would be limiting, therefore, to continue to conceive of the art of "writing back" to it as a straightforward linear affair. Rather, what we are dealing with is an intricate, polyphonous web of 'writing across' multiple cultural frontiers that both embraces highly regional and localized practices and cosmopolitan takes. (Eckstein 18)

This promising innovativeness of perspectives finds a final, exciting expression in one of the contributions included in the above-mentioned collection of essays by one of the early 'original' initiators of the postcolonial "writing-back" theory, Bill Ashcroft.[43] Most interestingly Ashcroft prizes the potential aspects of processes such as "transformation" (or in Eckstein's terms "writing across") as a necessary element of resistance, of "imaginations," of the "everyday" and "ordinary people" – all factors pointing towards the same interdisciplinary literary spaces that inform transcultural imaginaries (Ashcroft, "Resistance and Transformation" 16-17).

Interdisciplinary Literary Spaces

The perspectives on globalization and the new insights they have provided within other disciplines, as well as the interrelations of processes, selectively displayed in the two previous subchapters, make it necessary to return to the interactive, interdisciplinary

[41] Cp. Huggan, "Derailing" 60-61.
[42] On the simultaneity of developments, cf. also Schulze-Engler in "Von ,Inter' zu ,Trans'."
[43] Cp. Ashcroft, Griffiths, and Tiffin, *The Empire Writes Back: Theory and Practice in Post-Colonial Literatures*.

developments at the crossroads of globalization theories, postmodern and postcolonial theories and cultural studies. A structured summary of these processses – some of which were partially highlighted earlier – I hope will clarify my stance in this debate and sketch the point of departure for an understanding of a literary approach that involves what I term the transcultural imaginary.

As can be observed, the broad collectivity of contemporary cultural criticism displays significant tendencies toward a shifting perception of several aspects, all of which relate to the current impact of globalizing forces on cultures, identities, societies, and, eventually also, literatures and other cultural discourses. These tendencies are effectively linked to one another – but may, on grounds of greater accessibility, be broken down into two thematic clusters, each comprising two major aspects: cultures and individuals and transgressions and complexities.

Cultures and Individuals

At the center of the discussed developments is the changing concept of culture. With strong reference to sociologists such as Ulf Hannerz and Ulrich Beck, Frank Schulze-Engler has repeatedly underlined the transition towards an understanding of cultures as far more porous, flexible and interdependent formations in his many influential essays[44]:

> the idea that the social world is primarily made up of irreducibly different and possibly incommensurable 'cultures' has been heavily criticized in cultural theory for quite a while. Anthropological theory, for example, has become increasingly weary of 'culture' as a heuristic category for describing contemporary modes of living in and making sense of the world. [...]
>
> A primary issue in this context is the suspicion that 'culture' is "the essential tool for making other" (Abu-Lughood 1991, quoted in Hannerz 1996:31) and the evident inability of concepts of culture as a territorially fixed, collectively shared symbolic system to accommodate the sociocultural realities of an increasingly globalised world. (Schulze-Engler "What's the Difference?" 129)[45]

As indicated in the second part of Schulze-Engler's quote, one of the much discussed notions related to this re-conceptualization of culture is that of 'deterritorialization' and of 'nation' as the formerly major, yet today no longer sufficient point of reference for the definition of cultures. Despite all fears of globalization critics that the world is becoming one global place with one global culture, and despite the obvious fact that transnational organizations (WTO, UN, etc.) *have* gained more influence over the past decades, this neither means that 'nation' does not still play a significant part as source for identifications and power structures, nor that we are all floating in a soup of hybrid space. Instead, "[a]gainst all odds, the local posits the terrain of disjunctive global/local cultural flows, unpredictable outcomes, temporary autonomous zones, nonsynchronized

[44] Apart from the essay from which the quote that follows is taken, also cf. "Von ‚Inter' zu Trans'," and "Transnationale Kultur als Herausforderung" (both in German).

[45] Schulze-Engler cites Lila Abu-Lughood, "Writing Against Culture," in Richard G. Thomas Fox, ed., *Recapturing Anthropology* (Santa Fe, NM: School of American Research Press, 1991), 137-162, quoted in Ulf Hannerz, *Transnational Connections*.

spaces where indigenous imagination might achieve renewed social agency or a multicultural community, say, can articulate place-bound identity or construct ethnic survival" (Wilson/Dissanayake 8). It is these factors that also account for, or at least interact with, the increasing interest in the analysis of space and place in relation to global flows.

Patricia Yaeger has convincingly laid open the many complex reasons for why an analysis of space has necessarily moved to the center of our focus; not only does she name deterritorialization as one of the catalysts for this critical process (beside several others), but she also discerns the *re*-territorialized (cultural) space, which is "continuous, contradictory, convoluted, splintered, layered, and inconsistent" (16), "sanctions new forms of solidarity and identity" and effects "fresh markers of spatial community" (17). It is in the wake of this redefined notion of culture, which is invariably linked to fluid concepts of space and place, also strongly promoted by the British geographer Doreen Massey[46], that a number of scholars have begun to make stronger use of terms such as "translocal habitus" (Yaeger) or "transnational imaginary" (Wilson and Dissanayake), and "transculturalism" (i.e. Schulze-Engler, Eckstein) – though the usage and exact dividing lines of the terms remain yet blurred.[47] As Schulze-Engler once again brings to the point:

> As 'transnational connections' in a globally interlinked 'ecumene of modernity' come to the fore, 'transculturality' is emerging as an analytical tool geared towards exploring strategies of coping with cultural complexity on the level both of collectives and individuals. These strategies are intricately linked to far-reaching changes in the social world; what is thus at issue is not some vaguely utopian notion that cultural differences no longer matter, but the necessity to come to terms with a radically altered state of 'culture' and 'difference' in the contemporary world – for those engaged in cultural practices (including the production of literature) as well as for those seeking to develop analytical categories to describe and understand these categories. ("What's the Difference?" 131)

Within this process-oriented discourse surrounding the spatialization and fluidization of culture, some essential questions, which have indirectly come to occupy an increasingly important position, may be asked: what role do time and history play in this new cultural view? What happens within this cultural space? Who are the actors within, or is it self-functional? In fact, relating to the first issue, Patricia Yaeger has argued that space might have replaced time in importance, in a need to steady the postmodern world's non ethically focused instability.

> Have scholars turned to space in pursuit of an ever-receding prospect: the need for a stable home, an undissipated ground of being that might secure their analysis? As time's reliable design fades from view and its linear pleasures (winged with their dreams of cradles and closures) become less certain, suddenly space—time's earthy

[46] Cf., i.e., Massey, *On Space*.

[47] Wilson and Dissanayake, to give an example, use the adjectives "transnational" and "transcultural" close to interchangeably.

> twin and Enlightenment double—heaves into view as a potential site of physical continuity and analytical constancy. (12)

This turning back to fundamental issues of existence, as they are expressed in cultural productions, has become a more generally acknowledged concern within cultural and literary studies only recently.[48] Yet, even though we might have finally ceded our linear conceptions of time – as displayed especially in fictions of the past – it still remains a factor at least as important as space while simultaneously becoming part of its complexities. In a further step, we might turn to the second question, that of who or what – in the light of the nation's demise[49] – determines these cultural spaces and assigns meaning to their complexities. Even though vernacular notions of globalization and the criticism of 'globalization skeptics' might lead us to believe that the globalization debates are committed to communal structures and processes of transnational collectivities only, several other critics across the disciplines have discerned something very different. Contemporary realities, they claim, are characterized by an increasing agency of the individual in the formation of cultures and its imaginaries, instead of the other way around (culture forming people), which has been the predominant view so far (Schulze-Engler "Theoretical Perspectives" 28). Thus, Tomlinson observes on a more general level that "the idea of global governance is not just the business of nation-states – indeed cannot be left to them – but must involve the actions of much smaller groupings, even down to the level of individual people" (182); drawing from a postcolonial theory perspective, Bill Ashcroft claims that "the example of ordinary people in colonized societies reveals that the proletariat operates constantly in a dialectical and transformative mode" (18).
While Bhabha speaks of a "require(d) shift of attention from the political as a pedagogical, ideological practice to politics as the stressed necessity of everyday life – politics of perfomativity" (*The Location of Culture* 21), Featherstone observes that "[t]he lengthening and tightening of the chains of interdependencies and the integration of nation-states into a more closely knit worldwide network, hence holds out the potential of greater possibilities for individualization" (524). In other words, our attention ought to focus on the processes of globalization, as well as on the individual and its identity formation patterns and imaginaries, and its relationship to communal (local, global, regional, national) connections – thus again enforcing an attention toward the inevitable analysis of the "micropolitics of modernity":

> intimate questions of personal identity, gender relations and family life that turn out to be as decisive for the dynamics of modern societies as the macropolitics dominating public discourse that focus on questions of economic policy, political systems and ideological conflicts. The micropolitics of this "modernity at large" testify to the long-term consequences of core dynamics of modernity such as differentiation,

[48] Cf. Davis and Womack, *Mapping the Ethical Turn*, and *Postmodern Humanism in Contemporary Literature and Culture*. Cp. also the already mentioned study by Tomlinson, especially 181-207. I will return to this issue in the concluding chapter.
[49] Cf. for example, Benedict Anderson's *Imagined Communities*.

> rationalization and individualization for public and private lives. (Schulze-Engler, "From Postcolonial to Preglobal" 58)[50]

The intricate relations of the individual to globalization processes reverberate in the disintegrated and porous dichotomy of local versus global networks as well as their components; ultimately, even postcolonial critics like Bill Ashcroft have come to conclude that "agency" itself comprises a "two-way-gaze, the dual orientation, the ability to appropriate colonial technology without being absorbed by it," whereby "constructing new conceptions of modernity represents, in global terms, the most far-reaching and enterprising goal of [especially individual] post-colonial transformation" (18).

Transgressions and Complexities

The re-conceptualization of culture on the one hand and 'individualization' processes on the other, are not only strongly connected to one another but are also inevitably linked to two further critical tendencies, or primary intentions: the transcending of binary oppositions and discourses, and (consequently) the awareness of the complexity of cultural processes and structures.

The expressed need to transgress extreme positions and to allow for simultaneous either/and perspectives is not a recent recognition; at least since the 1980s, socio-anthropological cultural critics have repeatedly suggested such a reform of thought constructions.[51] Nevertheless, post-structural and postmodern deconstructive dynamics, as well as postcolonialism's and feminism's initial essentialism appears to have – until recently – blinded literary critics against this inevitable critical turn, while even here, as Patricia Yaeger accurately observes in relation to her vision of the poetics of the geography of identity, we must allow for several approaches to operate simultaneously:

> But while the hermeneutics of suspicion turns practitioners away from essentialism, universalism, and other forms of metadiscourse, the metanarrative turn has not vanished altogether in contemporary spatial cartographies—nor should it vanish.[52] New local conditions and the pressures of globalization require both skepticism and inclusive theorems capable of exploring the place-centeredness of social being. (14)

Within this new discursive setting, which interacts with the study of the impact of globalization on cultures, the relativization of the global/local dichotomy – "this fast imploding heteroglossic interface of the global with the local" (Wilson and Dissanayake 3) – receives the required attention, especially when related to the individualization of cultural agency.[53] This 'relativizing turn' also indirectly accounts for the increased interest in in-between spaces and hybrid formations, such as Bhabha's "third space" or Marwan Kraidy's detailed analysis of hybrid formations. Nonetheless, not all critics

[50] The first part of this quotation appears verbatim in another essay by Schulze-Engler, "Theoretical Perspectives" 28, which is also quoted in Ch.4.2.

[51] Cf. Bové; Ashcroft, "Resistance and Transformation"; Wilson and Dissanayake "Introduction."

[52] As Yaeger adds in a footnote at this point: "In other words, there is room in the new geography for both "macrotheory" and the work of deconstruction" (13, Footnote 18).

[53] Cf. Wilson and Dissanayake 6.

seem fully aware that the perspective must be approached cautiously as it bears the danger of neglecting the continuing major significance of 'difference' for the successful (trans)cultural dia- and polylogue – reflected, for example, in the expression adopted by Homi Bhabha of "difference in equality" (*The Location of Culture* xvii).[54]
The local/global dynamics of pluralized and kaleidoscopic cultural space, not only effect a change in the cultural imaginary[55] but also call for the above-mentioned increasing questioning of revised ethical values. Wilson and Dissanayake's formulation of the effects of what they term the global/local "heteroglossic interface" captures these various levels of dynamics:

> What we would variously track as the "transnational imaginary" comprises the *as-yet-unfigured* horizon of contemporary cultural production by which national spaces/identities of political allegiance and economic regulation are being undone and imagined communities of modernity are being reshaped at the macropolitical (global) and micropolitical (cultural) levels of everyday existence. Given these macroeconomic transformations underway, can there emerge strategies of "transnational solidarity" within such a space? (Wilson and Dissanayake 6)

As becomes obvious in this quote and in the present chapter as a whole, these critical shifts inevitably interact with an increased awareness of the complexity of processes and, most importantly, the need for new critical stances. Such a new cultural and literary criticism, as that applied in this study through the reading of transcultural imaginaries, implies the acknowledgement of the simultaneity of degrees of development – be it in relation to the impact of globalization, creating variable modernities, or the degree of exchange and alteration in transcultural processes. Additionally, these developments are active on various levels of society (local, communal, national) and in diverse spheres (politics, economics, culture, etc.) to differing degrees, and there are also differences within separate spheres (as will become obvious in the analysis of fictions of the past), alongside with an obvious interconnectedness of processes, all of which justify the search for new ways of understanding these processes and their effects. Patricia Yaeger thus speaks of "the quest for a public language" and an "overwhelming need to invent a new space-time imaginary" (11), while Schulze-Engler suggests,

> It might indeed make sense to talk of the resurgence of modernity – not as a triumphant Western project, but as a set of shared problems and predicaments that increasingly need to be addressed in global contexts. By the same token, the exhaustion of the

[54] As Bhabha explains: "The vernacular cosmopolitan takes the view that the commitment to a 'right to difference in equality' as a process of constituting emergent groups and affiliations has less to do with the affirmation or authentication of origins and 'identities,' and more to do with political practices and ethical choices. Minoritarian affiliations or solidarities arise in response to the failures and limits of democratic representation, creating new modes of agency, new strategies of recognition, new forms of political and symbolic representation" (*The Location of Culture* xvii-xviii). The expression "difference in equality" is quoted from a text by Etienne Balibar.
[55] In the quote that follows, Wilson and Dissanayake refer to "transnational imaginary" – which is not clearly defined in their introduction but can obviously (with some alterations) be related to my use of the term transcultural imaginary.

postmodernist challenge to modernity – which has inspired so many varieties of postcolonialism – becomes apparent […] there can be little doubt that the transition towards new, transcultural forms of public discourse and political agency has long since begun. The future not only of postcolonial studies, but also of cultural and literary studies in general, may well depend on whether they will be able to find the critical and methodological resources needed to engage and critically accompany this transition. ("From Postcolonial to Preglobal" 62)

4 From Multi to Trans. The Rise of Transcultural Studies

In 1991 the Department of Multiculturalism and Citizenship and the SSHRCC[1] commissioned a "State of the Art Review of Research on Canada's Multicultural Society" (Berry and Laponce 10). In this renowned collection of studies on Canadian "ethnicity and culture" the authors introduce their observations by affirming, or rather envisioning, the crucial role of ethnicity for contemporary sciences and societies alike:

> Ethnicity is likely to be to the twenty-first century what class was to the twentieth – a major source of social tensions and political conflicts; hence it will be a major focus of attention for an academia that will be asked to provide facts, explanations, and theories. But ethnicity is also likely to be, increasingly, a source of creation and diversification – from life-styles to constitutions to literature – that will sustain the interest of the social sciences and humanities alike. (Berry and Laponce 3)

The opening paragraph of Berry and Laponce's study, which was published in 1994, is significant for especially one main characteristic of Canadian multiculturalism and the debates surrounding it in the past decades: the focus on ethnicity as the major defining factor of the nation's diversity and its multicultural identity.

The 1990s saw the introduction of a growing academic debate on multiculturalism – as both subject and object of social change in Canada; during these years in literary academia, anthologies on multicultural writing and studies focusing on specific ethnic and racial groups were increasingly published.[2] At the same time, it was also the decade in which authors and intellectuals belonging to socially marginalized, 'minority' groups (as well as those intellectuals supporting them) – having successfully established their own spaces and voices – began to question the norms and practices of official Canadian multiculturalism, thus initiating vibrant, or in some cases vehement, controversies between extreme positions.[3] Today, many of the debates remain acute and continue to contribute to a dynamic discourse on Canadian multicultural society and literature; however, on a general level – and in some cases also on a more specific level – multiculturalism has come to be accepted as an integral part of Canadian identity: "Indeed, over the decades, multiculturalism, the support and encouragement of

[1] SSHRCC stands for the Social Sciences and Humanities Research Council of Canada; the fact that the research council commissioned the study is strongly felt in its 'report-like' character as well as its inclination toward social science approaches, cf. Lorriggio 192-193.

[2] Of these anthologies, Linda Hutcheon's and Marion Richmond's *Other Solitudes* (1990) was one of the first (Golfman 178); other important anthologies include Smaro Kamboureli, *Making a Difference*, and Greenstein, *Third Solitudes*; cf. the essays in the special issue on "Idols of Otherness. The Rhetoric and Realtiy of Multiculturalism," *Mosaic* (Vol. 29, No 3, Spetember 1996), and Huggan and Siemerling, "U.S./Canadian Writers' Perspectives On the Multiculturalism Debate" for more references.

[3] Bissoondath's *Selling Illusions* can be regarded as one of the first controversial studies; a more recent example is Kamboureli's *Scandalous Bodies*; for a diversity of critical perspectives on multiculturalism – positive and negative – cf. Verduyn, *Literary Pluralities*.

atomized cultures, has become ingrained in Canadian identity and nationalism. Ask someone on the street what it means to be 'Canadian,' and very often 'multicultural' will be the response" (Chung 306).[4] Despite or even *because of* the 'establishment' of the overall term of multiculturalism in Canadian public (identitary) discourse, definitions of the elements involved in this phenomenon and the phenomenon itself remain multiple and vague. For a long time, Canadian multiculturalism was not only most naturally equated with multi-ethnicity – a fact which seems ironic in relation to its historical origins in bilingualism policies and also if one considers the major influence of feminist and other theories on its later conception.[5] 'Race' was often merged with the term 'ethnic' (Berry and Laponce 5), leaving both realms, ethnicity and multiculturalism, with very narrowly defined grounds. The attempt to open up the discourses on ethnicity to include not only "the other," meaning minority groups but all Canadian citizens has been debated for decades and remains an important factor in the multicultural discourse today.[6] Yet, a broader approach to the understanding of multiculturalism – not only as political policy but as an abstract concept for academic discussions – beyond terms of ethnicity remains far from being established despite the increasing acknowledgment of inclusive conceptions of culture.[7] Not all factors of this "inclusive conception of culture," such as age, class, and sexuality can be fully taken into account in this study, however, an awareness of an open understanding of culture and thus of multiculturalism too, represents a crucial basis for the reading of transcultural features in literary texts.

The fact that today a larger number of Canadian critics and authors, including those belonging to groups which have been marginalized for long periods, see more positive effects and possibilities in multiculturalism than a decade ago, might point toward a Canadian literature and criticism that is introducing a new phase of multiculturalism;[8] a multiculturalism that has come a few steps closer to what Augie Fleras, in an article on racism in Canadian media, calls the "post-multicultural" phase, in which egalitarianism, or in the terms that he uses, "mainstreaming", has been achieved at least to a certain degree (Fleras 285). Such an observation – idealistic as it may be – underscores the

[4] See also Bennett, "Postcolonial Complexities" 193.

[5] Cp. Grace 287, also Hutcheon "Introduction" (to *Other Solitudes*), Kröller "Introduction" (to *The Cambridge Companion of Canadian Literature*) 5-10; on the influence of feminist and other theories on the increasing questioning of the essentialist labels fostered by the multiculturalist vision, cf. Golfman 177, and Lorna Marie Irvine, who claims that "The 1980s was a decade of literary deconstruction. Theorists and critics paid increasing attention to race, class, gender and sexual orientation as they argued about how to give voice to traditionally silenced groups. [...] Feminist theory in particular undertook to raise critical consciousness about everything from generic categories to reading practices to the place of the body in the act of writing" (Irvine 141).

[6] Early positionings of that kind are to be found in publications dating from as early as the 1970s: cf. Cornelius J. Jaenen, "Introduction" xi-xii; later examples can be found in Hutcheon and Richmond, *Other Solitudes* and Kamboureli, *Making a Difference*; discussions on this issue are also included in Berry and Laponce, and Verduyn, *Literary Pluralities*.

[7] Cf. the final section in Chapter 3; furthermore, Irvine discusses some recent, more innovative studies that suggest a new understanding of multiculturalism, 148-152.

[8] See, for example, the critical though still overall more optimistic evaluations by the "Africadian" author George Elliott Clarke and Chinese Canadian writer Paul Yee in Huggan and Siemerling, "U.S./Canadian Writers' Perspectives On The Multiculturalism Debate" 99-105.

pressing actuality of questions, repeatedly posed by critics in the past decades, asking what should the literature of such an 'ideal' multicultural society be defined by in the broadest sense. Thus, Evelyn J. Hinz asks, "what form the multicultural text should take" (xiii), while Huggan and Siemerling demand:

> What are the relationships between this business of national culture (which still seems to frame many discussions of multiculturalism) and affiliations of gender, race, and ethnicity, affiliations that cut across the nation, even the postcolonial nation, and often across languages like French or English? And what kind of a role do any of these affiliations play not just for literature as an institution but in the process of writing itself? (87)

In the same contribution, Québécoise feminist poet Nicole Brossard in her arresting response to the issue, suggests one possible answer to Huggan and Siemerling's above quoted questions, thereby underlining the necessity for a refocused perspective:

> Multiculturalism is a reality. Policies have been made to accommodate different cultures, but I do not think that it will be enough without what we call, and especially Edouard Glissant calls, *le métissage culturel*, or cultural *métissage*, which means interpenetration, fluidity, new configuration of identity, and continuous movement. (98)

Aligning itself with Brossard's thoughts, the following chapter seeks to make observations on the evolution of diverse aspects of multiculturalism in Canada, as well as their influence on the emergence of a transcultural imaginary.

Canada's Multiculturalisms

In 1971, when Pierre Elliott Trudeau announced his intention to integrate Canada's "other ethnic groups" – whose "cultural contribution" to Canadian society and culture was considerable[9], as had been found by the Royal Commission on B&B – multiculturalism became a paramount concern for Canada. Since the official integration of the Multiculturalism Act into the constitution in 1988, diversity and heritage management in the name of multiculturalism has developed into a national project. 'National project' here seems the most accurate designation as multiculturalism nowadays represents, on various levels of social, political and cultural life, and in various forms, the very concept that both unites and diffuses the Canadian nation; it is a concept that is constantly debated, revised and developed – a controversial and idealistic project.

In her essay on the "Nation and Its Discontents" Donna Bennett differentiates between the notion of 'nation' as referring to "a politically defined entity; or a cohesive social

[9] The last volume of the report that resulted from the research done by the Royal Commission on Bilingualism and Biculturalism (short "Royal Commission on B&B", cf. Berry and Laponce 7) was entitled *The Cultural Contribution of Other Ethnic Groups*. Cf. Hutcheon, *Other Solitudes* 13.

unit uniting the people of a certain geographical region; or a unifying culture that gives its members a sense of a belonging and identity" (15). Taking this triad as a guiding element for an approach towards the nation's major project, it becomes obvious that multiculturalism, too, must be divided in various (similar) spheres in order to be adequately mapped. In this sense, Canadian multiculturalism can be seen, on the one hand, as a national, therein functioning as a political, concept, which attempts to control ethnically and racially plural democratic power relations, governmental money distributions and culturally diverse individual as well as communal fundamental rights. As the following five paragraphs of the Canadian Multiculturalism Act underline:

> 3. (1) It is hereby declared to be the policy of the Government of Canada to
>
> (*a*) recognize and promote the understanding that multiculturalism reflects the cultural and racial diversity of Canadian society and acknowledges the freedom of all members of Canadian society to preserve, enhance and share their cultural heritage;
>
> (*b*) recognize and promote the understanding that multiculturalism is a fundamental characteristic of the Canadian heritage and identity and that it provides an invaluable resource in the shaping of Canada's future;
>
> (*c*) promote the full and equitable participation of individuals and communities of all origins in the continuing evolution and shaping of all aspects of Canadian society and assist them in the elimination of any barrier to that participation;
>
> (*d*) recognize the existence of communities whose members share a common origin and their historic contribution to Canadian society, and enhance their development;
>
> (*e*) ensure that all individuals receive equal treatment and equal protection under the law, while respecting and valuing their diversity; (Department of Justice Canada; *online resource*, n.pag.)

On the other hand, multiculturalism also figures as a major multifunctional copula in the commitment to a cohesive social unit – especially in opposition to the nation's mighty southern neighbor, whose sense of diversity must be seen in strong opposition to official Canadian multiculturalism (Huggan and Siemerling 83-87). However, both this social unit and the third element of the triad, a unifying culture, on which the former very much depends, have been called into question through the diversity of voices established through the very policy of multiculturalism. Thus, we might add a further level of meaning to multiculturalism in Canada, one that unites the three other elements despite the deviations and at the same time makes the term more dynamic: the set of discourses that evolved out of multiculturalism, which have been dominant in popular media and academia alike; we may consider them as fields of research and dispute, echoing and influencing Canadian cultural manifestations, creating a circle of unity and disunity, which represents Canadian identities and every day realities in its most authentic form.

One of the reasons that multiculturalism holds such a central position in Canadian society, in political culture and in academia is not only that it represents the marketplace at which public and academic discourses are discussed and coordinated; it has also come to function as an overarching expression of various theoretical tendencies developed within the critical debate, especially within literary-cultural criticism. Consequently, the emergence of multicultural policies and literature relates strongly to the rise of post-structural and postmodern theories in Canada since the 1980s and postcolonial critical debates since the 1990s.[10] This tendency is strongly reflected in the majority of the essays included in a special issue of *Mosaic* on "The Rhetoric and Reality of Multiculturalism," which Evelyn J. Hinz introduces by contemplating that "[i]f it is true that within the past decades we have experienced what Thomas Kuhn would call a "paradigm shift," then multiculturalism is probably the best umbrella term for the kind of re-conceptualizing that has occurred. Certainly, multiculturalism seems to be the index term that appears most frequently in various forms of discourse" (vii). Donna Bennett in "English Canada's Postcolonial Complexities," which has become one of the standard essays of earlier Canadian postcolonial discourse, basically equates contemporary Canadian multicultural developments (and especially literature) with the rise of postcolonial discourse in Canada[11]; while Francesco Loriggio when describing the overall tendencies of Canadian academia in a more cynical mode, observes that

> the multiculturalist moment is that phase of criticism which best presents academic criticism in its ambivalence, forever caught between the desire to escape itself, to be relevant, to participate in the discussions of value to society at large, and the constraints that it must impose on itself. (Loriggio 190)

In which ever way we choose to evaluate the "multiculturalist moment" in Canada, it must be acknowledged that both the policy and the discourse is unique to the Canadian nation and people, though similar strategies were introduced, for example, in Australia and New Zealand;[12] the specific Canadian multicultural situation has been influenced by its history and position as a former settler-colony that, in contrast to the United States, did not establish its national consciousness early on through a revolution.[13] In fact, not only is the interpretation of this heritage very different in America (consider the famous opposition of the 'melting pot' vs. 'mosaic'), the actual debate on multiculturalism is also far younger in the U.S. Graham Huggan and Winfried Siemerling, who held a round table discussion at Harvard to assess the differences between the two neighbors' multiculturalisms, explicate how debates in the U.S. that developed as late as in the 1990s, mainly focused on the academia and discussions around university curricula, and were particularly defined via race (Huggan and Siemerling 85-86). In Canada, where

[10] This relation has partially already been highlighted in the last section of Chapter 1.

[11] Of course, Bennett does not completely equate the two, but to a certain degree she presents simplified perspectives on both developments. To give an example from "English Canada's Postcolonial Complexities" (1993) – of which the second half partially also appears in "Nation and Its Discontents": "This is a literature that, in its accounts of immigrant experience and cultural otherness, may resonate with Canada's preexisting postcolonial condition partly because the ethnic writers' backgrounds are often already postcolonial. These writers from other postcolonial countries now find themselves relocated within a new postcolonial society" 189.

[12] Cp., for example, Gunew, *Framing Marginality*.

[13] Cf. i.e. Nelles 74-88.

the official debates already evolved during the 1970s in all academic and public spheres, more emphasis was from the beginning put on the issue of ethnicity, as well as on the nation's bilingualism and -culturalism, out of which the discussions had originally developed – while in the United States the linguistic aspect has been marginal (Huggan and Siemerling 83-87).

As both the authors of the essay and the Canadian writers who contributed to the round table at Harvard point out, today, we can observe not only various forms and strands of multiculturalism outside Canada, but also within the country, where it thus becomes possible to differentiate between several spheres of development. From a historical perspective, we must be aware, for example, of several periods of immigration since the beginnings of the colony, and more importantly, even before European settlement. Though some critics have highlighted the positive effects of multicultural policies for Natives in Canada, these policies have still only partially been integrated into official (and also the less official) discourses – despite the fact that indigenous peoples have been contributing to the North American cultural heterogeneity far longer (Hutcheon, "Introduction" 8; Kamboureli, "Introduction" 7-9, Bennett "Postcolonial Complexities" 174-175). Additionally, as underlined by Siemerling and Brossard among others, "there are several different strands of multiculturalism besides official multiculturalism, and they meet at various constellations. [...] different regional and cultural locations have motivated a considerable variety of responses" (Huggan and Siemerling 85) and "Canada has actually several multiculturalisms, official and unofficial ones, with possibly more to come" (87).[14] Most prominently, Quebec (and in general Canada's francophone communities) must be regarded as a major force within the development of Canadian multiculturalisms; French Canadians have been vital both for the concrete enactment of the official policies in the 1970s (at a time when Québécois nationalism was at its highest and represented a problem for the federal state) and as a counterforce, producing within its provincial context an even more flexible multiculturalism of its own.[15] As Siemerling affirms, Québécois literary and cultural criticism has in fact produced more advanced approaches to the understanding of heterogenic identities and socio-cultural productions than found in (and on) English-Canadian discourses (Huggan and Siemerling 86).[16]

As Berry and Laponce already noted in 1993 on the reception of multicultural policy, "opinions range from strong hostility to strong endorsement" (10). The major debates

[14] In the round table contribution, the two author's perspective gives an academic overview, while all of the following reactions by Canadian and U.S. writers, most stunningly Nicole Brossard's, display creative expressions and interpretations of the very plurality of these "unofficial" multiculturalisms.

[15] Kröller, "Introduction" (to *Cambridge Companion of Canadian Literature*), 5; Grace 287.

[16] Siemerling refers to Sherry Simon's *Le Trafic des Langues: Traduction et culture dans la littérature québécoise* (Montréal: Boréal, 1994); Pierre Nepveu, *L'Ecologie du reel: Mort et naissance de la littérature québécoise contemporaine,* (Montréal: Boréal, 1988). One might also add more recent publications, such as Harel, *Les passages obliges de l'écriture migrante;* Giguère, *Passeurs Culturels*; or Ertler, *Migration und Schreiben in der Romania*; Ertler, and Löschnigg, *Canada in the Sign of Migration and Trans-Culturalism*. See also the contributions by Lucie Lequin, Jean Jonassaint, Nadine Ltaif, Mair Verthuy in Verduyn; and Dupuis, "Transculturalims and écritures migrantes."

surrounding the broad realm of multiculturalism in the past decades have been based on the realization that "multiculturalism has its limitations" (Bennett, "Postcolonial Complexities" 193). The most disturbing of these limitations, and the one most controversially discussed, evolves around the issue of ethnicity and the questioning of multicultural essentialist attitude. Smaro Kamboureli summarizes this complex issue:

> Thus while multiculturalism is expected to facilitate the process of decolonizing the inherited representations of Canadian history, the literary tradition, and other forms of culture, it is also seen as essentializing race and ethnicity, namely assigning to racial and ethnic differences, as well as their various expressions, attributes that are taken to be 'natural', and therefore stable. (*Making a Difference* 12)

The emergence of critical voices, as Kamboureli indicates in the first lines of the preface to her more recent study, *Scandalous Bodies*, began at the end of the 1980s. Examples of early contributions are Linda Hutcheon's and Marion Richmond's *Other Solitudes* (1990), in which the authors display an awareness of the danger of "stereotyping" and "fossilizing cultures," as well as "reducing 'otherness' to singing and dancing or exotic food" (Hutcheon "Introduction" 14), and also Donna Bennett's "Postcolonial Complexities" (192-193). In her anthology from 1996, Smaro Kamboureli already calls for the deconstruction of concepts of minority and thereby the creation of a space for dialogue that would at the same time admit difference (*Making a Difference* 1-6). Three years earlier, Neil Bissoondath had already contributed one of the most discussed polemical studies, *Selling Illusions: The Cult of Multiculturalism in Canada*, in which he argues – in a fairly casual fashion, as some critics observed[17] – that multiculturalism fostered nothing but the exotification and commodification of ethnic minorities in Canada. In fact, both popular and academic reactions to Canadian multiculturalism have been controversial on several levels.[18] Critics such as Smaro Kamboureli and Neil Bissoondath have been expressing an "anxiety [...] about any homogeneous image of Canadian culture" (*Making a Difference* 6) as suggested by multicultural policies, and they have also criticized the unaltered marginalization of 'other solitudes';[19] other critics maintain the complete opposite, namely "that this support of pluralism, instead of fostering unity, keeps cultures apart or that multiculturalism pays lip service to culture – that no one truly understands someone outside of his or her ethnic group despite the feel-good sloganeering" (Chung 306).
The ever-antagonistic debate on multiculturalism, however, seems to have taken a new course since the 1990s – whereas especially the discourse on difference appears to have triggered alternative perspectives, as Kamboureli observes in 1996:

> I believe that within this complex web of historical changes, cultural differences, and politics there still remains the fundamental question of what constitutes Canadian identity. But in the 1990s this question has been reconfigured, and, I think, irrevocably so. For we can no longer afford to think of Canadian identity in singular terms. Its

[17] Cp. Golfman 175-181.
[18] Cf. also the reaction of Paul Yee in Huggan and Siemerling's round-table, 102-105.
[19] For further critical approaches cf. Gunew, *Haunted Nations* and Bannerji, "On the Dark Side of the Nation."

> imaginary cohesiveness has already collapsed upon itself. Nor can we afford to cavalierly dismiss the current interest in cultural differences as a mere fad, or an obsession. The recognition of cultural difference in the 1990s marks yet another beginning in Canadian multicultural history, the beginning of an attempt to understand how distinct identities can converge and dialogue with each other within Canada, how boundaries of difference must be repositioned—not in relation to the signs of 'centre' and 'margins' but in relation to new and productive alignments. (*Making a Difference* 12)

This more diversified approach to Canadian culture and multiculturalism, which, as Smaro Kamboureli emphasizes, still represents the core issue of Canadian identities, has been advanced since the beginning of the new century, strengthened by the realization that new modes within the debate were necessary – modes that represent a more future-oriented view.[20] In this sense, Andrew Chung in his essay on "Mixed Race and Nonbelonging in the Multicultural Nation" writes

> Canadians simply haven't thought about what their country will look like in the post-multicultural era. As the fast-paced mixing quickens and deepens, that day is not far off. […] But the decades-old policy of official multiculturalism in Canada has not evolved with these changing times. It is an outmoded concept that needs renovation. It does not yet recognize the emerging reality of mixed-race citizens. Quite apart from encouraging the successful cultural retention of the state's many nations, multiculturalism must now be flexible enough to accommodate the blurring of boundaries. (308)

With the prospect of a more flexible form of multiculturalism, comes the equally pressing need for an adapted reading of Canada's multicultural literature. Discourses on Canadian literatures have – in a similar manner as the multiculturalism debate displays – in general rather focused on notions of separate, essentialized notions of ethnicity and race, or on the aspect of marginalization with all the troubles and inequalities it inherits, which must be taken seriously. Yet, it are also these discourses that require an extensive revision in order to find new spaces for dialogue and convergence. In the critical words of Roy Miki:

[20] The rethinking that is currently taking place in regard to such issues as multiculturalism, identities and Canadian literature at large, are best exemplified in the recent innitatives and accomplishments of the TransCanada Project, developed by the above-quoted scholars Smaro Kamboureli and Roy Miki, among others. The Project also included the organization several conferences, the innovativeness of which is documented in the conference proceedings, *Trans.Can.Lit: Resituating the Study of Canadian Literature* (Ed. Miki and Kamboureli). The intriguing diverse perspectives brought forward in this collection are united by a critical investigation that moves beyond an analysis of "multiculturalism": it rather questions belonging as well as 'national' literary production in terms of citizenship and institutions. Kamboureli writes in the Preface: "Since the national, multicultural, and postcolonial idioms are affected by globalization in ways that make it imperative we confront how citizenship, in its different configurations, is controlled and performed today, it was important to make citizenship one of the operative terms in our proposed investigation of CanLit. […] The task, then, was to undertake a major rethinking of the assumptions that had goverened the field of CanLit studies and to rejuvenate the field through a renewed sense of collective purpose" (xiii).

> To counter this pedagogical thrust of the existing nation-state there needs to be a large-scale effort to rethink its historical formation to make visible the articulatory practices that enabled its difference-making. Since difference-making in whatever configurations it may take, whether through differentiations based on ethnicity, race, class, or through any other classificatory system, always works in the interest of order and stability, and thus defaults to existing relations of power, *new critical models and practices are required* [my emphasis]. What is necessary are critical practices that can make visible the multiple effects of contradiction, incoherence, and conflict in the body politic without insisting on unity and order as ends. Without such an approach to cultural processes, the "citizen" as a formation will remain at the mercy of governmental mechanisms that defuse the open-endedness of existence in the local sites where embodied citizens perform their lives. ("'Inside the Black Egg'"15-16)

'Multi' vs. 'Inter' vs. 'Trans'-culturalism(s)

Despite the multiple forms of multiculturalism represented within and outside Canada, we may still at least be able to temporarily define its basic function and sphere of influence by relating it to the demographic, political, and identitary texture of a "society consisting of varied cultural groups" (Bennett, Grossberg & Morris 226); invariably it also engenders "a social doctrine that distinguishes itself as a positive alternative for policies of assimilation, connoting a politics of recognition of citizenship rights and cultural identities of minority groups (Kymlycka, 1995; C.Taylor, 1992) and, more generally, an affirmation of the value of cultural diversity" (ibid. 226). However, if we extend these ideas and include the terms *inter-* and *trans*-culturalism, which are nowadays often applied in the same context, it becomes more difficult to trace generally acknowledged definitions. What we might, more or less, easily agree upon is the observation that while multiculturalism also denotes the 'mind set' of a society, it most prominently refers to a governmental policy, while inter- and transculturalism might well be considered as mainly referring to culture and cultural identities as well as the critical approaches that deal with them; however, they definitely do not denote an official doctrine. Yet again, in opposition to the term 'multiculturalism' and its derivate 'multicultural,' they are more common in academic discourses as descriptive terms for dialogic cultural forces such as those found in literary texts.

As one attempts to grasp the usage and connotations of 'interculturalism' and 'transculturalism,' one is first of all confronted with the problem that both are widely spread across the disciplines and in literary and cultural critical analyses; they may also be classified as the kind of expressions that are frequently used but often not defined or discussed in detail; some critics probably assume that their meaning is obvious or standardized, which is not the case – especially not in relation to each other.[21] Exceptions to this practice are seldom – though the essays and studies that represent the

[21] Heinz Antor, for example, mentions that interculturalism is in some cases used as conceptual umbrella term for both multi- and transculturalism, in others the term transculturalism is completely rejected in favor of the thus all-encompassing expression interculturalism, cf. "Multikulturalismus, Interkulturalität und Transkulturalität" 26.

fundamental basis of this examination might eventually trigger some revisions in the field.[22]

What Heinz Antor's own contribution to the above indicated collection of essays *Inter- und Transkulturelle Studien* makes clear – with reference to a further exceptional examination of the field and its termini, an essay by Wolfgang Welsch[23] – is that while interculturalism is conceptually close to multiculturalism in that it reflects a similar understanding of cultural diversity and side-by-sidedness (of its separate components), transculturalism differs in that it acknowledges difference and at the same time lays stronger emphasis on complex cultural interactions and the resulting hybridizations:

> Ausgehend von Begriffsbestimmungen des Philosophen Wolfgang Welsch unterscheidet Antor einen partikularistischen von einem hybridisierten Kulturbegriff. Diese Differenzierung erlaubt eine Definition der drei zentralen Konzepte, wobei ‚Multikulturalismus' und ‚Interkulturalität' noch eine Vorstellung von Kulturen als seperaten Entitäten und deren Nebeneinander beziehungsweise dialogischem Miteinander zugrunde liegt, während ‚Transkulturalität' die Komplexität von Kultur und die zahlreichen hybriden Übergänge, Binnendifferenzierungen und kulturellen Vernetzungen reflektiert, die ein Denken in getrennten kulturellen Einheiten problematisch werden lassen. (Antor 9)

As the passage shows, this definition of the terms is strongly linked to the already discussed turn in the perception of culture as a highly complex, porous construct characterized by "the fluidity and impermanence of cultural distinctions and relationships" (Bennett, Grossberg and Morris 68).[24] In other words, as underlined by Antor in his analysis of Welsch's approach, while both multi- and interculturalism are most often based on a stronger perception of culture in terms of Johann Gottfried von Herder's fixed entities (Antor 27-28), or "containers,"[25] transculturalism is assumed to echo postmodern non-essentialist, as well as postcolonial de-contructive alternative and dialogic conceptions of culture*s* (Antor 31-35).

The discussions and analyses brought forth in the present study endorse the definitions outlined in Heinz Antor's collection as well as the included essay (along with subscribing to the concepts developed by Frank Schulze-Engler in several contexts), yet do so with a special emphasis on the original etymological meanings of the prefixes 'inter' ('between') and 'trans' ('across,' 'beyond'), the latter thus evocating Latin derivates such as *transire* ('go across,' 'transcend,' 'exceed'), or *transferre* ('to carry across'), and related English expressions such as 'transfer' and 'translate.' In this respect one of the experts on transculturalism in Quebecois literature might be quoted, whose definitions of inter- and transculturalism follow similar lines of differentiation:

[22] Cf. i.e. Antor, *Inter- und Transkulturelle Studien. Theoretische Grundlagen und interdisziplinäre Praxis*; the essays by Frank Schulze-Engler and Janice Kulyk-Keefer; contributions by Eckstein; Vautier; Dupuis; and Siemerling.

[23] "Transculturality – the Puzzling Form of Cultures Today," *online resource*.

[24] Cp. Chapter 3.

[25] Cf. Schulze-Engler, "Von ‚Inter' zu ‚Trans'."

> It may be argued that interculturalism, as discourse, occurs whenever two cultures are present and engage in dialogue together. The purpose of this exchange is the attempt to understand the Other represented by each culture and to be reciprocally recognized as "one." In exchange, which might fail or only partly succeed, each cultural exponent engaged in the dialogue remains more or less the same, the ultimate goal of this engagement being mutual acceptance, as opposed to being changed by the exchange itself. [...]
>
> [...] Transculturalism takes place when at least two – and sometimes three or more – cultures are not only engaged in dialogue, but partake in a more profound and often contradictory process, in which enlightenment, misunderstanding, and continuous reassessment of identity are at play. The ultimate aim is to transform each other's identity through a long, arduous, and sometimes painful negotiation of Otherness. (Dupuis, "Transculturalism and *écritures migrantes*" 500)

There are two features that I would like to stress in opposition to prevalent notions of multi-, inter- and transculturalism as well as in addition to Antor's and Schulze-Engler's more detailed perceptions. The first one is that transculturalism should not be seen as replacing either of the two other concepts but rather as an extension of them.[26] Instead of one superseding the other, one should think of the concepts as building upon each other; in fact, as long as there is neither an awareness of multiculturalism within a society, nor official policies that regulate the equal rights of a multicultural society, both intercultural dialogue and transcultural exchange can hardly develop. The second point that must be emphasized is that intercultural and transcultural are in some instances difficult to separate, insofar as they both represent forms of cultural dynamic discourse; the differentiation of the two terms strongly depends on a necessarily subjective measurement and evaluation of the degree, complexity, and extent of consequences of interaction processes.[27]

Both of these crucial factors, the interdependency between all three concepts and the complex transition between the inter- and transcultural flows are intrinsically connected to the discourse on difference, which is a crucial issue in cultural studies and other critical fields. A superficial perspective on multi-, inter- and transculturalism could promote the view, insinuated by critics of either concept, that the first and partially the second concept would underscore the maintenance of difference, while the third would effect (or echo) the complete loss of any cultural differentiation effected by the continuing process of hybridization. In response to this possible problematization, Heinz Antor stresses the necessity to practice both inter- as well as trans-cultural modes of analysis and perception (36) and also advocates the "positioning" of a cultural identity (comparatively different or similar to others) as a *prerequisite* for cultural

[26] In the introduction to *Inter- und Transkulturelle Studien* Antor indicates the insufficiency of the categories of multi- and interculturalism and the necessity to replace it through transculturalism (10); however this potentially problematic suggestion is discussed more critically in his contribution "Multikulturalismus, Interkulturalität und Transkulturalität."

[27] Both of these features – the non-linear development of these concepts, and their partial crossings, which make them hard to differentiate – are also observed by Gilles Dupuis, though his discussion is firmly tied to the development of immigrant and migrant writing in Québec, cp. "Transculturalism and *écritures migrantes*" 499-501.

dialogue or hybridization; this view is also advanced in the investigation of transcultural imaginaries in the present study.[28] In a critique of Werner Sollors's proposition toward an "openly transethnic procedure" (Sollors qtd. in Schwenk 2)[29], Katrin Schwenk suggests a perspective that "shifts the emphasis within the argument. The shift avoids an opposition of *either* single-ethnic *or* transethnic attitudes and instead tries to elaborate a basis of "both and" for questions concerning multiculturalism (and also the concept of gender)" (Schwenk, "Introduction" 2). Or, as Wolfgang Klooss notes when he discusses intertextuality – a feature closely related to transcultural imaginaries – in the concrete context of the New Literatures in English:

> Despite the inevitable impact of tradition, the new literatures tend to employ a dynamic reading of culture, which fosters social process and transition, thus promoting transcultural rather than intercultural modes of communication. Writing and reading across borders becomes a dialogue which reveals both differences and similarities. It thus cannot suffice to make a plea for intertextuality as a merely decolonizing form of deconstruction; one should, rather, conceive of it as a strategy to communicate meaning across cultural boundaries. (Klooss, *Across the Lines* i)

The diverse features of transcultural approaches to culture and literature, as highlighted above and fortified by perspectives of renowned scholars, become even more acute when applied to the reading and analysis of texts. However, as the following pages will show, these ideas on transcultural processes were conceived in their original form at the beginning of the twentieth century and have since developed in diverse directions. In order to dissect the specific kaleidoscopic features that nurture a criticism of transcultural imaginaries in fictions of the past, it will first be necessary to trace the meandering emergence of transcultural theories.

Transcultural Theories

In an essay entitled "Rereading the Nation: Cultural Difference, *Transculture*, and Literary History in Canada and Quebec" published in 1993, Winfried Siemerling comes to the promising conclusion that "the wealth of writing and of cultural positions currently emerging in what is now Canada and Quebec produces increasingly relational and transnational procedures that may actually exceed that model [of the Canadian multicultural nation], and may in the process also reposition and refunctionalize aspects of literary studies in the future" ("Rereading" 200). I am pointing out the year of publication because it seems curious that the reactions within the critical discourse

[28] For a further example of this argument, cf. Kalogeras et al. xiii.

[29] The quote is taken from Werner Sollors, "A Critique of Pure Pluralism," *Reconstructing American Literary History,* ed. Sacvan Bercovitch (Cambridge: Harvard UP, 1986), 250-279. The essay is referred to by the editors of *Cultural Difference*, Winfried Siemerling and Katrin Schwenk, as the text which inspired the publication. Once again we may note the emphasis on ethnicity in a discussion focusing on difference and multiculturalism.

prophesized by Siemerling have yet remained scarce – in spite of the detailed analysis of several original sources and concepts related to contemporary transculturalism.

To speak of 'contemporary transculturalism' might be misleading as there is not one coherent strand or linear development of a single transculturalist approach, let alone a 'transcultural theory.' Siemerling's "rereading" is of interest for the present chapter in that it depicts several fundamental issues and developments within the Canadian literary and critical context that can be taken to explain the complexity underlying the hesitant emergence of transcultural perspectives in Canada.[30] Not only does Siemerling remark that "[d]espite the constant impact of cultural difference on Canadian writers, cultural plurality has become a central topic in discussions of Canadian and Québécois literature only in recent years[31], when issues of literary canons, ethnicity, multiculturalism, *transculture*, and postcolonialism were ushered in" ("Rereading" 188); more importantly, these notions and "issues," which are so strongly related to the concept of transculturalism – multiculturalism, difference, and ethnicity – were also received and dealt with in a completely different manner in Québécois culture and identity politics, thus in a 'minoritarian' context compared to the rest of Canada ("Rereading" 192). A vibrant 'school' of transcultural theorists, as well as a *littérature* that strongly reflected and affirmed this mode of cultural thinking emerged far earlier in Québec than elsewhere – though predominantly in the context of *littérature migrante*.[32] As observed by Siemerling and several other scholars, the year 1983 represented a turning point in the Québécois cultural scene with the publication of Régine Robin's *La Québécoite* and the first issue of *Vice Versa. Magazine transculturel,* which together with some critical studies led to an exemplary renegotiation of ethnicity in more positive terms ("Rereading" 192).[33]

The discourse on *transculture* within the Québécois literary scene, and especially in the context of the multilingual magazine *Vice Versa*, which was founded by a group of Italo-Québécois writer-critics, evokes several strands of elaborate ideas that are strongly related, and thus crucial, to an understanding of transcultural imaginaries.[34] However, *Vice Versa*'s concept of *transculture* can hardly be discussed without a further short digression to its original source of inspiration: the concept of "transculturation," introduced as a neologism by the Cuban anthropologist Fernando Ortiz in his remarkably innovative study of 1943, *Cuban Counterpoint: Tobacco and Sugar*. Ortiz was a regionally acclaimed, though, at the time, internationally marginalized South American scholar; thus, his work was acknowledged only hesitantly in anthropological circles and even less in literary circles, especially outside the Americas. In *Cuban Counterpoint*, Fernando Ortiz attempted to rewrite Cuban history by, on one hand,

[30] The essay is of additional interest as it represents an impressive earlier example of Siemerling's work, already pointing to his later publications, such as Siemerling and Schwenk, *Cultural Difference and the Literary Text*; Siemerling, *Writing Ethnicity*; and especially *The New North American Studies*.

[31] Siemerling is consequently referring to the end of the 1980s, beginning of the 1990s.

[32] Cf. Dupuis, "Transculturalism and *écritures migrantes*" for similar observations.

[33] Cf. also *The New North American Studies* 130-133; Dupuis, "Transculturalism and *écritures migrantes*" 500-502.

[34] The founders of *Vice Versa* were Lamberto Tassinari, Fulvio Caccia, Antonio D'Alfonso and Bruno Ramirez. Cf. Renzi, "Identity and Transculture in *Vice Versa*" 110-111.

elaborating metaphorically on the role of the natural resources of tobacco and sugar, and on the other, by describing the complex developments related to immigration and the impact of cultures on Cuban society and culture. As Ortiz makes clear at the beginning of the second part of his study, transculturation, which stands as an inclusive term for several complex processes of cultural layering and transfer, is meant to replace the term of "acculturation," which was more common in anthropology at the time. Ortiz refers to it as "the process of transition from one culture to another" (98), and as Fernando Coronil adds in his introduction, "[implying] the acquisition of a culture in a unidirectional process" (xxvi). However, transculturation, not only helped describe "the highly varied phenomena that have come about in Cuba as a result of the extremely complex transmutations of culture" and "these continuous, radical, contrasting geographic transmigrations, economic and social," it also extended the discourse on acculturation and deculturation[35] by adding the notion of "neo-culturation," which also points towards Ortiz's acknowledgement of an at least two-directional nature of transcultural processes:

> I am of the opinion that the word *transculturation* better expresses the different phases of the process of transition from one culture to another because this does not consist merely in acquiring another culture, which is what the English word of *acculturation* really implies, but the process also necessarily involves the loss and uprooting of a previous culture, which could be defined as deculturation. In addition it carries the idea of the consequent creation of new cultural phenomena, which could be called neoculturation. (102-103)

As fully shown in Fernando Coronil's introduction, Ortiz's concept of transculturation involved many innovative ideas that are still current today – its critical, flexible nature and historical orientation will reverberate in chapters to come. However, later readings and applications of his study either underrated or misinterpreted his original concept, as is also to some degree the case in M.L. Pratt's highly regarded postcolonial study on the 'contact zone,' which relegates transculturation (despite its reference to Ortiz) back into a unidirectional process (Pratt 6).[36]

As genuinely demonstrated by Jean Lamore's contribution to *Vice Versa* in 1987 (quoted both in Pierre Nepveu's famous questioning article "Qu'est-ce que la transculture?" and in Siemerling's "Rereading"-essay with reference to Nepveu, as well as in his recent more detailed *New North American Studies*), the intellectuals belonging to the circle of *Vice-Versa* also regarded Ortiz's transculturation as the original source for their understanding of *transculture*:

[35] Both concepts were included in transculturation (98).

[36] Mary L. Pratt claims "[e]thnographers have used this term to describe how subordinated or marginal groups select and invent from materials transmitted to them by a dominant or metropolitan culture. While subjugated peoples cannot readily control what emanates from the dominant culture, they do determine to varying extents what they absorb into their own, and what they use it for. Transculturation is a phenomenon of the contact zone," 6. In a footnote that refers to Ortiz (FN4) she mentions acculturation and deculturation, but not neoculturation.

> En fait, le sens exact et créateur de la transculturation selon son "inventeur," F. Ortiz, est clair et doit être rehabilitée: la transculturation est un ensemble de transmutations constants; elle est créatrice et jamais achevée; elle est irreversible. Elle est toujours un processus dans lequel on donne quelque chose en échange de ce qu'on reçoit: les deux parties de l'équation s'en trouvent modifiées. Il en emerge une réalité nouvelle, qui n'est pas une mosaique de caractères, mais un phénomène nouveau, original et indépendant. (Lamore qtd. in Siemerling, *New North American Studies* 133: 19)[37]

As the passage shows, "la transculture" takes up Ortiz's notion of neoculturation; however, there are several features that the *Vice Versa* group simply adopted, while others were specifically added or given more weight. An additional aspect that connects the Québécois school with Ortiz's original concept is the awareness that transculture and transculturation (which can in the context of *Vice Versa* be read as the process leading to a transculture) are not new developments but have been a part of human cultures and societies as long as they have existed and are thus also historically applicable concepts. However, Pierre Bertrand also argues in his 1988 essay that transculture used to be more a matter of the elites in former times (thereby linking it to earlier notions of cosmopolitanism[38]) but that it had become relevant for everybody in the age of globalization and migration:

> La transculture est donc une réalité du passé avant d'être une réalité de l'avenir. Mais alors que longtemps, elle ne concernait que l' « elite », elle est en passe, par des fluxs de migration et d'immigration désormais irréversibles, d'affecter la vie quotidienne de Monsieur-et-Madame-tout-le-monde. Ce qui était le privilège de quelques-uns devient, et deviendra de plus en plus, à une autre échelle, l'expérience de chacun. ("Le voyage immobile" 8)

The aspect that most prominently differentiates the *Vice Versa* concept from Ortiz's view is that it is written from a strong, in a double sense minoritarian (i.e. Québécois and 'ethnic') perspective. It advocates the transgression of national boundaries, as well as the questioning of notions of nationality and ethnicity as such, thereby proposing transculture as an alternative to the then still strongly promoted image of "québécité,"[39] and as a 'defense' against imposed U.S.-American values: "Alors la défense se ferait autrement: avec l'avènement d'une société autre, capable de devenir Indien, immigrant, Noir..." (Tassinari "Le pouvoir et ses fantasmes" 5). As this quote indicates, and as Pierre Bertrand and Lamberto Tassinari repeatedly emphasize in *Vice Versa*, the process leading to transculture in their eyes necessitates the transgression of one's own culture, the accessing of another culture that in return accesses one's own. This process opens

[37] The renowned definition by Jean Lamore is quoted from "Transculturation : naissance d'un mot," *Vice Versa* (N° 21, 1987), 19.
[38] Cf. During 91; in fact, the Italo-Québecois critics who were involved in the *Vice Versa* project were indeed all established intellectuals, even though the essays included in the magazine often dealt with the transcultural realities of everyday life (for example, Tassinari, "Le pouvoir et ses phantasms"). The editors of *Vice Versa* decided to renew the journal's concept in 1995 (cf. Vice Versa No 49) and to extend its program to include a transnational scope (Montréal-Toronto-NewYork), however its publication ceased soon after. Cp. Dupuis, "Transculturalism" 507.
[39] This issue is discussed particularly in Pierre Nepveu's essay "Qu'est-ce que la transculture?"

up a circle of "becoming" in which each individual discovers the "Other" that is not opposed to the self, but rather defines that part of identity that was not yet known:

> Transculture signifie bien traverser sa proper culture pour accéder à une culture étrangère, cette culture étrangère effectuant le même parcours en sens inverse. Il ne s'agit pas de reniement, mais d'ouverture. [...] Il s'agit d'un phénomène de « devenir » : je deviens l'autre, et l'autre devient moi, non pas dans un processus d'identification, d'assimilation, mais au contraire de différenciation, de diversification. En fait, je ne peux pas devenir l'autre, je ne peux que devenir un autre, autre que moi-même, et autre que l'autre. Et de même pour l'autre. Double devenir, double capture, pour la création d'une réalité originale, nouvelle, *sui generis*, réalité éclatée, douloureuse parfois, mais pleine et positive, pleine d'elle-même et suffisant à elle-même. Et c'est cette nouvelle réalité qui fait que l' « identité » ne peut plus être ce qu'elle était. Il s'agit d'une identité multiple, et non plus homogène. (Betrand 8)

Vice Versa 's visionary call for a diversified and cosmopolitan (québécois) society enriched by transculturality that would shed the mosaic-oriented "osmose symbolique des differences" (Tassinari 5) was, however, eventually also strongly criticized for the one-sided, fluid nature of its concepts (Latouche 44-45). Even though the magazine became less popular with readers in the 1990s, its ideas reverberated strongly in québécois literary and cultural criticism.

Regarding the theories that developed out of the cultural discourse initiated through *Vice Versa,* it is interesting to observe that the already existent focus on the minority perspective and migrant voices became predominant, while others, such as the general claim for an alternative layout for the conception of pluricultural societies (thereby including non-migrant citizens), became less important. In his 1989 essay, "Qu'est-ce que la transculture?" Pierre Nepveu raises several essential critical questions; he addresses certain elements of the issue by discussing three types of expressions in Québécois immigrant texts all of which despite a "pratique concrète, critique, du dépaysement et d'un certain 'territoire imaginaire' de la culture" were "loin d'épuiser la question de la transculture" (21).[40] Nepveu also insistently extended the perspective by devising the necessity to analyze "en quoi le texte québécois lui-même, à travers un certain pluralisme, rédéfinit aussi à sa manière cette expérience" (25), consequently exemplified in his reading of works by, for example, Jacques Poulin and Nicole Brossard as "texts transculturels" (21-29).

In contemporary Québécois literary criticism, contrary to the anglophone Canadian critical discourse, "transculture" and "transculturel" have become common designations for recent complex developments within society as depicted in literary texts – even though here, too, the focus of the term and its critical use remains largely limited to *littérature migrante*; at the same time, the inflationary use of the notions has elsewhere led to a loss of original, very specific meanings as well as a partial amnesia of the intentions behind the introduction of the term and to a lack of precise, renewed definitions. The more and more often indiscriminate usage of transcultural approaches – by now richly communicated in academia internationally and across the disciplines –

[40] Nepveu takes the expression "territoire imaginaire" from Michel Morin et Claude Bertrand, *Le territoire imaginaire de la culture* (Montréal: HMH, 1979).

which in some instances has effected its critical devaluation, constitutes an increasing problem for the phenomenon of transculturalism as criticism, as it often neglects the profound background of transcultural perspectives found in Québec. Apart from this, the major problem in the reception of the notions related to transculturalism lies in the genesis of its usage: moving from Ortiz's "transculturation" as anthropological process that can affect nations and their societies (in positive and negative ways, whether wanted or not), to *Vice Versa*'s "transculturation" as an active process leading to "transculture" in terms of a minoritarian vision of an alternative society; via Nepveu's description of transcultural aspects as characteristic of (Québécois) immigrant texts, the term finally moved on to denote the fairly indefinite notion of "transcultural" circling across diverse disciplines, as well as concepts recently brought forward within Central European schools of New Literatures and other mainly postcolonial literary criticism.

Reacting to the debates on "reasonable accommodation"[41] shortly before the Quebec elections in 2007, one of the founders of *Vice Versa,* Fulvio Caccia, insisted on reminding readers of *Le Devoir* of the former project of *transculture* initiated by the magazine in the 80s and 90s. He contended that a "renouvellement de la réflexion" was desperately necessary, as contemporary approaches to diversity in Québec – complicated by a crisis of the nation-state in the light of expanding transnational markets and technologies – were blocking solutions to the conflict of mutual cultural recognition. In a final paragraph Caccia underlines that his "conviction réside dans le fait que c'est justement dans cet espace transculturel à equidistance entre le repli communitaire des fondamentalismes et la derive d'une identité univoque et consumeriste que peuvent s'élaborer les nouveaux dispositifs du vivre ensemble" (Caccia, "Diversité culturelle et transculture ou Vice Versa?", *online resource*, n.pag.). Those scholars, who in recent years have been seriously working with the concept of transculturalism and have initiated new approaches to transculturalism, appear to have felt similar problems as those summarized by Caccia and reacted to them in the very way he had hoped for.
Contemporary growing interest in the potential of transcultural theories, has been influenced – even if this influence is not always acknowledged or actively discussed by researchers – by the increasing difficulties to accommodate discourses on the "recognition" (Charles Taylor) of ethnic, religious, racial and other cultural identities with discourses on the nation as a homogenizing and imaginary (Benedict Anderson) force of identification; both the acknowledgement of differences and the construction of unifying mind-maps must be seen in the context of the ever-increasing impact of globalization flows, and closures.[42] The yearning for flexible theorizations that grasp the

[41] The issue of "accommodation raisonnable" led to heated debates especially in Québec, where, eventually even a traveling "Commission sur les pratiques des accommodements raisonnables" headed by the sociologist Gérard Bouchard and the renowned philosopher Charles Taylor was initiated, dealing with "Quebec's term for a global dilemma: how far should local populations adjust their rules and habits to make immigrant newcomers feel comfortable practicing their own traditions?" (Wells, Aubin, and Patriquin, "Election 2007 Changes Quebec's Political Landscape," *online resource*, n.pag.); Cf. also Patriquin, "Canada's Renown for Tolerance Is Breaking Down," *online resource*, n.pag.
[42] Cf. Meyer and Geschiere, *Globalization and Identity: Dialectics of Flow and Closure*.

connection between possible new, revised visions of national representations and constructions of the self, and the complex, fragmentary imaginaries of generations of often forcibly cosmopolitan writers and readers is reflected in contemporary publications, especially those dealing with ethnicity and its literary representations. As Kalogeras et al. diagnose in relation to *transcultural localism*, which once again echoes an interest in the interaction of large-scale developments with small-scale spaces, "today's global culture cannot integrate 'everything,' thus it remains a terrain open to contestation so that its edges are constantly in flux" (viii). The impact of this new global culture on communitary, familiar cultures and their literature, especially those with a 'heritage' of former colonial mental structures, has effected a justified turn toward transcultural theories which embrace the recognition that "deterritorialized spaces and individuals can be actualized in between the dominant arrangements of social space 'as a local-global correlation of becomings-other' disorganized around the counterlogic of the *both/and*" (Wilson and Dissanayake 7-8).[43] The approaches which are discussed in some detail on the following pages are representative of these tendencies; however, depending on their disciplinary and theoretical background, they set different, specific emphases on the various aspects underlying transcultural reflections.

One of the most devoted defenders of the transcultural perspective in the North American context has been the Canadian writer Janice Kulyk Keefer, who was among the first scholars to use the term systematically (after Ortiz's conception of the original term and its popularity in Québécois intellectual circles of the 80s and 90s), especially in relation to anglophone Canadian literature. As early as 1991, Kulyk Keefer collected her thoughts, which she connected with her experiences as a Canadian-born scholar, teacher and writer with Ukrainian heritage in the intriguing essay "From Mosaic to Kaleidoscope. Out of a Multicultural Past Comes a Vision of Transcultural Future," which was, in the course of the 90s, followed by several other contributions on the issue.[44] Her stance on the emergence of transcultural writing in Canada is linked to two major aspects that were in one way or another also included in the earlier francophone versions of the concept: the starting point for transcultural writing in Canada was the increasing influence of the "ex-centric," ethnic, or racial minorities, mostly immigrants, in any case, marginalized, perspectives on Canadian literature ("From Dialogue to Polylogue" 60); and that "Canada has a long history of writing that is expressive of difference" (66), by which she indicates that transcultural processes, in the sense of cultural exchange across 'borders' of difference are not 'new': they did not develop only in the twentieth century, but long before Canada's introduction of multicultural policies. This aspect of transcultural theory – the historical component – had already

[43] The text quoted within is taken from Brian Massumi, *A User's Guide to Capitalism and Schizophrenia: Deviations from Deleuze and Guattari* (Cambridge: MIT Press, 1992), 141 and 112.

[44] As for example, "From Dialogue to Polylogue. Canadian Transcultural Writing During the Deluge," and "Writing, Reading, Teaching Transcultural in Canada."

been emphasized by Ortiz and remains essential, despite the increased attention the concept has received in the light of contemporary globalization processes.[45]
As far as the former aspect – the 'immigrant experience' component – is concerned, the positions, especially in the younger debates, diverge in fundamentally different directions. While the intellectuals behind the *Vice Versa* 'project' had used Ortiz's term to forward their vision of a (revised) migrant positioning, a perspective adopted by most contemporary Canadian literary and postcolonial critics, several other individual scholars have questioned the assumption that the concept should be limited to marginalized writers of 'othered' ethnic and racial backgrounds.[46] Janice Kulyk Keefer has also articulated doubts concerning this issue, in that she maintains that "while we can speak of a dominant group within Canadian society [...] that group, whether its members are of British or French descent, is as much an *ethnos*, or distinctive people and culture, as would be a group of Ojibway or Pakistanis" ("From Dialogue to Polylogue" 65) – an observation which leads her to define transcultural as a "comprehensive" term, "so that the texts of a Davies and a Munro, for example, could be read as examples of ethnocultural difference" (ibid. 65).[47] Not only does the attribute transcultural, as viewed by scholars such as Kulyk Keefer, transcend the debate between ethnicity and race so prominent in the 1990s ("Writing, Reading, Teaching" 183, 187-191; "From Dialogue to Polylogue" 68-69), it also acknowledges the diversity and plurality of liminal experiences of individuals situated between several cultures, across generations and across differences within cultural groups ("Writing, Reading, Teaching" 194-195; "From Dialogue to Polylogue" 67; "From Mosaic to Kaleidoscope" 15-16).
The very simultaneity of these contradicting aspects is inherent to the transcultural concept, whereby, it also opens up the potential to transcend and resolve the conflicting binary structures and other theoretical limitations of the past decades. Thus, even though Kulyk Keefer repeatedly speaks of transcultural texts as cultural products that express "ethnocultural difference" ("From Dialogue to Polylogue" 65), she also claims "the most important feature of the term 'transcultural' is its prefix, 'trans,' emphasizing mobility and change" ("Writing, Reading, Teaching" 194). This oppositional tendency that unites the articulation of differences with the crossing of borders as well as cultural exchange and the exposure of similarities, also lies at the heart of the present transcultural approaches. Therefore, it also tackles several other complex, interrelated issues debated in recent publications with a transcultural focus: the general questioning

[45] Cp. Welsch "IV. Supplements and Outlooks: 1. Transculturality – already in history," *online resource*; and Oonk, *online resource*.
[46] In the context of Québécois criticism, Gilles Dupuis has for example suggested the term "écritures transmigrantes" in order to acknowledge transcultural dynamics across texts, the interaction between migrant and non-migrant writers; by introducing this term he also highlights the emergence of this development through the influence of migrant authors on Québécois writing; cf. "Le commis voyageur," and "Transculturalism and *écritures migrantes,*" esp. 508.
[47] Kulyk Keefer similarly asks in another essay: "By designating certain Canadian writers, like Fred Wah and Myrna Kostash, as 'transcultural' and others, like Margaret Atwood or John Steffler, as plain Canadian, is one introducing a hidden hierarchy which privileges one group over the other, depending whether one is a purist or a devotee of hybridity?" ("Writing, Reading, Teaching" 193).

of the boundaries of cultural difference and, in relation to this, of popular binary oppositions based on concepts of self and other, the crisis of postcolonial theory, the impact of globalization on cultures and literatures, and the rethinking of traditional concepts of cultures, societies, and nations – all of which have been discussed in earlier chapters.

In the final paragraph of her essay in which she describes her "writing, reading and teaching" experiences, Janice Kulyk Keefer, once more captures the potential of the transcultural for writers, readers and critics alike when she says that

> [t]he act of moving across borders and connecting disparate voices into what I have elsewhere called polylogue – this is the *sine qua non* of 'transculturalist' aesthetics and multiculturalism itself. Border-crossing, not in order to arrive at some totalized, monolithic ideal of Canadianness, but rather to establish a dialogue rather than oppositional field of discourse, to conflate margin and mainstream, dominant and emergent group into an everchanging choreography of differences. As ideas, information and experiences move across cultures through the medium of film or theatrical performance or literary text, an awareness may result that where 'difference' or 'otherness' exists, so too does significant similarity. For those who write and read across a field of cultural differences, an empowering common ground may emerge [...]. ("Writing, Reading, Teaching" 197)

Of the scholars discussed here who evaluate the transcultural feature of border-crossing and cultural transfer processes, Kulyk Keefer is the one most directly routed in the Canadian literary context. The German philosopher Wolfgang Welsch writes from another, more general angle, but his claims are similar to those of Kulyk Keefer:

> It's just that now the differences no longer come about through a juxtaposition of clearly delineated cultures (like a mosaic), but result between transcultural networks, which have some things in common while differing in others, showing overlaps and distinctions at the same time. The mechanics of differentiation has become more complex – but it has also become genuinely cultural for the first time, no longer complying with geographical or national stipulations, but following pure cultural interchange processes. (Welsch, *online resource*, n.pag.)

However, also scholars who bring forward arguments from a stronger postcolonial or 'New Literatures' perspective especially in recent publications (Marie Vautier, Lars Eckstein, Frank Schulze-Engler), or those who integrate interdisciplinary approaches (Frank Schulze-Engler) have traced these assets of transcultural theory in varying contexts.[48] In this sense, critics have repeatedly saluted transcultural approaches as the possible solution to the unresolved discrepancies within postcolonial studies and as the Leitmotiv for a new generation of postcolonial criticism, as "today's most pressing transcultural concerns [...] tend to transcend the explanatory logic of postcolonialism" (Eckstein 17).[49]

[48] Cf. Vautier 271, Eckstein 16-17, and all essays by Schulze-Engler.
[49] Cp. also Schulze-Engler, "From Postcolonial to Preglobal."

These "pressing transcultural concerns" that Lars Eckstein refers to, and thus also the conceptual crisis of postcolonial criticism, are developments affected by the impact of globalization on individual and national cultures and identities. As Frank Schulze-Engler has repeatedly highlighted in his essays on transculturalism, the intensification of inter- and transnational interactions has broken down the concept of the nation-state. The idea of a singular entity containing one national culture no longer suffices as identificatory reference for present day complex social networks and the individuals that move within them ("Von 'Inter' zu 'Trans'" 42).[50] Thus, globalization seen from a more positive socio-cultural perspective, has multiplied the factors by which societies and individuals can build their identities and thereby has challenged critics to consider new ways of understanding these constructions on both macro- and microlevels (Welsch, *online resource*, n.pag.). Once again, we may point to the crucial ambivalence within transculturality – which represents precisely the envisioned "analytical tool" for contemporary cultures and literatures – between the birth of novel diversities, complexities, and similarities and continuing differences, as "notwithstanding globalization, boundaries remain distinct, or are constantly redrawn" (Kalogeras et al. vii).[51]

The perspectives gained by a transcultural approach to literature thus become especially relevant for texts that dispute the formation of identities, whether communal or individual, ethnic or racial, or determined by other cultural markers. Not only does "adopting a trans-ethnic and trans-national perspective [...] offer keen insights into the processes of self- and community-transformation, processes that result not only from trans-national contacts, alliances, and influences, but also conflicts" (Kalogeras et al. xiii), it also calls for an opening up of literary criticism discourses to intra- and interdisciplinary dialogues.

As the aspects delineated above indicate, the range and potential of the transcultural concept open up a great number of fields for critical debate, and literary and cultural critics interested in coming to terms with it are challenged to cover immense ground – in the words of Frank Schulze-Engler:

> Transcultural authors are not simply representatives of 'their' cultures; their texts challenge readers and critics to come to terms with processes of negotiation and change between and within cultures, and to move beyond the rigid understanding of cultures as self-contained normative frameworks. Opening up a transnational public sphere of dialogue, communication and political agency in a world allegedly determined by the incommensurability of cultures remains a major challenge at a time when participatory democracy and the self-organization of societies have yet to catch up with rapid

[50] See also Schulze-Engler, "Transnationale Kultur als Herausforderung."

[51] A further theoretical approach that was introduced fairly recently and also takes up many of the issues discussed here, has been developed in the context of term of "transdifference." The discussion was initiated by a circle of scholars and has in the meanwhile led to a number of publications: see Allolio-Näcke, Kalscheuer and Manzeschke; Breinig, Gebhardt, and Lösch. Despite many converging interests, the transdifference school appears to regard itself as clearly separated from transcultural criticism, which it acknowledges superficially (i.e. Fernando Ortiz or *Vice Versa*). For a detailed and highly interesting discussion of the transdifference approach, cf. Schulze-Engler, "What's the Difference?"

> economic globalization. English literatures across the globe have arguably already made a major contribution to meeting that challenge; it now seems time for criticism to follow suit. (Schulze-Engler, "Towards a Transcultural World Literature" 30)

In order to arrive at some conclusive observations, we need to reconsider and structure the manifold theoretical reflections that emerge from the realms of transcultural thought developed in the course of the twentieth century; the meaning and theoretization of the transcultural concepts for the present study can be captured on three levels.
First, transculturalism is comprehended as a *phenomenon of modernity*[52] that acknowledges the differing degrees, levels and plurality of cultural transfers in a globalized world, a world of "multiple modernities" (Schulze-Engler "Threoretical Perspectives" 29).[53] In this context it does not function as a category, nor does it designate a specific (historical) period – it simply offers a comprehensive, yet case-sensitive theorem to describe and analyze the multitude of possible cultural expressions born out of contemporary liminal positionings:

> The views of cross-cultural exchange in such texts are myriad and indeed transcend any unified body of aesthetic and political theory; art may deliberately set out to police the ugly undertows of globalisation, but it may also celebrate the chances and as yet unfulfilled promises of a small world; it may deliberately shun the global for the local, but just as well take refuge in aestheticist universalisms. (Eckstein 18)

Secondly, transcultural here also refers to a *state of mind* that is as much a process as it is a mindset that allows for this process to take rise and continuously evolve. While some specific pictures, symbols, songs, smells, languages, myths, memories, and other identity defining constituents may stay the same within an individual's lifetime and mark cultural 'traditions' – thus, constructed differences of communities and cultures –, others may well reappear, change, be deconstructed or forgotten. To be aware of the transcultural, means to accept the flexible, fluid conception of cultural constructions that define one part of present day individual and collective identities – while the other, possibly even stronger part might well strive for at least temporary identitary stability, emotional security (however it may be achieved), and the fulfillment of (moral) values. Thereby an adequate interpretation of transcultural processes – as any other process involved in the constructions of identities – of the (individual or collective) mind can and must *not* be reduced to markers of ethnicity and race, but should equally consider other spheres such as gender, sexuality, class, age and religion. This claim also touches upon the problematic reduction of resistance to a general revolt against imperial domination – much discussed within postcolonial discourse – which pushes aside other

[52] I here refrain from a discussion on whether it is really still a phenomenon of modernity, or whether it might in fact already be the symptom of a newly developing period – such as *trans*modernity. Ultimately, this question will be of significance for future investigations.
[53] See also Schulze-Engler, "Von ‚Inter' zu ‚Trans'" 41; and Featherstone, "Postnational Flows" 487-488.

levels and forms of reactionary forces of marginalization (Vautier 274).[54] As Lars Eckstein puts it with reference to Mary L. Pratt's much-quoted term:

> The transcultural dynamics of the 'contact zone' in our globalised modernity encompasses many encounters, of which that between coloniser and colonised is really just one (if a paradigmatically important one). Reading literature as a site in which the dynamics of the 'contact zone' are acted out therefore requires allowing for perspectives beyond imperial centres (as metonymically represented by Buckingham Palace or Pentagon) and their peripheries. (Eckstein 17)

This understanding of the transcultural is invariably linked to a concept of cultures and identities that grants stronger agency to individuals. For Frank Schulze-Engler, this agency is one of the most important features within the conceptual movement from 'inter-' to 'trans-cultural' readings of identities and cultures; whereby cultures are not seen as constitutive of individuals but instead as a globally accessible collaborative resources ("Von 'Inter' zu 'Trans'" 46).[55] This assumption is also the basis for Arjun Appadurai's complex ethnographical analysis of "modernity at large";[56] this approach is also used and extended by Wolfgang Welsch who assesses the construction of transcultural identities as a necessary competence for future generations:[57]

> Whenever an individual is cast by differing cultural interests, the lining of such transcultural components with one another becomes a specific task in identity-forming. Work on one's identity is becoming more and more work on the integration of components of differing cultural origin. And only the ability to transculturally cross over will guarantee us identity and competence in the long run [...] (Welsch, *online resource*, n.pag.)

Obviously, there are also limits to this prominent role of agency as, on the one hand, some processes happen subconsciously and are hard to navigate even if in present times an increasing amount of information is open to individuals to (consciously) choose from; on the other hand, following up on this latter aspect, one must not forget that not all people around the globe have the same degree of access to cultural 'collaborative'

[54] Marie Vautier refers to Stephen Slemon's understanding of the "complicity/resistance dialectic" originally used with reference to the relation of women to empire (Simon Gikandi). She cites Slemon ("Climbing Mount Everest"), who argues that it is never possible to resist to only one axis of domination "within the multiple and interwoven axes that comprise discursive formation (race, class, gender, sexuality, etc.)" (Slemon qtd. in Vautier 280, FN 12: 63). For Vautier, who introduces religion as a valuable component (or axis of resistance) in the transcultural analysis of postcolonial texts, "[t]he unpacking of Catholicism in contemporary transcultured Canadian and Québécois fiction, which generally flaunts an acceptance and a celebration of the indeterminacies and uncertainties of nation, culture, history, memory, and identity, allows for such an ambivalent but generative production of change" (274).

[55] As discussed in earlier chapters, he is mainly referring to Ulf Hannerz's *Transnational Connections*; See also Schulze-Engler, "Theoretical Perspectives" 29.

[56] "There is growing evidence that the consumption of the mass media throughout the world often provokes resistance, irony, selectivity, and, in general, *agency*" (7, the author's own emphasis).

[57] Note that in the quotation, Welsch expresses this agency by using terms such as "task in identity-forming," and "work on one's identity."

resources, whether for economic or political reasons, while others do not have the freedom of choice due to social constraints.

Thirdly – to return to our list of meanings that transculturalism represents in the present study – against all odds, or because of them, the transcultural is in several regards also understood as a *visionary concept*. The term 'transcultural,' which does not have a categorizing function and (thereby) presents an idealistic solution to both theoretical and cultural dilemmas, should be, based on the already described characteristics, seen as an ethical option within contemporary socio-political, artistic, or any other (inter/trans-) disciplinary discourse. It may be too naïve to maintain that the transcultural, even as a visionary concept, could ever be completely neutral, or apolitical; yet, in its attempt to transcend cultural boundaries (beyond, for example, the opposition between ethnicity versus race), it certainly can be regarded as a "multipolitical" theory (Kulyk Keefer, "Writing, Reading, Teaching" 192).

By referring to transculturalism as an "ethical option," I am suggesting, on the one hand, a connection between this term and what has been identified as an "ethical turn" in theoretical criticism;[58] on the other hand, I am also asserting that very often specifically transcultural texts display a strong ethical undertone. The potential and desire for the expression of temporary values, potential certainties, maybe even universalisms, is facilitated by one visionary feature of transculturalism: the ever-present potential for the creation of altered, alternative identities. Individuals and communities under the growing impact of multiple cultural images and discourses, negotiate the self and the other through processes of imagination, selection, exchange, layering, awareness of similarities, transfer as well as resistance and conflict, by which they arrive at identity constructions defined by what will in the next chapter be referred to as transcultural imaginaries.

In his essay on transculturality, Wolfgang Welsch strongly emphasizes that "[o]ur understanding of culture is an *active factor* in our cultural life" (*online resource*, n.pag.) and that the scholarly promotion of "descriptively adequate and normatively accountable" concepts of culture is not only a possibility but foremost a responsibility (n.pag.). The following and final theoretical chapter will take on this responsibility by sketching possible spheres and methods of literary analysis that could foster an understanding of transcultural identities and imaginaries, as "active factors" in kaleidoscopic histories.

[58] Cf. Davis and Womack, *Mapping the Ethical Turn*. As the editors of the volume remark in the Preface, "it would be ludicrous to imagine that [postmodern] readers of literature over the past several decades somehow disengaged their ethical faculties as they encountered their culture's grand narratives. What *has* changed over the course of the twentieth century in our discussion of ethics and literature is the simplistic, uncomplicated prescription of external ethical forces regarding so many different literatures and cultures," X.

5 Transcultural Imaginaries

We have come a long way to arrive here at this intermediary chapter, which intends to call to mind and reassemble reflections from past chapters and to unite them with suggestions for the literary analysis in the chapters to come. In earlier sections, I delineated how Canada's complex internal (re-)negotiations of identity related to the increasing popularity of the genre of historical fiction, especially in interaction with the rise of a postmodern, post-colonial – distinctively Canadian – 'national' literature. With an interdisciplinary take on contemporary socio-cultural developments and on theories of modernity, further chapters traced the impact of globalization on contemporary societies – the effects of which are to be found in literatures around the globe. The planetary pluralities and complexities discussed in Chapter 3, such as issues of race and ethnicity, agency, and the recognition of difference as well as similarities, already suggested intersections and counter-reactions with developments in the genre of historical fiction, particularly in relation to Canadian identities. Chapter 4 added another intricate angle, on multiculturalism as a policy and only a partially successful social ideal. It also went a step further by explaining a growing tendency toward transcultural, socio-cultural phenomena and, related to this, the emergence of alternative critical approaches – a development that appears logical though not completed, in the context of the presented phenomena. In order to move toward a concrete and more thorough understanding of the interrelations proposed in this study, I would like to turn to the two major terms brought forward here, both approximate in their function and intention: *fictions of the past* and *transcultural imaginaries*. Both are broadly defined, hard-to-pin-down concepts. It should be emphasized, however, that the reason for my introduction of these terms is rooted in an observed, natural interconnectedness of the two, even if each displays a dynamic and effective logic of its own.

The generic development toward what I refer to as 'fictions of the past' must be understood as the sum of multiple developments in the genre of historical fiction toward a remarkably open fictional form that unites postcolonial contents and postmodern aesthetics – two enormous spheres and subjects of criticism, the problems and boundaries of which I have already attempted to portray. Furthermore, it is a mode of writing that strongly questions the assumed boundaries of time in order to do justice to the interaction of history and the past with the present and the future; thereby it includes collective and individual memories, especially highlighting the role of individuals within this interplay. Most importantly, fictions of the past is seen as writing that dissects, negotiates and evolves identities as constructions of the past in the provoking context of contemporary extended as well as densified cultural choices and identitary building blocks. This process is achieved through continuous – though not necessarily endless – devisions and revisions of complex, constructed cultural spaces of existence that function as discourses in the tense struggle between global and local forces. Thus, these characteristics and the genre itself – if we can continue to call it a genre – are not only seen in the light of various established critical discourses, but additionally and fundamentally are evaluated as results of the impact of globalization on human existence. Fictions of the past are taken as exemplary modes of writing that express and describe the changes, constructions, emotions, and idealisms that these forces stimulate in literature, in both form and content.

As fictions of the past reveal human constructions of self and community across space and time, the complicatedness of which intensified over the course of the twentieth century, they represent a literary form with a great potential for the discovery and naming of transcultural phenomena. However, just as the tracing of the transcultural modes in fictions of the past functions as only one possible angle of analysis, the transcultural can be found in all kinds of literature. As my own arguments and the case studies will show, the transcultural is independent of the author's heritage and the 'national' or critical affiliation of the text.[1]

It is at this point that I would like to bring in the concept of 'transcultural imaginaries' – of which the second part, 'imaginary,' still requires some clarification. Two aspects influenced me to introduce this term. On the one hand, the necessity to find a mode of understanding for the influence of contemporary modernities on identities and, consequently, on literatures. It is in this sense that Arjun Appadurai, in his study on "modernity at large," underscores the new role and power of imagination – as an individual choice – in contemporary societies:

> What is new is that this world is a world in which both points of departure and points of arrival are in cultural flux, and thus the search for steady points of reference, as critical life choices are made, can be very difficult. It is in this atmosphere that the invention of tradition (and of ethnicity, kinship, and other identity markers) can become slippery, as the search for certainties is regularly frustrated by the fluidities of transnational communication. As group pasts become increasingly parts of museums, exhibits, and collections, both in national and transnational spectacles, culture becomes less what Pierre Bourdieu would have called habitus (a tacit realm of reproducible practices and dispositions) and more an arena for conscious choice, justification, and representation, the latter often to multiple and spatially dislocated audiences. (44)

As Appadurai himself indicates in some instances, to speak of a whole new form of imagination might lead to a misunderstanding of the term[2] – even if his definition of the concept as a process involves several levels: "The image, the imagined, the imaginary—these are all terms that direct us to something critical and new in global cultural processes: *the imagination as a social practice*" (31).[3]

[1] However, I might here underline more clearly that in earlier chapters, I have attempted to highlight that the Canadian social, political and literary context (and its historical development) present an especially fertile ground for the analysis of transcultural imaginaries and fictions of the past.

[2] See, for example, Appadurai 54.

[3] As he explains in more detail, "[t]he world we live in today is characterized by a new role for the imagination in social life. To grasp this role, we need to bring together the old idea of images, especially mechanically produced images (in the Frankfurt School sense); the idea of the imagined community (in Anderson's sense); and the French idea of imaginary (*imaginaire*) as a constructed landscape of collective aspirations," Appadurai 31.

On the other hand – I am now turning to the second argument regarding the term – imaginary, in a way, simultaneously extends and limits the idea of "imagination as social practice" as proposed by Appadurai. A further driving force behind its conception, from my perspective, is to introduce a term that exceeds a 'mere' understanding and description of contemporary mindscapes and the dynamics that shape them by suggesting a strategy for its possible analysis. When used as a noun, the 'imaginary' not only moves away from the connotation of being merely "made up" or "unreal,"[4] it also appears to be much more present in the (individual and collective) mind and not only part of the individual's "unconscious" described by Lacan.[5] In the sense in which it is applied here, imaginary does not necessarily describe a new social practice (Appadurai), yet it presupposes a social *awareness* of imagination as a possible social practice. Especially in connection with the adjective transcultural, it must be seen as more than a global phenomenon: as a tool for individuals that might be applied deliberately by some, and unknowingly by others – a space where conscious and unconscious, fact and fiction *productively* collide. The transcultural imaginary is thus employed as an overall term for a cluster of collective and individual processes and constitutions.[6] On a macro level, it refers to the acceptance of the constructed nature of identities, a taking over of agency (the possibility of which Lacan denies), and the impact of multiple levels and expressions of culture for the active construction of complexly layered cultural identities. This assumption of increasing agency and cultural choices is accompanied, however, by both a supposed freedom for some and a growing pressure and confusion for others.[7] On a micro level, transcultural imaginaries stand for specific dialogic reconstructions of self and other by individuals and groups alike. The expression imaginary (or imaginaries) thus accentuates the creative element of the imagination, the concrete impact of images (as well as discourses), and the fictional and constructed facet of the imaginative within the realm of identity constructions; in this context the addition 'transcultural' expresses the movement and creative momentum that provokes a transgression of the identification with one 'separate' and 'distinctive,' harmoniously normed culture.[8]

[4] The *Concise Oxford Dictionary* suggests: "existing only in the imagination," Pearsall 708.

[5] Lacan's psychoanalytical theories, which rely strongly on structuralist thought, claim that the unconscious desires to create an illusion of a complete self ("the imaginary") – an illusion, which humans overcome (in the "mirror stage") as the structures imposed by the outside, by language ("the symbolic") interfere with the imaginary to create a given order and identity. The self, in Lacan's view, can thus never be autonomous and does not hold any agency. Cp. Frosch, "Jacques Lacan." His most important works were published as *The Seminars of Jacques Lacan* (his 27 seminars were published in French between 1953 and 1980, and some of them in English translation starting in the late 70s).

[6] The term 'cultural imaginary,' has been applied by (literary) critics here and there, as for example by James Skidmore, "Urquhart's Fairytale: The German Cultural Imaginary in *The Stone Carvers*." However, it has arguably not yet received the attention it deserves.

[7] Cf. also Schulze-Engler, "Literature in the Global Ecumene of Modernity" 383.

[8] Cp. to Vautier's concept of "l'imaginaire de l'identitaire" in "Religion, Postcolonial Side-by-sidedness, and *la transculture*."

In many ways, my understanding of transcultural imaginary strongly relates to what Aleida and Jan Assmann have specified as cultural memory[9], with the one difference being that it is perceived and lived both on a diachronic *as well as* a synchronic axis. This means that we must not only assume that the transcultural imaginary has a strong temporal basis and is functional on various levels of society – individual, communal, regional, national.[10] Additionally, within these levels, – and here one finds another divergence in emphasis from the Assmannsian perspective – it is not made up of one clear-cut set of discourses but of several conflicting, regularly adapted and presumably hybrid forms of mindscapes.

As already discussed, scholars studying the effects of globalization on cultures and societies can be roughly divided into three groups: those that fear the rise of one globally homogenized culture, others that see endless cultural hybridizations as a promising ideal[11], and those that salute an age of newly constructed alternative cultures. Once again I would like to emphasize that the concept of transcultural imaginary can be integrated into neither of these positions convincingly – ultimately it stands for an openness to cultural metamorphosis without negating more separatist – or, in other terms, essentialist – approaches to dialogue. From this perspective, as Heinz Antor rightly claims, inter- and transcultural processes do not imply unreflected assimilations and hybridizations but instead invariably demand a positioning of the self before anything else – before any interaction with the other can take place.[12] We might at this point once more recall Janice Kulyk Keefer's suggestion for an alternative image of Canadian cultural identity: the kaleidoscope. Its characteristics are akin to those ascribed to transcultural imaginaries here: "separate pieces, none of which is more privileged than any other" create "a changing and infinitely variable pattern" and "suggest ongoing process rather than fixed and finished product" ("From Mosaic to Kaleidoscope" 16). The ever-changing pattern is generated by separate stones that stand

[9] Cf. the definition proposed by Jan Assmann: "The concept of cultural memory comprises that body of reusable texts, images and rituals specific to each society in each epoch, whose 'cultivation' serves to stabilize and convey that society's self-image. Upon such collective knowledge, for the most part (but not exclusively) of the past, each group bases its awareness of unity and particularity," Assmann qtd. in Rimstead I (One must note that the last aspect mentioned, that of "unity and particularity," does not necessarily apply for transcultural imaginaries); for further resources, cf. Jan Assmann, "Collective Memory and Cultural Identity," trans. John Czaplicka, *New German Critique* (N° 65, 1995): 125-33. Cp. also A. Assmann "Zur Mediengeschichte des kulturellen Gedächtnisses," as well as Jan and Aleida Assmann's numerous monographs.

[10] I hesitate to include the level of a global community, which is, if we are honest, today still the least developed communal sphere.

[11] Cp. Pieterse, *Global Mélange*.

[12] In Antor's German-language publication on inter- and transculturalism he writes: "Es kann in der inter- oder transkulturellen Begegnung nicht um kritikloses Bejahen, um die angestrengte und letzlich unreflektierte, weil ideologisch gewollte Akzeptanz alles Anderen gehen. Vielmehr verlangt eine solche Begegnung, um eine solche Beziehung überhaupt wert zu sein, eigene Positionalität, d.h. eine eigene kulturelle Identität, die man im Zusammentreffen mit dem Anderen auch nicht zu verbergen sucht, da diese in ihrer eigenen Alterität zum Anderen diesem wiederum erst eine interkulturelle Begenung ermöglicht." Antor, "Multikulturalismus, Interkulturalität und Transkulturalität," 34.

in constant interaction with each other, in fact their relational positioning only makes the colourful images possible. As formulated by another scholar in the vein of *ViceVersa*'s reflections from the Eighties: "The pluralistic idea of transculturalism (*seeing oneself in the other*) [my emphasis], basically relying on the forces of society (not politicians), has a more interactive (for citizens) and egalitarian approach" (Cuccioletta 1).

The characteristic of attempting to and allowing oneself to "*see oneself in the other*" underscores another significant aspect in the concept of transcultural imaginaries: the ethical dimension, which is not to be underestimated in its significance. Not only is it expressed in a (presumed) willingness and openness to communicate, to find similarities and defend or negotiate differences, but it is also frequently guided by a desire to bring together the disparate political, social, and emotional threads of life, to assuage the universal longing for a deeper sense. What might be termed a pull toward "transcendental cosmopolitanism"[13] within transcultural imaginaries, is an expression of the desire to understand our reality as one that moves beyond complete fragmentation and nurtures the belief in a transcendental meaning of existence:

> After all, as we read and interpret, as we attempt to make meaning, the possibility for connection, for community, for relationship looms before us. What binds human to human, community to community, country to country are our stories. The chasm of everyday existence can only be bridged as we listen to one another, as we judge the relative worth of differing artistic and scholarly voices. (Todd and Womack xvii)

In an earlier section, I considered the transcultural as a three-tiered concept: as a mindset, as an overall phenomenon, and as an idealistic vision. Similarly, individual and collective imaginaries displayed in Canadian fictions of the past reflect transcultural characteristics whether they are regarded as a conscious opening up (of both writers and the public), as subconscious, unstoppable processes effected by contemporary globalizing impacts on cultures and individuals, or as visionary interpretations of contemporary intercultural existence. Whether it is Marie Vautier's idea of a transcultural "imaginaire de l'identitaire," which she links to "the abstract, the mind, the spiritual, and even the soul" (270), Nicole Brossard's passionate arguments related to Eduard Glissant's *metissage culturel* (Huggan and Siemerling 98), or Elspeth Cameron's outlook on a "utopia of complexity" (xiii); these recent critical expressions all relate to transcultural imaginaries, particularly as they support an opening up of new possibilities when thinking about the increasingly dynamic and agentive mindscapes of the Canadian literary and non-literary self.

[13] Pin-Chia Feng uses the term "transcendental cosmopolitanism" in her essay "Transcontinental Writing: Reconfiguring the Politics of Home in Maryse Condé's *The Last of the African Kings*," 2. She takes the term from Hal Wylie's "The Cosmopolitan Condé, or Unscrambling the Worlds." In this essay Hal Wylie claims in regard to Maryse Condé's transcultural writing: "Still, Condé's ambitious insistence upon seeking the links between generations, and between the ethnic groups, must be seen as a quest for the meaningful factors of our time. We must learn how to make the ghosts work for us rather than being haunted by them. [...] Condé seems to be groping beyond identity to look for the universal meaning, the touchstone values that may have been lost sight of or even that may remain to be defined," (final paragraph, *online resource*).

On the following pages I will attempt to extend the scope of this emerging discourse by suggesting some possible elements for concrete readings of transcultural imaginaries in fictions of the past.

Space, Place, and Time

A reading of transcultural imaginaries in fictions of the past first of all requires that we become aware of the diversity, fluidity, and unpredictability of spatial and temporal spheres that define contemporary (collective and individual) identities. In the wake of globalizing forces that today both exacerbate and enrich the negotiation and understanding of self and other, it is hardly possible to ignore approaches to space, which effectively unite the hard-to-grasp interaction of time, place, distance, social structures, existence, and the mind. In her remarkable study *For Space*, Doreen Massey articulated the following propositions for her arguments towards an understanding of space:

> *First,* that we recognise space as the product of interrelations; as constituted through interactions, from the immensity of the global to the intimately tiny. […] *Second*, that we understand space as the sphere of the possibility of the existence of multiplicity in the sense of contemporaneous plurality; as the sphere in which distinct trajectories coexist; as the sphere of coexisting heterogeneity. […] *Third*, that we recognise space as always under construction. […] It is never finished; never closed. Perhaps we could imagine space as a simultaneity of stories-so-far. (9)

Space as a complex entity can be understood as a major activator and mediating device for transcultural imaginaries, which, as we know, are reflected strongly in fictions of the past. The genre itself becomes representative of the spaces that Massey characterizes as expressions of and reactions to present day modernities. In contrast to traditional historical novels, which were often set in exotic historical periods so remote they could clearly be distinguished from the present, contemporary fictions that deal with history and incorporate historical settings dissolve clear-cut temporal boundaries.[14] Historical fiction of the latter half of the twentieth century has also deconstructed the long-held belief of an objective representation of history: historiographic metafiction emphasizes the revelation of discursive misrepresentations due to inequalities of power through the dissemination of linear temporalities and causalities. The most recent examples of the historical genre, fictions of the past, continue to use this deconstructive mode; however, they also imply partial reconstructions of truth and reinterpretations of the past that constitute intermediary, often transcultural alternative identities – which, in a further process, effectively determine existences in the present and future. Similarly, fictions of the past do not restrain their view on the past to a single local setting. This allows those

[14] Though, of course, retrospective narrators, movements in time and metafictional devices have also appeared in earlier literary periods, and certainly in modernist fiction.

involved to come to terms with individual, familial, or communal movements around the globe and continuous 'manipulation' by either unequal, forced power relations or peaceful intercultural dialogue, all of which makes it necessary to productively evaluate the multiplicity of cultural 'traditions' that change across generations. Considering these trajectories allows us to identify the transhistorical and translocal levels of transcultural imaginaries.

In fictions of the past, the local represents the intermediary space in which the individual (or communal) and the global meet. While the local (in terms of those images and discourses with which one is in more immediate contact) provides the individual with flexible and direct possibilities of identification, the global opens up even greater possibilities for the consideration of several further loci (i.e. specific places) that may define individual or collective identities, the particularities of which are negotiated within the cultural imaginary. As Doreen Massey explains:

> On this reading, the spatial, crucially, is the realm of the configuration of potentially dissonant (or concordant) narratives. Places, rather than being locations of coherence, become the foci of the meeting and the nonmeeting of the previously unrelated and thus integral to the generation of novelty. The spatial in its role of bringing distinct temporalities into new configurations sets off new social processes. And in turn, this emphasizes the nature of narratives, of time itself, as being not about the unfolding of some internalized story (some already-established identities) [...] but about interaction and the *process of the constitution of* identities. (Massey, *For Space* 71)

This cycle does not pit the local against the global, as they resonate within each other without crushing cultural distinctiveness, which is determined by actual places and individuals. History and space, local and global, and individual and community all reciprocally acquire meaning through a constant interaction and renegotiation of signifiers that eventually may also include transcultural elements. Thereby, the aspect of change and transformation becomes a significant facet in the concept of transcultural imaginaries.[15]

In the interpretation of space, place, and time in fictions of the past, we may thus question how both historical and socio-cultural space (thus both on a diachronic and synchronic axis) are envisioned and overcome in the narratives discussed. Further explorations should reveal what specific places mark the (historical) space in which individual and collective identities evolve, and how they interact to form transcultural imaginaries. If we note that individual and local identities are formed through movements across time (via memory and history) and that the individual makes sense of the global through the collection of a wide range of information that is interpreted in the local context, the following considerations may be added: what pluralities of time and place constitute individual cultural spaces? What individual cultural markers make up the transcultural space and how do they interact with the parameters of collective spaces, and what role do they play in the constructions of identities?

[15] Cp. also Sugars, "The Hands of Chance and Change."

Voices and Perspectives

The density of spaces, places, and of the dimensions of time characteristic of fictions of the past is inevitably accompanied by an equally overwhelming amount of voices and perspectives that speak from within and, at the same time, form these interlocking realms from the outside. The existence of a plurality of voices in works of fiction is, as we know, not a recent phenomenon; we may, however, observe an intensification of this feature as well as a shift in the development and function of these diversities of perspective in Canadian historical fictions in the past decades.
Considering this 'intensification' and 'shift,' it stands to reason that scholars have continued to refer to Bakhtinian theories as a way to approach contemporary fiction. Janice Kulyk Keefer, for example, has related the "carnivalesque" directly to her reading of transcultural texts:

> The present mode of transcultural writing in Canada is, I would argue, a postmodernist form of the Bakhtinian carnivalesque, combining both the celebratory aspects Bakhtin observes in late-medieval and Renaissance manifestations of "grotesque realism" and expressions of hostility and alienation he connects with what he calls the modernist grotesque. The carnival features of transculturalism are present not only in its rejection of monologic forms of discourse and its preference for polyphony and heteroglossia, but also in transculturalism's interrogating of established social and cultural hierarchies, its increasingly insistent transgression of the code of "good behaviour" demanded by the Department of Multiculturalism [...] ("From Dialogue to Polylogue" 68)

Obviously Bakhtin's concepts harmonize well with both postmodernist aesthetics of irony and polyphony, as well as with the postcolonial and general minorities' call for the deconstruction of former hegemonic structures. However, as the features mentioned by Kulyk Keefer indicate, Bakhtin's carnivalesque also essentially resonates in transcultural literature. Gabriele Helms, in her fairly recent publication on "dialogism and narrative techniques in Canadian novels," as the subtitle goes[16], also most convincingly applies Bakhtin's theories in order to show "how multiple [independent and unmerged] voices[17] are interrelated in contemporary Canadian novels and [how] they can challenge constructions of Canada" (7). Helms's emphasis lies on the deconstructive and subversive power that Bakhtin's carnival of voices implies, which, taking into account the novels (partially also historical novels)[18] that she discusses, is not only perspicuous but also in line with current Canadian literary and cultural criticism. There are, however, several aspects in Bakhtin's theories discussed in the

[16] Helms, *Challenging Canada: Dialogism and Narrative Techniques in Canadian Novels*.

[17] A few lines further down from the passage quoted here, Helms cites Bakhtin's definition of dialogism, which particularly insists on "independent and unmerged voices and consciousnesses" (7).

[18] Helms includes in her analysis Joy Kogawa's *Obasan*, Sky Lee's *Disappearing Moon Café*, Daphne Marlatt's *Ana Historic*, Aritha van Herk's *Places Far from Ellesmere*, Jeannette Armstrong's *Slash*, Thomas King's *Green Grass, Running Water*, and Margaret Sweatman's *Fox*.

above-mentioned approaches that should be reconsidered in regard to a reading of transcultural imaginaries. Most importantly, the Bakhtinian carnivalesque in contemporary fictions of the past no longer 'only' challenges collective or individual constructions of identity (or other imaginative constructions such as that of the nation – Canada, in the case of Helms); instead, it takes subversion as a *prerequisite*, yet also *goes beyond* deconstructive modes – thereby attempting to exstract at least one provisional song of truth from the polylogue of voices: a melody that only rises through the parallel performance of several tunes. The inquisitive, revolutionary voices of the carnivalesque have shifted their perspective away from the subversion of largescale hegemonic power structures to the increasing empowerment of the individual subject, which is also elaborated in the stronger representation of individual perspectives on the past and history in 'historical fiction'.[19]
Another major difference between Bakhtin's dialogic principles and the narrative voices that convey transcultural imaginaries is established in the primary assumption that the consciousnesses of independent characters may in some instances merge, and that they are realized as being dependent or mutually influential in a positive sense, regardless of whether they are culturally radically different, partially similar, or the same. From this perspective, dialogue and polylogue become constructive in as much as they may also be deconstructive.[20] Thus, next to the movements in space and time, and the consequent redefinition of self and other in place, it is the impact of the carnival of voices that marks changes in the individual, through which it structures new, alternative identities. The characters that voice or indirectly perform transcultural imaginaries must therefore not only be analyzed in terms of the multiple cultural markers that define them, by which they construct their individual and collective maps of belonging: age, generation, sexual affiliation, gender, ethnicity, race, class, etc. The source of their transcultural imaginary lies in the interaction with 'other' individuals and 'othered' fictions of collective identification.

Returning to less abstract observations regarding possibilities for an analysis of the transcultural in voices and perspectives expressed in fictions of the past, I would like to consider three specific aspects. First of all, Frank Schulze-Engler's claim of a contemporary focus on the "micropolitics of modernity" is, in my opinion, certainly a beneficial point of departure – a focus apparent in literature but not yet acknowledged in literary criticism. By turning our attention to these "decisive dynamics of modern societies" ("From Preglobal" 58), which happen on a microlevel of identity discourses, we should come to understand how these texts question family relations and structures, debate gender conflicts, search for alternative forms of identification, and transgress and transform cultural stereotypes and imaginaries in the context of globalized modernities. To listen carefully to the harmonies and dissonances, similarities and differences of the many voices that compose the micropolitics of a text is one of the ways I propose to approach transcultural imaginaries in fictions of the past.

[19] Cf. Vautier 271.
[20] Also Gabriele Helms notes the equally positive potential in dialogue (8); she insists, however, on the importance and maintenance of difference to deconstruct power hierarchies (9).

A concentration on the concrete effects of modernity – in terms of new media and other communication technologies or developments in transportation – on identities could produce further insights into contemporaneous forms of transcultural imaginaries, which interact with these fictions' interest in the past. Also, instances of intermediality and the (meta)reflections of protagonists on aspects of globalization or the problems of modernity promise to open up new views on potentially dissident transcultural voices and perspectives.

Finally, I would like to suggest that we might also note the appearance of what could be referred to as transcultural figures, who stand between two, or several, differing cultural consciousnesses (i.e. generational, sexual, ethnic, racial, immigrant etc.). On one major level, these personae in their own right attempt to deal with their positions and very often navigate between and especially across poles of extremes in order to arrive at some temporary, alternative state(s) of stability. On another important level, however, these transcultural figures also mediate and translate between various cultural spheres and thereby often develop into creative, structuring forces for the people surrounding them and the communities they belong to.

Once again, there are numerous questions that the above-described reflections on voices and perspectives provoke for an understanding and possible extended examinations of transcultural imaginaries in fictions of the past: in how deeply are protagonists with different cultural backgrounds integrated into texts? How do voices move through space and time, and what impact does this have on (their) transcultural imaginaries? Do different cultural voices and consciousnesses stand in opposition or merge, and how? Is the agency of individuals reflected in texts and, if so, how, and finally, does the transcultural voice convey an ethical intention?

Transfer, Exchange, and Resistance

It cannot be emphasized often enough that focussing on the transcultural essentially means to focus on change, a moving beyond former binaries of self and other, and a flexibility in terms of the interactions of local and global, individual and collective, as well as the past, present, and future. The information, notions, images, and discourses accessible to individuals have become so dense and overwhelming that processes of identity formation by necessity become selective (sometimes maybe even simplifying) and follow dialogic principles of transfer, exchange, layering, and possibly resistance.

Just as we cannot speak of one modernity or one globalization due to differences in the pace, intensity and contents of cultural (and obviously also economic, political and so on) developments in different regions and societies – also cultural imaginaries reveal diverse degrees and forms of change – either toward or away from the transcultural. The degrees of transcultural approximations can be detected in many ways; for example, by integrating images and discourses that interact and are applied de- or re-constructively next to each other: myths, memories, histories, fairytales, oral tales, family stories, and so on. These, as we discussed above, might be communicated through cultural filters, and via various media, thereby being effective and effected in different degrees.

Transcultural approximations can also be expressed through the respective complexification of cultural identitary systems that relate belonging to personal interpretations of gender, class, race, age, ethnicity, and sexuality. All of these elements, which are combined individually, leave us with a rich tapestry of cultural imaginaries, which we might attempt to analyze in their entirety or pick apart for particularities of the micropolitics of existence.[21]

In her essay "Religion, Postcolonial Side-by-sidedness, and *la transculture*," Marie Vautier proposes – in terms of her focus on religion – that in order to understand what she calls a "transcultural sense of flexible, contingent identities" (277), one ought to distinguish three contributing factors: linguistic, rhetorical and ideological code-switching; iconography; alternate religious systems and mythologies. The possible analytical spheres and methods that might help us comprehend the numerous dimensions of transcultural imaginaries in fictions of the past are as vast as imaginaries are unpredictable; it is for this reason that the examination of processes of transcultural layering, exchange, and other positive or negative interaction remains forcibly reductive and incomplete. However, in order to give some ordering structure to the various forms and functions of transcultural collage that might be found in fictions of the past, despite all variables and complexities, there is one analytical strategy of interest: in one of her essays of the 1990s, Janice Kulyk Keefer notes (in the narrower context of texts by marginalized authors) "a question which applies to all 'transcultural' writers. What position does one adopt to one's community of origin – that of faithful representative or rebel; of champion or transgressor? [...] I would suggest that the dialectic between the salvaging or preservation of a culture or the opening up of that culture to critique and change forms a prime concern for 'transcultural' writers" ("Writing, Reading, Teaching" 194). The different modes, levels, and degrees of exchange discussed above might be interpreted as expressions of grades of commitment to either "preservation" of established boundaries or an "opening up." Such a perspective would also sensibly integrate the disputed dichotomy of similarity versus difference, as well as the argument that this opposition should be revised critically without necessarily diluting the significance of distinctive identitary fictions. Similar perspectives, though more from a postcolonial criticism position, have been expressed by Marie Vautier, who refers to Rowland Smith when she argues for complexly related spaces of identitary discourses that (in her case represented by Catholicism) "[are] at one and the same time a site of resistance, a site of complicity and a site of generative creativity" (275). Resistance, from this perspective, is transformed in one of several enabling creative forces, which provide individuals with new agency. In the recent words of Bill Ashcroft,

> a difference which resists domination through the transformative capacity of the imagination is one which, ultimately, moves beyond these [colonial binary discursive] structures. The importance of transformation should not be regarded as diminishing the struggle for political freedom and self-determination, or refuting the active 'resistance'

[21] However, transcultural layering, exchange, and resistance must not be confused with postmodern pastiche or ironic deconstruction, even if they might in some instances create similar effects; instead, the functional emphasis of these transcultural modes lies on active self-formation and the acquirement of cultural agency.

> to imperial power. Nor should it be regarded as contrary to the spirit of insurgence. Rather it demonstrates the fascinating capacity of ordinary people, living below the level of formal policy or active rebellion, to foment change in their cultural existence. It is this change which makes active resistance meaningful. (17)

It is in a similar vein that we should envision the role of transcultural imaginaries, as moving between potential variations of transformative (non-)belongings and emotions in fictions of the past. The central issues that will attend this analytical sphere in the chapters to come are, thus, how are identity-founding cultural constructs integrated, re-written, or re-defined within a narrative? How are cultural transfer, exchange and layering reflected in thematic constellations and temporal movements? How does an accepting or rejecting of transfer and change, extend or replace former identitary manifestations; and how do these processes and modes of belonging influence transcultural imaginaries in fictions of the past?

Part 3 – Case Studies

The third part of this study now turns to a number of literary texts that display characteristics which allow us to refer to these texts as 'fictions of the past.' Characteristics such as transhistoricity, the focus on individual histories and memories, transgenericity, the depiction of postnational, plurihybrid identities, the challenging of dualities, and a post-deconstructive, ethical mode should become more obvious in the following analyses. All discussed fictions obviously also intend to present to the reader a more in-depth account of examples of the genre in its present expression as well as an insight into various degrees and forms of transcultural imaginaries. However, before approaching the texts I would like to add some comments in respect to the choice, organization, and analysis of the following 'case studies.'

Looking back on the development of historical fiction in Canada and specifically its criticism – as already discussed in earlier chapters – one notes an indirectly voiced but still visible tendency toward a classification of historical fictions on two levels. On the one hand, they are most often understood as postmodern historiographic metafictions or postcolonial rewritings; on the other hand, critics tend to differentiate between 'ethnic' (i.e. hyphenated-Canadian, as which a number of authors resist to be classified), versus 'non-ethnic' fictions (in the sense of, to borrow a controversial québécois term, "pur-laine") on the other.[1] In the following readings of the genre, I strictly avoid categorizations according to these criteria and actively deconstruct them through the two central concepts of fictions of the past and especially, transcultural imaginaries. The selection of texts thus follows the main principle of an attempt to portray a wide selection of different kinds of fictions of the past, specifically those presenting a variety of forms and degrees of transcultural imaginaries. The case studies do not argue for the homogeneity of the genre but instead insist on its diversities.

Nonetheless, any analysis of such a large number of texts has to be structured in some way or another. The criteria that inspired the organization of this final part are strongly related to the two major concepts of this book. The basic argument underlying the grouping of texts in the following chapters is a broad division of authors based on the transcultural impact that their lives and texts display: into authors with stronger migrant influences, closer to the experience of immigration (Chapter 6); then, writers of all ethnic, racial or any other specific cultural background who are generationally, temporally or emotionally more detached from the migration experience (Chapter 7); and finally, writers with a Native or Métis heritage, who hold a special position regarding their transcultural imaginaries (Chapter 8). I discuss migrant writers first because of their vital role for the revived popularity of the genre of historical fictions and especially for its movement toward fictions of the past, in which individual memories and postnational histories interact. Apart from that, in many cases these texts strongly echo ramifications of the transcultural, this being a group most obviously having to deal with problems of acceptance and integration, othering, the crossing of cultural spaces, memories of migrancy, dis- and re-placements. While the impact of migrant writers has been an accepted feature of the Canadian literary production since at least the 1940s, with commanding popularity by the 1980s, Native authors, in

[1] Cf. Gross, Klooss and Nischik 393-394; Moisan and Hildbrand, *Ces étrangers du dedans*, especially "Conclusion" 305-328.

comparison, appear to have been the last to be fully integrated as non-dependent artists into the world of Canadian literature. For a long time after their gradual acknowledgement, authors of Indigenous heritage showed little interest in the historical genre, being reluctant to re-write a history that was not theirs. Interestingly, it is this group of texts that most strongly still resists transcultural imaginaries (the maintenance of native tradition holding a stronger position), as the analysis in the final case study chapter will show; in contrast, migrant authors were those most re-active in the implementation of transcultural imaginaries especially in fictions of the past. The order of the chapters, if anything, reflects – from my perspective – the progression of the initial importance of the group, which the authors belong to, for the development of fictions of the past and the prominence of the transcultural imaginary within the genre.

Finally, I would like to emphasize once again that the concept of transcultural imaginary must be understood as an extremely complex and relational concept that can generate a great number of perspectives on literary texts, of which only a very limited selection can be included here. A focus on a selection of aspects in each of the texts makes room for some comparisons and cross-references to the authors' other works.

6 Understanding Migrant Pluralities – Rewriting Hi/stories

Earlier examples of fictions by postmodern authors often featured playful examinations of the functions and constructed nature of history;[1] however, since the 1980s, migrant authors have had a considerable impact on CanLit in general and on the genre of historical novels in particular.[2] Their work succeeded in establishing the perspective of cultures from outside Canada contributing to 'the culture' inside – a perspective that insisted on a rewriting of the master narrative of Canadian history, which had so far excluded other histories and stories from its design. Cultural difference as a theme in literature, which is often reduced to meaning ethnic difference, becomes a focus of genuine interest – in an attempt to embrace more open concepts of culture. The reading of 'difference' as it has been used to classify Canadian writers is increasingly regarded as a paradox, and continues to spark debates in the present:

> However, in contrast to aboriginal Canadian writers who explicitly claim and affirm the specificity of their literatures with regard to their ethnic origin, grouping writers and their works along those ethnic lines is not without problems. Neil Bissoondath and Michael Ondaatje, for instance, regard themselves as Canadian writers and criticise the notion of hyphenated Canadian literary identities as ethnic ghettoisation; in this view, "difference is no longer a strategy of self empowerment wielded by the minority, but a prison policed by the majority" (Samantrai 1996, 41). Other writers affirm their ethnic origins and/or their status as 'hyphenated' Canadians in their personal identification as well as in their literature. (Lutz 314)[3]

The positions taken within the ethnicity and race debate differ exceedingly from author to author, just as the immigrant experiences that determine these writers' fictions vary from personal trauma to stories passed on by parents or relatives; to what degree and in which form these memories are then integrated in texts, constitutes other specific features. This plurality is also to be found in the lives of the three authors discussed in this chapter. Thus, Michael Ondaatje was born in Sri Lanka (then Ceylon) during WWII, and moved to England in the 1950s before arriving in Canada in 1962, where he began to teach at York University after extensive studies. The ten-year younger Dionne Brand was born in Trinidad, and immigrated to Toronto in the reactive period of the

[1] Cp. for example, Robert Kroetsch, *The Studhorse Man* (1969) and *Badlands* (1975); Timothy Findley, *The Wars* (1977) and *Famous Last Words* (1981); Leonard Cohen, *Beautiful Losers* (1966); Margaret Atwood, *Surfacing* (1972); Rudy Wiebe, *The Blue Mountains of China* (1970), *The Temptations of Big Bear* (1973), and *The Scorched-Wood People* (1977).

[2] As repeatedly noted, the publication of Joy Kogawa's *Obasan* is most often regarded as the crucial turning point in this development. Cf. i.e., Gross, Klooss, and Nischik 321; Kröller 7.

[3] The quotation within the passage refers to Ranu Samantrai, "States of Belonging: Pluralism, Migrancy, Literature" in Siemerling, *Writing Ethnicity* 33-50.

1970s while still in her teens and then studied there before becoming an acclaimed scholar and writer; while, the youngest of the three authors, Madeleine Thien, now in her thirties, was born in Vancouver, as the daughter of Malaysian-Chinese immigrants and got her M.F.A. in creative writing at the University of British Columbia.

In my grouping and analysis of the texts, an awareness of the problematic nature of the above-mentioned debate, especially in the context of such a heterogenic genre is implied. It is for this very reason that I refer to the transcultural authors discussed in this chapter as migrant writers, rather than ethnic, hyphenated-Canadian, or immigrant writers. After all, all Canadians are immigrants[4] or descendants of immigrants, except First Nations and Inuit – and even within this group one could argue along various lines, apart from the fact that clear-cut classifications would be illusory in any case. In her encompassing essay on Dionne Brand's fiction, Johanna Garvey, with reference to the "cross-cultural" nature of Brand's texts (*online resource* 495), mentions Iain Chambers's take on migrancy – a definition which retrospectively speaks for the intentions underlying this chapter: "Migrancy, on the contrary [to travel], involves a movement in which neither the points of departure nor those of arrival are immutable or certain. It calls for a dwelling in language, in histories, in identities that are constantly subject to mutation" (Chambers qtd. in Garvey, *online resource* 501).[5] However, not only are we as readers and critics, but also the authors that will be analyzed in the following sections, well aware of the changing nature of the discourse on identities and the necessity to adapt this debate. As Dionne Brand writes cleverly,

> Too much has been made of origins. And so if I reject this notion of origins I have also to reject its mirror, which is the sense of origins used by the powerless to contest power in a society. The overstrong arguments about "culture," which are made both by defenders of what is "Canadian" as well as defenders of what is labelled "immigrant."
>
> These are mirror/image-image/mirror of each other and are invariably conservative. Because they must draw very definite borders both to contain their constituencies as well as, in the case of the powerful, to aggressively exclude the other and, in the case of the powerless, to weakly do the same while waving a white flag to the powerful for inclusion. Each of these arguments select [sic] and calcify origins. [...]
>
> How do we read these complicated juxtapositions of belonging and not belonging and intrabelonging. In a place such as this, so full of immigrants, everyone is deeply interested in belonging. (*Map to the Door* 69-71)

In the spirit of Brand's reflections, the following readings indeed offer revisionary approaches to the debate while displaying a broad spectrum of transcultural features within fictions of the past comprised by migrant writers.

[4] Cp. Hutcheon, "Introduction" 2. See also Staines "Canadian Literature at the Millennium," who quotes a passage from Atwood's *The Journals of Susanna Moodie* on that issue, 32. A similar observation was made by W.H.New during a private conversation in 2006.

[5] The text that Garvey is quoting from is Iain Chambers, *Migrancy, Culture, Identity* (New York: Routledge, 1994).

How Families Haunt, And Histories Heal– Michael Ondaatje's *Divisadero*

Most literary critics would argue that Ondaatje's most recent masterpiece, *Divisadero,* could hardly be classified as a historical novel. I, too, subscribe to this perspective, however with one major limitation. It might not be a historical novel, but it most clearly can be read as a 'fiction of the past.' History, memory, and the past in general are what carries the novel from the first page to the last – even if many sections of the book are basically set in the present and recent past (around the 1970s). This specific feature as well as the intertwined narratives and circular structure found in the novel prompted one critic to interpret *Divisadero* as a new fictional form termed "hybrid novel" (Löffler, "Ein Hybrid-Roman," *online resource*, n.pag.).

The novel centers on a family, which is in many regards disrupted, living in Northern California close to the city of Petaluma – a region vibrant in the gold rush era, as also shortly alluded to in the novel.[6] It tells the story of three unrelated siblings: Anna, the main protagonist and narrator; Claire, a girl whom Anna's father adopted in the hospital, as the girl's mother, just like his own wife, had died giving birth; and Coop, the neighbor's boy, taken in even earlier by Anna's mother after his family had been brutally murdered. Coinciding with this motley family constellation, there are several interwoven narrative strands that evolve and revolve around the central character of Anna, who looks back on her unsettled life, studies the life of others and struggles to define her identity in the present. Ondaatje devides the dense patchwork of stories into three major parts, which roughly reflect the focus on three different narrative 'perspectives' (Part One, "Anna, Claire, and Coop"; Part Two, "The Family in the Cart" Part Three, "The House in Dému"). We first get to know Anna's life and her family as a young girl, which is essentially, as most of the novel, described from Anna's distanced adult perspective. Here we learn about the event that unhinged the children's lives and led to their separation.

While several sections of the first part are also dedicated to the equally restless life of Coop – he becomes a professional poker player – the sections of the novel, which are essential for the present analysis, focus on Anna, now a historian, doing research in France on the French writer Lucien Segura ("Le Manouche" 63-95 and "The Person Formerly Known as Anna" 135-148). Yet a further narrative level is added as a large segment of the novel (most of Part Two and Three) also fictionalizes this historical figure's life and experiences – presumably reconstructed and re-imagined by Anna; this element of the story shall be the subject of the following pages, too.

What is different in *Divisadero* in comparison to Ondaatje's previous novels is that the historical sections do not rewrite the story of some factual hero or an event from *H*istory, as was the case in *The Collected Works of Billy the Kid* (1970) (on the infamous American outlaw), or in *The English Patient* (1992) (set before and during WWII and based on the adventures of the historical figure of the Hungarian Count

[6] A short section describes this historical background in relation to Coop's rather short-lived obsession to get involved in the gold-digging business. Cf. *Divisadero* 12-15.

Almásy); nor does it shed new light on a neglected aspect of Canadian history, as in *In the Skin of a Lion* (1987) (a fictionalized account of Toronto and its immigrant communities in the 1920s and 30s), or on that of Ondaatje's country of origin, as in *Anil's Ghost* (2000) (which is set in present-day Sri Lanka and explores the atrocities of the civil war). Instead, *Divisadero* is set in California's diverse regional landscapes, cities and highways, as well as in rural France; it is not interested in the study of the role of history for collective imaginaries but rather in its interpretation of the forces of memory and history, looking to the individual and forgotten, the marginal *fictional* personae in the great picture of history.[7] In this recent work, Ondaatje prominently sketches personal rewritings of the past, family histories, the complexities of identity in relation to one's family and loved ones, and the quest for inner calmness – in short what Schulze-Engler identifies as the "micropolitics of modernity."[8] As he put it: "[…] when I look back on it now it is a very private book, it's not about being in a public space, on a public stage. The public stuff, the wars that happen throughout the book, are happening a long way away, even though it influences people. So I think it was a kind of intimacy and privacy of people in solitude offstage that interested me" (Koval, *online resource*, n.pag.). However, in its self-reflected desire to unveil hidden histories, we must still acknowledge the continuing proximity of the novel to what has in the past been referred to as postmodern historiographic metafiction, displayed, for example, in the fact that the historian Anna collects and reads material on and by the poet Segura. Thereby she re-imagines his life, just as she scans her memories and mentally constantly re-drafts her own family – fact and fiction are once again disclosed as being close allies.

If we start by turning our attention to the central theme of the novel, the reconstruction of individual identities and the vital yet fragile position of memories and histories for this process, one should first observe the (narrative) coupling of four of the five main protagonists into two pairs: Coop and Claire, and Anna and Lucien Segura. Coop, Claire, and Anna have all three, as they well know, been affected for the rest of their lives by the day their father nearly killed the boy he raised. While Anna evades her memories by fleeing into other countries, historical worlds, and other people's lives, both Coop and Claire do not completely leave the area in which they grew up in – in fact, Claire is the one who has stayed behind to take care of their taciturn, ageing father. Claire has accepted her lot in the story, suffering from the fragmented emotions that she has been left with; she is leading a double life, as an assistant in the Public Defender's Office in San Francisco during the week, and on the weekends, as the adventurous horse-rider she has been since her youth on her father's farm – a passion that in its tightrope walk to danger helps her forget the past: "She and the horse climbed into the hills that some part of her had always believed were her true home. Here she was uninterpreted by family life, could be dangerous to herself" (*Divisadero* 100). While Anna and Coop were especially close as youngsters and came to experience their

[7] Collective identity is only very marginally discussed in relation to American history and myths, 144, 9-10; also note that the individual, marginal perspective on history, was also prominent in other of Ondaatje's novels, such as in *In the Skin of a Lion*. However the emphasis on the personal, familial past in relation to identity constructions is even stronger in *Divisadero*.

[8] Schulze-Engler, i.e. "From Postcolonial to Preglobal" 58-59, and "Theoretical Perspectives" 28.

affection sexually for two months, it is Claire who saves Coop twice: the first time, when he gets caught in the storm after having been severely injured by their father, who at that moment is already desperately looking for Anna, who has disappeared; the second time, when she senses that something has happened to him after briefly having met him in Tahoe. Indeed, she finds him again beaten up, more dead than alive, all his memories lost. She not only helps Coop escape from his enemies, she also takes him back with her to their father's farm, realizing that to take advantage of this (possibly only momentary) eradication of the past in Coop's mind and to gamble with this gap in time, not only gives Coop and her father a second chance, it also lets her hope for her own recovery of self:

> Driving to San Francisco, Claire reaches for Coop's hand.
>
> I need you to meet my father.
>
> Your father … Why?
>
> He brought you up, Coop. And he's old now. So old. […]
>
> She did not want to explain any more to him, knowing this act could be terrible, even brutal. Or it would be generous. Or break her father's heart again. All of these things were possible. But so much had been wasted. She had only a distant father, and now Coop, like this, a boy remembering nothing. She wanted to fold the two halves of her life together like a map. (164)

What happens at their encounter, we do not learn – the story of Claire and Coop ends with their arrival at the old farmhouse. Obviously, Claire's and Coop's fate is very strongly rooted in the present – one section mentions "[t]welve years after the American bombing of the Gulf in 1991, America was poised to attack Iraq again" (160) – as a narrative, this sections strongly removes the novel from any relation to the historical genre, even if individual past and memory, as I have tried to show, is decisive for the protagonists' developments. Anna's story, however, reverses this generic positioning by a strong connection to history.

Anna's self-reflexive musings on her life and her family, and on the haunting aspects of biography emerge throughout the novel, be it whilst doing her historical research or when she spends time with the young gypsy Rafael, whom she meets at the house she lives in in Dému, which, by the way, is the house the writer she is working on spent the later part of his life.

> *Everything is biographical*, Lucien Freud says. What we make, why it is made, how we draw a dog, who it is we are drawn to, why we cannot forget. Everything is collage, even genetics. There is a hidden presence of others in us, even those we have known briefly. We contain them for the rest of our lives, at every border we cross. (16)

We see here how Anna understands that, in a certain way, we are all always not only constructed by ourselves but also by the people that surround and have surrounded us. At the same time, she admits that she is not capable of intimate relationships (71-76), and never talks about her family past; yet this changes when she gets to know and love the mysterious Rafael – the free-spirited *gitan*, who in contrast to Anna grew up well cared for by his mother. He tells Anna stories about his parents, how they met, and their life together. However, what intrigues Anna most, as well as the reader who can only understand the importance of this detail as the novel proceeds, is that Rafael knew the writer Lucien Segura when he was a boy, and so he can also tell Anna stories about what he remembers. This intimate information that she receives from Rafael is essential for Anna, as the story of the writer and her re-imagination of it, help her settle the 'new' person she wants to be. She wishes to let go completely of her old self – since the moment of her escape from home, she has no longer regarded herself as "Anna"[9]; however instead of denying her past, she comes to see with the help of Lucien's story that she must also partially recover her old self – which she does by eventually also telling Rafael about her own life. In this way, Anna finally finds some sense and peace in the vicious circle of memories that she describes: "For we live with those retrievals from childhood that coalesce and echo throughout our lives, the way shattered pieces of glass in a kaleidoscope reappear in new forms and are songlike in their refrains and rhymes, making up a single monologue. We live permanently in the recurrence of our own stories, whatever story we tell" (136). She escapes this endless recurrence of her own story through her commitment to the story of Lucien Segura, who is connected to her through this very trauma of constantly reliving a haunting past.

The similarities between Lucien's life and Anna's are striking, and allow us to see them historically seperated yet connected as a pair in the narrative and thematic structure of the novel: both grew up in a complicated and unusual family situation; both had only one parent (in the case of Segura, his real father had left his mother early on, she had remarried and his stepfather had died not long after); both grew up with 'adopted,' unrelated family members, who also become the cause for unresolved or dramatic love – that is Coop, and in Lucien Segura's story, Marie-Neige, a girl his age married to a man considerably older than her – the two become neighbors when he is sixteen. While Anna left her home as a young girl, Lucien Segura spends an unhappy life experiencing a love-less marriage, witnessing the war and later his beloved Marie-Neige's death before he deserts his increasingly alienated family in order to find peace.

Throughout his life Lucien Segura hides behind words, first as an obsessive reader in his youth (a trait that strongly connects him to Marie-Neige), later as a writer: after the war and Marie-Neige's death, he can only free himself by writing several novels containing the adventures of Marie-Neige's fictional alter ego in a row. After finishing, he decides to never write again and leaves his family. Anna, is not only fascinated by Segura's life, she is also obsessed with the past in general – and has thus made it her profession; similarly to Segura she knows that to write biographies of artists, working in archives and studying histories is her way, and only a temporary method, to escape her troubling memories:

> Those who have an orphan's sense of history love history. And my voice has become that of an orphan. Perhaps it was the unknown life of my mother, her barely drawn

[9] The prologue (1) and a subtitle in the first part of the novel, "The Person formerly known as Anna" (135), suggest that Anna might have actually changed her name.

> portrait, that made me an archivist, a historian. Because if you do not plunder the past, the absence feeds on you. My career exhumes mostly unknown corners of European culture. [...]
>
> [...]
>
> This is where I learned that sometimes we enter art to hide within it. It is where we can go to save ourselves, where a third-person voice protects us. (141-142)[10]

Ultimately Anna and Lucien's identities are, however, not redeemed by their obsession with the past and history; what eventually makes a re-establishment of self possible and also invariably links the two protagonists, is their friendship with Rafael. Lucien meets the traveling family while he is still searching for a house to live in – they, too, are looking for a place to temporarily settle with their caravan. The writer is touched by the harmonious and at the same time restless nature that the small family displays, and with awe observes their flexibility and openness, reflected, for example, in the father's refusal to settle on a name for himself (175).[11] As long as the family stays with him, Lucien accepts the boy Rafael as if he were his own son. In fact, when the 'gitans' finally do leave, the writer feels that the little bit of structure and love that he had left in his life, given to him to a large degree by Rafael, leaves with them and soon after, we are led to assume, he drowns in the nearby lake:

> The lake throws up a sparkle between the trees. Lucien takes a moment to struggle into his cardigan and walks into the shadows of the oaks. He does not feel this present life is real without the boy. The essential necessity of Rafael. They have shared things cautiously. He has reached for some fragments of his life to give to this almost adopted boy, and in return Rafael has described the eclipse he and his mother witnessed near Plaisance, its terrible wind that was more terrible than the darkness. And what Lucien wants now is a storm. (272)

Rafael also becomes an "essential necessity" for Anna, who re-constructs her identity through the history of Lucien; he represents the final, direct link that closes the circle of haunting pasts that allows the constraining boundaries of family, emotional dependency and time to, at least partially, dissolve. The questions as to the possibilities of events, the present reality, and details of existence of Coop and Claire remain open to Anna;[12]

[10] The pages following the quoted passage refer to the text sequence inserted at the very beginning of the novel, the prologue (a very common feature in Ondaatje's novels), which describes Anna's favorite moment in history (the day Colette died, Paris 1954); it also offers an explanation for the title of the novel: "I come from Divisadero Street. Divisadero, from the Spanish word for 'division,' the street that at one time was the dividing line between San Francisco and the fields of the Presidio. Or it might derive from the word *divisar*, meaning 'to gaze at something from the distance.' (There is a height nearby called El Divisadero.) Thus a point from which you can look far into the distance" (142-143).

[11] Cp. also 176, 182, and 187-188.

[12] The novels open-endedness is also discussed in a review by Elizabeth Wadell, as are some other aspects observed in my own interpretation, such as the thematic structuring of stories and

however the necessity to accept the inexhaustibility of imagination for the reconstruction and understanding of past, present, and future is the most vital realization that she takes with her from Rafael and Lucien's story.[13] In the end, the historical narratives and her relationship to Rafael will provide Anna with an agency that nurtures what might be seen as an opening up of imaginaries that eventually also helps her to accept the calamities of her family's past – despite continuing uncertainties. As this passage in which the narrative perspective moves from Segura's imagined reflections, over a narrator's comments to Anna's thoughts shows:

> He will never know what becomes of his children. He will not know whether he has nurtured them or damaged them. A girl travels down the long California valley in a commercial refrigeration truck, hardly able to speak, as a result of her fear or her bravery, listening to every word of the good stranger. Lucette in Paris sips absinthe with her lover. The boy Rafael will meet me, a woman from the New World. . . . And Coop? And Claire? Will these children, in their eventual cities, turn out to be the heroes of their own lives? (272)[14]

Ondaatje's *Divisadero* acts out a transcultural imaginary through the translocal and transhistorical movements that permeate the narrative structure; its setting in California and France, movements partially also effected by a postmodern questioning of the boundaries between history and story, fact and fiction, memory and imaginary. However, an unusual, even more captivating feature is detectable in the theme of generational transgressions of culture, or rather, the difficulties involved in carrying wisdom and imaginaries across generations. The inter-familial struggles and complexities of relationships between parents and children are the cause for the protagonists' scramble for identity and emotional security: Anna's father, who has himself lost his wife, ends up traumatizing his daughter in his desire to protect her; Lucien emotionally disturbed by the tragic happenings in his own life and in his love for a woman, watches his own daughter, who has tried to help him escape his estranging world of words, have an affair with a poet who is a suitor to her sister, while she is already married. As Lucien acknowledges at some point in his life: "Sometimes truth is too buried for adults, it can be found only in hours of rewritings during the night, the way metal is beaten into fineness. Whereas children are a generation with immediate clarity" (230). In the process that leads to the trans-generational de-traumatization, once again, Rafael is attributed the key position in accepting Lucien as a second father, and later passing on this man's knowledge and history to Anna, who subsequently learns to forgive her own father.

Themes of ethnic and racial cultural transfer and exchange, or issues of gender and sexuality do not play an obvious role in this novel – *Divisadero* is not a political

characters, and the focus on identities. Cf. Wadell, "*Divisdero* by Michael Ondaatje," *online resource*, n.pag.

[13] Cp. also to the prologue, which foreshadows Anna's voice: "The raw truth of an incident never ends, and the story of Coop and the terrain of my sister's life are endless to me. They are the sudden possibility every time I pick up the telephone […]" (1).

[14] The drive in the refrigeration truck refers to Anna's escape; Lucette is the name of Lucien Segura's daughter.

novel;[15] nor does it obsessively insist on the contrasting of communal and individual history. Nonetheless, the transposition of the past (be it as historical research, fictional rewritings or personal memories) across individual cultural spaces reduces the presupposed limits of time and place, thereby developing a basic vision of transcultural imaginaries as a solution for individual trauma. In the constellation of characters, Rafael's position is not entirely that of a transcultural figure, yet he surely appears as a mediator between the intermingled stories – through him the temporal levels are linked and become transhistorical.

Divisadero's value as a fiction of the past ultimately lies in its depiction of history and memory as containing both haunting and deconstructive, as well as healing and reconstructive powers for the individual's construction of self. The protagonists, particularly Anna, achieve their personal empowerment of identity through an individual recreation of the images and voices that circle their mind. They can only accept and recollect their fragmented selves by realizing the interdependence and omnipresence of others in the self:

> With memory, with the reflection of an echo, a gate opens both ways. We can circle time. A paragraph or an episode from another era will haunt us in the night, as the words of a stranger can. The awareness of a flag fluttering noisily within its colour brings me into a sudden blizzard in Petaluma. Just as a folded map places you beside another geography. So I find the lives of Coop and my sister and my father everywhere (I draw portraits of them *everywhere*), as they perhaps still concern themselves with my absence, wherever they are. I don't know. It is the hunger, what we do not have, that holds us together. (268)

It is with this unsettling note on a longing for love and our loved ones, a desire that both completely dissects and "holds us together" with which Ondaatje leaves us at the end of the novel: "Oh this older need for a lullaby, not a storm" (273). Until the very end, the riddle of existence remains unresolved, save for the understanding that a certain truth lies alone in the possibility of fact.

[15] Cf. the interview with IPS correspondent Mark Weisenmiller, which indicates that Ondaatje is less conscious of his novels' relation to human rights, identity and migration and that he acknowledges his ethnic heritage as "lucky" asset, while he is more conscious of "virtual erasing of national borders" in his work; Weissenmiller, "We Live in an Age of Migration," *online resource*, n.pag.

The Impossible Art of Mapping the Past – Dionne Brand's *At the Full and the Change of the Moon*

There are some authors within the Canadian literary scene that are easier to separate from the discursively charged context of multicultural belonging, cultural inequalities and the rights of minorities, even though they have a heritage of migrancy and display the discrepancies and hybridities lived at the crossroads of cultural identifications. Both Michael Ondaatje, who has always been more strongly dedicated to reflections on aesthetics and art than on politics in his work and interviews[16], and Madeleine Thien, belonging to a younger generation of migrants, for whom family pasts represent a very personal realm of quest, can be counted among this more 'moderate' group of writers. With Dionne Brand, however, the situation is different. At the usual risk of over-simplifying or generalizing, one can state that she is a feminist, lesbian Afro-Carribean Canadian writer – giving her at least three reasons to have and express a strong opinion on matters – a writer who has throughout her life been politically active. "[…] [A]rt is politically charged, because it is, because we are living in a politically charged moment, that's suffused in race and racism and the ideas of land and border and belonging" (Olbey 100), Brand argues in an interview. Indeed, her art focuses our attention right on the center of the discourses around the multiculturalism debate, feminist issues and, even more so, on the histories and struggles of the Black Diaspora.

With an author like Ondaatje, it is possible to observe that each time he writes a novel he is moving in a language and world of its own (Koval, *online resource*, n.pag.), Dionne Brand's work is hard to separate from the author's own experience. Apart from that, all the individual works must be read as interrelated, as being part of a bigger picture – a fact that becomes especially obvious when reading her memoir-related *A Map to the Door of No Return. Notes to Belonging* (2001), which I will refer to repeatedly. The present analysis, however, will focus on *At the Full and Change of the Moon*, which apart from its mostly historical setting, considers several other themes pervasive in Brand's work, and in Carribean fiction in general: (collective) memory, identity, rootlessness, space, body, and belonging.[17] In seemingly more optimistic words she comments, "I love this notion of wandering forever to find a place. That search is a way of reaching beyond boundaries" and mysteriously adds somewhere else, "I am

[16] Cp., for example his rather casual explanations in the interview by Weisenmiller, "We live in an Age of Migration"; when asked, "Do you believe that your characters have a firm sense of their identity?", he replies: "I don't think so. I don't think that they think about it. I just don't believe that people do that. So the characters in my books don't do that either." Or: "How does the migration of your characters within the stories fit into the overall scheme of your writing? Does the sense of home, and actually owning and having a house, play an important part in both your personal and professional life?" – "I think that any writer, every writer wants a base where you're at. You want both a firm sense of where you are, but also want a sense of adventure." (Weisenmiller, *online resource*, n.pag.). Apart from that there are about as many books on the politics of Ondaatje's novels, as on their aesthetics, or on their depiction of art.

[17] Cf. Condé, "Introduction" 3.

directed by rootlessness [...] I want to draw new maps" (Methot, *online resource*, n.pag.).

Maps are central to Brand's fiction – it is a metaphor for the one-dimensional forces of colonial imperialism as well as for the problem of mapping identities in terms of the often sweeping multicultural discourse. The image of the map also permeates *A Map to the Door of No Return*, a book that represents Brand's personal attempt to map her thoughts, memories and critical perspectives:[18]

> One drives through lost paths, one asks the way redundantly, one floats and looks, one looks and floats – all marvel at their ability to learn and forget the way of lost maps. We all feign ignorance at the rupture in mind and body, in place, in time. We all feel it. (*Map to the Door* 221)
>
> [...]
>
> 5 To Travel without a map, to travel without a way. They did, long ago. That misdirection became the way. After the Door of No Return, a map was only a set of impossibilities, a set of changing locations.
>
> 6 A map, then, is only a life of conversations about a forgotten list of irretrievable selves. (ibid. 224)

The awareness of the impossibility of mapping in any logical, linear way is an insight that she gives not only in relation to "the door of no return" (thus the history of the Black Diaspora) but with regard to all (especially marginalized) identities in the past and present – as also reflected in the structure of the memoir. Even though it is not the subject of our analysis, I would like to emphasize the importance of *Map to the Door*; it is in itself a transcultural text that helps one to understand the potential textures of transcultural imaginaries. Reflecting this imaginary, the memoir includes snippets from historical texts, memories from her childhood, discussions of literary texts that strongly influenced her, and many other textual ramifications – this transcultural mode of expression is the only way for Brand to draw a map of her complex feelings of belonging and of Afro-Carribean history:

> "Some of us want to tie the world down into spaces that we own. You can map a place, and write observations, but that's strictly a reflection of your own point of view," Brand asserts. "If that point of view is rigid enough, that's all you see. A map should be a larger place – a place filled with the endlessness of living, the hugeness of the imagination." (Methot, *online resource*, n.pag.)

[18] Cf. the interview with Mavjee, in which Brand explains: "To make a map is to create a definition of a place. Some maps are made to places you don't know even exist — to a new place. I wanted to lift that idea of map-making. I want to live in another kind of world. In a sense, that is the map I am writing," Mavjee, *online resource*, n.pag. Also qtd. in Goldman, "Mapping the Door of No Return" *online resource*, n.pag.

Brand adopts this position for all her work, however it becomes especially meaningful in both *At the Full and Change of the Moon* and *Map to the Door*. The latter also gives insight into material that influenced two of her novels and the processes of thought and observation that accompanied their writing and conception.[19] It also gives considerable insight into experiences that led to *At the Full and Change of the Moon*, such as visits to museums in the Caribbean, several historical sources and a trip to Amsterdam in 1992 (*Map to the Door* 196-211).

At the Full and Change can be seen as an exemplary fictionalization of this issue of mapping identities and histories and the above mentioned difficulties of doing so. As discussed by Johanna X. K. Garvey, the family tree that precedes the novel announces this theme, while at the same time its focus on a maternal perspective (it excludes fathers from its mapping) and unconventional complexity as well as anonymous form, indicate the alternative transgressive spaces that permeate this novel.[20]

The narrative frame of the novel is the starting and end point of this transhistorical mapping: it tells the story of Marie Ursule, a slave in Trinidad in the early nineteenth century, who initiated a mass suicide on her plantation before being executed herself;[21] her only daughter Bola escapes the act of violence and eventually Marie-Ursule's offspring is scattered all around the world. The novel evolves the turbulent life of Bola and that of some of her many grand- and great-grandchildren. It finally arrives at her great-great-grandchild Bola born in 1982, before the concluding chapter of the novel returns to the world of "old" Bola and Marie Ursule. The following overview of the separate chapters' main protagonists and approximate settings underlines the novel's complex translocal and transhistorical structure:

[19] In the interview with Maya Mavjee Brand says, "The book is a map. The form, the sketches and ruminations, as early maps were, allowed me the freedom to pick up an idea and examine it in many different ways. The way it travelled was in some ways the way a poem travels. I could reach out and follow an idea. I could drop one thread and then pick up another one. The form allowed the book itself to become a map to my journey for a new kind of identity and existence. Whether it's a poem, a newspaper article, a piece of music, a novel, a piece of my own writing, a childhood memory — all these signposts come together to drive the journey," Mavjee, "Opening the Door," *online resource*, n.pag. Those who have read *In Another Place, Not here* – a novel also discussed in terms of a fiction of the past – will through a reading of *Map to the Door* come to understand that Brand herself, similar to her character Verlia, experienced the tragic attack of U.S. bombers on Grenada in 1983 (*Map to the Door* 154-169). Cf. McCallum and Olbey, "Written in the scars: History, genre, and materiality in Dionne Brand's *In Another Place, Not Here*," *online resource*, n.pag.

[20] Cf. Garvey, "'The Place She Miss' – Exile, Memory, and Resistance in Dionne Brand's Fiction," *online resource*, 494-495. This essay presents a highly informative and complex reading of Brand's work (with a focus on the sea metaphor and the author's placement in the general context of Black Diaspora criticism).

[21] In the acknowledgements to *At the Full and Change of the Moon* as well as in *Map to the Door*, Brand explains that the idea for the character Marie Ursule came from V.S. Naipaul's *The Loss of Eldorado: A History*, which mentions a similar, true story. It is also from this story that Brand takes the last words, which Thisbe, Marie Ursule's model, is supposed to have said at her hanging: "This is but a drink of water to what I have already suffered" ("Acknowledgments" *Full and Change* 302); cp. *Map to the Door* 205-206.

Chapter I	"...But a Drink of Water" – Marie Ursule (Bola, Kamena) / Trinidad / 1810s-20s
Chapter II	"At the Full and Change of the Moon" – Kamena, Bola / Trinidad / 1830s-70s
Chapter III	"Tamarindus Indica" – Private Samuel Gordon Sones (grandson of Bola and an Indian sugar cane worker, son of Augusta) / Trinidad, England, Palestine / 1910s-40s
Chapter IV	"A Sudden Big Lust" – Cordelia Rojas (great-grand-daughter of Bola, married to a man whose grand-father was Cordelia's grandmother's halfbrother) / Venezuela, Trinidad / 1953 and earlier
Chapter V	"Priest" – Carlyle (great-grand-son of Bola), Eula (his sister), Adrian / Trinidad, India, Canada, America / presumably 1960s-70s
Chapter VI	"A Soft Man" – Adrian Dovett (great-great-grandson of Bola), Maya (his sister) / the Carribean, South American coast, various parts of North America, Amsterdam / 1980s-90s
Chapter VII	"In a Window" – Maya / Curaçao, Amsterdam, Brugge / 1980s-90s
Chapter VIII	"Blue Airmail Letter" / Eula (great-grand-daughter of Bola, sister of Carlyle) / Toronto / around 1980
Chapter IX	"Bola" – Bola (great-great-grand-daughter of Bola, daughter of Eula, living with her grandmother and aunts – who she believes are her mother and sisters) / Trinidad / later 1990s
Chapter X	"At the Full and Change of the Moon" – 'old' Bola / Trinidad / around 1900 (d.1921)

The chapters of the novel, which each develop separate plots, are strongly rooted in both postcolonial as well as feminist discourse. As Garvey observes, "[t]hat Bola's partners have origins not only on the island but also in Venezuela, India, Africa, and elsewhere, and that her children reside not only near Culebra Bay or in Terre Bouillante, but also in places such as Curaçao, England, Amsterdam, New York and Toronto, vividly illustrates the possibilities for a new mapping of cultures and a concomitant decolonization" (*online resource,* 495). Brand's postcolonial perspective is expressed in the descriptions – which are at times distressing – of the tragic fates and struggles of Marie Ursule's descendants, their forced dispersion across the world, leaving them rootless and very often hopeless. There is, for example, Private Sones who dreams of being equal to others (white people) but after he rebels against discrimination in the army and is sent back from WWI for misconduct, is broken for the rest of his life; or Adrian who flees across the Caribbean Sea to Florida, New York and later to Amsterdam where he, however, drowns his sorrows with drugs, and his sister Maya who desires nothing but her freedom as a woman but is forced to settle and have a child with a white man. On the whole, Marie Ursule's descendants are incessantly haunted by a history that is so devastating it can only be healed by forgetting, which disrupts their sense of belonging – a fact that Marie Ursule already senses on the morning of the mass suicide, in spite of her own drained imaginary[22] it is the choice she makes over complete extinction:

> The lives of her great-great-grandchildren, their lives would spill all over floors and glass cases and the verandas and the streets in the new world coming. Their hearts would burst. When asked they will say that they had no reason at all for sitting numb, with cocaine or gin or music coursing through their fingers. Singers will pierce them dipping into their ribs. They would come to be whatever impulse gathered the greater in them, like threatened forests flowering. (20)

The lives of Marie Ursule's and Bola's descendants display the conflicting role that history and memory take in relation to an understanding of self in the specific contexts of Afro-Carribean hauntings of disembodiment and postcolonial longings for agency, space, and place, particularly in the context of the present world's modernities. Imperialistic rule and the slave trade of former times and its consequences – a historical trauma for the black community – is hardly overcome in the globalized metropolis of the present, which is full of decay and forgetting:

> I am living in a city at the end of the world, Mama. It is rubble. It is where everyone has been swept up, all of it, all of us are debris, things that a land cleaning itself spits up. It is the end of the world here. The office buildings and factory buildings and houses and shops and garages all wreathed in oil and dust and piled on top of themselves. It is as if some pustule erupted from the ground and it is this city. It is bloated and dry at the same time, crumbling with newness, rubbled in glitter.
>
> [...]
>
> Don't think that I'm sad. I'm just trying to explain it to you so you will know why I did not write sooner. I'm forgetting you even as I write this letter. The more I write the more I forget. Perhaps that is why I never wrote until now. (238-239)[23]

[22] Marie Ursule is described as a woman gone reckless and broken by slavery, for whom death is the only place left to find freedom, the only way to forget: "She could not think of escape for herself. She could not imagine the mountains, or Arauc or Terre Bouillante where they said life was free. She could not imagine or believe any place like that. She was ruined already," 6. In another passage she asks: "Hadn't life ceased to be certain long ago, hadn't every turning stood still, hadn't every stillness turned to motion long long ago? And what was memory when she felt it loop and repeat, when what she was about to do she had imagined done already, like a memory," 9.

[23] In comparison to this passage, one might consider the depiction of the Ursuline nuns who owned Marie Ursule before she was sold to DeLambert and who continue to haunt the region they lived in long after their deaths. They come to represent the decadent history of colonial invasion and brutality, cf. *Full and Change* 35-38.

The historical fate of the members of the Black Diaspora causes a restlessness that is linked to the unrelenting antagonistic confrontation between memory and forgetting: thus, on the one hand, the desire – which however is not a matter of choice – to forget one's origins, one's family past, and all the ancestral stories; on the other hand, the natural longing to remember, to have something to hold on to. As Brand herself commented on this matter, "[p]erhaps what's most significant about all the characters in *At the Full and Change of the Moon* is their wanting to be released from history, from both personal as well as public history. If I could think of an emotion coming out of that book, it would be this desire for release" (Olbey 101); at the same time Brand also acknowledges, that "[t]he ruin of history visited on a people does not wipe out the steadfastness of beauty. [...] Beauty, it seems, is constantly made" (*Map to the Door* 193).[24] This contradictory feeling becomes so dominant in the lives of Marie Ursule's and Bola's great-great-grandchildren that it either breaks them, makes them go mad, or both. It is for this reason that Maya feels safest in a framed window, even though she is selling her body[25] – at least she can create a minimal space in which time dissolves and she has control over her fate:

> Maya is standing in the window. This is where she is. Framed in a window. This second. Not what comes after and not what came before. She wishes that this moment were all she must live. Right here in the window, framed just so. The left corner, glass and air and the wooded shafts angled to the right and the end of the floor mat. This moment framed in a window, every area of space and air composed. (207)[26]

In some instances, the protagonists (some more, some less) also find a way to achieve peace; however, this way often leads to a completely non-linear perception of the world, which, as will be discussed a little later, at the same time obviously comes to be regarded as a turn to madness from outside. Thus, Brand's approach to history unsettles linear perspectives through a view on the fates of individuals who have been affected long-term by the forces of History and through a poetic, close to magical, reading of ancestral memory[27] that troubles or, in some cases, enchants and strengthens these individuals.[28]

[24] Beauty, or "[d]esire in the face of ruin," *Map to the Door* 193, is here interpreted as an ethical value, a form of steadfastness in hope, a repeatedly renewed longing for "[m]aking sense [...] putting the senses back together," *Map to the Door* 195. In relation to her earlier years, Brand also describes her own longing for release: " I wanted to be free. I wanted to feel as if history was not destiny," *Map to the Door* 168.

[25] For some time she works in the red light district in Amsterdam, which is famous for its 'casual' riverfront windows, in which the women display themselves. Brand describes her encounter with the character "Maya" during her visit to Amsterdam in *A Map to the Door of No Return*, 210.

[26] For further descriptions of the feeling of power and inner peace this window gives to Maya, cf. 218-219.

[27] Maureen Moynagh sees Brand as "present[ing] cultural memory as a spiritual and bodily knowledge inscribed by the material forces of history, including by its silences," *online resource*, final paragraph.

[28] Goldman in "Mapping the Door of No Return" opposes the colonial, linear view of history as progress, to the "drifting" concept of space and memory of the Diaspora; Brand's rooting in the

As Marlene Goldman has argued, Brand not only questions notions of nation and belonging, to a large degree she also deconstructs the assumed power of communal bonds and family, though she only proposes limited alternatives (Goldman, *online resource* n.pag.).[29] This issue is connected to the second major political slant in the novel, and Brand's work in general: the feminist perspective. The portrayed women do not only enforce the disintegration of familial and communal feelings of belonging (through the rejection of maternal bonds)[30], they in fact become representative of the Afro-Carribean historical fate and its fight for freedom: "Struggling with the consequences of a colonized past in the Caribbean as well as with contemporary realities of global economics, these women express a repeated need to leave the place they occupy—where their bodies may resemble occupied territory—and to find a place of empowerment" (Garvey, *online resource* 486).[31] Brand's women – or at least those that come to some resolution of their restlessness – live their sexual desires: Bola, Marie Ursule's daughter, embodies unrelenting desire through her many affairs (each of her children is fathered by another man) and her strong connection to the sea;[32] Cordelia Rojas, her granddaughter born in Venezuela only comes to true pleasure in the later years of her life:

> And then in her fiftieth year, Cordelia burst from her own seams. She had gone to her window with a sudden remembrance of pink shells and Culebra Bay. She had not meant to remember. All the years she had been taken up with ordering her thoughts. The vigour she had used all these years to contain her memory, to clean her house and maintain her children, had turned on her. She was greedy for everything she had not had.
>
> What she had not had was the enjoyment of her body clear and free. (121)

These women do not only display physical and emotional strength[33], they are also capable of transcending history, to "see beyond the conclusion that flesh can come to" (*Full and Change* 38) by dreaming the future or seeing the past, and in doing so

postcolonial discourse has also been evaluated as leading to a one-sided, too biased and negative portrayal of white people, cp. Teelucksingh, "Carribean Rebels," 392-393.

[29] For similar arguments on Brand's novel *In Another Place, Not Here*, cp. Joanna Luft, "Elizete and Verlia Go to Toronto"; Luft, like several other critics, relates Dionne Brand to Paul Gilroy's famous study *The Black Atlantic: Modernity and Double Consciousness*, which argues that "black cultural identity emerges through the dynamics of diaspora multiplicity," Luft 33.

[30] Cf. Goldman, final paragraphs, and Garvey, both *online resources*, n.pag.

[31] Brand also comments on the relation of the Black/female body to agency in *Map to the Door* 35-42.

[32] The sea is very important in Brand's novels; also in *At the Full and Change of the Moon*, where it represents freedom, female sexuality, the past and the future, and the Middle Passage, cf., i.e., 44-47; Cp. the essays by Luft, and Goldman.

[33] Note, for example, descriptions of Marie Ursule (10), which have been referred to as the characteristics of African warrior women (Cf. Teelucksingh), or of Maya: "She sculpted her calves for running and her thighs for lifting, she pruned the biceps and triceps and she cultivated the deep river running down her back hardening the ridges on either side. She made herself strong and liquid," 221.

perform the only way of coming to terms with the confining anxieties of the present, as the following description of 'old' Bola shows:[34]

> Old and gone, dropping all her pieces of conversations and laughter. She lived now in the best of places, where everything happened at the same time. Her days were full of all her living, everything she had done and seen and heard, all her children and her childhood and Kamena and the red birds and the blind man and the golden man and the man whose scent was too sweet and her mother, Marie Ursule. All happening at the same time. In all of it the present was small and just a part. [...] Sones heard her singing sometimes. Marie Ursule. Just these two words were her whole song. But only sometimes could she leave the water and the nuns and the trumpet fish and all her living to hear something heaving like a coming whale. (83)

Thus, within the context of both a postcolonial and a feminist discourse, *At the Full and Change of the Moon* can be seen as a transhistorical and translocal novel. However, while the diverse narrative settings represent the black diaspora's *forced* displacement in history, the ability of some protagonists to dissolve the boundaries of time and space suggest a solution to this forced-upon state.

Despite this small possibility of release, on the whole, 'place,' 'home,' and 'identity' remain concepts of the imagination with no direct association to an actual country: home is everywhere and nowhere, it is emptiness and forgetting, always "in another place, not here."[35] This fact is explicitly dramatized in Marie Ursule's close friend Kamena's everlasting and unpredictable search for home and freedom, represented by the marooned camp of Terre Bouillante – he dies exhausted from his fruitless attempts to collect and memorize the directions to its possible location;[36] Eula, some generations later, however, collects maps from places around the world and employs them for her own ends, by using them randomly, no matter where she is, where she is heading and whether it is the right map or not:

> I collect maps of all kinds, old ones and newer ones, ordnance maps and road maps. That was how I found my way out of America after leaving Carlyle and Gita on the road to Florida. In the trunk of the car I had brought all my maps and when I was so tired that I did not know my way, I would pull off to the side of the road and search my maps. Any one would do, even a map of France or Guyana. Their steadiness steadied

[34] Also Marie Ursule and 'young' Bola have such transcendental qualities, cf. 15, 36, 40, 266, 285.

[35] As in the title of Dionne Brand's earlier novel, *In Another Place, Not Here* (1996); in *Map to the Door* Brand also writes about this in-between-space: "There is a sense in the mind of not being here or there, of no way out or in. As if the door had set up its own reflection. Caught between the two we live in the Diaspora, in the sea in between. Imagining our ancestors stepping through these portals one senses people stepping out into nothing; one senses a surreal space, an inexplicable space. One imagines people so stunned by their circumstances, so heartbroken as to refuse reality. Our inheritance in the Diaspora is to live in this inexplicable space," *Map to the Door* 20.

[36] Cf. esp. 53-60. His yearning for this place of restfulness is later echoed in Adrian's confused straying through Amsterdam, 180.

> me, it did not matter that they were not where I was. Their definite lines brought order to my head. (231)[37]

The reconstruction of selves through identification with place is in these situations frustrated by the impediments of history. In this instance, Brand's novel differs strongly from Ondaatje's *Divisadero*, in which the reconstruction of past and biography is eventually inscribed into place and identity; thereby home becomes a choice. For Brand's protagonists' choice is limited; home and individual agency are only found in the in-between-places of the mind for which no maps can ever be drawn.

In a similar manner, the transcultural imaginary that the novel displays must be understood, to a large degree, as a forced-upon state of being and of the mind. Here, the transcultural mode is the result of displacements, it becomes more paralyzing than enabling if the positioning of the self never had a chance of being completed or was disrupted due to historical circumstance. At first sight, there seems to be no possibility to acquire agency in the overwhelming presence of a history that is endlessly echoed in the miniscule movements and thoughts of the black diaspora represented by Marie Ursule's descendants. However, all protagonists do eventually acquire – in varying degrees and forms – an ability to transcend their situation through a performance of transcultural imaginary, in terms of what Goldman calls "aesthetics and politics of drifting" (*online resource,* n.pag.). Carlyle, the cruel man called Priest by others for his ability to exert power over others, for example, survives by being able to change his personality all the time (161), while Cordelia releases herself from personal (and inevitably also the communal) history by escaping her role as a wife and transgressing the socially constructed limits of sexual desire (121-128). In several cases "drifting" takes on more of a bitter note: thus, Maya's constant state of drifting can hardly make up for her unwanted fate, just as Private Sones's self-imposed incessant pilgrimage to the *tamarindus indica* tree cannot heal the man's heart, broken by the consequences of history's rigid racializations: "'Misconduct, my ass,' he mumbles each day to the *Tamarindus indica*, since no one else will hear him. No one wants to listen again to the story and anyway all who knew it have passed away and those who remain think he is off his head" (75).

The extreme experiences of transhistorical and translocal imaginaries, such as those undergone by Marie Ursule, her daughter Bola and the Bola of the 1980s – experiences that are hard to separate from madness – on the whole, appear to be the only possible way to peace. The great paradox that limits all characters is that history, which engendered the loss of agency in the past, also opens the possibility for the recovery of agency in the present. As mentioned above, Marie Ursule and Old Bola are able to look into the future – the hope that is anticipated by Marie Ursule and strongly lived and felt by old Bola, then lost for several generations, comes to some resolution in the young Bola; the release from history is achieved by timetravel, settling, or rather drifting between boundaries of reality and imagination.[38] As Brand has noted of Bola: "'The difference we normally place – to differentiate this existence from that one, dead from alive – is not a concern to Little Bola. The boundaries are movable, they're

[37] Cp. also 52.
[38] Also cf. 278, 289, and 297.

exchangeable, they're equally symbolic, and she can move through them. This is the thing about the book,' Brand says. 'Boundaries are pliable.'" (Brand qtd. in Methot, *online resource*, n.pag.). There is no map to "drifting," to forgetting or not forgetting – to accept that is inevitable for the descendants of the slave rebel Marie Ursule.

Both the issue of individual identity (which in this case is hard to separate from communal history) and the issue of 'self' in relation to 'other' becomes even more complex as it is invariably related to postcolonial discourse; thus, Gordon Collier remarks:

> "Indeed, the token concepts of 'self' and 'alterity' (which is a smart word for 'otherness') may be set up in opposition to each other, like '*wir*' and '*das Fremde,*' but in a postmodern world which is suspicious of such binary oppositions it is surely quite possible to imagine another dialectic – a dialectic of *Rückkoppelung*, an epistemological feedback system in which the self and the other meet at, and are both mutually and reciprocally defined by, the interface of cultural contact. We discover ourselves reflected or distorted in the Other. And the Other surrenders to or struggles against our colonizing gaze; and so often, or all too often, the image of him- or herself that the Other glimpses in our eyes is not a self of the Other's own making." (Collier 225-226)

The understanding of individual identities is enforced by the other through the power structures of history. As a consequence, as Brand makes clear in this novel, if the inequalities of history stay inscribed on the self, or rather continue to be inscribed by the other, through the inequalities of the present, it becomes difficult to voice an identity that is transcultural in a positive way. Thus, though young Bola might be happy for herself in her world, her situation appears rather hopeless from the outside, and it is equally hard to say what will become of Maya's daughter, who resents her mother's "drifting" yet at the same time feels so much understanding (224-226). To fully understand Brand's open-ended take on the construction of black diasporic identities it would be counter-productive to come to a final conclusion from the reading of *At the Full and Change*; instead, a continued reflection on it in the works that followed becomes necessary.[39]

As she expresses in her memoir, the author feels her own desperation at the reality and heaviness of history that is so strongly intertwined with her fictional worlds:

> I feel like sitting there, right there beneath the statue covered in pigeon waste, I feel like sitting there and crying, I feel bereft. I feel abandoned by Marie Ursule to city squares and windows and public places where I am on display and must make my display, like exotica. I feel marooned like Kamena. Marooned now in outposts and suburbs and street corners anywhere in the world. I am adrift, spilled out, with Adrian and Maya at the end of this century in any city all over the world with nothing certain as Marie Ursule coming. We are all abandoned, all scattered in Marie Ursule's hopelessness and her skill. (211)

However, as other sections in the memoir allude, even if the protagonists of *The Full and Change,* and sometimes also Brand herself, do not really succeed in grasping their

[39] I am referring to Brand's recent novel, *What We All Long For*, in particular.

fragmented selves, as they are overwhelmed by sadness and despair, there is still hope for a transcultural imaginary that evolves through positive forces of creativity. The transcultural burden described above becomes more fluid and inspirational only two pages further:

> And it doesn't matter where in the world, this spirit is no citizen, no national, no one who is christened, no sex, this spirit is washed of all this lading, bag and baggage, jhaji bundle, georgie bindle, lock stock, knapsack, and barrel, and only holds its own weight which is nothing, which is memoryless and tough with remembrances, heavy with lightness, aching with grins. They wander as if they have no century, as if they can bound time, as if they can sit in a café in Brugge just as soon as smoke grass in Tucson, Arizona, and chew coca in the high Andes for coldness. (*Map to the Door* 213-214)

Thus the reconstructions of cultural space and individual empowerment might also be achieved through an acceptance of the creative potential of the transcultural imaginary underlying the Afro-Carribean identity – or any other identity, in any other place. The responsibility to activate one's own agency correlates with the realization of the power of contemporary imaginaries to "challenge the idea of constantly having to fix oneself as a way of finding identity," and to "[…] disturb the deeply troublesome labels that admit no complexity, no range but which come to represent us in the world" (Mavjee, *online resource*, n.pag.). Thus, in *At the Full and Change of the Moon* Brand might be regarded as initiating an act of transformation that could engender this new awareness of transcultural agency and creativity. This hope is expressed by the author in the following two passages:

> My city was a city in my imagination where someone suddenly and plainly appears as if belonging and not belonging, where someone may disappear also into nothing and everything. […]
>
> I stepped into the cool opening of the Door of No Return. My feet landed where my thoughts were. This is the trick of the door – to step through and be where you want to be. Our ancestors were bewildered because they had a sense of origins – some country, some village, some family where they belonged and from which they were rent. We, on the other hand, have no such immediate sense of belonging, only of drift. (*Map to the Door* 118)

> This dreary door which I've been thinking about, though its effects are unremitting, does not claim the human being unremittingly. All that emanates from it is not dread but also creativity. This comes to me as I am standing, listening to the music, mouthing an inane soca lyric that commands me to jump or shake. (ibid. 42)

The Poetics of Orientation: On Truths and Certainties – Madeleine Thien's *Certainty*

While Michael Ondaatje's and Dionne Brand's approaches to the transcultural elements of the imaginaries that their novels display still appear strongly influenced by the complexities of postmodern deconstructive aesthetics in the one and discourses of postcolonial identities in the other case, Madeleine Thien's reflections and fictional transcultural movements in space and time, seem to take an entirely new direction. Even though not in complete contrast to her senior writer colleagues, Thien's writing is rooted in "families and immigration" (Mudge, *online resource*, n.pag.), she tends to ask existential questions that are even more strongly disconnected from the critical 'political' debates on multiculturalism, or rewritings of (Canadian) official history but instead long for a general understanding of identities within globalized modernities. As she notes in the above quoted interview:

> What I do in my work is not what someone like Amy Tan does. I tend to leave off physical descriptions and the sense of writing from a specific ethnicity. I think I'm sort of existing between both worlds and trying to find a way to tell a story that encompasses those worlds and has a sort of give-and-take between both. [...] My sense of place is slightly different. I'm the child of immigrants without being an immigrant. (Mudge, *online resource*, n.pag.)

Inspired by the sad experience of her mother's sudden death and her own desire to overcome the pain, Madeleine Thien's mapping of spaces and identities "raise[s] all those existential questions—why are we here, what is the point, what happens afterwards?" (Mudge n.pag.) and relates this quest with an essential turn toward the "inner perspective" (J. Eckstein, *online resource*, n.pag.).[40]

Thien's novel also applies the 'art' of cartography as a metaphor for the understanding and reconstructions of memories and identities, similar to Brand's *Map to the Door*, though to a lesser extent. It tells a number of intrinsically interwoven stories and histories centered on the quests of the young protagonist Gail and her parents who immigrated to Vancouver, Canada from China and Malaysia (similar to the author's own parents).[41] The mapping of memories and the spaces and places that molded them and especially the search for truth and meaning in life are dominant themes in the novel,

[40] In this interview in German she observes: "Ich wurde gefragt, warum ich nicht explizit über Immigration schreibe. Wichtig finde ich es, meine Charaktere nicht nur von der Außenseite zu betrachten, nicht allein aus der Perspektive ihrer Vergangenheit, der Immigration. Mir geht es um die 'innere' Perspektive, wie sie ihr eigenes Leben sehen, wie ihr Leben durch die Vergangenheit, Familie, Freunde beeinflusst wurde. Jemand ist ja nicht primär Immigrant, oder Ausländer, und so weiter," Interview with Eckstein, "Auf Lesereise in Deutschland," *online resource*, n.pag.

[41] Cf. "Madeleine Thien: Author Bio," *online resource*.

which are reflected in the title, *Certainty,* and the naming of the chapters, which are sometimes supplemented by settings and dates:[42]

"Chaos" – Vancouver, Canada

"Pieces of Map" – Sandakan, British North Borneo; Sept. 1945

"A New Geometry"

"Aloft"

"A Bird Feather" – Jakarta, 1957

"The Garden of Numbers" – Vancouver, Canada

"The Island" – Ysbrechtum, The Netherlands

"Certainty" – Ysbrechtum, 1992

"The Glass Jar" – January

There are two characteristics particular of fictions of the past which stick out in Madeleine Thien's *Certainty*. First, the multi-leveled mappings that one finds in this novel are less based on the concept of 'national' identities, or ethnic and racial affiliations – nor on a deliberate desire to deconstruct them. This is implied in terms of movements across the Canadian borders to settings in other former colonial territories and histories, through identifications with specific places. These local settings are defined by the individuals' perception and emotions, and not by political boundaries or a specific location on the map. This tendency is supplemented, as already indicated above, with a turning inward, which speaks for an increasing longing for the outlines of an internal, individual map in the context of an increasingly pluralized reality. This leads to the second most prominent point in *Certainty*, that this search within, this search for meaning and understanding of existence does not reveal a mosaic of multicultural fragments alone, one next to the other, but additionally fosters an increased awareness of a partial layering and consequent polybridity of identities.

The transcultural complexity of the various narrative strands is prefigured by the fact that they are set across the world, in different periods of the twentieth century: they move between Borneo in the 1940s and Jakarta, Hong Kong as well as settings in Canada and Australia in the 1960s to Vancouver and the Netherlands of the present. These events of the past and present are positioned around the main protagonist, Gail, who is already dead at the beginning of the novel. A young, creative woman in her early

[42] Most chapters that bear no reference to time and place, focus on the fictional present or very recent past, with the exception of Chapter 4, "Aloft" that to a great extent recapitulates Gail's mother's memories of her childhood in Hong Kong of the 1950s, and later her studies in Australia and emigration to Canada with Gail's father, Matthew – though I must add that narrative movements in space and time can be found in every chapter of the novel.

forties, she died unexpectedly from a lung infection during a research trip to Prince Edward Island. In the course of the novel we are introduced to her life, which led her to places all around the globe. Doing research as a freelance radio journalist, she first travelled to Amsterdam, Prague and then other European cities during her studies and later to several destinations within Canada and again back to Europe. The transhistorical and translocal movements in the novel are intensified by two major elements, narrative as well as thematic, that come to dominate the novel: memories, on the one hand, and Gail's inquisitive projects on the other, both of which are interconnected by the persona of Gail, who triggers most of them before and after her death.

The high degree to which memory figures in *Certainty* underscores the arguments made by Birgit Neumann toward what she refers to as "fictions of memory," in which the prominence of individual remembering (as opposed to a rewriting of historical events typical of historical fictions) effects "a constant oscillation between past and present which indicates that memories are dynamic processes linking different temporal layers" (Neumann "Narrative Constructions" 193).[43] Several sections in *Certainty* are completely situated in the past, told from what appears to be an authorative perspective, such as the first part of the second chapter entitled "Pieces of Map" (Sandakan, British North Borneo, *September, 1945*), which depicts Gail's father's, Matthew's, childhood (23-46). Even within the episodes that focus only on past events and settings, the narration does not follow a chronological order but moves across temporal and spatial boundaries. In other sections, the link to the present is upheld; the fact that we are reading one of the character's memories is made clear by short references to present situations and processes. A turn to such a mode occurs in the above-mentioned chapter, which opens its second part with the words: "There are mornings when Matthew wakes and he forgets that he is old. He thinks that he is seven, perhaps ten years old, but then it is like being on a hilltop in the fog" (46); shortly afterwards the chapter moves on to describe memories which are particularly emotionally disturbing for the old man, especially the moment he wittnessed his father's murder by Japanese soldiers. Finally, in other sections, characters situated in the present jump across time moving from one memorized moment to another – here events of the present, memories of the past and future dreams substantially come to influence each other. As Ansel, Gail's partner, reflects while grieving Gail's death: "He knows it is impossible, irrational, but he is lifted away from the present, set down in a different timeline. The details of their lives, all the habitual acts, the cherished conversations, continue to accumulate, day after day, into the future" (94-95). History or actual historical events, as such, remain marginal, and if they turn up they are filtered through the limited perception of individuals. Additionally, instead of self-reflexive remarks on the writing of history or elements that deconstruct the hegemony of master narratives, we also find memory as an explicit theme within the novel. All protagonists (including Gail who is also given a voice in the novel) repeatedly think about how memories work, how they influence lives, how memories change over time, about how time itself appears to be a construct, and how our mind is under a constant strain to make sense of it all. As Gail's mother, Clara,

[43] Cf. also her publication *Erinnerung-Identität-Narration: Gattungstypologie und Funktionen kanadischer Fictions of Memory*. It was however published in German, which is why I quote articles by her on the same topic that were published in English.

contemplates: "Time, Clara believes, is the great mystery. Since Einstein, physicists have argued that time is merely a convention, that only the speed of light is constant everywhere in the universe. If one traveled fast enough, time would bend, and one person's past could theoretically become another person's future" (117-118).[44] Many of these thoughts are in fact evoked by Gail's death – both her partner and her parents think of the deceased woman incessantly and understandably find it hard to accept that she is gone. Early on in their relationship, Ansel remembers, Gail in fact worked on a report on memorials:

> Gail was sitting cross-legged on the floor. "I have all these outtakes," she told him. "These reels and reels. Just tapes of people talking, but I can't throw them away. Sometimes, people remember things they haven't thought about in years, a private memory, a story. You know that feeling when you're moving house, going through boxes, and you find something unexpected? That's what I feel is happening to them. (84-85)

Gail's occupation with radio as a medium of communication is not insignificant for the reading of this novel. People are stirred by Gail's inquisitive nature, the questions she asked her parents, and her research on various, often related topics. Her work is very prominent throughout the book, and on several occasions her family and friends continue to talk about the issues she worked on, both her partner Ansel and her mother sometimes listen to some of her recordings, only to hear her voice. At the same time, the medium becomes representative of several important aspects that underlie the novel. On the one hand, I am referring to the historical role of radios as a means for social 'interaction,' as well as a device that connected 'separated' communities (whether due to location or to the political situation) to the outside world. In this context, in which the radio represents freedom (especially for Matthew's father under the Japanese regime, during which radios were forbidden), passages that describe the social importance of radios, such as the following, remind us of Dionne Brand's descriptions of similar family rituals in Trinidad:[45]

> Around noon, she woke to the sound of voices. Someone had wheeled the neighbourhood radio out. She could hear the footsteps of children running towards the sound. When she stood up and looked through the curtains, she saw them standing pressed together, transfixed by the voice, their mouths open as if to taste the words. The dial was fixed to Radio Sabah in Jesselton. When the announcer introduced a song,

[44] This passage, as well as the general tendency in the novel towards a relative perception of time, is anticipated in the first epigraph, a quote from Albert Einstein: "For we convinced physicists the distinction between past, present, and future is only an illusion, however persistent" (n. pag.).

[45] Cf. *A Map to the Door of No Return* 13-15. Note the ironic, postcolonial tone in Brand's text in comparison to Thien's: "The news of the BBC is a door to 'over there,' it is the door to being in the big world. Your grandfather positions the radio so that the sea's spray does not rust out the wires. He twists and turns the aerial for cleaner reception. Your grandmother and grandfather silence all when the BBC is on. […] Something important is about to be said" (14).

> "Goodnight Irene," the children scuffed their bare feet in the dust, bringing up small clouds, the particles expanding as the first chords began. (160-161)[46]

For Gail, it is also a medium that allows her to come very close to the thoughts of individuals as well as a medium that captures the sounds specific to a place or situation. With her headphones on, she hears far more details than one would normally hear; recording people and their surrounding draws her attention to the small-scale details of life and memory. The layers and specificities of sounds, the different formats of contributions as well as the deep personal insight (indicated earlier) relate to the relevance of history and memory in the novel. Gail's recordings succeed in capturing the miniscule elements of moments, the feelings of individuals, and their relation to a larger context so that they become accessible and remain 'alive' for the future. The novel thereby enables a completely revised perception of the past through an interaction between imaginaries and contemporary globalizing forces represented – as well as it is called into question – by the medium of the radio.[47]

> She has fragments spliced together, dozens of conversations gathered on a single reel. Soundscapes, features, interviews. [...] For Gail, the devotion lies in more than the words spoken. It is the words spoken at a specific moment in time, in a particular place. A child singing in the background, a pause in the telling, an old woman wetting her lips, smoothing her dress. (195)

One can come to the conclusion that the topics that Gail worked on, in a way, speak for the whole novel; they bear a single message, that of a desire to understand the meaning of our present existence and of our functioning within it. Gail collected material on the history of the mind, produced a piece on tuberculosis and, before she died, was doing intensive research on a secret diary written in numbers. All these issues are linked by the observation that so many aspects of our existence, including history and personal experiences remain an uncertain terrain, hardly accessible through logical understanding. This uncertainty, especially for those traumatized by their fate and by historical circumstance, which Thien characters appear to experience, is intensified by the effects of contemporary modernities. Ani, describing her immigration from Tarakan explains this discrepant feeling vividly: "From there, she had felt the wish to be part of something greater, to lose herself in the city, and so she had continued to Jakarta. 'People come here from all over the world,' he had said," (177) – however only a few lines further she prefers to stay in the photo studio she works in, "protected for a brief while from her memories, from the chaos and uncertainty of Jakarta" (177).

By trying to understand her parents' (especially her father's often haunting) memories and the histories of other people, Gail does not try to deconstruct some dominant

[46] The section is presented from the point of view of Ani, Matthew's childhood friend and life-long love; it is set in Sandakan in approximately 1953, when Matthew returned for a while before leaving for Australia.

[47] I here regard the radio as standing for twentieth century modernity; however, by the time Gail uses this medium, thus towards the end of the twentieth century (which is also the time this passage is set in), it is already rather considered as an outdated communication medium, in comparison to the Internet.

narrative or to reconstruct all the alternatives. Gail, like other characters for instance her partner, Ansel, her parents, or the Danish photographer, Sipke Vermeulen, who married her father's childhood love, Ani, is trying to locate herself and her existence within the many-layered spaces of time and place in the present world. Gail describes this by referring again to her work as a journalist:

> In radio, in the countless scripts she has written, Gail works with the belief that histories touch. Follow the undercurrent and you will arrive at the meeting place. So she weaves together interviews, narration, music and sound in the hope that stories will not be lost in the chaos of never touching one another, never overlapping in any true way. Each element a strand, and the story itself a work of design. Out of the disparate pieces, let something pure, something true, emerge. Let it remain there, visible. (209-210)

The audio-electronic medium and Gail's studies on fundamental issues of modernity are, however, not the only way that Madeleine Thien subscribes to this perspective. Photography and the role it plays for the understanding of contemporary complexities of existence and the desire of the person using it to come closer to grasping some elements of 'truth' features prominently in *Certainty*. Sipke Vermeulen depicts himself (when he meets Gail and talks about his life) as a cosmopolitan character, especially in his youth. Talking about how he came to be a famous war photographer, he describes the desire to essentially grasp the world around him as his initial influence:

> Walking home under the street lamps, through the crowds of people, he came to believe that only in stillness, only if he were able to step outside of time, could he begin to make sense of the world.
>
> […]
>
> Later on, others told him that he had a gift; he was able to catch and distinguish the defining moment. When he was working, he had the sensation of walking into a deep tunnel, the edges of his body dissolving into the scene around him. Yet he was capable – he does not know how or why – of pulling something tangible from the deep. (229)

Sipke traveled a lot and was commissioned to capture dramatic scenes of world politics, the gruesome results of wars and conflicts; his images sold worldwide. However, for him as a person, it became more and more difficult to objectively filter meaning as he was taking more and more pictures of death, murder and suffering. "Nothing made sense, and he tried to separate himself from his emotions, focusing on the sight of his camera to dull the turmoil, the sickness" (230). Only some years later does he find peace in his relationship with Ani, who gives him something to believe in – she herself had lost both her parents during the war and insisted on forgetting the past, in order to focus on the present. Together they settle in Jakarta, where Sipke begins to work as a portrait photographer. In 1963, Sipke returns to the Netherlands, where he was born, and Ani follows him with her son shortly afterwards.

In the many personal histories that we get to know, all of which are interconnected across continents and histories and extended by the insight given by Gail's work, the truth will eventually be found in the relationships that the characters have to the people that surround them and to those they love. This truth becomes especially stinging for Ansel after Gail's death.[48] His partner's death indirectly relates Ansel to Sipke, whom Gail had tracked down and visited in Ysbrechtum half a year before her death: Sipke had suffered tremendously after Ani's death from cancer. To Gail, whom he tells the story that her father had not managed to tell her, Sipke explains during her visit the nature of his relationship to his wife – a relationship truly transcultural in nature, as it succeeds in transcending individual cultural differences and histories and in connecting similarities:

> He and Ani had moved easily between Dutch, English and Indonesian; they had many languages within their reach. When they were younger, the exchange of words, of ideas, was important. But later, less so. He believes that the human body has other means of communicating, some way that is yet to be categorized by science, or by language itself. Two people can swim in the same memories, the same dreams; that is how it had become for him and Ani. (233)

Matthew and Clara, Gail's parents, are less separated by cultural differences – they both emigrated from an Asian country, and Matthew's father had had Chinese origins. Nonetheless, they struggle to come to terms, to find a 'transcendental' meaning in their relationship due to their conflicting personal histories. The one person who keeps them together, who possibly represents their version of truth, is their daughter Gail.

Despite the fact that she is dead, Gail is situated at the center of the novel; all the threads of stories lead toward her as well as away from her and before her unexpected death she wants to uncurl each one of them. In her work, as well as in her relationship to her parents, she becomes a transcultural figure, who not only collects stories and is altered by them, but who also functions as an active agent between the cultures and histories, changing people who surround her through her in-between presence – thereby also forging her own transcultural identity. Especially telling is the relationship to her father, to whom she was a kind of anchor in the blur of past and present:

> When Matthew and his daughter walked together, along Keefer, then Pender, she used to whisper the street names under her breath. Matthew would tell her stories about his childhood before the war, about Sandakan, until he realized that she remembered so much. […]
>
> Six months ago, his daughter died suddenly in her sleep. […]
>
> Now, when he walks through this neighbourhood, he loses track of the streets. In his mind, he hears his daughter singing the names to herself, Keefer, Pender, Adanac, but his sense of direction has become confused. When he looks around, nothing he sees is familiar. He has lived here for most of his life, but if he picked up a pencil, out of the small islands of memory he could draw the streets of his childhood. (18-19)

[48] Ansel had had a short relationship with another women only a year before. He later confessed it to Gail who then consequently distanced herself from him.

Even after her death, Gail remains an anchor for her family and friends, an agentive force that enables the transgression or even elimination of potential borderlines between cultural imaginaries. Her radio documentaries help Ansel to overcome both his own grief and the hardships he faces in his job as a doctor, even though he can hardly accept the certainty of her death. During one of her visits to her daughter's grave in a Vancouver cemetery, Clara performs a Chinese ritual during which carefully folded paper objects representing valuable items are burnt as symbolic offerings to the dead, who might make use of them while traveling through the land of the dead; however, instead of objects she burns the pages of a book she read in her childhood, one of the classical Chinese novels, *Journey to the West*: "The ritual occupies her hands as she releases her mind, sets it down beside the idea of her daughter. The remembrance of her presence in the room, her heart beating quietly and in its own solitude – the physical form of the girl that she misses" (130).

As trite as it might seem on the surface, love and death are the two most dominant themes in the novel; they are, however, by no means treated as romantic issues, on the contrary, Madeleine Thien carves them out for the reader secretly, most dramatically, with fragile, barely visible contours like that of a glass figurine. The increasing skepticism toward the ever-deconstructive mode is, too, reflected in the novel, thereby pointing toward the growing yearning for and expression of a renewed shift toward meaning. Existential values of life and human relationships are accentuated by the many deaths described in the novel. There are characters who experience the loss of their family and struggle to find their way in the emptiness created by such a tragedy: there is Gail's father, who saw his own father being shot by Japanese soldiers as a child, or Sipke Vermeulen, who can only keep going after his wife's early death by decorating his house with memories in the form of photographs and, of course, Gail's family and her partner Ansel, who struggle to redefine their maps having lost the most important point of reference in their life, their daughter and partner, respectively. There are also other deaths, those of strangers, less proximate yet equally depressing for those who witness them: the death of the little boy flying a kite on a roof, whom Gail's mother as a young girl could not save from falling off the building, and the young tuberculosis patient Alistair, whose fatal infection is diagnosed by Ansel. Again, the connections woven by the author through the narrative strands that relate Gail's work in the past with her family's struggles in the present highlight a further essential set of links between existential questions that individuals face and the globalized modernities they are living in. Before meeting and examining Alistair, Ansel listens to one of Gail's documentaries:

> Sitting in his office, [Ansel] turns to the cassette player he keeps beside his desk. [...]
>
> "The history of tuberculosis, the white death, is deeply embedded in the history of the modern world." Gail's radio voice is much the same as her usual voice. Only here the pauses are more deliberate, her tone intimate. "Influenza, the Black Plague, syphilis and AIDS – these diseases, like tuberculosis, have their own personalities in much the same way that nations have historic periods. Tuberculosis rose with the Industrial Revolution, in a time of poverty and cramped living conditions [...]."

> A year after they met, Gail had begun working on this documentary. Since its completion, he has kept a copy in his office, lending it to students, colleagues or interested patients. Now, occasionally, he plays it to hear her voice, preserved and distinct, as if she is in the room there with him. (88-89)

Alistair, the tuberculosis patient, is the same age as Ansel – his case is especially dramatic for the young doctor; yet his own grief eventually helps him build up a friendly, consoling relationship to the terminally ill man and his only remaining relative, his sister. Again, the drama and pain of reality can only be resolved through the embrace of inter-human communication and relationships.

Each entangled in their stories and memories, the protagonists try to draw maps of their existence, to break the 'secret' code in order to reveal the hidden, true meaning. This theme is not only represented in Gail's attempts to find answers through her work on radio documentaries and Sipke through his photography, it also appears in the recurrent metaphor of the deciphering of codes and mathematical problems, which often remain mysterious and inaccessible. Cryptography and the decoding of a secret diary play an essential role in Gail's last documentary about the Japanese war prisoner, William Sullivan, who composed the encrypted diary. Shortly before her unexpected death, she visits her friend Harry Jaarsma in Amsterdam, who finally succeeded in breaking the code of the diary; however, her documentary is never completed. It is Harry who observes, "I think codebreaking is part of a very human desire, the desire for revelation, for meaning" (205). What is central to this subplot is the repeated observation of the relativity of the concepts that we create, and especially the necessity to question the equally constructed boundaries that accompany them. Harry Jaarsma, philosophizing on the Mandelbrot Set[49], a complex graphic object of a simple quadratic equation, elucidates:

> "Do you know how birds fly in formation? As far as we know, they hold no picture in their minds of the V formation, let alone the vast pattern of migration. They are aware only of the other birds in their immediate proximity. And the same is true for me; I respond to what is immediately around me. But the pattern that I cannot see, that I have no knowledge of, exists. [...] We glimpse a part of the puzzle and intimate, however vaguely, an answer. But if we read a book about geography, or the history of the Earth, or the universe, for that matter, how does that change the way I place myself within this formation?"
>
> She gazes at the boundary, the intricate details. "It changes nothing and everything."

[49] The Mandelbrot Set is indeed a fascinating mathematical phenomenon; one need not be a mathematician to understand or feel the mysterious, fascinating pull that the images, which the equation produces, exert. As Harry Jaarsma explains to Gail: " The Mandelbrot Set,' Jaarsma says, running his fingertips over one of the prints. 'A collection of points derived from the quadratic equation $z = z^2 + c$. The equation itself is very simple, but the Mandelbrot Set is one of the most complex objects in mathematics. See this boundary here,' he says, indicating a shape enclosed by a band of colour. 'Any part of this edge, this carotid, no matter where, no matter how small, will, if magnified, reveal new points. And these, if further magnified, will also reveal new points, *ad infinitum*'" (218). To see examples of such images Cf. Burbanks, "The Mandelbrot Set" *online resource*, n.pag.

> Jaarsma smiles, delighted. "Precisely." (219)

Once more, as this passage indicates, the protagonists can only find the solution to the riddle of life by defining their position in relation to and relationship with other humans[50] and by holding on to fixed points of reference, which they discover in their belief and in their reliance on emotional ties that cannot be mapped by human understanding: "Knowing another is a kind of belief, an act of faith" (273), as one of the protagonists observes. In her interviews, Thien confirms this when she refers to *Certainty* as "a very optimistic book because, while in the end there are many things the characters don't know about each other, they do know things that transcend the particularities of their experiences and connect them despite the unknowns" (Mudge, *online resource*, n.pag.).

Eventually, sorrow and pain transcend all realities of time and space, eliminating given cultural and social boundaries, and the individuals are left with nothing but the faith in the possibility of "certainty." Thus, as Gail's father recapitulates: "So many things [...] that we carry all our lives, in the hope that we know will finally redeem us, that we will find something that abides, even now, in the indefinite, the uncertain, hereafter" (306). However, it is precisely this hope, this belief in that which remains even after loss that might console and relieve the state of uncertainty: "Now, [Ansel] feels the same vertigo, a sense that he is falling. He gets to his feet, imagining her near. Love, this heaviness, this weight, holds him steady" (303).

Of the three fictions of the past discussed in this chapter, Madeleine Thien's *Certainty* is the one in which the expression of transcultural imaginaries is accomplished in the most explicit degree on several levels of the novel. The dissolution of temporal and spatial boundaries, strongly present in the settings and narrative strategies of the novel, is extended to the development of the characters' identities, which strongly rely on the personal histories and memories of either their own lives, of family members, or those of others. The construction of an individual space in which the complex, or often not so complex but simply hurtful, unavoidable events of life acquire meaning can only be achieved through the unremitting belief in the other. Even if art forms and media featured in *Certainty* carry the potential to re-adjust attention to the miniscule moments of truth or sounds of life, a re-creative empowerment is always only enacted by the interaction and communication between and the admitted interdependence of humans. Thien most formidably displays how the basic nature of transcultural imaginaries, which require communication, exchange, and the transgression of the boundaries of time, space, cultures, and histories, often affects, rather than dissolves, uncertainty. At the same time these imaginaries open up possibilities for a solution to this very uncertainty through mutual understanding and the sharing of similarities instead of differences.

> The boundary encloses a finite area, but the boundary itself is infinite. No matter how much we increase the magnification, the same shapes appear and reappear in the border,

[50] It seems no coincidence that the key phrase that William Sullivan used to encode his diary was composed of the names of his family, cf. 193.

though never quite the same. The image reveals a kind of symmetry, not left and right, but of large scales and small ones.

"Imagine that we are standing here," he says. Unexpectedly, he takes her hand, ever so gently, and places it on a corner of the print. "I can imagine what the rest of the picture is like because this is a fractual image, and it is self-similar. It repeats. But to imagine the entire picture is akin to standing on a street corner and trying to imagine what England looks like from an airplane or from Mars. I can extrapolate, but what I see at this level may not conform to my expectations of what it will look like as we move in space and time. (218-219)

7 Canadian Polybridity and the Reinvention of Pastness

The popularity of migrant literature, which radically increased from the 1980s onward, has had a substantial impact on the Canadian literary landscape. Migrant authors have contributed to the gradual establishment of a diversified and far more representative literary canon that has, to a large degree, overcome outdated power-relations. Today, the divergent voices of migrant writers stand for a multicultural Canadian nation, where a large percentage of people live who have migrant backgrounds, which they have experienced either directly or indirectly. The following literary analysis demonstrates that the transcultural imaginaries, so diversely interpreted in the fictions of the past by migrant writers, have substantially influenced the writing of 'non-migrant' authors (or those less affected by migration) too. Parallel to this influence, the works discussed in this section also bear features that point toward the general impact of predominant critical theories, but even more so, of present day global modernities – as one of the main arguments of this study claims. Which of these developments was more influential in the writing of the authors discussed here, or which formed which detail, when, and to what degree, does not essentially have an effect on our reading of these texts. However, what must be recognized is the fact that the discussed works can be regarded as transcultural fictions of the past.

Here we arrive at the center of an issue that still partially appears to represent a hurdle within contemporary literary criticism. Most studies working with concepts of the transcultural, or those which apply it as a label for specific texts, continue to relate it mostly to the works of hyphenated, marginalized, or – in a postcolonial sense – 'othered' authors, also outside the context of Canadian literature; most surprisingly, they do so despite their awareness of the paradox that is inherent to the classification of literary works in – to use the popular simplifying terms – 'minority' or ethnic versus 'majority' or non-ethnic writing. The contribution of Andrea Lutz in the overall remarkable, recent collection of studies *New Literatures Across the Globe,* provides an example of this misunderstanding. Here, the recent developments in Canadian literature since the 1960s, are grouped – surprisingly unconventionally – into "four major trends: regionalism, postmodernism in literature and literary criticism, aboriginal literature, and multi- or transcultural literature" (Lutz 311-312). The last trend, as Lutz suggests, might be subdivided "along the lines of ethnic origin" (313). Lutz is well aware of the problems that this subdivision involves, and also acknowledges that

> [i]n view of these issues, it is therefore essential for the reader to recognize that Canadian transcultural literature is as varied as the individual literary texts and possible positions in the literary and political debate, the individual experiences, the imaginative scope and aesthetic interests of their authors; and that dialogue with these texts requires the reader also to reflect on and examine his or her own position. (315)

The problem here is – and this is the overall point I would like to make – that even if the nature of transcultural imaginaries and the questions it relates to are precisely captured in Lutz's exemplary critical excerpt, the perspective on transcultural writing still remains a limited one, which does not necessarily include "mainstream and majority" texts (Lutz 315).[1]

The selection and grouping of texts in this study (in migrant and non-migrant authors – and later Native texts) show how categories such as 'mainstream' or 'ethnic/non-ethnic' might be questioned and successfully deconstructed in favor of a more encompassing vision of transcultural literature. This becomes obvious when we compare the texts included in Chapter 6 and 7: Michael Ondaatje, for example, is conventionally regarded as a mainstream Canadian author, despite his migrant background, while George Elliott Clarke is often classified as African-Canadian, although his ancestors immigrated to Canada in the early nineteenth century.[2]

The authors presented on the subsequent pages, as explained in the introduction to these case studies, are Canadian writers who are more strongly (or sometimes completely) detached from the immigrant experience. Thus, Jane Urquhart, who is the first to be discussed, was born in Ontario – a region that she has used as setting in close to all of her work. However, her family's past has also inspired the writer to fictionalize Canadian immigrant experiences and histories outside Canada. George Elliott Clarke, too, in his writing considers himself a representative of a specific Canadian region and history; born in Nova Scotia in 1960 he refers to himself as an 'Africadian' – "a term he coined to describe the descendants of black United Empire Loyalists who came to the Maritime provinces in the late 18th century" ("Clarke, George Elliott," *online resource*, n.pag.). Guy Vanderhaeghe, who studied history and worked as a historian before becoming a writer, was born in a mining town in Saskatchewan. Of the three writers considered here, he is the one whose family heritage neither features in his writing nor is it mentioned in interviews. His fictionalizations of history and his interpretations of the North American settlement past are, however, not only highly successful but also – as the analysis will show – intricately transcultural.

As writers, Urquhart, Clarke and Vanderhaeghe find themselves less caught in the hybrid identitary interspaces of transnational migrations. Apart from that (or probably in most instances in relation to this) their texts often focus more strongly on the Canadian or North American histories and settings. This does not mean that some sections of their texts might not include or refer to settings in Europe or elsewhere – in terms of the final workings of the texts the main attention, however, remains within the realm of North American histories. However, concerning the features of fictions of the past as well as those of transcultural imaginaries, the following studies nonetheless reveal ample controversial insight.

[1] Cp. Lutz 323-324.
[2] Cp. "Author's Note to the U.S. Edition" in *George and Rue*, v-vi.

The Recreation of Artists, Ancestors and Her/stories – Jane Urquhart's *A Map of Glass*

Already in her early fictions such as *The Whirlpool* (1986), *Storm Glass* (short stories, 1987), and *Changing Heaven* (1990), Jane Urquhart began to concern herself with regional histories, and family histories that are passed on as oral tales, and the psychological depths underlying processes of remembering, forgetting, and feelings of belonging.[3] This interest was inspired by her own family, as she remarks: "The past is important to my life and therefore, I suppose, important to my fiction. I come from a multi-generational family that pays a lot of attention to generations that have preceded them. Long stories are told concerning people who have been dead for years, mementos are kept" (Wyile, "Confessions" 80). All of her novels, but particularly her more recent ones, including *Away* (1993), *The Underpainter* (1997), *The Stone Carvers* (2001) and the here-discussed *A Map of Glass* (2005), display features of fictions of the past and also point toward an awareness of transcultural imaginaries in varying degrees and forms.[4] "It is kind of astonishing the number of visual images we store in our minds without even trying. They're just sort of there" (O'Shea Bonner 89), she explains describing the importance of landscapes, places, and histories in relation to her writing.

In *A Map of Glass*, Urquhart presents an extended vision of the past that she masterly reimagined in her previous works: in her story, which centers on local Ontario history, she prominently includes a perspective given from the present. The novel is set in Toronto and rural southeastern Ontario. Sylvia, the main protagonist, is a middle-aged woman, who suffers from an unidentified sociopathic disorder.[5] She escapes from the Ontario countryside and her paternalistic, parochial husband to Toronto, where she looks for the young artist Jerome, who found the corpse of her lover Andrew Woodman, who had gone missing over a year earlier. Eventually, the two meet and both succeed in overcoming their haunting memories through their prolonged and increasingly intimate conversations. The story set in the present is interacts with the middle section which represents a historical account and family history written by Sylvia's dead lover: Sylvia

[3] Characters and locations in *The Whirlpool* were based on a notebook belonging to her husband, Tony Urquhart's grandmother. There is a character based on the Confederation poet Archibald Lampman and others relate to several historical figures of the area around Niagara (cf. Wyile, "Confessions of a Historical Geographer" 80-82; Canton, "Ghosts in the Landscape" 195), while *Changing Heaven* interpreted the history of the region in which Emily Bronte lived, and integrated a character (Arianna Ether) which was inspired by a tombstone that Urquhart had come across in the region (cf. Canton 194-199).

[4] *Away* is set in Ireland and Eastern Ontario telling the story of Irish immigrants, *The Underpainter* and *The Stone Carvers* are also set in various regions in Ontario and in France, both focusing on World War I experiences, and the latter especially on that of German immigrants. (cf., for example, Wylie, "Confessions of a Historical Geographer," and O'Shea Bonner, "Finding Your Place in the Story").

[5] The description of Sylvia's disorder remains vague throughout the novel; reviewers have related the mysterious "condition" to autism (Schiefer, Sugars) and Asperger's syndrom (O'Grady).

will give this section, which is referred to in the other parts as a collection of notebooks, to Jerome to read; it also plays an important role in the psychological recovery of the two protagonists. Through these transhistorical narrative constellations Urquhart juxtaposes younger, open-minded urban people who feel adrift in a world of mediated perception and fast living and forgetting, with a slightly older generation that struggles to overcome outdated conceptions of identity. As it moves across several temporal spheres of local history and includes a diversity of characters, transcultural figures, and discourses, the novel presents a striking example of the genre of historical fiction in its contemporary form as 'fiction of the past.'

The central interest of this novel – which is at the same time the factor that also allows us to read it as a fiction that displays transcultural imaginaries – is the renegotiation of identities via the past, the struggle to define the present self, and the potential that is found in (trans)cultural dialogue between individuals to deconstruct preconceived, established notions of belonging and existence. The two main protagonists, Sylvia and Jerome, are important for this observation: they not only establish the inherent symmetry in the novel; they are also the initial and concluding points of development and of histories; their dialogue allows them to depart from old and arrive at new complex spaces of identification. As central characters, the two stand in complete opposition at the beginning of the novel, their identities are dichotomous in terms of the cultural spaces of age, gender, locality and landscapes, and their social roles.[6] Yet in the course of the novel they move across conflicting spaces of difference and time in order to come to terms with their present realities.

One of the most obvious oppositions, which is also gradually deconstructed, can be observed in that of the "bounded localities" of rural and urban space (Kalogeras et al. xiii). Sylvia is from rural Ontario, a place represented in her early life by the house, which she hardly left during the greater part of her life. Sylvia only comes to transgress the boundaries set for her and to explore the diverse landscapes of the county when she gets to know her lover, the landscape historian, Andrew, who later develops Alzheimer disease and ultimately dies because of it. The chaotic urban space, the city of Toronto, contrasts the 'controllable spaces' in which Sylvia lives; there the conceptual artist Jerome lives in a basement apartment with his girlfriend of South East Asian descent, Mira:

> "I've lived," [Sylvia] said, "all my life in the same house. And my father's people lived there before me." […]
>
> Jerome looked at her with interest. "Really?" he said. "Then you are settled," he continued, "a settler." He looked at the girl beside him. "We haven't lived together two years yet, and we've moved three times."

[6] The last aspect refers to both Jerome's active role in and intellectual contribution to society as an artist, in opposition to Sylvia's limited perspectives and confined spaces of life due to her 'illness.'

> Sylvia could not imagine these moves, this drifting from one place to another. What she wondered, had they been leaving behind?
>
> "It's very hard," Mira said. "Very hard to find good studio space." She waved one arm in the direction of the red door Sylvia had noticed earlier. "This was just luck, really, that and word of mouth. When you hear about something you have to act fast."
>
> The sound of a siren pierced the room and Sylvia found herself becoming conscious of the vastness of the city, of people talking – *word of mouth* – of plans being made and carried out, of accidents taking place, of events unfolding while she sat in a white room with two young people she had never met before. Finding it cruel in its arbitrariness and impossible for her to control, the multiplicity of places and relationships connected to other people's lives was something she tried to avoid thinking about. (*Map of Glass* 48-49)

The rural landscape, in opposition to the urban, is also more obviously connected to the past, to Canada's settlement history, rendered in the novel in the middle part through a story that – though connected to Sylvia through Andrew – spins an independent narrative. It recounts the life of the owner of a timber business, the Irishman Joseph Woodman (Andrew's great-great-grandfather), situated on an island in Lake Ontario, and the life of his two children, Branwell and Annabelle, who were Andrew's ancestors. It is a sweeping narrative about art (Branwell becomes a mural painter and his sister Annabelle, too, likes to paint), love (he falls in love with the French-Canadian orphan Marie), landscapes (we are presented a haunting vision of Ontario during and after the settlement period) and decay (eventually Marie and Branwell's son, Maurice, causes the downfall of the family through his greed). In Urquhart's vision of Andrew's reimagined family histories, English and Irish traders live side-by-side with French 'coureur du bois.' As already indicated, this middle section represents not only the stories that Andrew told Sylvia in the course of their relationship but also the contents of the notebooks, the result of his intensive research, which he gave to Sylvia to take care of.[7] Even though the depiction of the past in this central part of the novel appears in many ways stereotypical and romanticized[8], we must not forget that this story within fictionalizes Andrew Woodman's notes and subjective re-creation of his family's history as well as – though this is not specifically stated, we must consider the possibility – Sylvia, Jerome, and Mira's, Jerome's girlfriend's, interpretations. The interaction of the three parts is considerable especially as the first and third sections constantly refer to (memories of) stories told in the second. The expression and rewriting of local history must essentially be seen in relation to its perception in the present: the struggles of the characters depicted in Andrew's journals, their positioning

[7] It is interesting to note that again a protagonist who recently died and the work that dominated his life occupies a central role in the narration, reminding us of Gail in Thien's *Certainty*.

[8] Interestingly, most reviews that appeared after the publication of the novel criticized the narration set in the present as being implausible, and rather praised the middle section. Cf. Sugars, "The Hands of Chance and Change," and Christian House, "A Map of Glass by Jane Urquhart," both *online resources*, n.pag.

within a local history of settlement that faced existential problems of survival, helps its readers (Sylvia, Jerome, Mira) to define their own position and locate their selves, to filter substantial values from the complex labyrinth of globalized, cosmopolitan identities, which depend far more – as Jerome will come to realizes – on a person's initiative than on circumstance. It is Andrew's study of landscapes and histories, and the story of his family's past that initially not only brings them together and later continues to connect Sylvia and him, but also dominates the conversations and friendship between Jerome and Sylvia in the present.

The same rural landscape depicted in Andrew's 'histories,' plays an important role in the present for the cosmopolitan artist, Jerome - the mentioned island was adapted as artists' retreat, and this is where he goes to spend a few weeks alone, away from the bustling lights of Toronto, in order to work on a new project. It is also there that he finds Andrew's body, who had lost his way and frozen to death. The dichotomous structures of the local and rural versus cosmopolitan and urban spaces are tightly knit in *A Map of Glass*, with individual human remembering as well as collective narratives of the past – all point toward the (de)constructions of difference within these fictions of the past as essential building blocks of identities. Next to the opposition of rural and urban space, however, Jane Urquhart's novel displays a number of other dichotomies, of other binary constructions of difference, in various identity-defining spheres. These are not only related to the past and also linked between each other, they are also continuously deconstructed and redefined in the course of the protagonists' dialogues and relational development:

> Outside was the constant hum of the city, the unknown world. Inside the young man shifted his position now and then on the old couch, leaning forward, or nodding to indicate that he was listening. Sylvia found herself speaking slowly and carefully, as if rehearsing a speech she had memorized.
>
> "The day that you found Andrew you became the present, the end of the story, the end of my story, the reply to the last unanswered question," she told him. "And you were the end of Andrew's story as well. You were, in a way, the last thing he told me. Toward the end, one of the very last things he said aloud was something about a hook of the past sewing us together. (74-75)

As we only come to understand as the novel proceeds, in the course of the conversations between Jerome and Sylvia, the initial boundaries of temporal and cultural spaces eventually break away as the cycle of history, memory, and narration is momentarily completed. It is this cycle that also comes to reveal the difficult position occupied by Sylvia as a woman, a position complexified and restrained by the rural surroundings she grew up in, described earlier, and by her personality disorder.

As a child Sylvia grows up completely imprisoned and isolated due to her mysterious illness. Nevertheless, Sylvia herself takes several steps toward the deconstruction of her constricted identity, the first by establishing a secret relationship with the landscape historian Andrew. On the one hand he drives around with her in the countryside and shows her places he is studying, thereby liberating her spatially. On the other he also tells her the history of the places which are strongly linked to his personal family history, thus introducing her to a new space, one that allows for a dialogue with the past. Their relationship liberates her sexually, emotionally and spatially from her husband:

> "What was it," asked Jerome, "what was it you were grateful for?"
>
> "I don't think I'd ever really felt anything before ... before him." Sylvia said. "And then there were the stories he told about his family, his ancestors." She leaned over and reached into the bag at her feet, running her fingers for a moment over the smooth leather of one of the journals. "They were like a gift, really these stories, a gift from him to me." (136)

Some time after Andrew's disappearance and assumed death, Sylvia reads about Jerome's discovery of the corpse and finally decides to take another step, which ultimately leads to the final deconstruction of her restrained identity. She runs away from her husband and travels to Toronto all by herself where she wants to meet this artist, with whom she shares a connection through the death of her former lover: "I am now in the world," she whispers to herself at her arrival in the city (41). In an opposing direction, Jerome basically feels very much at home in the city and only decides to go to the countryside because he is suffering from a creative blockage. Even though he is fascinated by the multitude of transcultural inspirations that the urban space offers, for him, as it turns out, it is the rural space that will have liberating effects, for his art and also for himself; however, only after he gets to know Sylvia:

> He was still reluctant to develop the films from his time at the island – as if he believed the dead man he had found might appear in the wavering images that swam into focus in the darkroom […] Long walks through the streets and alleyways of his neighbourhood had yielded only a new admiration for the miniature front gardens of the Italian and Portuguese immigrants who had settled in this part of the city, […] He had photographed the gardens in the lushness of late summer, and then again during their decline in the fall, and had thought that he might somehow reproduce them – or at least the idea of them – in shadow boxes, but nothing tangible had come from any of this. It put him in mind of his father […]. (61)

The actual de- and subsequent re-construction of identities, is only achieved when the two characters meet. In long conversations, the strange, middle-aged woman Sylvia and the young, cynical artist Jerome talk first hesitantly and, as they gradually become more self-assured, they exchange memories and stories. It is in this complex process of re-telling the diverse discourses of the past and the crossing of multiple space- and timeframes that the two succeed in leveling binaries and re-creating their identities. Thus, the historical space not only evokes a commonplace of understanding for the two protagonists, their dialogues about the past initiate a positioning in the present, which subsequently also generates a transcultural opening. For Sylvia the urban space becomes a space of freedom and liberation from her memories as well as from patriarchal structures, despite the fact that she decides to return to her husband in the end. Jerome – through Sylvia's narrations and the reading of Andrew's family history –

is rid of his own haunting childhood memories and also of negative emotional and patriarchal structures rooted in his childhood and in the bad relationship to his father, an alcoholic, who died tragically during a quarrel. Toward the end of the novel, he finally begins to open up, a reaction, which is triggered by Sylvia's (and Andrew's) stories.

> "Stability was what I always wanted," said Sylvia, "More than you know."
>
> "Perhaps. But you … you lost someone. And I'm worried." He cleared his throat. "I worry about that." He paused. "About you."
>
> "Oh, don't," said Sylvia quietly. "You're so young. And all of this … it's well …" For the first time it occurred to her that she might have troubled this young man. "You'll forget this," she said.
>
> "No. No, I won't." Jerome looked solemn for a moment, then glanced at Sylvia and smiled. "I won't want to forget. Not the story. Not the things we've talked about." He moved over to the couch and slowly sat down. "And the truth is, I want to know, I guess I always wanted to know what happened to him. And now I want to know about you." (327)[9]

The movement between cultural differences and the transgression of binaries is also evident on another level of the novel. The aspect of change and transformation that is inherent in the concept of the transcultural is not only strongly expressed through the medium of time, through longer and shorter movements between pasts and presents.[10] It is also reflected on a thematic level through the metaphor of change that repeatedly emerges: both Andrew and Jerome are depicted as being obsessed with the impact of time on objects and on landscapes.[11] While Andrew was committed to the investigation of settlement history and the signs and traces left behind on landscapes, Jerome relentlessly attempts to capture change and the effects of time passing in his art. At one point, Jerome tells Sylvia about a train ride that inspired his interest in changing landscapes:

> When the tracks had swung away from the highway, Jerome had become aware of the fencelines of the fields that were passing, one after the other, by the train window. It seemed to him that these frayed demarcations made up of rotting cedar rails, fieldstones, rusting wire, and scrub bush were the only delineating features in an

[9] Incidentally, this passage also refers to the transgression of another, far too often ignored marker of difference, that of *age*.

[10] Cp. also Sugars, "The Hands of Chance and Change."

[11] Several reviewers of *A Map of Glass* strongly criticized the too overt emphasis on this theme; as Carry O'Grady, for example, puts it, "[a] ludicrously portentous paragraph kicks off: "And so, time, it seems, will always apply its patina to human effort," and ends: "Each decade insists on its own particular changes." In fact nearly every act performed by the characters furthers the development of this theme, whether it's baking a cake (sand in the icing!) or washing one's hair (the water looks like tears!). You rather wish these poor people, so heavily burdened with import, could take an evening off and watch a nice drama on the CBC," "Sweeping All Before" *online resource*, n.pag.

> otherwise neutered landscape. [...] He had reached for his sketchbook, had drawn a series of overlapping lines on three or four pages, had made some notes about how these lines might be transformed into a three-dimensional installation within the confines of a rectangular room [...]
>
> He quickly became obsessed by the ruined fences, and a few weeks later he had borrowed a car, driven out of the city, and begun to search out remnants of rails, boulders, and stumps [...] He began to think of fences as situations rather than structures. Like an act of God or a political uprising, they seemed to him to mark the boundaries of events rather than territories. (16-17)

Jerome's perception of the landscape and the rotting "fencelines" and his transformation of his view into a three-dimensional installation illustrates an imaginary that accepts borders "as situations rather than structures," that realizes space in terms of "events rather than territories," and is intrigued by the dynamic potential for change. The notion of change is also prominent in the stories of Branwell, Annabell and Marie. Here, however, progress and decay are depicted as primarily deconstructive forces: their father's timber industry, for example, has to eventually close down as new industries emerge, and Branwell's paintings in the tavern are painted over and forgotten after some time. As the final paragraphs of the second part dramatically exemplify:

> Eventually, parts of the inn would be leased to spinster sisters trying to make a living by serving home-cooked meals to motorists on what was now a paved highway between Guelph and Goderich. A cairn would be erected nearby to mark and memorialize the blazing of the Huron Trail, now more than hundred years old. Halfway through the twentieth century, the provincial government would decide to widen the highway and would expropriate much of the front yard. [...]
>
> With each change of ownership – and sometimes even without change of ownership – a new layer of patterned wall-paper would be slapped over both the mural of the Niagara Fall in the upper room on the brookside and the mountain scene across the hall. Finally the fractured wall paintings would be covered by no fewer that ten layers of paper flowers and paste and the landscapes would be forgotten altogether. (292-293)

Sylvia stands in contrast to these perspectives on change. She is initially imprisoned by her own desire for order and an obsession with consistency and stagnancy. Eventually she comes to understand that she can only change her situation by accepting changes in her surroundings and by taking over agency, for example, by writing down her own version of the last part of Andrew's notebooks. The following passage articulates this liberation, which she finally achieves in the urban environment:

> No one paid any attention to her, and she knew then that the city had opened its indifferent arms to her, that she could move or stand entirely still, respond, or refrain from responding, and a strange calmness came over her. The feeling was not foreign, not new to her, but here in the city she did not recognize it for the contentment that it was. It was not happiness; she had experienced that particular exhausting state of alert only three or four times, always in the company of Andrew. Now in the midst of the kind of constantly altering stimuli she had believed she could never incorporate into her

> life she knew only something she had always known: that this kind of tranquility could never be brought to her in the hands of others. (149)

The development of reformed identities and the transgression of cultural boundaries that evolves during Jerome and Sylvia's conversations is substantially aided by the presence of Mira. Portrayed as a devoted, friendly, open-minded, and curious person, Mira can be interpreted as representing a mediator figure in *A Map of Glass*. Not only does she display a diversity of cultural mindscapes, being equally concerned with her own South-East Asian heritage and Jerome's European roots as well as the prevalent religions, which in fact are a greater concern to her than they are to him:

> "The lion," Mira said suddenly. "Saint Jerome in the wild with his lion."
>
> Along with a tiny plaster figure of Krishna, Mira had tucked into his pack a small poster of Joachim Patinir's sixteenth-century *Saint Jerome in the Wilderness*, an image she always insisted Jerome take with him when he disappeared into what she called "the wild," which, to her mind, was located anywhere beyond the city limits. Brought up as a Hindu, she was fascinated by the Christian saints and their stories were, for her, as distant and compellingly exotic as the various Hindu gods and warriors were to him. When they began to get to know each other, she had been delighted to discover that his mother and father had given him the name of a famous saint, though he assured her that religion would have been the last thing on his parents' mind. (25)

Mira also has an impact on those surrounding her, changing them as she mediates between the binaries that initially separate Andrew and Sylvia, and pushes them towards the dialogue that eventually changes both of them. She is the missing link that breaks the solitudes in an actual and in a metaphoric Canadian sense. After their final encounter, and with the help of Mira, the story culminates in an ultimate resolution of memories or, in this specific case, personal history appropriated into her-story, through which an affirmative reconstruction of identities is achieved. This resolution finds its expression in Sylvia's imagining and writing down of the final part of Andrew's story, Mira's reading it out loud and Jerome's listening to it. Initially Jerome does not understand why Sylvia decides to return to her life as a well-guarded wife and hesitates to let her go, the woman who reminds him so much of his own mother who had suffered under his father's tyranny and alcoholism. However, after hearing her version of the 'story's' ending, Jerome comes to understand this newly achieved freedom of imagination. He allows for his own memories to resurface and reconciles himself with his present identity:

> Jerome remained silent while Mira folded up the papers and placed them on the arm of the couch. He was trying to remember the last time he had been read to, who had done the reading. It would have been during his childhood, but the feeling associated with the faint memory was good, warm. There had been an encircling arm, so it would have been early on – his early childhood. Sometimes there had been stories, he suddenly knew, sometimes poetry.

> "God," said Mira. "How sad, how terribly, terribly sad. Do you think we'll ever see her again?"
>
> [...]
>
> "Wait," he said, not looking at her, then slowly turning his eyes wide. "I think it was him."
>
> Mira was searching his face.
>
> "I think it was him." He closed his eyes, then opened them again and grabbed Mira's arm. "It was my father," he said with amazement, the shock of something resembling pain, or perhaps joy, making it necessary for him to have to steady himself. "He read to me," he said with wonder in his voice. "It was my father who read to me." (369-370)

The narration and communication of histories becomes a creative space, a space of agency – whether this agency allows for a person to question and overcome her own cultural preconceptions, thereby loosening rigid social boundaries and roles, or in an opposite direction, enables individuals to rethink their position in relation to others, and in this process stabilizing formerly inexplicable, random, 'too' fluid identifications. We may thus observe that what is at stake here is not (or not predominantly) a desire to reveal the constructed nature of historical discourses, but the protagonists' gradual ability to activate it as a creative space and use it for present situations.

Not all critics who reviewed Urquhart's novel, were all that pleased with the complex juxtapositions and the symbolic de- and re-constructions analyzed in this chapter – even though all unanimously agreed on the author's poetic skills. As one reviewer commented, "[a]lthough Urquhart writes well, her novels are often overwritten. Lush imagery can be cloying and unlikely circumstance irksome. Some events in the novel's convoluted plot seem contrived, the characters symbols, stand-ins for ideas rather than people who bind the reader to the story" (Schiefer, *online resource*, n.pag.), while another added "[it] turns out to be an extraordinarily, implausibly symbolic tale. Urquhart has knitted up these interlinked stories so tightly that none has room to breathe. Everything is freighted with meaning, from the rafts carrying the timber to market to the family hotel that is gradually submerged in drifting sand, a legacy of mismanagement and greed" (O'Grady, *online resource*, n.pag.). Even though the criticism might be applicable to some parts of the novel, Urquhart's contribution to a reformed understanding of cultural translation between different modes of life, between histories and imaginaries remains significant.[12]

In Urquhart's *A Map of Glass* de- and reconstruction of identities are effected by the juxtaposition and mutual influence of differing cultural imaginaries and spaces. This is reflected in the depiction and interaction of various narrative perspectives, and the transhistorical relation of a narration set in the present with a further internal story situated in the past. Through the dialogue of past and present, between young

[12] One might also note, to give a final example, Sylvia's intimate friendship with the blind woman, Julie, for whom she creates tactile maps.

cosmopolitan man and middle-aged woman from the countryside, the 'self' is re-positioned in relation to the 'other' and initial dichotomies are eased or even merge. History functions as a part of the cultural imaginary, as potential transcultural force that initiates transgression and relativization of former definatory boundaries. The communication between individuals, which is in this case mainly processed on transhistorical and transcultural levels, allows them to acknowledge and activate new understandings of identity and truth.

Tracing the Lyrics of the Unvoiced – George Elliott Clarke's *George And Rue* and *Trudeau: Long March And Shining Path*

If one scans critical essays and studies on writing 'black' in Canada, there appear to be two major features that all literary theorists agree on: the one, that the identitary space from which these authors write is highly heterogeneous, continuously contested from outside *and* within (in contrast to the U.S., where "blackness" is conveyed and accepted as a more unified discourse[13]); and, the other, that this multiplicity of voices[14] allows for new forms of understanding and dealing with cultural categories – race, obviously being the most acute one but also others.[15] As Clarke comments with reference to this multi-levelled Black space, "the 'New Provinces' that I have in mind are those being created by *les écrivains de couleur*, those insisting upon new, more inclusive definitions of Canadianness" (Clarke, "Introduction" xxiii).

In an earlier chapter, we already encountered one voice of black Canada, Dionne Brand, whose reflections and fictions of the past reveal several traces of transcultural imaginaries from the perspective of the contemporary black diaspora. By portraying the haunting presence and presentness of the history and narrative of slavery for contemporary black identities in Canada, and across the world, she conveys the necessity to rethink one-dimensional labels of color and belonging in order to acquire new forms of agency. The world of George Elliott Clarke reveals again different aspects of Canadian contemporary identities, however equally sparked by a transcultural imaginary. Born and raised in the North end of Halifax, his demarcations of home, identity, and belonging might appear considerably clearer, though they are in no way less complex than that of Brand's conflicting, hybrid notions of self. G.E. Clarke has

[13] Cf. Clarke, *Eyeing the North Star*, "Introduction," xv-xvv. As Clarke repeatedly emphasizes, the openness and flexibility of identifications in Canada allow for more hybrid, alternative definitions of self, however at the same time they make it more difficult to argue in terms of race (for example, in cases of racial discrimination) and to 'organize' Blacks as a coherent community, with which one might identify. See especially Compton and McNeilly, "The Crime of Poetry."

[14] Clarke in fact, to give one example, not only underlines the "palette of discourses" ("Introduction" xviii) but also differentiates between what he calls "aboriginal (descendants of early settlers)" vs. "naturalized (immigrant)" African-Canadian writers, xxii.

[15] Cf. Clarke, "Introduction"; Cuder-Dominguez, "African Canadian Writing and the Narration(s) of Slavery"; and especially Chiandry, "'Canada in Us Now': Locating the Criticism of Black Canadian Writing," which argues that a special (possibly transcultural) potential is to be found in criticism of black Canadian writing and discourses of race.

made it his duty to create an awareness for African-Canadian history and literature in Canada, and his role for the emergence of an established criticism of black writing in Canada, specifically of the Eastern regions (compared to Wayde Compton in the West) has been significant.[16]

The focus on the history of blacks in Canada and on the deconstruction of myths (of Canadian history and identity) has been central not only to his criticism and scholarly activism but also to his literary works[17]; as he argues, since "African-Canadian history is ignored in Canada, African-Canadian writers are forced to act as historians" ("Introduction" xx). Thus, in his poetry, drama, operas and prose, Clarke has repeatedly turned to the past, particularly that of Africadia[18]: to give some significant examples, *Whylah Falls* (1990), a poetic collection later adapted as a play, was set in Nova Scotia of the Depression era; *Beatrice Chancy* (1999, drama) re-imagines the situation of slavery in nineteenth century Canada; and *Execution Poems* (2000) already dealt with the story of his two cousins, George and Rue – the work won the Governor General's Award for Poetry in 2001.[19]

The multi-facetted nature of the imaginary revealed in Clarke's work appears hard to grasp from the reading of one work alone – to make this intricacy visible for the present analysis, I have decided to compare two completely divergent works of G.E.Clarke, of which the second is in fact not a novel, but a dramatic poem: *George And Rue* and *Trudeau: Long March And Shining Path*. To understand the transcultural imaginary that is drafted in the texts they must, from my perspective, be read in relation to each other, as complimentary works.

George Elliott Clarke sets his only novel so far, *George and Rue*, in the 1920s to 1940s in the region that he grew up in, Three Mile Plains in Nova Scotia, three kilometers

[16] As it says on the official homepage of Nova Scotia, in a listing of recipients of the Order of Nova Scotia in 2006: "Through his work, he has given a voice to the voiceless and fought for equality of rights for African Canadians, or, to use a term he coined, Africadians. He has helped to establish the academic study of African-Canadian literature," Government of Nova Scotia, "Order of Canada: Recipients 2006," *online resource*, n.pag.; Cf. also Wyile, "We Have to Recover Their Bodies" 133-134.

[17] His most important critical contributions were "Africana Canadiana: A Primary Bibliography of Literature by African-Canadian Authors, 1785-1996, in English, French, and Translation," *Canadian Ethnic Studies* 28.3 (1996): 106-209 (extended in his later publication *Odysseys Home*); *Fire on the Water: An Anthology of Black Nova Scotian Writing* (1991); *Eyeing the North Star: Directions in African-Canadian Literature* (1997); *Odysseys Home: Mapping African-Canadian Literature* (2002), which contains his most important critical essays.

[18] As mentioned at the beginning of Chapter 7, 'Africadia/n' refers to the communities of Blacks in the Maritimes, which immigrated to Canada before the American War of Independence; Clarke also uses the term African-Canadian instead of the more common term Black Canadian; as Chiandry explains, "His critical dispositions seem to be consistent with his apparent preference for the term *African Canadian* over *Black Canadian* (used by other critics), and one could tentatively argue that the former term tends to imply and emphasize cultural self-assurance or "immanence," while the latter term, especially in the writings of Stuart Hall and Paul Gilroy, often emphasizes the constructedness of "blackness" (often deliberately written as uncapitalized or non-proper noun) within a relational and thus potentially unstable, discursive economy," 199.

[19] Cf. Wyile, "We Have to Recover Their Bodies."

southeast of Windsor. It fictionalizes, as Clarke clearly states in an afterthought entitled "Verdict," the fate of his "matrilineal cousins once removed" (*George and Rue* 219), who in 1949, in desperate need of money, murdered a white man and were hanged the same year. The novel first sets out with a dark glimpse of the night of the murder, yet then moves back in time, in the first and longest section entitled "Whip," to depict the two brothers' poverty and their violent childhood. George and Rue's parents, Cynthy ("part Mi'kmaq Negress" 5) and Asa (a "fifth-generation Hamilton in Nova Scotia, and the third-generation to call Three Mile Plains home" 10) meet and marry in 1923; George is born in 1925, Rufus, called "Rue," one year later. The boys' father is a brutal man, who beats his wife and children, seeks the company of other women, and drinks instead of working:

> A nightmare of a dream, Asa made their lives a rum-splashed Damnation; he was Satan to Cynthy and their sons. The belt touched them so much, it was like their best suit of clothes. The wanton rage inside him was a lake of fire and melting rocks, as volcanic as alcohol, his one true faith. [...]
>
> Polluted by their papa's mean drunkenness, the boys grew like poisonous weeds. (22)

From the start George and Rue's circumstances lock them in an inevitable circle of poverty and crime, with violence, sex, and "rum" as the only means to temporarily suppress or express their frustration. Even though they both try to evade their fate, they cannot bear the hardships that society thrusts upon the underprivileged and discriminated Black communities. Racial divides stifle any (trans)cultural dialogue and an escape from their doom is rendered impossible.

The second part of the novel, which is entitled "Hammer" with reference to the tool that the brothers used to kill the white taxi driver, thus focuses on George and Rue's murderous act. The driver turns out to be a friend of George's – however, when George begins to feel doubts and protests against the killing, his brother Rue, "cash-famished [...] an ebony piano key sharply out of key with the surrounding ivory ones" (115) determinedly commits the murder. The final section "Rope" describes the young men's arrest, interrogation, trial, and their time in jail, during which the brothers develop completely opposing ways of dealing with their situation and their death sentence. It includes a variation of perspectives, that too rather emphasizes the cultural differences than allowing for any exchange: newspaper clippings, a description of the racist white judge who sentences them, as well as of the coffin maker, and a letter that George composes to the Governor General of Canada and some journal notes.

In the long interview included in Herb Wyile's recent collection of conversations with Canadian authors of historical fiction, George Elliott Clarke describes the difficulties that arose while writing the novel: the family of the actual victim that was killed by Clarke's relatives had asked Clarke not to write the story; when the *Execution Poems* came out, they remained calm, yet when *George and Rue* was published they called upon the media for protest (Wyile, "We Have to Recover Their Bodies" 148). However, Clarke's intention in writing this novel had been to trace this unbelievably brutal aspect of his family's past and to try to understand the circumstance that would cause humans to commit such a horrid act. As he describes the wider scope of this desire to understand the past and its ironies:

> He [the man murdered by the Hamilton's] was surely a victim of the Hamiltons as much as the Hamiltons were victims of their circumstances—including racism. Yet, history—even fictional history—demands facing unlovely, ugly truths, such as the probability that, somewhere along the line, Burgoyne [Silver's real name] was an innocent beneficiary of the invasion of North America by his ancestors and the creation of vast wealth—wealth that drove the Renaissance and created Modernity—sapped from South American gold mines and the blood of Aboriginal and African slaves. Still, in writing this story, I had to be sensitive to the clear, immediate fact that an innocent man was struck down in his prime by two guys acting on animal instincts—to fill their guts and clothe their backs using somebody else's means. But again, the irony is that that was what slavery was all about too—filling guts, clothing backs, all based on violence or the real threat thereof to a class of slaves. (Wyile, "We Have to Recover Their Bodies" 147-148)

Clarke's 'political' agenda in the writing of this historical novel becomes obvious in the above-cited passage but is also expressed in several other interviews:[20] *George and Rue* doubly exposes unknown or neglected details of the past, of Clarke's ancestors and, on a larger scale, of Canadian history; through the revealed details Clarke wants to direct his readers' attention towards the injustices, neglect, and partial mythification[21] that Black communities in Canada experienced in the past: "it's about the society, and it's a society that existed back then and may still exist in certain ways today" (Wyile "We Have to Recover Their Bodies" 146).

In line with the intentions behind this novel, which can clearly be related to concerns discussed within postcolonial theories, its scope of settings in time and place are limited to a very specific cultural space. One may mention that to a certain degree, even this narrowly focused setting of Three Mile Plains' depicts a multi-racial community, of Mik'maq, Blacks and Acadians – however all are united by the constricting 'culture' of poverty, violence and discrimination that dominates the novel. Such a view on 'culture,' and in fact the dramatically inescapable fateful nature of such a culture itself, does not allow for anything like transcultural exchange. On the whole, the novel's descriptions rely on a clearly defined period of time and hardly move outside the limited scope of its protagonists. There are only two exceptions: one in regard to place – George travels around as a soldier in the Canadian Army and with the Merchant Marine; occupations which, however, do not make him more respected in society, except with his future wife who on their re-encounter muses, "George did look roguishly handsome, and he had been to London and he had seen war; he had seen Buckingham palace [...] George was a living cosmopolitan" (84). The other extension of the scope of setting concerns the sphere of time; here the authorial narrator at one instance allows the reader some insight into the history of the Africadians of Nova Scotia:

[20] Cf., i.e., Compton and McNeilly.

[21] In terms of a long persisting amnesia in Canadian society of the injustices inflicted upon African-Canadians.

> What neither Asa nor Cynthy knew was how much their personal destinies were rooted in ancestral history—troubles. Their own dreams and choices were the passed-down desolations of slavery. African Nova Scotia and, specifically, Three Mile Plains were the results of slave trade and slave escape. [...] The Negro—Coloured—people come from black slaves freed by redcoats down in Maryland and Virginia, then transported, like convicts, to "New Scarcity" during the War of 1812. [...] They arrived just like two thousand black others who came with nothing to nowhere. (14)

The understanding of history communicated by Clarke in this novel attempts to locate discrepancies at the crossroads of individual fate and communal *H*istory; as Clarke, in the words of Barbara Chase-Riboud, who is quoted as an anagram in the notes further back in the novel asks: "Did history really repeat itself? Or only family history?" At the same time, in contrast to any possibility of understanding history, the narrator's slightly blackened voice observes: "They was so poor, they supposedly didn't even have history" (14).
Circumstances render the existence of transcultural figures impossible, not to speak of individual empowerment – no matter whether characters accept constant discrimination and adapt to the role forged out for them by society, or whether they resist assimilation, degrading obedience and an inhuman existence, eventually they all remain within the vicious circle of (in-)difference. Neither their own opinion nor the opinion of other more powerful groups of society (white Anglo-Canadian) changes to the better. Thus, it appears that *George and Rue*, instead of propagating transcultural imaginary, depicts extreme positions of contrary cultural imaginaries; these deny any possibility of a mingling of self and other, of cultural transfer – in both directions –, layering, mixing of images, and discourses, thereby resisting a process of transcultural renegotiation of identities and histories. However, even if this is what Clarke depicts and what he lays emphasis on in terms of what it was like, his view is that of a person who is aware and certainly wants his readers to become aware, too, of the transcultural visionary current that flows beneath the Canadian identitary shield:

> This fusion and fission of various minority cultures *was* and is what confirms the *uniqueness* of the majority anglophone and francophone populations—and, thus, of Canadian culture as a whole. Hutcheon's assertion, then, that "Canada has experienced no actual 'creolization' that might have created something new within a split racial context" (*Splitting* 76) is not necessarily so, for the Métis emerged from liaisons and marriages between the French and First Nations peoples; Irish Catholics became francophones in Quebec; and francphone and Aboriginal demands for equality have served to shape the nation's constitution. In the end, Canadian "creolization" is reflected in the adoption of a federal multicultural program in 1971 [...] and the encouragement of federal bilingualism (beginning in 1969). (Clarke, "What Was Canada?" 34)[22]

It is at this point that we might turn our attention to Clarke's more recent work, *Trudeau: Long March and Shining Path,* which is not only based on the author's

[22] The quotation within is taken from Linda Hutcheon, *Splitting Images: Contemporary Canadian Ironies* (Don Mills, ON: Oxford UP, 1991).

fascination with the political figure who introduced multiculturalism and bilingualism in Canada, but also significantly complements the dark reality rendered in *George and Rue*.

In an introductory essay to *Trudeau*, George Elliott Clarke explains why he "as a 'visible minority' person (my official identity in white-majority Canada), [seizes] the right to 'write what [he] like[s]' (to cite Steve Biko), including this libretto about a wealthy, European male" (20) – he presents his literary appropriation of one of the major figures of Canadian political culture of the twentieth century as an appraisal of Pierre Elliott Trudeau's achievements as Prime Minister from 1968 until 1984. He thereby emphasizes his role as "a cult figure for many Canadians *de couleur*" on the one hand and as a "*citoyen de monde*" (20) on the other.[23]

If we see *George and Rue* as a reproachful question posed to Canadian society, one highlighting the racist reverberations in Canadian history, then *Trudeau* could be regarded as the answer that Clarke himself suggests. This response, rendered in an idealizing poetics, emphasizes Clarke's personal *transcultural* reading of this central historical persona, who is indeed a *transcultural* figure:

> Eschewing sociology, political science, economics, and constitutional law, this libretto avoids definitive realism. It is a paean to the liberationist mood of 1968: Prague's "Spring," Paris's "May," and Canada's "Tory" version—namely, "Trudeaumania." Yet, my Trudeau is not the now-deceased immortal, but rather the Warhol silkscreen; not surreal, but sidereal: an insubordinate reality, half-Plato, half-Chaplin. *My* Trudeau is *the* slapstick contrarian—with Pound's *brio*, Mao's ascetic aesthetic, Layton's macho assertiveness, Davis's sunglasses, X's sass, and Dylan's alluring mystery. (*Trudeau* 24)

Obviously, of all the works discussed in this study, *Trudeau* breaks most radically with traditional perceptions of historical fiction; first and simply because it is not prose but a dramatic poem, which, second, was performed as an opera enriched by the music of jazz composer and performer D.D. Jackson.[24] However, even if the novelistic form is still the most common genre for fictional histories, I see no necessity to exclude other genres from examination. They can be termed fictions of the past just as convincingly – especially in this case, which gives so much insight into the transcultural imaginary of "Africadia."

As David Tough observes in his review of the text, "[a]s far as the narrative goes, Clarke sticks fairly closely to the standard touchstones of Trudeau's life" ("Trudeau Through the Looking Glass" III, 3rd paragraph, *online resource*). Thus, Clarke deals with a period lasting from 1949 until Trudeau's death in 2000; he portrays some early decisive moments (Trudeau's travels to China, his meeting with J.F.Kennedy), dramatizes his rise in 1960 and the most popular phase, "Trudeaumania" in 1968 from various angles, moving on to his marriage, the October Crisis of 1970, and his personal and political struggle around the eighties, before finally describing his political return,

[23] In his critical review of *Trudeau* David Tough argues that Trudeau should not be re-imagined but valued as "the real Trudeau, the one we find in his words" and claims that Clarke does not "[bother] to say why Trudeau is worth mythologizing," "Trudeau Through the Looking Glass," *online resource*, n.pag. This is however exactly what Clarke does in his introductory essay.

[24] Cf. "Réalité" and "Hansard," *Trudeau*, 119-122.

old age and death. This "path" is, however, painted by Clarke in very bright nickelodeon colors, using the highly poetic-oralized slang so characteristic of Clarke's work – language and depictions that move Tough to speak of Clarke as portraying a "topsy-turvy Trudeau" (I, last paragraph, *online resource*), "playfully tipping his hat to the canonical Trudeau as he flips the bird to its authors. It's all rendered a little off, with a very Lewis Caroll-like delight in the nonsense of common sense" (III, 3rd paragraph).
However eccentric the depicted Trudeau may be, how far from or close to the 'real' historical persona, he stands at the center of this fiction of the past as a transcultural figure and as an appropriated hero of Africadian cultural identity. Just as Clarke views the cultural and racial group he is writing from as well as its literature as "a species of hybridity" and "a patchwork quilt of voices. Its creators are, like their forebears, exiles, refugees, fugitives, pilgrims, migrants, and natives" ("Introduction" xii-xiii), he also depicts Trudeau and his life with an emphasis on his multiple mundane, cosmopolitan features and experiences. Clarke's Trudeau moves rapidly in space and time; he meets and converses with several important political and cultural figures of the time all over the world. Clarke also allows for him to become a figure within which the individual, personal spheres cross, or at times clash with, the larger communal, national (Canada), and global spheres.
The questioning and dissolving of ethnic and racial boundaries that such an approach ideally prompts – an approach which makes up for what had not been possible in *George and Rue* –, becomes obvious before the opera even begins in G. E. Clarke's description of the "dramatis personae." Therein, Clarke loosely suggests that Mao Zedong "may be Chinese or Cuban or Québécois," Pierre Elliott Trudeau "an Aboriginal / First Nations (or Métis) person," and his wife, Margaret, "Indian (out of Kashmir or Bihar) with a command of Indian vocal / musical traditions. Or she could be Italian. Let her identity be as indeterminate as Canadian actress Rae Dawn Chong in Jean-Jacques Annaud's film *Quest for Fire* (1981)" (27-28).[25] However, it is especially Trudeau who is depicted as, "in-between" (Tough III) figure, "a white Negro clone" (2.2, 53), as he himself states early on: "Crossing river and mountain pass, / I jettison my race and class" (1.1, 34)[26]; repeatedly Trudeau ridicules the principle of being labeled or forced to fix his political view; thus, being asked by Mao if he is a Capitalist or Communist, he replies "Truthfully, I'm just a canoeist" (1.1, 35), or when Neruda and Fidel Castro want to know whether or not he is a Marxist, he playfully evades by answering: "I like Groucho Marx…" (2.1, 49). Especially the people surrounding him in the dramatic poem continuously describe Trudeau as a complex, double-faced visionary acting beyond the color of skin, even if these voices become more skeptical later on.[27] In a scene set in 1960 the musician Robertson observes in conversation with

[25] This is also observed by David Tough; not only that he "re-imagines key personalities of the 1960s-70s cultural politics as ethnic in-betweens" but also that "the point of this is to re-claim Trudeau as a visible minority icon – as an icon, in fact, of ethnic in-between-ness," "Trudeau Through the Looking Glass," III, 2nd paragraph, *online resource*. Clarke partially confirms this intention in an interview with Kristina Kyser, "George and Ruth," 871.
[26] The numbers here refer to act and scene, and then the page (instead of lines).
[27] Cp. for example Act 4, Scene 1-2, 88-94 both set in 1970.

Simone Cixous[28] (and by including references to African American writers Richard Wright and Ralph Ellison):

> ROBERTSON: Simone, Pierre's a Montrealer—as
>
> Unpredictable as free jazz.
>
> From Native Son to Invisible Man,
>
> He shifts like ectoplasm—or Peter Pan.
>
> His life *is* art; a canvas
>
> Shimmering black-and-white contrasts. (2.2, 52)

And as Cixous adds in an attempt to capture the politician's conflicting appearances:[29] "Adonis—or Don Quixote? / Don Juan—or Wile E. Coyote? / An enigma, a prodigy? / A most eccentric oddity?" (2.2, 53). At the same time, Trudeau is not idealized solely in his role as "Mr. In-Between" (3.2, 68) – the depiction also mentions his politically inappropriate measures regarding Natives[30] and his problematic relationship with Québéc (3.5, 79; 4.2, 91; 4.4, 94-99).

Obviously, due to the time it is set in, media play a significant role in the text not only as a contextual reference but also as constructing forces that were essential for Trudeau to build up and disseminate his contested image, as well as for the people perceiving him: "It looks like he's stepped from a T.V. And into a Beatles concert" (3.5, 78).[31] The references to the impact of the media as well as those to personalities (and works) of the arts and popular as well as intellectual culture of the time, next to allusions to other literary works or political writings create a dense intertextual and transcultural discourse. Thus, Clarke not only constructs "mixed" characters, such as the Québécoise journalist Simone Cixous (Simone de Beauvoir / Hélène Cixous), the African-Canadian jazz pianist Roscoe Robertson (Robbie Robertson / Oscar Peterson), and the Québéc

[28] As mentioned a few paragraphs further down, Clarke uses mixed historical personalities. Cf. also Tough, III.

[29] These conflicting appearances, by the way, are also reflected in Trudeau's clothes that change from scene to scene, varying between, for example, elegant suits, a karate outfit, military clothes and flower-print Tahitian shirts.

[30] Cf. Van Toorn, "Aboriginal Writing": "Jean Chrétien, Trudeau's Indian Affairs Minister, disregarded Native advice on how best to redress long-standing disadvantages in Native communities, and proposed in his controversial 1969 'White Paper' that Indian status be abolished, Native services be mainstreamed, and Aboriginal peoples become just another element in Canada's multicultural society. The White Paper provoked a flood of anger that did not abate when Trudeau and Chrétien abandoned the White Paper's key proposals" 31.

[31] See also 3.2, 68. However, just as the media were essential for the acceptance and popularity of Trudeau as a flamboyant national political figure, they eventually also undermined his reputation: "TRUDEAU. Reporters, when will you stop / scheming up nightmares from ink and Scotch? / Whatever I defend, whether black or white, / not one of you feels I'm ever right" (4.4, 97).

liberationist Jacques Fanon (Frantz Fanon / Jacques Rose).[32] He also relates Trudeau to Shakespeare's Caesar (3.5, 83) and Macbeth (4.4, 95), or Black Panther Founder Huey P. Newton (4.4, 94); he refers to the work of Italian film music / Jazz composers to describe the atmosphere in Monte Carlo of 1969 (4.1, 85), and lets Roscoe Robertson cite lines that remind of Bob Dylan's "Like A Rolling Stone" to describe Trudeau ("A *Playboy* swinger, / A 3-D thinker, / A white Negro clone: / He's a rolling stone!" 2.2, 53);[33] and, he also integrates references to Norman Mailer, Austin Clarke (3.2, 68) or Alice Munro (2.2, 54). Finally, Trudeau himself is depicted as mixing languages in conversation and mingling cultural references, for example, when he calls upon the Chinese poetress, Yu: "Let's go forth now, chanting haikus / And albas and sonnets and epics and blues" (1.1, 39).[34]

The variety of cultural discourses and images layered in the text speaks for a cultural imaginary that defies one single perspective and instead transgresses the 'other/ed' realm. Since this transcultural imaginary is encapsulated mainly in the figure of Trudeau, and Trudeau represents such a milestone in the twentieth century cultural and political identity of not only Africadia but Canada as a whole, this imaginary appears to be extended as a transcultural vision of Canadian identity in the text:

> TRUDEAU. Here I am, in my sixties,
>
> But I announce the 1980s—
>
> A new Canada, a new Canaan,
>
> A gilt, sparkling Constitution,
>
> Sunning a Just Society,
>
> A rainbow of minorities—
>
> Multicultural, bilingual, at peace.
>
> *Sagesse* lights my bright policies.
>
> CIXOUS. That is your generous theory.

[32] Cp. Tough, III, 2nd paragraph.

[33] There is a further reference to Bob Dylan in Act 4, Scene 1, 87.

[34] For a passage where languages are mixed (French, English, Chinese), see 2.4, 61. The quoted passage from Act 1, Scene 1 (31), as well as the fact that languages are mixed, of course, reminds one of Clarke's description of the Africadian heritage: "The King James scriptures melded with East Coast spirituals, New Orleans jazz, Bajan calypso, and Nigerain jit-jive. Steel drums and steel guitars harmonized. A discourse diced with Motown slang, Caribbean Creole, approximated Queen's English, gilt Haitan-French, Canuck neologisms, and African patois" Clarke, "Introduction" xii.

It may collapse in history.

TRUDEAU. True. No *pays* can be constructed

To outlast deathless pyramids.

The only eternal policies

Are love and snow and death and ice.

[...]

TRUDEAU. There's no cultural purity.

Truth is there never was.

What we call humanity

Is a beautiful mess. (5.2, 104)[35]

The obviously idealized perspective of Canada as "a Just Society" made up of a "rainbow of minorities" is the extreme counterpart to the Canadian society portrayed in *George and Rue* – and it is significant that G.E. Clarke presents both. In the one work, the main figures are detested by society and forgotten in history (George and Rue), while in the other, the protagonist is one who is loved, remembered, and idealized – yet both are portrayed to have been misunderstood. Seen together, the two works display a remarkable example of Canada's kaleidoscopic potential positionings, while each work in itself still displays individual transcultural dynamics.

The issue of transculturalism in terms of an idealistic means to transgress cultural differences and to trace similarities is developed even further in the view of history that pervades *Trudeau*. Clarke depicts history as being altered by the revolutionary hippie-spirit of the time, in which love is the alternative to the repressive forces of history. Again, the aggressive, disuniting elements of human existence are questioned ("How can men fire guns at others? / In such fog, aren't all men brothers? / Who is fighting whom? Why? What for? / In history's fog and fog of war?" 1.1, 33), while those aspects that bring people together on a peaceful, respectful, or loving basis are described – tongue-in-cheek – as a solution to the existential tragedies of human kind ("Love history, and it loves back" 1.1, 40; "If only we could make history / Just by making love. / Then maybe all human history / Would chronicle love." 1.1, 41). However, in the case of Trudeau's relationship and marriage with Margaret, the spell is soon gone. While at the beginning they are still convinced that their love might withstand the burdens of time ("We'll touch, retouch, until *touché*, / We marry *poutine* and sushi. /

[35] Cf. Act 3, Scene 3, 72.

Everything we do, we'll make news—/ Our love will make history muse." 2.3, 56), Margaret a few years later has to accept that "[...] Canada is his real lover / [...] I give him only love, but love / Merely bores our historians" (4.5, 100). Trudeau's true commitment, thus, was to "the new Canada," in which any relation to the past had to be one that would be future-oriented, or 'transhistorical' – as he says in 1968: "Our responsibility to the past / Is to be contemporary" (2.3, 56).[36]

One main feature of Clarke's libretto is, of course, the strong postmodernist slant. Intertextuality, a deconstructive, re-imaginative approach to history, self-reflexive remarks, and a mise-en-abyme (Roscoe Robertson is shown to be tempted to write an opera on Trudeau in a scene set in 1984, 5.2, 106-107) are obvious traits of the revisionist, metafictional form of historical fictions. Especially the epigraph that is placed before the introductory essay, prepares the reader for what is to come and anticipates what Tough in his critical tone calls "the choose-your-own-adventure brand of postmodernism" (*online resource*, n.pag.):

Damn each history! Each bio!

There can be but the one "Trudeau."

But *your* Trudeau? And *my* Trudeau?[37]

On doit chercher l'homme dans ses mots.

Each portrait's une belle infidèle:

Blame the artist? Blame the model?

Perspective veers, look after look:

Both film and play betray the book.

Rhyme's, too, *déja vu*—medieval—

[36] See also 3.4, 75; towards the end Clarke's Trudeau comes to reflect upon and revise his commitment and his view on history, cf. 5.2, 103; 5.4, 108-110; 5.5, 113.

[37] Here Clarke adds the following reference in a footnote: "Cf. Pound, Canto II." The Canto begins in the following manner: "Hang it all, Robert Browning, / there can be but the one "Sordello." / But Sordello, and my Sordello? / Lo Sordels si fo di Mantovana," Pound 6. "Sordello" is a poem by Robert Browning, and a figure that reappears later in Pound's *Cantos*, cf. Cookson 6-7. The relation of Clarke's *Trudeau*, as he hints at, to Pound's *Cantos* project is obvious if one considers Pound's numerous references to historical figures and other literary works, or his integration of other languages in the epic poem (Chinese, and European languages other than English), cf. Cookson xiii-xv.

Even in octosyllable

Doubled as couplet (so I hear)—

Art as *avant-garde* as Chaucer.

But Trudeau—*ours*—opposed, through verse,

Posed versions of our universe. (17)

Yet, this revisionist perspective on identities and histories coupled with the innovative (postmodern) narrative strategies and thematic concerns, bears again specific features that give the text an additional – transcultural – emphasis. First of all, the transgression of racial, ethnic, and, on a more general level, cultural boundaries appears as a central concern – be it expressed through bold interdiscursive complexity, mixed characters, language and wordplay, or concrete visionary stances. Secondly, George Elliott Clarke transcends the extreme 'limited' minoritarean perspective employed in *George and Rue*, to self-consciously and self-confidently appropriate a prominent figure of (majoritarean) Canadian politics, culture, and identity. However, Clarke's interpretation of Trudeau does not limit him to the cosmopolitan persona he surely was, or restrict him to a revisionary figure in relation to Canadian national history; instead, the author juxtaposes the 'global' Trudeau with the intimate, personal Trudeau by repeatedly referring to the politician's longing for his father.[38]

Compared to the "rootedness" that has been ascribed to Clarke's work, "his commitment to the local and his grounding in a specific historical community" (Cuder-Dominguez 65) – which also comes to the fore in *George and Rue* – his literary sphere and identitary perspective is dramatically broadened in *Trudeau*. The analysis of these two historical fictions in different literary forms should, thus, "compel us to pursue more interpretation, more thought, on what cultural identities mean today; they inspire us to rethink the conventional limits of identity and to explore hybrid and pluralistic ways of interpreting and effecting social and cultural relations" (Chiandry 198). From this perspective, the works of African-Canadian authors such as Clarke "signal many understandings of Canadian blackness, many venues of intervention in the new century. By interrogating the past, these authors open paths into the future" (Cuder-Dominguez 56) – the future of transcultural Canadian identities.

[38] For example, Clarke lets Trudeau reflect at the end of his life: "I have merely been a traveller, / All this lonely life, a wanderer, / Searching always for my father" (5.5, 112); for other examples, cf. 1.2, 43; 2.3, 56. This interest in father/son relationships is something that Clarke himself observes as being a link between *George and Rue* and *Trudeau*; cf. Kyser, "George and Ruth" 871.

Crisscrossing Wild West Borders and Identities – Guy Vanderhaeghe's *The Last Crossing*

At the beginning of his literary career in the 1980s Guy Vanderhaeghe, as he admits today, strongly resisted writing about history. Being a graduate in history, he was reluctant to integrate historical material in his work, instead preferring a focus on contemporary settings and issues.

> I always felt that because I had done an MA in history, I would be too inclined to steer to the facts of any sort of historical topic or theme that I was interested in. [...] [However,] [b]ecause I'm a writer and because I studied history, I've always had an interest in the historical novel. That interest sometimes is distaste, sometimes it's an enormous source of pleasure for me. (Mouat, *online resource*, n.pag.)

Not only regarding his earlier professional background, Vanderhaeghe's positioning as a writer of historical fiction appears exceptional. Compared to other authors that emerged in that period, he might well be regarded – as he does himself – as writing more "conventional" fiction (Wyile, "Making History" 29). This might not be completely true of his award-winning novel, *The Englishman's Boy* (1996) – an impressive fictionalization of events surrounding the Cypress Hill Massacre[39] as well as a depiction of the Hollywood era of the 1920s. Yet *The Last Crossing*, which is partially set in the same period (late nineteenth century) and place (North-West Territories, Whoop-Up Country[40]), does indeed strongly display modernist narrative techniques. The content of the novel, however, reveals intriguing transcultural ideas, which echo three of Vanderhaeghe's literary concerns: his skepticism towards extreme postmodernist perspectives especially in relation to historiography, a resistance to the complete "atomization" as well as commodification of history[41], and a special interest in the ethics of individual identities (Mouat, *online resource*, n.pag.; Wyile, "Making History" 35, 39-41, 48-49). Guy Vanderhaeghe's understanding of history plays an important role here; not only is he interested in alternative interpretations of history, he also displays a heightened awareness toward the interactions, crossings, and subsequent development of societies over time:

[39] During this incident in 1873 a group of Natives were attacked and killed by white traders – an event which eventually led to the establishment of the Royal Mounted Police; according to the Canadian Encyclopedia, "in 1873 a gang of American wolf hunters massacred some Assiniboine there. The incident spurred Prime Minister John A. MacDonald's government to establish quick passage of the recently introduced bill to create the North-West Mounted Police," "Cypress Hills," *online resource,* n.pag.

[40] The North-West Territories designated around the 1870s more or less all the land between Ontario and British Columbia, and even large sections of what is today part of Ontario and Quebec; cf. "North-West Territories, 1870-1905," *online resource,* n.pag.; Fort Whoop-Up (1869-74) was the centre of illegal trade until the RCMP arrived in the area of what is today Southern Alberta, "Whoop-Up," *online resource,* n.pag.

[41] History as a commodity was especially a theme in *The Englishman's Boy*, cp. Wyile "Dances with Wolvers."

> I also feel that history is a narrative about intersections among peoples, cultures, economic forces, etc. It's what brings about change and modifications of the status quo—some good, some bad, depending on the perspective. But if history is anything for me, it's the story of how intersections and collisions work themselves out in surprising and startling ways. (Wyile, "Making History" 47)

Embedded within these transcultural intersections – prominently captured in *The Last Crossing* – lies a further aspect in Vanderhaeghe's work: the oppositional paradox between the role of individuals as passive 'victims' of history, as "creatures of context" (Wyile, "Making History" 51) as opposed to the view of individuals that can acquire agency, "the notion of personal acts, personal decisions, and the ability to make moral choices, ethical choices, and different ways of thinking" (ibid. 51); the latter especially being a prerequisite for the construction of identities based on a transcultural imaginary. In his play *Dandock's Dance* (1995), which captures the happenings in an insane asylum during the flu epidemic of 1919, Vanderhaeghe already began using historical material as a source of inspiration. *The Englishman's Boy* and *The Last Crossing* represent a major shift in his work, the two novels being part of a larger project on the settlement era in Canada's (less 'wild') 'best West.'[42] What connects the two novels is not only the specific time in which they are set (approximately the 1870s); it is also the area: the indefinite and unguarded borderland between the Canadian territorties and the U.S. For Vanderhaeghe the unboundedness of this region, the free movement and encounters of diverse groups and individuals across the landscapes becomes representative of an open discursive space of identities: "So there's the question, which is becoming popular in literature, the idea of borders, political borders, borders of ethnicity, race, all the rest of it. This is kind of a borderless region" (Mouat, *online resource*, n.pag.) – a region in which "it's all very fluid, and, culturally, it's very mixed" ("Making History" 31). This strong symbolic emphasis in the two novels' settings is taken even further in *The Last Crossing,* as it depicts the journey of a heterogeneous group of individuals across this borderless land.

As Patricia Linton has highlighted, "*The Last Crossing* is a novel about different kinds of crossings" (*online resource* 1) – not only the (transatlantic and transcontinental) crossing of "geographical territory" but also the crossing and thereby challenging of several identitary (cultural) spheres. In 1896 Charles Gaunt, a painter and also recently successful poet belonging to the British upper-class receives a letter from Canada in which somebody called Custis Straw mysteriously urges him to return. As we learn, Custis was one of the members of the group traveling through the American and Canadian West sixteen years earlier. Back in 1870, Charles Gaunt, and his brutal, sexually obsessed military brother, Addington, had been sent across the Atlantic by their father in search of Charles's twin brother, Simon. The two brothers set out for the North together with a mixed group of 'locals.' All members of the party are on a personal identitary quest: the Métis guide Jerry Potts; Lucy Stoveall, a strong-headed earthy woman in search of the murderers of her younger sister, who is put in charge of

[42] As Vanderhaeghe has mentioned the project might even develop into a trilogy (Mouat, *online resource*, n.pag.).

cooking for the men; Custis Straw, a local intellectual, Civil War veteran, and Lucy's suitor; as well as his friend, the saloonkeeper Aloysius Dooley, and the journalist Caleb Ayto. Even though Simon is eventually found living in a camp with Natives, the journey turns out to be more than a transcontinental quest for all its participants. Lucy and Charles have a passionate relationship, which however ends when Charles returns to England and Lucy, finding herself pregnant, decides to marry her suitor Custis. A quarter of a century later, Jerry Potts, who is based on a historical figure[43], has passed away, and so has Custis Straw. Custis's last wish was to inform Charles of his daughter and initiate a possible re-union with Lucy: thus, Charles's "last crossing." These diverse crossings interfere with the protagonists' existing conceptions of self, even if they do not always support the postmodern ideal of hybrid identities: "Vanderhaeghe's novel exploits the complexities of its historical setting to construct a series of possibilities for fluid or alternative identities" (Linton 1). *The Last Crossing* is especially impressive in this respect, as it captures within its narrative such a great variety of identitary passages, by which it negotiates notions of class, race, ethnicity, gender, sexuality, and colonial power relations.

If one scans the categories of social identification that are transgressed in *The Last Crossing*, it soon becomes obvious that several of them are, due to the setting of the novel, strongly linked to the final notion mentioned – that of colonial power relations. Thus, if we begin by looking at the depiction of class differences, which are temporarily overcome in Charles's and Lucy's relationship, we may note that the two are not only separated by obvious financial and educational differences (Lucy, who is a hapless widow and washerwoman, has difficulties understanding the language of her upper-class British lover). Their contrasted social positions are initially rooted in their belonging to different social segments, one to the imperialistic Old World and Victorian society, the other to the uncivilized New World frontier. However, whether or not the novel is read more strongly in contemporary postcolonial terms, Lucy and Charles's love affair most obviously suggests a breaking up of the rigid Victorian class distinctions and the superficial values attached to them.[44] Charles, who feels socially and sexually liberated and at ease in Lucy's presence ("[t]he sensation of being exposed – no walls, no curtains – the immodesty of an animal, naked of everything but instinct and need, there is only this," 195-196), believes that they will find a place and means to live together; while Lucy realizes from the beginning that the social constraints are too hard for Charles to overcome. After having read Charles's explanation for his temporary return to England and his desire to come back for her later, she observes:

> It took me a good while to spell out all the words, work them through to sense. But when I did, I could read plain between the lines of that clear hand. He's a deep well of pain and confusion, more than I reckoned. My heart breaks for him. I know something else. Every word Charles wrote he thinks he believes because he's got to blind himself. But I can see the truth of it. I have no other choice but to look on it steady.

[43] Cf. Vanderhaeghe's interview with Herb Wyile which also includes two pictures of the 'real' Jerry Potts – a half Kanai, half Scottish scout, who famously assisted the North West Mounted Police as a guide, translator and negotiator, Wyile, "Making History" 43-46; cf. also Linton 3-5.
[44] Cp. also Wyile, "Doing The Honourable Thing," *online resource*, n.pag.

> In so many words, he said his brother [Simon] threw himself away on an Indian woman. Charles's circumstances are no different. He can't raise me up, but I can damn sure pull him down. I won't do it.
>
> [...] I don't fault him for what I know is going to happen. (365-366)

Thus, in this case, as it seems, the prospect of crossing social boundaries has failed and Charles "essential self" is not only "revealed" (279) but remains unaltered. What has not been considered so far in critical studies of the novel, is that Charles, on the one hand, breaks the rigid codes of his social surroundings back in England by publishing a scandalously revealing book of love poetry (which becomes a great success); and on the other, and more importantly, he is considering a return to Lucy many years later. As the ending suggests, a turn of events in favor of a transcultural revision might be possible:

> Gaunt imagined a different ending for his book. The man at the foot of the stairs takes one step, then a second, then a third. He lacks the courage to look up during his slow ascent, afraid to see that once again she has disappeared. But still, is it not better to make the climb, whatever the outcome? And what if, on gaining the top, he lifts his eyes and finds her still standing there, waiting, despite how very long it has taken him to reach her? (391)

The questioning of gender roles and predetermined conceptions of sexuality that already resonates in the plot around Charles's and Lucy's love for each other, is even more strongly carved out in the opposition of the characters of Addington and the two frontier-men Custis Straw and Jerry Potts, as well as in the story of Simon Gaunt.[45]
As Herb Wyile points out, the reformed standpoints on gender roles, especially those of men, in *The Last Crossing* go hand in hand with a deconstruction of stereotypes of the amoral, lawless "Wild West" as opposed to the virtuous, dutiful, flawless Empire, represented by the ideal of the Victorian family (the Gaunts) (Wyile, "Doing the Honourable Thing," *online resource*, n.pag.). Thus, Custis and Jerry on several occasions come to display a high sensibility for honorable behavior towards both the other sex as well as to any othered person (be it friend or foe). Custis not only defends the Métis Jerry when he is insulted by Addington (thereby provoking his being brutally beaten up by the latter), he also heroically helps Lucy several times, most memorably when he accepts her proposal to marry him to save her from complete social disgrace. Jerry Potts, from his side, even rises above all the discrimination experienced through Addington's insulting remarks and helps him – as he believes he was asked to do – to come to an honorable death while hunting. Addington, in extreme contrast to the two, not only endangers the party's well-being through his irrational decisions and aggressive mood, he is also discovered by Custis to have been Lucy's sister's murderer: "[his] standing upon honour, however, seems to be contradicted by a more deepseated discomfort with his bloodthirsty behaviour, suggested by recurring nightmares [...] symbolizing his psychological, moral and physical decay" (Wyile, "Doing the

[45] Herb Wyile's essay, "Doing the Honourable Thing: Guy Vanderhaeghe's *The Last Crossing*," focuses on the depiction and de/constructions of masculinity in the novel; his considerations give a well-researched and thoroughly argued insight into this topic.

Honourable Thing," *online resource*, n.pag.). As the novel shows, the questioning and re-defining of borders in relation to gendered stereotypes is strongly related to the re-establishment of values. This feature, which points toward Vanderhaeghe's concern about the ethics of individual identity, implies that "traditional conceptions of honour value status over moral, ethical and spiritual integrity and that, consequently, doing the truly 'honourable thing' often requires resisting social dictates grounded in rigid assumptions about class, race, and gender" (Wyile, "Doing the Honourable Thing" n.pag.). What Linton indicates in a slightly different context, is to a certain degree also applicable here, that "[i]n any particular cultural context, individuals are offered a narrow spectrum of identity categories. But they have choices, or in some cases create options for themselves, that express essential elements of their subjectivity" (2, *online resource*). One person in the narrative who obviously takes advantage of his choices and insists on his right to redefine his individual (sexual) identity is Charles' lost brother Simon. Charles finally finds him living in a Crow camp together with a *bote*:

> The trapper called her a *berdache*, the name the French had given them, but every Indian tribe has their own word for such persons. *Bote* in Crow, *wintke* in Sioux, *he man eh* in Cheyenne. If you translate them into English, they come out roughly the same, Two Spirit, I told Gaunt. I said that an old Crow man once informed me that it's the mystery of two spirits in one body that make a *bote* holy, a creature both male and female, yet more than either. It gives them extraordinary spirit power. (355)

Simon decides to stay with his spirit lover and to adapt to Native cultural practices since the world that he comes from – Victorian society – does not offer any space for such transcultural, in this specific context transsexual, development and exchange. However, as Wyile has pointed out, this instance, too, does not ultimately sanction complete transcultural openness, as Simon insists that the *bote* be *his* only (especially sexually), and not, as Crow culture prescribed, belong to all (Wyile, "Doing the Honourable Thing" n.pag.).

As observed by Wyile in one of the interviews (and confirmed by Vanderhaeghe), the Métis guide Jerry Potts occupies a special position within the novel: "There are multiple heroes, one might say, in *The Last Crossing*, but obviously Jerry Potts sticks out for his subtle subversion, his forbearance, his unsung accomplishments" ("Making History" 43). On the one hand, he is as an individual stuck between two cultures, two races (Native and White), struggling with a *desire* for hybridity that can not be fulfilled due to imperial power structures; on the other hand, he functions as a mediator figure, on both a figurative and actual level of the story. Even though he knows that ultimately he is only accepted by his Native tribe as a full member (despite his being a half-breed), while the Whites do not accept him as an equal; that his identity can thus only be rooted in his Native heritage – Potts, as an individual, still has the agency to at least base his *acts* on transcultural decisions. On one occasion, the party is considering crossing an area called Sand Hills; since they do not realize that it is a 'haunted' place, Potts decides to tell them a traditional story about it. However, Potts's thoughts after having told the story reveal that he did not recount a genuine Native myth but a story adapted both to his naïve audience and his own desires:

> He could not tell of it in a way the Englishman could understand, so he told him a story, one he had heard many times in the lodges of the Peigans. It was the tale of how the sacred bundle of the Worm People was brought to them by the man who had gone to seek his wife in the Camp of the Dead. But he had decided not to speak of the bundle or the sacred things that an unbeliever, an Englishman, could never accept.
>
> […]
>
> But still he could not stop himself from talking. He hurried on, wanting to end the story as quickly as possible. He trimmed it here and there, but as he did, it became more and more his own story. Then suddenly he could not go on, could not unstick his tongue to tell the last terrible part. (183)

There are also other figures in the novel who are, like Potts, entangled between cultures, yet contrary to Potts they do not struggle to embrace their multi-leveled heritage. When Charles Gaunt and Lucy have the opportunity to watch a Métis caravan pass by, Charles notes their mixed appearance:

> They shyly smile at Lucy and shake her hand with grave courtesy. To my mind, the Métis closely resemble a tribe of wandering gypsies. Some are very light-complexioned, while others are as dark as any of the Indians I laid eyes on in Fort Benton. Their costumes are like Potts's own, a motley of native and European dress. I see an assortment of blue coats, jackets of dressed skin, wide-brimmed floppy hats, wool trousers, and beaded buckskin pants. All the men wear long bright sashes cinched to their waists, a dash of Gallic élan to challenge the flamboyance of their Indian beadwork. (278)

A further instance of, as Linton calls it, "a powerful public expression of hybrid subjectivity" (7) is rendered through the figures of two half-breed brothers that Potts kills during a battle against the Cree. At the moment of death the two courageous warriors aware of their fate both begin to sing a traditional death chant – while the one sings in Cree, the other joins in with an English prayer (335).

Even though, as both Linton and Wyile rightly claim, Vanderhaeghe's protagonists do not – and in most instances *cannot* – succeed in constructing hybrid identities, their interaction across cultural (and geographical) boundaries does have an impact on their conception of self and other. As a fiction of the past, the imaginary of the novel still displays a considerable degree of transcultural processes. As both interviews and the novel itself show, Vanderhaeghe's approach to history is obviously one that deconstructs the myth(s) of a peaceful settlement of white people in the West, it does so also by questioning the limits of transculturality: "[it] can be read against continuing debates about the relationship between subjectivity and social or cultural identity, especially challenges to the ideal of hybridity in some versions of postmodernism and renewed debates about essentialism in postcolonial theory" (Linton 2); thereby, it represents a partially more critical view on transcultural imaginaries. Despite *The Last Crossing*'s partial skeptical stance, which opens up further perspectives, the novel exemplifies not only an enormous spectrum of identitary spheres, but also that the crisscrossing and questioning of their borders can become a viable ethical choice for individuals.

8 The Reappropriation of AlterNative Past

The decision to add this final section on the contribution of Native writers[1] to the development of transcultural imaginaries and fictions of the past might in many ways appear audacious – foremost because it is hardly possible to do this vital and many-layered branch of Canadian literature justice in the limited scope of this chapter.[2] Precisely because Aboriginal literature today represents an integral element in the nation's literary production, criticism, and identity, this final case study chapter presents indispensable insight. As a matter of fact, Indigenous writers have hesitantly but all the more distinctively also contributed to fictional rewritings of history – the more recent developments concerning this literary involvement have, however, hardly been an issue in critical studies.[3]

As has been comprehensively explicated by Penny Van Toorn, the mutual influence of Aboriginal narrative traditions and Canadian dominant cultures has not only been considerable (and painfully one-sided in terms of power structures) but also diverse and diversely interpreted over time, for example in regard to the demarcation of the starting point of a written Native narrative tradition in Canada:

> While it is universally accepted that the Aboriginal peoples of North America have long practiced the oral arts of narrative, song, oratory, and prayer, the question of when they began to write elicits a range of possible answers. Depending on how authorship and writing are defined, Aboriginal writing has several alternative beginnings. (Van Toorn 26)

[1] Obviously, this study only covers English-language writing, thereby also excluding the remarkable contributions of French language écrivains amérindiens from its analysis. However, the analysis in the second section of this chapter does also consider one story by a Québécois Aboriginal author that is included in English translation in the collection discussed. For a recent critical study on Native authors in Quebec, cf. Maurizio Gatti, *Etre écrivain amérindien au Québec: Indianité et création littéraire* (Montréal: Editions Hurtubise HMH, 2006).

[2] The adjective "Native" and even more so, the noun "Native" as well as the collective reference "First Nations" are, according some critics no longer the most adequate terms to use for the peoples that were colonized by the White settlers from the 16th century on (cf. for example, Penny Van Toorn). Instead, more general terms such as "aboriginal" and "indigenous" should be favored, and the individual preferences of writers respected. In the present chapter, the expression "native," as an adjective, (and sometimes First Nations) is used interchangeably with Indigenous and Aboriginal, which refer to Native Indian, Métis and Inuit people.

[3] "AlterNative", in the title of this chapter, refers to one of Drew Hayden Taylor's hilarious yet thought-provoking plays. *alterNatives* describes an evening dinner that three couples (Native, Non-Native, mixed) spend together, and ironically exposes the superficialities and misconceptions of all three. The Native couple refer to themselves as "'alterNative warriors,' that is, Native activists who challenge accepted orthodoxies about Native identity and history held by both the Native and non-Native communities, 'a new breed of warriors who have an allegiance to the truth, rather than tradition'," Falkenstein, "Angry (Nice) Young Men," Review, quote within from Drew Hayden Taylor, *alterNatives* (Vancouver: Talon Books, 2001).

Yet, as scholars of Canadian culture and literature nowadays would insist, it is one thing to speak of the beginnings of Aboriginal written tradition[4] and another to speak of its actual acceptance in Canadian society; as again Van Toorn observes, "[t]he decades between Johnson's death and the late 1960s were a barren time for Aboriginal literature and culture" (31)[5], while one of the earlier anthologists of Native writings, Italian-Canadian scholar and author Penny Petrone in her critical study mentions the "formal recognition in Canada's new constitution" in 1982 as a significant date in the process of acknowledgement of the nation's Aboriginal peoples and their heritage (*Native Literature* 3).

The rise and growing acceptance of Aboriginal literary activities coincided with Native communities' increasing intervention in Canadian politics in the 1960s, culminating in the rejection of P.E. Trudeau's and Jean Chrétien's initiative towards the assimilation of Aboriginal peoples: "Since the White Paper, Indian political activity has greatly increased awareness of Indian problems and goals among the general public and the Indian population itself" ("Native People, Government Policy," *online resource*, n.pag.). Correspondingly, the first anthologies and critical studies of Native-Canadian literature were only to appear by the 1970s (poetry) and 1980s (fiction) (Van Toorn 33, 36). However, the struggle toward a 'contemporaneous' version of Native literature and voice continued: before writers like Drew Hayden Taylor, Thomas King, Basil Johnston, Jeanette Armstrong, or Eden Robinson could become successful with their own specific (postmodern) mixtures of humour, tragedy, innovative narrative form, and traditional heritage, earlier creative writers of Aboriginal descent first had to fight the constraints of Western realist generic traditions as well as existing confines of voice. The dispute on the appropriation of Native voice, which reached a peak in the late 1980s, eventually led to the demise of the tradition of collaborative works and a more respectful exposure of Native perspectives and narrative 'rights.'[6] As recently as 1990, W.H. New introduced a special issue of *Canadian Literature*, in which he also mentions a list of newly established organizations, institutions, and publishing houses by and for Native artists, with the hopeful words: "This collection of essays and poems is a speaking-place. Because boundaries are processes of interaction as much as they are lines of demarcation, it is also a series of opportunities to begin listening" (New, "Learning to Listen" 8).

As one contributor in Jeannette Armstrong's early collection of critical essays by First Nations scholars and artists (published at Theytus, one of the young publishing houses mentioned by W.H. New) brings a main concern in Native literatures to the point: " 'Who we are' has been constructed and defined by Others to the extent that at times we too no longer know who we are" (Damm 84). It is this particular identitary struggle caused by a history of cultural oppression that provokes Native artists to study, highlight, and challenge the lives and cultures of Native communities, as they are

[4] Aboriginal oral narrative traditions in contrast have been an essential part of Native cultures ever since, cf. Gruber, "Aboriginal Oral Traditions" 27-37; Van Toorn 22-26.

[5] Van Toorn is here referring to the famous Native poet Emily Pauline Johnson (1861-1913).

[6] For a more detailed insight into the appropriation debate in Canada cf. Smyth Groening, "Introduction: Writing 'Indians' and the Manichean Allegory," in *Listening to Old Woman Speak: Natives and Alternatives in Canadian Literature*, 3-27.

experienced in contemporary, everyday life. Thus, since the introduction and slow establishment of Native voices in the Canadian literary landscape, Native authors have mainly been dealing with fictional renderings of the *present* rather than with rewritings of the past. As Thomas King explains this phenomenon in his CBC Massey Lecture Series:

> What Native writers discovered, I believe, was that the North American past, the one that had been created in novels and histories, the one that had been heard on radio and seen on theatre screens and on television, the one that had been part of every school curriculum for the last two hundred years, that past was unusable, for it had not only trapped Native people in a time warp, it also insisted that our past was all we had.
>
> No present.
>
> No future.
>
> And to believe in such a past is to be dead.
>
> Faced with such a proposition and knowing from empirical evidence that we were very much alive, physically and culturally, Native writers began to use the Native present as a way to resurrect a Native past and to imagine a Native future. To create, in words, as it were, a Native universe. (King, *The Truth About Stories*, 106)

In the course of the conquest of North America, the perspective white settlers had of Indigenous people shifted several times, from naïve but helpful exotic creatures to graceless, cannibalistic savages.[7] What Thomas King is mainly referring to above is the romanticized image of the dying Indian popular since the nineteenth century, which was firmly established during the American Romantic Period, and persisted far into the twentieth century; as Penny Petrone mentions, "[a]s late as the 1930s it was assumed that Canada's Indians would become extinct" (*Native Literature* 2). The over-simplified image of the mythic representative of North American past, the "National Indian," as King calls it (*Truth* 79) had to be overcome through an affirmation of the existence and the complex identities of Natives in the Canadian present – and as one might argue, this resolution is now bearing fruit.

Having reclaimed their righteous position in Canadian society as well as redefined their present selves, Native Canadians have only very recently begun to challenge the history constructed by the oppressors of Aboriginal cultures, to narrate their own perspectives and to offer retellings of the North American past. This re-telling of history by Native authors – which by the very nature of Native traditions of story telling and orature is more strongly interwoven with a concept of histories as stories – appears to be a decisive step for an understanding of contemporary non-Native and Native-Canadian identities alike. However, the analysis of transcultural imaginaries in Aboriginal fictions of the past remains a delicate terrain. Aboriginal peoples had for centuries continuously

[7] These images are discussed at several stages in Thomas King's *The Truth about Stories,* for example, 74-88. Also cp. Smyth Groening, *Listening to Old Woman Speak* and Francis, *The Imaginary Indian*.

been forced to adapt their cultures and identities to the desires of colonial intruders; at some points in time the cultural exchange might have been welcome, at others, the reaction very understandably led to resistance, which has ensured a certain amount of continuity and maintenance of traditions in Native cultures. This chapter thus faces one major discrepancy:[8] contemporary Native literature, on the one hand, displays a continuing resistance, or insistence on difference to non-Native cultures – a resistance so strong it questions any possibility of transcultural interaction; on the other hand, alongside is an obvious desire to rewrite, retell and reconstruct a past and present dominated by non-Native realities, at times we can also observe a revision (that ironically accompanies this literary prospect) of this extreme version of resistance. Native-Canadian fictions of the past are, as a result of being based on Aboriginal traditions and conceptions of the world, more openly related to transcultural imaginaries than many other cultures; at the same time, the Native heritage of the past and the globalized present, as well as colonial history and contemporary Canadian modernities, too, need to be mapped; thus, the struggle of First Nation writers to come to terms with a complex array of hybridized identities also explains both the critical occupation with the past as well as the development of a transcultural imaginary.

In writing this chapter on transcultural imaginaries in Native-Canadian fictions of the past, I am fully aware of the difficulties and limitations of perspective that my non-native reading entails. Especially in regard to history, and Aboriginal perspectives on the past, it becomes hard not to slip into an oversimplifying analysis of an issue so varyingly interpreted across the many Nations and tribes of Canada's Indigenous peoples.[9] This chapter intends to offer only some tentative observations 'from the outside,' some reflections on this crucial component of Canadian cultural identity, the creative contributions of which enrich the perspective of all groups involved in an (attempted) understanding. The following two sections will touch upon several of these issues. The first, "The Truth About Histories" captures possible features of Native rewritings of history by referring on a more general level to the work of Canada's most celebrated Aboriginal author Thomas King; while the second section debates the contingency of transcultural imaginaries in Aboriginal fictions of the past through an analysis of a representative variety of stories, from the collection *Our Story: Aboriginal Voices On Canada's Past*.

[8] A discrepancy, which, as we have seen, we find equally in the literatures of other discriminated and 'othered' cultures in Canada; however, in the case of Aboriginal cultures and their relation to 'post/colonial' Canada, the discrepancy appears especially drastic.

[9] As indicated in the first paragraph of the very first entry of Toye's *Concise Companion to Canadian Literature*: "Legends and tales are part of the oral tradition inherited by Canadian Natives from their forefathers and preserved through countless recitations. Because they are not a homogeneous people, because they speak a number of languages, practice many diverse customs, and hold many distinct believes, their mythology is varied and vast," "Aboriginal legends and tales," 1. Cf. also Nabokov, "Native views of history."

The Truth About Histories: Neopremodern Native Narratives[10]

In the introduction to the *Canadian Literature* special issue on "Native Writers and Canadian writing," New poses an intriguing question: "The paradigms and parallels of anthropology do not describe a single unifying tradition among the many Native cultures of northern North America; differentiating more than uniting, they look for cultural variation. But have the differences thus distinguished had any palpable effect on the paradigms of Canadian historiography?" ("Learning to Listen" 5). New's query and the comments that follow suggest that the effects that Native cultures could have had on the dominant society were for a long time suppressed, and by the time the special issue appeared were only beginning to develop. We might extend W.H. New's observation to ask: what role has the restitution of Native Canadian history, also in recent fictions of the past, had in the construction of contemporary Aboriginal identities, and does it entail a reciprocal impact of imaginaries?

As indicated above in the quote by Thomas King, Native writers indeed have hardly written fictions set in the past or dealing with historical topics. There are a few earlier exceptions, such as Beatrice Culleton Mosionier's *In Search of April Raintree* (1983; set in the 1950/60s), Lee Maracle's *Ravensong* (1993; set in a Salish community in the 1950s), and Tomson Highway's *Kiss of the Fur Queen* (1998; set in Manitoba of the 1950s).[11] However, all these fictional rewritings of the past share two main characteristics that clearly set them apart from some more recent examples: they are more often than not (semi-) autobiographical[12], and they put a strong focus on the traumatic experiences of individuals in Native/non-Native relationships – represented most dramatically by the maltreatment of Aboriginal children in residential schools.[13] Only since the 1990s have some authors such as Thomas King or the younger writer Joseph Boyden begun to approach history from a new angle.[14]

There are several features that these recent novels have in common and, which also show in how far fictions of the past by authors of Aboriginal heritage have opened

[10] "Neopremodern" is a term coined by Ridington ("Happy Trails to You" 105), discussed at the end of this section.

[11] Also Thomas King mentions some exceptions, however all written by Native-American authors, cf. *The Truth About Histories*, 107. Of course, history was already a prominent theme in Aboriginal texts published long before those mentioned, but these were mostly non-fictional texts, rendering "written histories, travel accounts, and autobiographies" (Gruber 413) in the nineteenth century, and traditional stories linked with personal memories around the 1970s; cf. Gruber, "Literature of the First Nations, Inuit, and Métis," 413-428.

[12] Penny Van Toorn refers to these novels as "life narratives," 32.

[13] Both Beatrice Culleton Mosionier and Tomson Highway fictionalize autobiographical experiences at residential schools in their novels. A more recent example can be found in the works of Robert Alexie, *Porcupines and China Dolls* (2002) and *The Pale Indian* (2005). Government officials decided to close residential schools in 1969, however, the last school only closed in 1996. Cf. "Residential Schools," *online resource,* n.pag.

[14] For an insightful discussion of Boyden's *Three Day Road* cf. Bölling, "'A Part of Our History that So Few Knew About': Native Involvement in Canada's Great War – Joseph Boyden's *Three Day Road*."

themselves up to an interpretation of transcultural imaginaries. The first of these traits concerns the importance of orature in Native traditions and the continuation of these oral elements in contemporary written texts (Petrone 3-7, Van Toorn 22-25). This use and translation of oral forms into written discourse has been widely discussed, and "is a concern because Indigenous cultures have never been static in time, nor uniform across the country that is now Canada" (Van Toorn 24). Yet the fluidity and diversity that oral forms of narration entail is nonetheless partially preserved in written accounts. The orality in native texts links up with a further feature that is especially important in relation to the fictionalization of history: the use of myths. Even if one looks at one of the most important early modern texts of Native-American literature, N. S. Momaday's ground-breaking *House Made of Dawn* (1968), which is set between 1945 and 1952, the text is full of native myth and other elements of oral story-telling. History, the present, myth, as well as visions of the future are tightly knit together in the Native universe; myths have a sense of past-ness in them, just as they reflect present-ness – they can change every time they are retold depending on the context. As explained in the *Concise Companion to Canadian Literature* with what appears like a slightly sarcastic tone,

> [f]or non-Native readers preoccupied with exact chronology and factual details, Native chronicles based on oral traditions are disappointing. The constant evocation of a confusing assemblage of mythological figures, and the frequent introduction of supernatural causes and interventions, have created a hodge-podge of details concerning historical origins. Countless variations of a single tale, even within the same tribe or band, are confusing: the treatment of a story may be altered by the taste, gender, or life-circumstances of the narrator, as well as by the place and time of the telling, and even the particular audience. ("Aboriginal legends and tales" 2)

Finally, we must also keep in mind that as opposed to the teleological traditions, indigenous cultures do not necessarily regard the past, present, and future as chronological structures. The a-chronological perception of time is something that is strongly reflected in many native texts, also those dealing with the past, and might be related to what Thomas King refers to as the "associational" characteristic of Aboriginal literature.[15] Apart from that, native history also spans a broader, non-Canadian stretch of time as it includes pre-colonial periods. All of the characteristics mentioned – the oral nature, the close relation to myth, and the circular, broadened conception of time – yield two further important qualities that differentiate Native literature from non-Native texts (and in the past also often led to a depreciation of the former by the proponents of the latter): the anti-climactic, episodic evolvement of narratives, and the frequent crossing of genres within a text (Van Toorn 25-26, Petrone 5). Thus, "some traditional Aboriginal stories can also prove difficult to pigeonhole in European genre categories because they combine farce, tragedy, religious allegory, secular history, didactic messages, and elements borrowed from foreign cultures" (Van Toorn 26). Taken together, this spectrum of characteristics is strongly evocative of the transgeneric,

[15] I will return to these features at the end of this section. Cf. Thomas King, "Godzilla vs. Post-colonial."

transhistorical, and transcultural features discussed in relation to recent fictions of the past.

The title of this section, "The Truth about Histories" as may have already become obvious, points towards Thomas King's intriguing lecture series, which he held in 2003: *The Truth About Stories: A Native Narrative*. The insight he gives into the complexities of the de- and re-constructions of Aboriginal universes is indispensable for any critic of Canadian cultures; in the context of Native identities, images and stories, the critical reflections and creative writing of Thomas King also prove to be revealing. One of the very clever observations that King makes, is that if one compares Native and non-Native (in his specific example Judeo-Christian) myths, one comes soon to understand that while the latter bases most of its myths and stories on hierarchical structures, the former imagines a universe that "is governed by a series of co-operations [...] that celebrate equality and balance" (23-24). Apart from describing King's cultural, or as one might claim, political convictions, this observation also indicates a basis of ethics underlying Indigenous cultures that radically differs from those that dominate the larger part of the world – ethics which may also advance transcultural imaginaries. An even more important insight conveyed in King's lectures – though this insight is not completely new – is the importance of storytelling as an oral form for Native cultures. Each of the five lectures starts with the same story; every time, however, a small detail, or the context in which it is told changes. King wants us to understand how exactly the same story can be told again and again and always be something different. The same, I would like to argue, holds true for histories, which, too, are in the Native universe no more than stories, the "truth" of which depends on the context in which they are told. As King emphasizes in every single lecture, "[t]he truth about stories is that that's all we are" (2, 32, 62, 92, 122).

The play between history and story is underscored in the title of another of Thomas King's works, this time a short story collection published in 2005: *A Short History of Indians in Canada: Stories*. The title is in fact misleading as the stories in this collection, and also the title story have hardly anything to do with history, in terms of Western or westernized cultures. In King's cultural imaginary the boundaries between history and story, reality and myth are blurred; especially as the constructed official realities and stories of the past had – and partially still continue to have – such a strong impact on the actual, present state of Natives.

There is one story in the collection that actually does deal with history: "Coyote and the Enemy Aliens." The story is an oral-style, Native retelling of a by now well-known dark moment in Canadian history: the internment of Japanese-Canadians at the end of and after World War II. Coyote is central to the story because he is taking advantage of the fact that there are new jobs due to the regulations and is helping White people. I am mentioning this story firstly because it exemplifies some features discussed above, such as episodic narration, oral style, and a deconstruction of conceptions of time. The following excerpt from the beginning of the story demonstrates all three characteristics:

> Okay, so I'm going to tell you a Coyote story. Maybe you hear that story before. Maybe not.

> Coyote was going west. That's how I like to start that story. Coyote story. Coyote was going west, and when he gets to my place, he stops. My good place. By the river.
>
> That was in European time . . . 1940. Maybe it was 1944. No, it was 1942.
>
> Coyote comes to my house in 1941. Hello, says that Coyote. (50-51)

Secondly, the story also contains two further elements that might be interpreted as features that relate to imaginaries that permit cultural exchange and 'layering' rather than essentialist positioning or hybrid chaos. The one element is that King rewrites a chapter of Canadian history that concerns another suppressed cultural group in Canada; the other that he uses what might be called a transcultural figure – even though it is a traditional narrative character. Coyote, as a trickster, represents an in-between figure, in this case not necessarily the friendliest kind, crossing between cultures, between the native narrator and non-native history. As Siemerling explains, "[t]he simultaneity and encounter of two systems of reference – a duality and form of double consciousness – leads to trickster performances and strategies that mark many written texts by Native authors" (*New North American Studies* 62).

As mentioned earlier, to discuss contemporary Aboriginal literature, including what we might refer to as Native versions, or "alternatives," of fictions of the past in terms of transcultural imaginaries might still be regarded as a bold venture. Yet the features described and exemplified do spur the following question: do examples of contemporary indigenous Canadian fictions of the past suggest that Native-Canadian authors are constructing a new kind of identity? A re-appropriated version of a (hi)story which (in the context of contemporary modernities) reflects new or reformed aspects of contemporary Native identities and imaginaries?

Most of contemporary Native texts may be referred to as postmodern without hesitation; surely, as is the case with other 'othered' literatures, the development of postmodern, deconstructive narratives in the twentieth century certainly helped Indigenous Canadian voices to break free and speak up.[16] Nonetheless, we must equally be aware of the fact that many of the 'postmodern' features in Aboriginal literature have always been there, as it has for long been multi-layered and complex in structure and contents. As Robin Ridington has claimed with reference to King's work: "I think he adds an Aboriginal dimension to the Western canon rather than simply using western writing strategies to describe Aboriginal experience. His work is neopremodern, not postmodern" (105). Her suggestion might well apply to most other contemporary Aboriginal literature. Resisting labels coined and applied mainly by non-Native critics – labels such as 'postcolonial' – Thomas King himself has come up with some quite precise and effective terms for grasping the very nature of Native texts without using the common labels 'postmodern' or 'postcolonial' (he especially resists the category postcolonial because for him it suggests a continuation of colonialism):[17] he describes them as "tribal" (literature that is

[16] Cf. Gruber, "Literature of the First Nations, Inuit, and Métis."

[17] His critical relation to New Literatures theories becomes especially obvious in his well-known essay "Godzilla vs. Post-Colonial"; it is however also conveyed in *The Truth About Stories*, 58

cultivated in the bounded context of a specific community), "interfusional" (blends oral and written literature), "associational" (avoids centering of character and narrative, more focus on everyday life and the community); the final adjective is "polemical" in the sense that Native literature reflects the clash of Native and non-Native cultures and resistance to cultural imposition ("Godzilla vs. Post-Colonial" 185-187). At this point I would like to propose an additional possible adjective for this list: "transcultural." The analysis of the following texts will show that contemporary Native fictions of the past are not necessarily always polemical, and they do not only depict differences; they also unite what might initially seem to be cultural differences, thereby implying extended "postindian" possibilities of identification.[18]

The Future of Speaking Back – *Our Story: Aboriginal Voices on Canada's Past*

If a major question underlying this chapter is, how do contemporary re-tellings of history by Native Canadian authors inform the (re)construction of Indigenous identities? The arguments elaborated so far have already indicated possible answers. For one, Aboriginal storytelling traditions exhibit a rich variety of narrative strategies that facilitate, or even foster an openness and respect for the (cultural) 'other' – features that not only encourage alternative forms of telling histories, they also break up lopsided cultural perspectives. Furthermore, present-day Native Indian, Métis, and Inuit constructions and identifications of self, require reformed, independent, and re-appropriated Aboriginal fictions and voices, especially in the context of a globalized multicultural Canada. One possibility to acquire this literary agency (I dare not judge actual social realities) might be found in fictions of the past – whether writers insist on cultural resistance or accept a transcultural vision. Thus the issues that should be dealt with on the following pages are: how do Native authors construct contemporary fictions

and 114-115. Most importantly, cf. Winfried Siemerling, who includes a very detailed discussion of Thomas King's (and Gerald Vizenor's) thoughts and works in his *New North American Studies*: "Native Writing, Orality, and Anti-Imperial Translation: Thomas King and Gerald Vizenor" 59-94.

[18] The term "postindian" was introduced by Gerald Vizenor and refers to the deconstructed version of the "imaginary/National Indian" (King) constructed by colonial invaders, as i.e. in *Manifest Matters: Narratives on Postindian Survivance* (Lincoln: U of Nebraska P, 1999); the term is discussed in great detail in Siemerling's chapter on Thomas King and Gerald Vizenor in *The New North American Studies*; as Siemerling writes with reference to Vizenor's understanding of the "postindian": "Like all emergence in the contact zone, however, the revisionary re-articulation of speech, thought, and consciousness of Natives in contexts of European/Western languages and writing is not an unmediated emergence *as such* [...] it is a relational process, a correlation of two forms of consciousness and expression. In this kind of translation, Native cultures make erstwhile non-Native writing and languages their own from different angles and perspectives," 60. From my perspective, the transcultural version of the postindian, however, might transcend Siemerling's understanding to include more than 'only' two levels and two parties in a cultural dialogue that might, furthermore, evince mutual cultural understanding and change.

of the past? How do they blend traditional and non-traditional aboriginal narrative strategies and themes? Can we observe a positive interaction of cultural imaginaries (in the sense of blending and mutual influence) or rather negative interaction (resistance)? My presumptive answer to all of these questions is that we are seeing a potpourri of several currents.

Our Story: Aboriginal Voices on Canada's Past, a collection of stories edited by the Dominion Institute[19], presents an ideal resource for the analysis of a variety of Native fictional perspectives on Canadian history that informs possible responses to the questions posed above. In itself, *Our Story* can be regarded as a transcultural project because it attempts and manages to present a variety of alternative views of history by bringing together contrasting (native and non-native) imaginaries. Rudyard Griffiths, founder of the Dominion Institute, explains the editors' goal in the Preface: "What we need to work on is finding new ways—after more than four hundred years of living together—to hear each others' stories anew, to step out of preconceived notions of not only what constitutes our history but how our history is constituted. *Our Story* is an important contribution to moving dialogue in this direction" (2).

The nine stories included in *Our Story* are as diverse as one would expect from such a pluricultural selection of ingenious Indigenous writers; together they present a dense fabric of histories that is held together by one significant feature – a continuing narrative impact on the reader long after the book has been put down. Each of the authors, who were asked to contribute stories about a defining moment in Canadian-Aboriginal history, display different modes and interests in the rewriting of the past; however, as Rudyard Griffiths observes, summing up three further important tendencies that these stories have in common: "In each of these fictionalized accounts we are exposed to the Aboriginal sense of place, the passage of time, and the complex relationship of myth and truth" ("Preface" 3).

What the stories reveal is a web of conflicting imaginaries and realities that are anything but simple. The "Aboriginal sense of place" is indeed strongly present in the stories, and as one of the contributing authors, Rachel A. Qitsualik, in fact insists that "[t]he persistence of this land forbids true time travel" (35).[20] The respectful relationship to "Mother Earth" together with the century-long, unjust 'loss' of land to White settlers, makes for the unbroken consciousness of a "sense of place" in the Aboriginal

[19] The Dominion Institute Website gives the following information about this organization: "Our mission is to build active and informed citizens through greater knowledge and appreciation of the Canadian story. In 1997, a group of young professionals, concerned about the erosion of a common memory and civic identity in Canada, formed the Dominion Institute – a national charitable organization dedicated to creating active and informed citizens through greater knowledge and appreciation of the Canadian story. Using groundbreaking public opinion research and innovative TV, new media and in-school programs, the Institute helps hundreds of thousands of Canadians connect in meaningful ways with the country's history, shared citizenship and democratic institutions and values. The Institute's programs fall under three themes: memory, democracy and identity." The Dominion Institute, "About," *online resource*, n.pag.

[20] Each of the stories is accompanied by a "Contributor's Note" which comments on the historical moment chosen for the story, or on any other general issue concerning the story, Native-Canadian history, present or future.

imaginary. This sense of place persists in the present and transcends generations to mark even those long displaced from the land of their ancestors. Such a persistence that travels across time becomes an unsettling component for Natives in the present, who consequently wrestle to identify themselves. This point is made in Lee Maracle's "Goodbye, Snauq" in which the protagonist, who constantly converses with his ancestors, who were forced to leave the land they originally lived on, struggles to accept that this land of his forbears is lost forever, even though ironically a court case had acknowledged them as the rightful "owners."[21]

> The hypocrisy marring Canada's behaviour toward us is still evident, but it struggles for maturity, and while it struggles for maturity I accord myself a place. This place is still at the bottom, [...]. Although today I must say goodbye, tomorrow I may just buy one of the townhouses slated for completion in 2010. Today I am entitled to dream. Khatsahlano dreamed of being buried at Snauq. I dream of living there. ("Goodbye, Snauq" 219)

The second concern enumerated by Griffiths is "the passage of time." Time indeed plays a less dominant role, but is at least equally vital – on various levels. First of all, it must be noted that the stories included in the collection display the variety of modes that fictions of the past may take in terms of their relation to pastness. While some narrators situate their stories in distant times, many of them prefer the more recent past (twentieth century), and several are even more or less set in the present. Thus, while Rachel A. Qitsualik's "Skraeling" is set at the time of the first contact between Inuit and Vikings, and Basil Johnston's "The Wampum Belt Tells Us..." relates events around the Battle of Queenston Heights in 1812, the stories by Lee Maracle ("Goodbye, Snauq") and Drew Hayden Taylor ("A Blurry Image on the Six O'Clock News") are set at the turn of the millenium and in 1990 respectively. Of the remaining stories, all except one are set in the twentieth century.[22] Yet all stories evidence not only that the dialogue with the past and with ancestors represents an important general feature but also how strong the impact of history has been on Native consciousness. They also underline how Aboriginal identities of the present can hardly eschew the dialogue with the past – even if for a long time, as Thomas King has argued, it was necessary to focus on the present. For Lee Maracle, the awareness of history and the passage of time in Native traditions also prescribe an acceptance of change – a change that, as some stories show, might carry transcultural potential; however, change is accompanied by a bitter note as the wounds inflicted upon Native identities in the past centuries are only in the process of healing:

> Raven has never left this place, but sometimes it feels like she has been negligent, maybe even a little dense. Raven shaped us; we are built for transformation. Our stories

[21] The problem here is, that in the meantime (since the protagonist's ancestors displacement in the early twentieth century) the land houses apartment buildings, industries and other institutions, whereby the descendents of the indigenous people are forced to accept redress instead.

[22] Of these, only one deals with the otherwise in Native texts often discussed issue of residential schools – Tantoo Cardinal's "There Is a Place." However, even here it is not the most dominant concern.

> prepare us for it. Find freedom in the context you inherit—every context is different: discover consequences and change from within, that is the challenge. Still, there is horror in having had change foisted upon you from outside. Raven did not prepare us for the past 150 years. She must have fallen asleep some time around the first smallpox epidemic, when the Tsleil Watuth Nation nearly perished, and I am not sure she ever woke up. ("Goodbye, Snauq" 205)

On another level, that of the narrative realization of history within the stories, the diverse interpretations show how time does not necessarily need to be understood as a linear concept. This notion reiterates the fact that within Indigenous cultures the tribes' past and ancestors are credited with a more significant position in everyday life and rituals, whereby the historical consciousness is emphasized in the form of storytelling, myths, dreams, and visions. These features are best exemplified in Basil Johnston's "The Wampum Belt Tells Us...". The story describes a meeting of Anishinaubae warriors, who assemble to listen to the pledge of Tecumseh's courier and join forces with the famous leader against invading American troops.[23] Before the courier speaks, however, the *mazhinawae* – the keeper of the Wampum Belt – is asked to tell the history of the people: "In the old days, the *mazhinawae* recited the history of the Anishinaubae peoples at the outset of winter and the storytelling season and on special occasions such as the present. With the Wampum Belt draped over his arm, Abeedaussimoh, pointing to two figures of two canoes with masts fore and aft worked into the belt, began" (77). In the course of his narration, the storyteller eventually focuses on the fate of two of Cartier's men, Parisé and Lebrun (later renamed Pau-eehnse and Nebaunaubae), who are adopted initially against their will by an Odauwau band and come to lead a fulfilled life within the community. Eventually they are even asked to participate in the storytelling ritual:

> By the third winter the two men were in demand as storytellers; people wanted to hear about their country and what had brought them to the Land of the Great Turtle. After three years both men were enough in command of the language to enable them to take part in the storytelling sessions.
>
> The storytelling season always commenced with the account of creation told by one of the leading narrators in the village. This long story was followed by a recitation of the history of the nation.
>
> Two weeks went by before the storyteller came to the prophecy that foretold the coming of bearded White men to this continent. It was this narrative that many older people wanted to hear, to see what their adopted White men would say and do. [...]
>
> And this is the story that he told. I've heard that it was Daebaudjimoot, our nation's first storyteller, who first told this story. ("The Wampum Belt Tells Us..." 87)

[23] Tecumseh was one of the Indigenous war chiefs who allied with the British and the Canadians to fight off American troops during the War of 1812, cf. "Tecumseh," *online resource*, n.pag.

In the following, the narration evolves into a complex storytelling session within the actual storytelling at the assembly, during which the two adopted white men not only narrate their past, as well as open up a dialogue with their Chief and their other listeners, but also the two levels of narration become intermingled (92). Toward the end of the story, also the extradiegetic narrator, having illustrated the events that occurred after the assembly and after the Battles of Queenston Heights and the Thames, comes to reveal his identity as a storyteller (100-101).

The dense interaction of storytelling modes and levels of narration, together with the already discussed close reliance on oral traditions, accounts for the transgeneric appearance of Native fictions of the past, which also convey history as a dialogue that is open to individual interpretation and input from outside.[24] As Qitsualik indicates in the comments to her story it is only through a drifting into other times and cultures – for example via stories – that differences can truly be overcome (35-36). The contemporary protagonist of Lee Maracle's "Goodbye, Snauq" also experiences multiple levels of historical consciousness: not only has she got a profound knowledge of her people's history, which she acquired as a student of Indigenous government and passes on as teaching assistant, she also imagines concrete situations inspired by her research and hears the voice of one of her ancestors, Khahtsahlano, speaking to her.[25] Finally she realizes during a session with her students, who will later assist her in saying "goodbye" to Snauq, her ancestors' lost land:

> "There is much more to history than meets the eye. We need to know what happened, and what happened has nothing to do with the dates, the events, and the gentlemen involved, it has to do with the impact." […]
>
> They all pull their seats forward. "We need to finish this story." They nod, as if for the first time they seem to know what's going on. Even the white students nod, affirming that they too understand. (216)

While some of the writers of *Our Story* decide to present a view of "official" Canadian history from a Native perspective, as Thomas King in "Coyote and the Enemy Aliens," which also appears in this collection, most of the contributors choose to set an emphasis on the micropolitics of histories from the perspective of modernity. This is not only the case in Lee Maracle's story but also in Drew Hayden Taylor's, in which he describes the thoughts of a white woman recently divorced from her Native husband, whom she unexpectedly spots on TV during the news coverage of the events at Oka. As Taylor explains in his comment:

> And that is why I ended up writing, in *A Blurry Image on the Six O'Clock News*, from the perspective of a divorced White woman. Not my usual messenger of storytelling. But it was that polarization that affected me, and the realization that, in the midst of

[24] In Johnston's story this becomes especially obvious through the integration of the White men in the Odauwau's storytelling process.

[25] It does not become obvious throughout the narration whether the protagonist is a woman or a man; however, as the author is a woman, I will here assume that the protagonist is too.

> socio-political upheaval, some emotions remain simple and highly recognizable, regardless of race or cultural background. (224)

Also Tomson Highway adds a personal perspective (that is in fact partially autobiographical)[26] to the collection of fictions of the past. His story is highly valuable for an understanding of transcultural imaginaries in Native fictions, as it portrays the transformational power of art (181) exercised by a young Cree Indian boy. In "Hearts and Flowers," Highway captures events set in the year 1960, in which the Native peoples of Canada finally gained the right to vote. He works out this historical moment by rendering the perspective of an eight-year-old Cree, Daniel Daylight, who is learning to play the piano and is in fact highly talented. He is practicing a duet, which he is going to perform together with a white girl of the same age, Jenny Dean. This transcultural exchange is made possible by his open-minded white schoolteacher, who believes in his talent and does not care about the prejudices the audience will have towards this collaboration. Daniel is not old enough to understand politics, but he knows, through explanations given to him by his schoolteacher, Mr. Tipper, that his parents are not accepted as humans and that this disrespect is also related to the fact that they cannot vote. It is his biggest wish to change this degrading law and he believes he can do so by giving his best and playing as beautifully as possible, together with the friendly white girl Jenny:

> For Daniel Daylight, two things happen. First, from where he sits, he sees four hands, two brown (non-human), two white (human), playing the piano. He is sure, somehow, that once he and Jenny Dean have mastered the piece and won first prize in the duet section of the music festival, he—and his parents—will be human. They will have the vote. Father Roy will *not* be able to turn Cheechup Daylight and his wife, Adelaide, away from the little voting booth at the little wooden church that overlooks the northern extremity of beautiful, extraordinary Minstik Lake with its ten thousand islands. ("Hearts and Flowers" 192)

The concert is a great success and as he is driving home in the car with Mr. Tipper they hear on the radio that the Aboriginal people of Canada were, on that very day, given the right to vote.

> "You see?" Daniel Daylight says to Mr. Tipper, his English, and his confidence, having grown quite nicely in just two months. "We are human. I knew it. And you know why I knew it, Mr. Tipper?"
>
> "Why Daniel Daylight?"
>
> "Because I played it." (199)

Through the power of his own will and musical imagination Daniel succeeds in overcoming the great gap created by dominant cultural constructions, by de- and reconstructing them, not only for himself but also for those watching and listening to

[26] Cf. Highway's comment to the story, 179-181.

him, by playing a piece together with a white girl. The achievement of the individual meets the historical and unites into a transcultural moment, maybe even momentum. Highway does not resolve whether this experience remains limited to Daniel's perception, or whether it also has an effect on the imaginary of other participants at the concert.

Another story that compellingly captures the positive forces and creative potential of transcultural imaginaries is Jovette Marchessault's "The Moon of the Dancing Suns."[27] Again, it is the younger generation (and partially the Elders) that succeeds in overcoming sorrow and hardship through the suspension of cultural or individual differences – gaps that adults only narrowly succeed in bridging, or often even widen under strained circumstances. The story describes the friendship of a diverse group of youths, not all yet in their teens, during the Second World War: there is Tobie, a Métis-Lakota boy who has to take care of his sick mother while his father is in the war; Anaie, a little non-status Cree Indian who has spiritual abilities; Jérémie, a Mohawk; David, whose family has been white for generations but has Ojibway ancestors; and Kateri, who too displays powerful spiritual and storytelling qualities. While the adults quarrel over the disappearance of two of their children, the latter not only find their companions, they in fact practice communal occupations that unite them despite their differences; in one instance, for example, Kateri acts as a storyteller as she explains her reasons for running away from home – her storytelling functions as a healing device for all the children:[28]

> As Kateri continues her narrative, Tobie observes his friends. They are all hanging on her every word, especially David, whose face, at certain points in the tale, is crossed by shafts of light.
>
> Tobie thinks he can remember that David once told him that in his family there was a long tradition of storytelling. "The finest gift that you can make to a friend or guests is the enchantment of a good story. You must take care always to have one ready."
>
> "My friends," muses Tobie, "are more alive than all the people I run across in the course of the day. ("The Moon of the Dancing Suns" 140)

The friends tell each other about their varying religious customs and beliefs, and in the story's culmination meet for a ceremony to celebrate Solstice. Together with a Franciscan monk from Russia – their parents and grandparents secretly watching them – they first share precious personal treasures and memories with each other and then dance and sing:

> At the instance of Solstice, Kateri is absolutely still. Quivering like a winged creature clad in a golden beam of light, she begins to sing the dirge "Death of a Warrior." The

[27] Jovette Marchessault is an author from Montreal writing in French (249). Since her story is included in the collection in English translation, I did not see any reason to exclude it from the analysis.

[28] Cp. Melchart "The Healing Potential of the Spoken Word," for a comprehensive recent diploma thesis on this issue.

> musical bow and the rattles accompany her as she intones the sad lamentation. All those present think they hear very clearly the beat of the drums along with the plainsong of the dead souls coming from the heart of the earth. When Kateri finishes her song, another voice arises … Appearing as a white shape, it descends from the Moon.
>
> The grandmothers think, "It is the magnificent Daughter of Heaven."
>
> The grandfathers think, "It is the White Bison Woman, who taught us the seven sacred ceremonies."
>
> Kateri's grandmother thinks, "It is the Great White Star, come from the Land of the Dead, to be a guide to our daughters and our sons."
>
> Brother Léon thinks, "It is Gabriel, the Angel of the Moon, the guardian of human and animal mothers and new-borns, who is beginning his task of tenderness and love. How the blessings enlarge and spread!" (152)

The children in this story and Highway's talented Daniel come to represent transcultural figures who not only find an alternative, enabling mode for themselves to survive in the midst of social tensions, they also act as mediators between self and other for their families and communities. A similar example can also be found in Qitsualik's "Skraeling," in which the half Inuit, half Viking boy Siku bears the role of a shaman, or *angakoq*, for his Tunit community. "Skraeling" describes the encounter of an Inuk called Kannujaq with a now-extinct tribe of the Canadian North called Tunit, and on another level their encounter with the first white invaders, the Vikings. Of course all those encounters are invariably linked to misunderstandings, prejudices, violence, and fear. Siku's father is a Viking who had been saved by the Tunit people, but later returned to his own people, only to come back repeatedly, brutally fighting for his son. However, Siku also becomes the missing link for the main protagonist Kannujaq's understanding of the similarities of such divergent cultures as those of the Vikings, Tunit, and Inuit (65). As Marchessault brings the message to the point by quoting the "words spoken at the conclusion of every Lakota tobacco ceremony" at the beginning of her story: "MI TAKU OYASIN: *We are all linked to one another*" ("The Moon of the Dancing Suns" 129).

Not all stories in the collection reflect this openness, instead communicating a certain degree of resistance to a transcultural imaginary or a belief in its potential to enable agency: Brian Maracle, for example, expressly resists the description of an event that involves the impact of White people, as this is precisely what has dominated First Nations' existence in the past centuries (13-14); and Tantoo Cardinal's story "There Is a Place" depicts indirectly, albeit more dramatically, how the reality of Métis people around the 1920s was determined primarily by cultural and social segregation that led to an absence of choices and often to a complete loss of agency.

Transcultural imaginaries, in the cases in which they do appear in the fictions of the past discussed in this chapter, thus additionally bear an idealist, visionary quality. Consequently, the transcultural does not necessarily describe past or existing realities but offers a future-oriented ethics of hope that may eventually render a healing across cultural differences possible:

> The first view of both town and reserve, to Daniel Daylight, always looks like a spaceship landed on Planet Earth, not unlike the spaceship in the comic book that his older brother, John-Peter Daylight, gave him as a Christmas present twenty-one days ago and that Daniel Daylight keeps hidden under his pillow in the dormitory at the residential school. Daniel Daylight likes, in fact, to imagine all those lights in the distance as exactly that: a spaceship come to take him to a place where exist not Indian people, not white people, just good people and good music. ("Hearts and Flowers" 186)

The rewritings of history drafted in *Our Story* suggest that Aboriginal authors are not just writing "speculative fictions" about Canada's past[29] – thus, narratives that "reflect the widespread skepticism [...] about historical knowledge and its literary representation" (Wyile, *Speculative Fictions* xii); they present something even more encompassing: *visionary* – possibly even *healing* – fictions of the past. In the most extensive survey of recent developments in Canadian historical fictions to date, Herb Wyile was forced to exclude Native Canadian voices due to, as he observed, a lack of fictional rewritings of the past by that group of writers. Although in 2002 he speculates:

> Nonetheless, given the increasing variety, innovation, and postcolonial complexity of the work by native writers, I would venture that it is just a matter of time (no pun intended) before we see native writers producing their own historical fiction. Given the dominant culture's continued ignorance concerning the significance of the historical context of land claims, the effect of residential schools on cultural practices and family structures, and the question of self-government, the past is bound to become more prominent a territory to which natives writers turn. (*Speculative Fictions* xvi-xvii)

Indeed, Wyile's prophecy has been confirmed in recent years as a growing number of Aboriginal writers have turned to this "territory" and produced remarkable rewritings – such as those discussed in the present chapter. Apart from these innovative, alter-native and most importantly, in several cases transcultural re-appropriations of the past, Native authors – Penny Van Toorn mentions this towards the end of her insightful chapter on Aboriginal writing – are beginning to "[lift] the gaze beyond the national arena [...] exploring the political predicaments of oppressed groups in the Middle East, Africa, and Central and South America" (44). Though this is not yet the case in *Our Story* (except for a short reflective gaze on the happenings across the world at the time of the Viking invasion in "Skraeling," 38-39), some authors do, as already indicated in relation to King's "Coyote and the Enemy Aliens," express their sympathy for the fate of other marginalized ethnicities within Canada. Thus, Lee Maracle's protagonist is well informed about the injustices inflicted upon Chinese population in the Canadian West; therefore she finds at least some satisfaction in the knowledge that the land of her ancestors is now owned by a Chinese multibillionaire: "It is such an irony that the first

[29] "Speculative Fiction" refers to the title of Herb Wyile's study on contemporary Canadian historical fiction; in his preface he explains that the title was inspired by "the recurring characterization of the historical novel as a mirror image or inversion of science fiction," xi – in his study, the term refers to historical fiction as historiographic metafiction, i.e. resisting "retrospective certainty," xii.

'non-citizen immigrant residents' should now possess the power to determine the destiny of our beloved Snauq. I know it shouldn't, but somehow it makes me happy, like knowing that Black Indians now people the Long Island Reservation in New York State" (218).

The fictions of the past produced by Aboriginal writers in the past decade exhibit an openness that not only lends its ears to *other* discriminated voices but also searches a reformed dialogue with the general mass of dominating, former colonial culture within Canadian society; yet the results of this initiative have yet to be observed: "By drawing non-Native readers imaginatively into Native and Métis life-worlds, literary texts can build bridges of understanding and empathy. Whether these bridges lead to real-world action and Native/white alliances is another question [...]" (Van Toorn 42). However, we must conclude that the (trans)cultural imaginary reflected in contemporary Native fictions of the past sparks the aspiration that contemporary Aboriginal citizens have established self-assured modern identities and will continue to speak up in order to articulate their vision of past, present and future; this might be the beginning of a new era of creative healing that applies the "power and sacredness [...] [of] the word as a force of change" ("Aboriginal Legends and Tales" 11).

Conclusion: The Necessity and Ethics of 'Trans'

The aim of this work was to explore the possibilities and actualities of 'transcultural imaginaries' in contemporary Canadian literature. It was argued that this extended mode of consciousness that fosters layering, exchange, and transformation of cultural information and images across identitary spaces of difference, does in fact exist, particularly as a marker of current forms of the historical genre, provisionally termed 'fictions of the past.' These claims were related to a further assumption, that the present development of societies and cultures under the influence of globalization forces has caused these particularly dense and complex processes and modes of identification. As David Chariandy observes in the more specific context of Black Canadian Writing:

> Given the fact that many contemporary theorists of race and ethnicity are now consciously endeavoring, in Cornel West's words, to embrace "diversity, multiplicity and heterogeneity" (3), the discursive complexity that has always been a special concern of critics of Black Canadian literature may now prove to be broadly significant, even exemplary, throughout the world. (Chariandy 212)[1]

To insist on the analysis of transcultural processes and expressions today does not imply that it is a new phenomenon; however, it does presume that recent planetary developments intensified its presence and engendered its becoming an integral part of present-day human (co-)existence. Another important assertion is linked to this development – already indicated in the quote above – that the emergence of the transcultural voice in literature would not have been possible without the persistent work of migrant authors. Nowadays, as the selection of texts discussed in the case studies suggest, the transcultural affects the works of authors of all origins. Thus,

> [i]n the end, considering a writer migrant, local, national, or universal does not really matter, since from a modern, or better still, a postmodern and postcolonial perspective, all writers nowadays belong to what Anglo-Saxon critics call 'World Literature,' a much broader and more inclusive concept than Goethe's Weltliteratur, which served as the prototype for a universal conception of culture where exclusion was, in fact, the norm. What does matter, at least for the future of literature in Quebec and Canada, is what the so-called migrant writers have achieved as art and how they have contributed not only to the mere remapping, but also to the reshaping of the literary canon. (Dupuis, "Transculturalism and *Écritures Migrantes*" 507)

The "discursive complexity" that Chariandy mentions and that accompanies the concept of transcultural imaginaries is also its key asset, insofar as it allows critics, authors, and readers alike to overcome established categories, to develop new forms of thinking

[1] The quotation within refers to Cornel West, "The New Cultural Politics of Difference," *Keeping Faith: Philosophy and Race in America* (New York: Routledge, 1993), 3-32.

across (disciplinary, cultural, and other) boundaries, and to reverse gridlocked understandings of self and other. This observation is most clearly evidenced in the work of the youngest author discussed in the case studies, Madeleine Thien. Influenced less by the Marxist and feminist theories in which authors like Dionne Brand engage, or the semi-strong, revised postcolonial thinking that underlies the works of George Elliott Clarke or Thomas King, Thien's *Certainty* vividly captures the uncertainties and desires of a younger generation that can no longer be termed Generation X, but rather 'generation Y' (why?) or 'W' (double you); belonging to a generation born into the arrays of a media-dominated, migratory and thus densified reality of a culturally hybrid world, Thien pleads that "stories will not be lost in the chaos of never touching one another, never overlapping in any true way. [...] Out of the disparate pieces, let something pure, something true, emerge. Let it remain there visible" (210).

As should have become obvious, the basic argumentation of my investigation, which focuses on the suggestion to read contemporary 'fictions of the past' in terms of transcultural imaginaries, is developed on two levels: one part of my observations are theory-based, the other part is grounded on the actual literary, textual level. While the one approach shows how fictions of the past and transcultural imaginaries 'make sense' from discourses within the academia, within the socio-political context of Canada, in terms of globalization, and its inherent discrepancies, the other, the close reading of a diverse array of texts, illustrates how authors elaborate, or in some cases question, transcultural, transgeneric, and transhistorical features in "space, place, and time," through a variety of "voices and perspectives," and via "transfer, exchange, or resistance." This examination argues for its approach by looking at both sides of the scene; however, these two perspectives also have implications for a larger-scale vision.
What is revealed on both levels – definitely for me, and hopefully for the reader – is, what one might call, the potential and, eventually, the necessity of 'trans.' Its potential through the interpretation of *trans*-cultural imaginaries lies in the opening up of new perspectives, of *trans*-lation between and across theoretical as well as identitary boundaries, and its ability to *trans*-cend binary oppositions. This potential is beginning to be probed, for example, in the very recently published collection *Transcultural English Studies*, edited by Frank Schulze-Engler and Sissy Helff. In it, critics such as Mark Stein, who investigates the work of transcultural Scottish writer Jackie Kay, productively accede to "focus on the location of transculture. The concept is not treated as a given but, instead, a series of questions is raised about what transculture is and how it can be identified" (252).
Even if one remains critical of the true *potential* of transcultural approaches, the '*necessity* of trans' or similar alternative readings has become an urgent project for literary theory as both critics and the texts they study, make clear. Innovative scholars across the disciplines who are discussed in this study, scholars such as Wilson and Dissanayake, Patricia Yaeger, Lars Eckstein, or Middleton and Woods, to name only a few, all express and theoretically substantiate this claim. What the present analysis thus underscores is that as a great number of thinkers, often working in very different theoretical realms, have indicated, here in the harsh words of Andrew Chung, "Canadians simply haven't thought about what their country will look like in the post-multicultural era" (308). This new "post-multicultural" citizenship that displays

"'territorialized cosmopolitan' subjectivities—subjectivities with multiple affiliations across axes of gender, ethnicity, class, and sexuality which are not unrooted or free-floating, but are principally and firmly located in the physicality of [place]"[2] and that "emphasizes mutability over authenticity" (Johansen 49) requires rethinking – a rethinking that might be assisted through transcultural approaches. As Winfried Siemerling puts it,

> [b]oth transcultural and dynamic (rather than essentialist) multicultural perspectives seem able to produce interventionist readings of multiple cultures and cross-cultural situations on an increasingly global scale; in this process they contribute to a displacement of horizons of expectation that seems necessary for cross-cultural communication, and generate, in other terms, dialogized 'reoriginations.' [...] Facilitating comparative perspectives and cross-cultural 'translations,' both *from* and *into* respective local circumstances seems to constitute a much-needed function and a more urgent task for universities than the elaboration of essentialist identities or the fulfillment of national missions (which of course cannot but gain from such transnational functions). (Siemerling, "Rereading the Nation" 199)

I think I have made clear enough that indeed a reading of transcultural imaginaries represents a promising option for future literary and cultural investigations. However, I would like to add two final thoughts that most stingingly emerged in the last stages of my work and therefore seem worth mentioning. The one insight gained is that of unresolved, persisting ambiguity that accompanied my research throughout the entire process and remains to be understood as the only discernable, possible answer to contemporary complexities of existence. The other is that the most important of these ambiguities, the most future-oriented is that of 'the ethics of trans.' Let me elaborate on these two final thoughts.

Ambiguity, or ambivalence, it appears is one of the few universals, if it can be called one at all, that remains in contemporary criticism. Even if this might be disappointing for some, I have come to regard it as a rather fruitful realization. Many of the concepts and theories that trouble literary and cultural theorists today – 'identity,' 'authenticity,' 'space,' 'genre,' and 'globalization' – are all marked by ambivalence and can only be applied satisfactorily if one acknowledges this very ambiguity. In fact, the concept of transcultural imaginaries, too, is beset by such contrariety. Yet as Siemerling suggests in his TransCan/Trans-Scan reflections on the prefix "trans," "such doubleness and doubt, however, speak to [our] sense of what is possible, and potentially valuable, in "TransCanadian" perspectives. They combine well with the idea that local positionality by definition is relational, and thus requires mediation, difference, and multi-perspectival recognitions" (131). That theories need room for this ambiguity, for in-between theoretical solutions was expressed in many of the theoretical approaches included here. Such ambiguity fosters creative space between "flow and closure"[3], as, for example, in reaction to the ambivalences underlying theories of identity

[2] In this essay Johansen analyzes Dionne Brand's *What We All Long For*; in the original wording she thus refers to the "physicality of Toronto," where the novel is set.

[3] Cp. Meyer and Geschiere, *Globalization and Identity: Dialectics of Flow and Closure*.

(postmodern arbitrariness and indeterminacy versus essentialism), which leads Paula M. L. Moya, in *Reclaiming Identity*, to subscribe to a postpositivist, realist framework that "shows how identities can both be real and constructed: how they can be politically and epistemically significant, on the one hand, and variable, nonessential, and radically historical on the other" ("Introduction" 12). Several aspects of this ambiguity arise out of the situation that many factors of our current existence – globalization, migrations, new forms of communication, etc. – are having an effect on our realities and identities; as a consequence to this present change, contemporary critical theories themselves are momentarily locked in a productive moment of process, of ambiguity, in which ideas are on the verge of being developed. Thus, as Bové observes about being "'between' because we are neither this nor that" (376):

> [T]he hybridity of the intellectual's work, the fact of being within modernity and the state while trying to be in but not of postmodernity and globalization produces as yet unfulfilled demands for thinking, a process that can only be satisfied in a movement that does not work within the tread-marks of previous intellectual systems. ("Afterword" 377)

Or, Smaro Kamboureli, who recently formulated this idea similarly, in the context of the ambitious TransCanada project:

> CanLit may thus be instrumentalized by and concerned with the Canadian state, but it also contests the stateness, and boldly points beyond it, to an elsewhere that is not yet legible, that defamiliarizes the tropes that produce transparency and its accompanying contentment and complacency. An alternative cognitive space, this elsewhereness demands epistemic breaks that require new tools to comprehend its materiality; it calls for an understanding of temporality and space that questions the assumption that knowledge is residual, always anterior to what has come before, the product of the same epistemological gestures that have cultivated the categories of 'proper' subject and 'other' in the first place. ("Preface," *Trans.Can.Lit* x)

This common call for alternative modes of thinking, whether a pledge for "elsewhereness" or a "hybridity of knowledges" (Bové 379) in this "'interregnum,' that place and time when there is as yet no rule, when there are ordering forces but they have not yet summoned their institutional rule into full view" (ibid, 385), these were desires that also projected the ideas in this book and remain inspirational even now.

In the course of the development of my understanding of transcultural imaginaries and possible readings of them in contemporary fictions of the past, I attempted to flesh out interdisciplinary literary spaces that comply with contemporary understandings of culture, echo the (re-)emerging defense of individual agency, and acknowledge the possibilities of (trans-)cultural transgressions and complexities. In doing so – again in view of both theories and literatures – the most intractable of all perspectives gained was that of what I referred to above as the 'ethics of trans.' If we speak of a poststructuralist ethical turn, we might surely think of the important role that structuralist theories played in the emergence of postmodern, postcolonial ethics that rejected and deconstructed former master narratives in favor of the marginalized voice.

Yet, as Wyile notes, with reference to more recent theorists of 'the ethical turn,'[4] there are further levels to be considered; his analysis of two novels, one of which is *George and Rue*, reveals "how the encounter with these novels involves a more genuinely and politically fruitful, engagement of our ethical faculties" ("Making a Mess of Things" 823). The described effect, once again, resides in the power of ambivalence – ethics, too, must be regarded here as a double-edged concept, whose effectiveness for literary theories only unfolds in an in-between far beyond essentialist moralism, in the "process of destabilizing a sense of empathy and blurring the lines between victims and victimizers [as] a recognition of the self in the other" (ibid. 834). Transcultural imaginaries themselves, as they are expressed in the discussed texts, suggest an ethical voice – a voice already inherent in the theories of *ViceVersa*'s intellectuals of the 1980s; this voice provokes the questioning, comparison, and transgression of difference, and thus a quest for conflicting *and* shared meaning, which presses those involved in the literary discourse to challenge their conceptions of self and other.

Transcultural theories as the one developed here, I have come to believe, might also be seen as an ethical responsibility that the literary critic must confront herself, as well as one confronted by literature and its readers. It resonates with the claim to "postmodern humanism" made by Davis and Womack, who point toward the impersonal, unsettling, and "out of touch with reality" nature of many contemporary literary theories that neglect "humanity's struggle to derive hope and meaning in a postmodern landscape beset by ethical contradictions and vexing moral dilemmas that offer no clear resolution" ("Necessary Negotiations" xxiii). In this context they argue:

> Once we witness the ways in which a story or a film or a song may come undone, word rubbing against word in the friction of (mis)reading, we are compelled to return to the commonalities of human experience and the overarching desire for meaning and relationship that offers not only hope for the future but in many ways also serves as the loadstone in the arch that carries us across the chasm of alienation as we confront the void [of contemporary globalized realities] (xxi)

Such a view can be applied to the concept of transcultural imaginaries and results in the 'ethics of trans,' which, again antithetically, acknowledges the constructedness of the world while at the same time taking a step forward, presenting a momentum of trust that allows for the development of new meaning in this "void" of contemporary existence. While the majority of fictions of the past discussed in this study display that a transcultural rethinking, a re-evaluation of existential situations, and an acknowledgement of ambiguous feelings and relations is well underway, the future will show whether more theorists of literature decide to, at last, follow suit.

[4] Wyile refers to critics such as David Parker, Davis and Womack, Wayne Booth, Martha Nussbaum, and Richard Rorty, cf. "Making a Mess of Things" 821.

Maps

The rufous hummingbird travels five thosand miles from summer home to winter home and back. This hummingbird can fit into the palm of a hand. Its body defies the known physics of energy and flight. It knew its way before all known map-makers. It is a bird whose origins and paths are the blood of its small body. It is a bird whose desire to find its way depends on drops of nectar from flowers. (Brand, *Map to the Door* 6)

Bibliography

"Aboriginal Legends and Tales." *The Concise Cambridge Companion to Canadian Literature*. Ed. William Toye. Oxford: Oxford UP, 2001. 1-4.

Achilles, Jochen, and Carmen Birkle, eds. *(Trans)Formations of Cultural Identity in the English-Speaking World*. Heidelberg: Universitätsverlag C. Winter, 1998.

Alexis, André. *Childhood*. Toronto: McClelland&Stewart, 1998.

Allolio-Näcke, Lars, Britta Kalscheuer, and Anne Manzeschke, eds. *Differenzen Anders Denken: Bausteine zu einer Kulturtheorie der Transdifferenz*. Frankfurt a.M.: Campus, 2005.

Anderson, Benedict. *Imagined Communities: Reflections on the Origins and Spread of Nationalism*. 1983. Rev. ed. London and New York: Verso, 1991.

Antor, Heinz, and Klaus Stierstorfer, eds. *English Literatures in International Contexts*. Heidelberg: Universitätsverlag Winter, 2000.

---. "Introduction: English Literatures – From National to International Contexts." ibid. ix-xii. Antor, Heinz, ed. Fremde Kulturen verstehen – fremde Kulturen lehren. Heidelberg: Winter, 2007.

Antor, Heinz. "Inter- und Transkulturelle Studien in Theorie und Praxis: Eine Einführung." ibid., *Inter- und Transkulturelle Studien* 9-24.

---. *Inter- und Transkulturelle Studien: Theoretische Grundlagen und interdisziplinäre Praxis*. Heidelberg: UV Winter, 2006.

---."Multikulturalismus, Interkulturalität und Transkulturalität: Perspektive für interdisziplinäre Forschung und Lehre." ibid., *Inter- und Transkulturelle Studien* 25-39.

Appadurai, Arjun. *Modernity at Large: Cultural Dimensions of Globalization*. Minneapolis: University of Minnesota Press, 1996.

---. "Sovereignity Without Territoriality: Notes for a Postnational Geography." Yaeger 40-58.

Appiah, Anthony. *Cosmopolitanism: Ethics in a World of Strangers*. New York: W.W. Norton, 2006.

---. *The Ethics of Identity*. Princeton (NJ): Princeton University Press, 2005.

Armstrong, Jeanette, ed. *Looking at the Words of Our People: First Nations Analysis of Literature*. Penticton (BC): Theytus Books Ltd., 1993.

Ashcroft, Bill, Gareth Griffiths, and Helen Tiffin, eds. *The Empire Writes Back: Theory and Practice in Post-Colonial Literatures*. London: Routledge, 1989.

---. *The Post-Colonial Studies Reader*. 1995. 2nd ed. London: Routledge, 2006.

Ashcroft, Bill. "Resistance and Transformation." Antor and Stierstorfer 15-27.

Assmann, Aleida. "Zur Mediengeschichte des kulturellen Gedächtnisses." Erll und Nünning, *Medien des Kollektiven Gedächtnisses* 45-59.

Atkinson, David W. "Canadian Historical Fiction: A Survey." *Canadian Children's Literature*. 23/24 (1981): 28-29.

Atwood, Margaret. *Alias Grace*. 1996. Toronto: Seal, 1997.

---. *In Search of Alias Grace: On Writing Canadian Historical Fiction*. Charles R. Bronfman Lecture in Canadian Studies. Public Lecture Nov 21, 1996. Ottawa: University of Ottawa Press.

---. Interview with Thomas King. "In Conversation with Thomas King and Margaret Atwood." Excerpt from an interview conducted for *Fine Print* in 2005. King, *A Short History of Indians in Canada* 5-17.

---. *Lady Oracle*. 1976. Toronto: Seal, 1999.

---. *Surfacing*. Toronto: McClelland&Stewart, 1972.

---. *Survival: A Thematic Guide to Canadian Literature*. Toronto: Anansi, 1972.

---. *The Blind Assassin*. 2000. Toronto: Seal, 2001.

Badami, Anita Rau. *Can You Hear the Nightbird Call?* 2006. Toronto: Vintage Canada, 2007.

---. *Tamarind Mem*. 1997. Toronto: Penguin, 2002.

Bak, Hans. "Writing Newfoundland, Writing Canada: Wayne Johnston's *The Colony of Unrequited Dreams*." Steenman-Marcusse, *The Rhetoric of Canadian Writing* 217-236.

Ball, John Clement. Interview with M.G.Vassanji. "Taboos." Daurio 200-209.

---. "Locating M. G. Vassanji's The Book of Secrets: Postmodern, Postcolonial, or Other-Wise?" *Floating the Borders: New Contexts in Canadian Criticism*. Ed. Nurjehan Aziz. Toronto: TSAR, 1999. 89-105.

Bannerji, Himani. "On the Dark Side of the Nation: Politics of Multiculturalism and the Sate of 'Canada'." Verduyn 125-151.

Beck, Ulrich. "What is Globalization." Held and McGrew 99-103.

Bennett, Donna. "English Canada's Postcolonial Complexities." *Essays on Canadian Writing*. N° 51-52 (1993/94): 164-210.

---. "Getting Beyond Binaries: Polybridity in Contemporary Canadian Literature." *Moveable Margins: The Shifting Spaces of Canadian Literature*. Ed. Chelva Kanaganayakam. Toronto: TSAR Publications, 2005. 9-25.

---. "Nation and Its Discontents: Atwood's Survival and After." *Canadistica Canaria (1991-2000): ensayos literarios anglocanadienses*. Ed. Juan Ignacio Oliva. La Laguna: Servicio de Publ., Univ. de la Laguna, 2002. 13-29.

Bennett, Tony, Lawrence Grossberg, and Meaghan Morris, eds. *New Keywords: A Revised Vocabulary of Culture and Society*. Malden (MA): Blackwell, 2005.

Berry, J.W., and J.A. Laponce, eds. *Ethnicity and Culture in Canada: The Research Landscape*. Toronto: UoTPress, 1994.

---. "Evaluating Research on Canada's Multiethnic and Multicultural Society: An Introduction." ibid. 3-16.

Bertrand, Pierre. "Le voyage immobile." *Vice Versa*. N° 22-23 (1988): 8-9.

Besner, Neil. "Beyond Two Solitudes, After Survival: Postmodern Fiction in Canada." *Postmodern Fiction in Canada*. Ed. Theo D'haen and Hans Bertens. Postmodern Studies 6. Amsterdam: Rodopi, 1992. 9-25.

Bhabha, Homi. *Nation and Narration*. London: Routledge, 1990.

---. *The Location of Culture*. 1994. London: Routledge, 2005.

Birkle, Carmen, ed. *Migration – Miscegenation – Transculturation: Writing Multicultural America into the 20th Century*. Heidelberg: Winter, 2004.

Blodgett, Eduard D. *Five-Part Invention: A History of Literary History in Canada*. Toronto: UoT Press, 2003.

Bölling, Gordon. "'A Part of Our History that So Few Knew About': Native Involvement in Canada's Great War – Joseph Boyden's *Three Day Road*." *Inventing Canada-Inventer le Canada*. Ed. Klaus-Dieter Ertler and Martin Löschnigg. Frankfurt a. M: PeterLang, 2008. 253-267.

---. *History in the Making: Metafiktion im neueren anglokanadischen historischen Roman*. Heidelberg: Universitätsverlag Winter, 2006.

---. "'You're Not the Indian I Had in Mind': Hollywood's Appropriation of the Native Other in Thomas King's *Green Grass, Running Water* and Guy Vanderhaeghe's *The Englishman's Boy*." *American and Canadian Literature and Culture: Across a Latitudinal Line*. Eds.

Klaus Martens and Paul Morris. Saarbrücken: Nordamerikanische Literatur und Kultur. Centre for Canadian and Anglo-American Cultures, 2008. 70-95.

Borgmeier, Raimund and Bernhard Reitz, eds. *Der historische Roman*. 2 vols. Anglistik & Englischunterricht 22. Heidelberg: Carl Winter – Universitätsverlag,1984.

Bové, Paul. Afterword. Wilson and Dissanayake 372-385.

Bowering, George. *Burning Water*. 1980. Toronto: Penguin, 1994.

Boyden, Joseph. *Three Day Road*. 2005. London: Phoenix, 2006.

Brand, Dionne. *A Map to the Door of No Return: Notes to Belonging*. Doubleday Canada, 2001.

---. *At the Full and Change of the Moon*. New York: Grove Press, 1999. (U.S. Edition)

---. *In Another Place, Not Here*. 1996. New York: Grove Press, 1997. (U.S. Edition)

Braun, Hans, and Wolfgang Klooss, eds. *Multiculturalism in North America and Europe: Social Practices – Literary Visions*. Trier: WVT, 1995.

Breitbach, Julia. "Politics and Literature between Nationalism and Internationalism." Nischik 149-158.

Brennan, Timothy. "From Development to Globalization: Postcolonial Studies and Globalization Theory." *The Cambridge Companion to Postcolonial Literary Studies*. Ed. Neil Lazarus. Cambridge: Cambridge UP, 2004. 120-138.

Brown, E.K. "Canadian Literature Today." ibid. 107-111.

---. "Our Neglect of Our Literature." ibid. 72-77.

Brown, E.K. *Responses and Evaluations: Essays on Canada*. Edited and with an Introduction by David Staines. Toronto: McClelland and Stewart, 1977.

Burbanks, Andy. "The Mandelbrot Set." *Loughborough University*. School of Mathematics – Homepage. 2 Mar. 2009. http://www.lboro.ac.uk/departments/ma/gallery/mandel/index.html.

Caccia, Fulvio. "Diversité culturelle et transculture ou Vice Versa?" *Le Devoir*. Jeudi, 1er mars 2007. 1 Dec 2008. http://www.vigile.net/Diversite-culturelle-et.

Cameron, Barry. "Theory and Criticism: Trends in Canadian Literature." New, *Literary History of Canada* 108-132.

Cameron, Elspeth, ed. *Multiculturalism and Immigration in Canada: An Introductory Reader*. Toronto: Canadian Scholars' Press, 2004.

Canton, Jeffrey. Interview with Jane Urquhart. "Ghosts in the Landscape." Daurio 194-197.

---. Interview with Thomas King. "Coyote Lives." Daurio 90-97.

Cardinal, Tantoo. "There is a Place." The Dominion Institute. *Our Story*. 103-122.

Carter, Lee. "Muslim Sitcom Debuts in Canada." *BBC News*. Toronto. Last Updated: Tuesday, 9 January 2007, 15:00 GMT. 20 Dec. 2008. http://news.bbc.co.uk/2/hi/americas/6244199.stm

Castell, Manuel. *The Information Age: Economy, Society, and Culture*. 3 vols. Cambridge: Blackwell, 1996-98.

"Centennial Celebrations, 1967." *The Encyclopedia of Music in Canada*. 7 Mar. 2008. http://www.thecanadianencyclopedia.com/index.cfm?PgNm=TCE&Params=U1ARTU0000644

Chariandy, David. "'Canada in Us Now': Locating the Criticism of Black Canadian Writing." *Essays in Canadian Writing*. 75 (Winter 2002): 196-217.

Childs, Peter, Jean Jacques Weber, and Patrick Williams. *Post-Colonial Theory and Literatures: African, Carribean and South Asian*. Trier: WVT, 2006.

Choy, Wayson. *All That Matters*. 2004. New York: Other Press, 2007.

---. *The Jade Peony*. 1995. Vancouver: Douglas&McIntyre, 1999.

Chung, Andrew. "The Peculiarity of Eracism: Mixed Race and Nonbelonging in the Multicultural Nation." *Canadas of the Mind: The Making and Unmaking of Canadian Nationalisms in the Twentieth Century*. Ed. Norman Hillmer and Adam Chapnick. Montreal: McGill-Queen's UP, 2007. 300-310.

Clarke, Austin. *The Polished Hoe*. 2002. New York: Amistad, 2004.

"Clarke, George Elliott." *The Canadian Encyclopedia*. 20 Apr. 2009. http://www.thecanadianencyclopedia.com/index.cfm?PgNm=TCE&Params=A1ARTA0010840

Clarke, George Elliott. *George and Rue*. 2005. New York: Caroll&Graf, 2006. (U.S. Edition)

---. Introduction. *Eyeing the North Star: Directions in African-Canadian Literature*. Ed. G.E. Clarke. Toronto: McClelland&Stewart, 1997. xi-xxv.

---. *Odysseys Home: Mapping African-Canadian Literature*. Toronto: UoT Press, 2002.

---. *Trudeau: Long March and Shining Path*. Kentville (NS): Gaspereau Press, 2007.

---. "What Was Canada?" Moss, *Is Canada Postcolonial?* 27-39.

Cohen, Leonard. *Beautiful Losers*. 1966. Toronto: McClelland&Stewart, 1991.

Collier, Gordon. "Identifications and Alterities: *Écriture* and Orality in the Carribean and its Diaspora." *Wir und das Fremde*. Ed. Philipp Wolf and Stefanie Rück. Nell-Breuning Symposium Rödermark, Oktober 2002. Münster: LIT Verlag, 2004. 225-244.

Compton, Wayde, and Kevin McNeilly. "The Crime of Poetry: George Elliott Clarke in Conversation with Wayde Compton and Kevin McNeilly." *Canadian Literature*. N°182 (Autumn 2004): 53-64.

Condé, Mary. Introduction. *Carribean Women Writers: Fiction in English*. Ed. Mary Condé and Thorunn Lonsdale. London: Basingstoke, 1999. 1-7.

"Constitutional History." *The Canadian Encyclopedia*. 7 Mar. 2008. http://www.thecanadianencyclopedia.com/index.cfm?PgNm=TCE&Params=A1ARTA0001873

Cookson, William. *A Guide to the Cantos of Ezra Pound*. London: Croom Helm, 1985.

Coronil, Fernando. Introduction to the Duke University Press Edition. "Transculturation and the Politics of Theory: Countering the Center, Cuban Counterpoint." Ortiz ix-lvi.

Crummey, Michael. *River Thieves*. 2001. Toronto: Anchor Canada, 2002.

Cuccioletta, Donald. "Multiculturalism or Transculturalism: Towards a Cosmopolitan Citizenship." *London Journal of Canadian Studies*. 2001/2002, Vol. 17: 1-11.

Cuddon, John Anthony, and Claire Preston, eds. *A Dictionary of Literary Terms and Literary Theory*. 4th ed. / rev. by C. Preston. Oxford: Blackwell, 1998.

Cuder-Dominguez, Pilar. "African Canadian Writing and the Narration(s) of Slavery." *Essays on Canadian Writing*. Issue 79 (Spring 2003): 55-75.

Cumyn, Joanna. "Reconfiguring the Nation: Intercultural Textuality and M. G. Vassanji's *The Book of Secrets*." *Beyond Comparison/Au-delà des comparaisons*. Ed. Roxanne Rimstead, Michelle Ariss, Simon Gilbert, and Suzanne O'Connor. Baldwin Mills: Topeda Hill, 2005. 201-209.

"Cypress Hills." *The Canadian Encyclopedia*. 5 May 2009. http://www.thecanadianencyclopedia.com/index.cfm?PgNm=TCE&Params=A1SEC819120

D'haen, Theo, and Pieter Vermeulen, eds. *Cultural Identity and Postmodern Writing*. Amsterdam: Rodopi, 2006.

Damm, Kateri. "Dispelling and Telling: Speaking Native Realities in Maria Campbell's *Halfbreed* and Beatrice Culleton's *In Search of April Raintree*." Armstrong 83-92.

Daurio, Berverley, ed. *The Power to Bend Spoons: Interviews With Canadian Novelists*. Toronto: The Mercury Press, 1998.

---. Interview with Dionne Brand. "Writing It." Daurio 31-41.

Davey, Frank. *Post-national Arguments: The Politics of the Anglophone-Canadian Novel since 1967*. Toronto: UoT Press, 1993.

---. *Surviving the Paraphrase: Eleven Essays on Canadian Literature*. With a Preface by Eli Mandel. Winnipeg, Turnstone Press, 1983.

Davis, Geoffrey V., et al. eds. *Towards a Transcultural Future: Literature and Society in a 'Post'-Colonial World*. ASNEL Papers 9.1. Amsterdam: Rodopi, 2004.

Davis, Rocio G. *Transcultural Reinventions: Asian American and Asian Canadian Short-story Cycles*. Toronto: TSAR, 2001.

Davis, Todd F., and Kenneth Womack, ed. *Mapping the Ethical Turn: A Reader in Ethics, Culture and Literary Theory*. Charlottesville & London: UP of Virginia, 2001.

Davis, Todd F., and Kenneth Womack. *Postmodern Humanism in Contemporary Literature and Culture: Reconciling the Void*. Basingstoke & NY: Palgrave Macmillan, 2006.

---. "Introduction: Necessary Negotiations." ibid., *Postmodern Humanism* x-xxv.

Demers, David Pearce. *Global Media: Menace or Messiah*. Cresskill (NJ): Hampton Press, 1999.

Department of Justice Canada. *Canadian Multiculturalism Act*. 1985, c. 24 (4th Supp.). An Act for the preservation and enhancement of multiculturalism in Canada. [1988, c. 31, assented to 21st July, 1988]. Multiculturalism Policy of Canada. Section 3. 19 Jun. 2009. http://laws.justice.gc.ca/en/showdoc/cs/C-18.7//20090918/en?page=1

Döring, Jörg, ed. *Spatial Turn: Das Raumparadigma in den Kultur- und Sozialwissenschaften*. Bielefeld: transcript, 2008.

Doyle, John. "Little Mosque Is Gloriously Canadian." *Globe and Mail*. Tuesday, 9 Jan. 2007. *Westwind Pictures*, homepage. 20 Dec. 2008. http://home.westwindpictures.com/_shows/littlemosque/jan0907e.html

Dragland, Stan. "*The Colony of Unrequited Dreams*: Romancing History?" *Essays on Canadian Writing*. N° 82 (2004): 187-213.

Dube, Rebecca. "Little Mosque on the Prairie: Globe and Mail Update." *Globe and Mail*. Created 9 Jan. 2007. Last Updated 3 Apr. 2009. 21 June 2009. http://www.theglobeandmail.com/news/opinions/article734029.ece

Dünne, Jörg, and Stephan Günzel, eds. *Raumtheorie: Grundlagentexte aus Philosophie und Kulturwissenschaft*. Frankfurt a. M.: Suhrkamp, 2006.

Duffy, Dennis. *Sounding the Iceberg: An Essay on Canadian Historical Novels*. Toronto: ECW, 1986.

Duncan, James S., Nuala C. Johnson, and Richard H. Schein, eds. *A Companion to Cultural Geography*. Blackwell Companions to Geography. Oxford: Blackwell, 2004.

Dupuis, Gilles. "Migration et transmigrations littéraires au Québec: L'exemple brésilien." Ertler, *Migration und Schreiben* 13-22.

---. "Transculturalism and *écritures migrantes*." Nischik 497-508.

During, Simon. *Cultural Studies: A Critical Introduction*. London: Routledge, 2005.Durnin, Katherine. "Archives and Truth in Fred Stenson's *The Trade*." *Canadian Literature*. 178 (Autumn 2003): 73-88.

Easingwood, Peter, Konrad Gross, and Lynette Hunter, eds. *Difference and Community: Canadian and European Cultural Perspectives*. Amsterdam: Rodopi, 1996.

Echterhoff, Gerald. "Das Außen des Erinnerns: Was vermittelt individuelles und kollektives Gedächtnis?" Erll and Nünning, *Medien des kollektiven Gedächtnisses* 61-82.

Eckstein, Judith. Interview with Madeleine Thien. "Madeleine Thien – Ein Interview: Auf Lesereise in Deutschland." *3Sat*. Online. Interview vom 22.März 2007. Interview Judith Eckstein, Redaktion Bettina von Pfeil. 25 Feb. 2009. http://www.3sat.de/3sat.php?http://www.3sat.de/denkmal/internet/106201/index.html

Eckstein, Lars, ed. *English Literatures Across the Globe: A Companion*. Paderborn: Wilhelm Fink Verlag, 2007.

---. Introduction. ibid. 13-19.

Egan, Susanna and Gabriele Helms. "Life Writing." Kröller 216-240.

Elias, Amy J. *Sublime Desire: History and the Post-1960s Fiction*. Baltimore: John Hopkins UP: 2001.

Elliott, Anthony, and Larry Ray, eds. *Key Contemporary Social Theorists*. Oxford: Blackwell, 2003.

Elliott, Anthony. "Anthony Giddens." Elliott and Ray 135-140.

Engler, Bernd, and Kurt Müller, eds. *Historiographic Metafiction in Modern American and Canadian Literature*. Paderborn: Schöningh, 1994.

"Eric R. Kandel: The Nobel Prize in Physiology or Medicine 2000." *Nobelprize.org*. Official website of the Nobel Foundation. 10 May 2008. http://nobelprize.org/nobel_prizes/medicine/laureates/2000/kandel-autobio.html

Erll, Astrid, and Angar Nünning, eds. *Gedächtniskonzepte der Literaturwissenschaft: Theoretische Grundlegung und Anwendungsperspektiven*. Berlin: De Gruyter, 2004.

---. "Gedächtniskonzepte der Literaturwissenschaft: Ein Überblick." Erll, Gymnich, and Nünning 3-27.

---. "Literaturwissenschaftliche Konzepte von Gedächtnis: Ein einführender Überblick." Erll and Nünning, *Gedächtniskonzepte* 1-9.

Erll, Astrid, and Hanne Birk, eds. *Medien des kollektiven Gedächtnisses: Konstruktivität – Historizität – Kulturspezifität*. Berlin: De Gruyter, 2004.

Erll, Astrid, Marion Gymnich, and Ansgar Nünning, eds. *Literatur – Erinnerung – Identität: Theoriekonzeptionen und Fallstudien*. ELCH 11. Trier: WVT, 2003.

---. "Einleitung: Literatur als Medium der Repräsentation und Konstruktion von Erinnerung und Identität." ibid. iii-ix.

Erll, Astrid. "Literatur als Medium des kollektiven Gedächtnisses." Erll and Nünning, *Gedächtniskonzepte* 249-276.

---."Medium des kollektiven Gedächtnisses: Ein (erinnerungs-) kulturwissenschaftlicher Kompaktbegriff." Erll and Nünning, *Medien des kollektiven Gedächtnisses* 3-22.

Ertler, Klaus-Dieter, and Martin Löschnigg, eds. *Canada in the Sign of Migration and Trans-Culturalism: From Multi- to Trans-Culturalism*. Frankfurt am Main: Peter Lang, 2004.

---. *Inventing Canada – Inventer le Canada*. Frankfurt am Main: Peter Lang: 2008.

Ertler, Klaus Dieter, ed. *Migration und Schreiben in der Romania*. Wien: LIT, 2006.

---. "Die Entwicklung der *écritures migrantes* vor dem Hintergrund des zeitgenössischen Diskursdesigns in Québec." ibid., *Migration und Schreiben* 43-54.

"Expo 67." *The Canadian Encyclopedia*. 7 Mar 2008. http://www.thecanadianencyclopedia.com/index.cfm?PgNm=TCE&Params=A1ARTA0002691

Fagan, Cary. Interview with Michael Ondaatje. "Where the Personal and the Historical Meet." Daurio 115-121.

Falkenstein, Len. "Angry (Nice) Young Men." Review of Brad Fraser's *Martin Yesterday*, David Gow's *Cherry Docs*, and Drew Hayden Taylor's *alternatives*. *Canadian Literature*. N°168 (Spring 2001). Mostly Drama: 143-145. 20 May 2009. http://www.canlit.ca/reviews.php?id=9756

Featherstone, Mike, and Scott Lash, eds. *Spaces of Culture: City–Nation–World*. London: Sage Publications, 1999.

Featherstone, Mike, ed. *Global Culture: Nationalism, Globalization and Modernity*. London: Sage Publications, 1990.

Featherstone, Mike. "Postnational Flows, Identity Formation and Cultural Space." *Identity, Culture and Globalisation*. Ed. Eliezer Ben-Rafael with Yitzak Sternberg. The Annals of the International Institute of Sociology. New Series Vol. 8. Leiden: Brill, 2001. 483-526.

Feng, Pin-Chia. "Transcontinental Writing: Reconfiguring the Politics of Home in Maryse Condé's *The Last of the African Kings*." Kalogeras et al. 1-14.

Findley, Timothy. *Famous Last Words*. 1981. Toronto: Penguin, 1996.

---. *The Wars*. 1977. Toronto: Penguin, 1986.

Fleishman, Avrom. *The English Historical Novel: Walter Scott to Virginia Woolf*. Baltimore: Johns Hopkins UP, 1971.

Fleras, Augie. "Media and Minorities in a Post-Multicultural Society: Overview and Appraisal." Berry and Laponce 267-291.

Francis, Daniel. *National Dreams: Myth, Memory, and Canadian History*. Vancouver: Arsenal Pulp, 1997.

---. *The Imaginary Indian: The Image of the Indian in Canadian Culture*. Vancouver: Arsenal Pulp Press, 1992.

Frosch, Stephen. "Jacques Lacan." Elliott and Ray 190-191.

Frye, Northrop. "Conclusion to a *Literary History of Canada*." (1st ed.) Frye, *Mythologizing Canada* 63-95.

---. "Culture as Interpenetration." Frye, *Mythologizing Canada* 137-146.

---. *Mythologizing Canada: Essays on the Canadian Literary Imagination*. Edited by Branko Gorjup. Toronto: Legas, 1997.

---. *The Bush Garden: Essays on the Canadian Imagination*. Toronto: Anansi, 1971.

Garvey, Johanna. " 'The Place She Miss' – Exile, Memory, and Resistance in Dionne Brand's Fiction." *Callaloo*. 26. 2 (Spring 2003): 486-503. *Literature Online*. 26 Jan. 2009. http://gateway.proquest.com/openurl?ctx_ver=Z39.88-2003&xri:pqil:res_ver=0.2&res_id=xri:lion&rft_id=xri:lion:ft:mla:R03410173:0

Gauthier, Louise. *La mémoire sans frontiers: Émile Ollivier, Naim Kattan et les écrivains migrants au Québec*. Québec: Les Presses de l'Université Laval, 1997.

Giddens, Anthony. *Modernity and Self-Identity: Self and Society in the Late Modern Age*. Cambridge: Polity Press, 1991.

---. *The Consequences of Modernity*. Cambridge: Polity Press, 1990.

---. "The Globalizing of Modernity." Held and McGrew, *Global Transformations Reader* 92-98.

Giguère, Suzanne. *Passeurs Culturels: Une littérature en mutation*. Québec: Les Presses de l'Université Laval, 2001.

Goldberg, David Theo, ed. *Multiculturalism: A Critical Reader*. Oxford: Blackwell, 1994.

Goldman, Marlene. "Mapping the Door of No Return: Deterritorialization and the Work of Dionne Brand." *Canadian Literature*. Issue 182 (Autumn 2004): 13-29. *Literature Online*. 17 Jan. 2009. http://gateway.proquest.com/openurl?ctx_ver=Z39.88-2003&xri:pqil:res_ver=0.2&res_id=xri:lion&rft_id=xri:lion:ft:mla:R03504099:0

---. *Paths of Desire: Images of Exploration and Mapping in Canadian Women's Writing*. Toronto: UoT Press, 1997.

Golfman, Noreen. "Locating the Difference: Ways of Reading Multiculturalism." Hinz (*Mosaic* Special issue) 175-185.

Gorjup, Branko. Introduction. Frye, *Mythologizing Canada* 9-21.

Government of Nova Scotia. "Order of Canada: Recipients 2006." *Nova Scotia*. Government homepage. 15 Apr. 2009. https://www.gov.ns.ca/prot/2006recipients.htm

Grace, Sherrill. "Sociopolitical and Cultural Developments from 1967 to the Present." Nischik 285-290.

Grant, George. *Lament for A Nation: The Defeat of Canadian Nationalism*. 1965. 40th Anniversary Edition. Carleton Library Series 205. Montreal: McGill-Queen's UP, 2005.

Griffiths, Rudyard. Preface. The Dominion Institute 1-3.

Grisard, Dominique, Jana Häberlein, Anelis Kaiser, and Sibylle Saxer, eds. *Gender in Motion: Die Konstruktion von Geschlecht in Raum und Erzählung*. Frankfurt a.M.: Campus Verlag, 2007.

Groening, Laura Smyth. *Listening to Old Woman Speak: Natives and Alternatives in Canadian Literature*. Montréal: McGill-Queen's UP, 2004.

Groß, Konrad, Wolfgang Klooss, und Reingard Nischik, eds. *Kanadische Literaturgeschichte*. Stuttgart-Weimar: Metzler, 2005.

Gruber, Eva. "Beginnings: Aboriginal Oral Traditions." Nischik 27-37.

---. "Literature of the First Nations, Inuit, and Métis." Nischik 413-428.

Gruber, Iris. "Transdifferenzphänomene am Beispiel der littérature migrante in Québec." *Trans – Internet-Zeitschrift für Kulturwissenschaft*. N° 14 (Feb 2003). 28 Jul. 2008. http://www.inst.at/trans/14Nr/gruber_quebec14.htm

Gunew, Sneja. *Framing Marginality: Multicultural Literary Studies*. Carlton: Melbourne University Press, 1994. Full text available online. 3 Aug. 2008. http://faculty.arts.ubc.ca/sgunew/biblio.htm

---. *Haunted Nations: The Colonial Dimensions of Multiculturalisms*. London: Routledge, 2004.

---. "Writing by Women." Kröller 194-215.

Hammill, Faye. *Canadian Literature*. Edinburgh: Edinburgh UP, 2007.

Hannerz, Ulf. "The Global Ecumene." Lechner and Boli 109-119.

---. *Transnational Connections: Culture, People, Places*. London and New York: Routledge, 1996.

Hardt, Michael and Antonio Negri. *Empire*. Cambridge: Harvard UP, 2000.

Harel, Simon. *Les passages obliges de l'écriture migrante*. Montréal: XYZ éditeur, 2005.

Hatch, Ronald. "Change and the Concept of History in the Canadian Historical Novel." *Tensions between North and South: Studies in Modern Commonwealth Literature and Culture*. Ed. Edith Mettke. Proceedings of the 8th Commonwealth Literature Conference. Würzburg: Königshausen & Neumann, 1990. 19-27.

---. "Narrative Development in the Canadian Historical Novel." *Canadian Literature*. N°110 (Fall 1986): 79-96.

Heble, Ajay, Donna Palmateer Pennee, and J.R.Struthers, eds. *New Contexts of Canadian Criticism*. Peterborough (ON): Broadview Press, 1997.

Heble, Ajay. "Contexts of Canadian Criticism: Democracy, Counterpoint, Responsibility." New *Contexts of Canadian Criticism*. Ed. Ajay Heble et al. 78-97.

---. "Sounds of Change: Dissonance, History, and Cultural Listening." *Essays on Canadian Writing*. 71 (Fall 2000): 26-38.

Heighton, Steven. *Afterlands*. 2005. Toronto: Vintage Canada, 2006.

Heilmann, Ann, and Mark Llewellyn, eds. *Metafiction and Metahistory in Contemporary Women's Writing*. Basingstoke: Palgrave, 2007.

Held, David, and Anthony McGrew. *Globalization/Anti-Globalization: Beyond the Great Divide*. 2nd ed. Cambridge: Polity Press, 2007.

Held, David, and Anthony McGrew, eds. T*he Global Transformations Reader: An Introduction to the Globalization Debate*. Cambridge: Polity Press: 2000.

Helms, Gabriele. *Challenging Canada: Dialogism and Narrative Techniques in Canadian Novels*. Montreal: McGill-Queen's UP, 2003.

Hepp, Andreas, and Martin Löffelholz, eds. *Grundlagentexte zur transkulturellen Kommunikation*. UTB 2371. Konstanz: UVK, 2002.

Hepp, Andreas. *Transkulturelle Kommunikation*. Konstanz: UVK, 2006. Hepp, Andreas, and Martin Löffelholz. "Transkulturelle Kommunikation. Enführung in die Grundlagentexte." ibid. 11-33.

---. "Transkulturalität als Perspektive: Medien- und Kommunikations-wissenschaft in Zeiten der Globalisierung." Karmasin and Winter 223-255.

---. "Translokale Medienkulturen." Hepp and Löffelholz 861-885.

Highway, Tomson. "Hearts and Flowers." The Dominion Institute. *Our Story*. 177-199.

Hildebrandt, Mathias. "Von der Transkulturalität zur Transdifferenz." Allolio-Näcke et al. 342-352.

Hilger, Annick. *Not Needing All the Words: Michael Ondaatje's Literature of Silence*. Montreal: McGill-Queen's UP, 2006.

Hill, Lawrence. "Rueing the Consequences." Review of George Elliott Clarke's *George & Rue*. 3 Feb. 2005. *CBC Radio Canada*. Online. 23 Apr. 2009 www.cbc.ca/arts/books/georgeandrue.html

Hinz, Evelyn J., ed. *Idols of Otherness: The Rhetoric and Reality of Multiculturalism*. Special Issue of *Mosaic*. Vol. 29, N° 3 (Sept. 1996).

---. "What is Multiculturalism?: A 'Cognitive' Introduction." ibid. (*Mosaic* Special Issue) vii-xiii.

Hodgins, Jack. *Broken Ground*. 1998. Toronto: McClelland&Stewart, 1999.

---. *The Invention of the World*. 1977. Toronto: Macmillan, 1983.Hoffmann, Gerhard, and Alfred Hornung, eds. *Ethics and Aesthetics: The Moral Turn of Postmodernism*. Heidelberg: Winter, 1996.

House, Christian. "A Map of Glass by Jane Urquhart." *The Independent*. Review. 30 October 2005. 15 Apr. 2009. http://arts.independent.co.uk/books/reviews/article322948.ece

Howells, Corall Ann. "'Home Ground / Foreign Territory': Transculturalism in Contemporary Canadian Women's Short Stories in English." Easingwood 71-77.

Hubbard, Phil J., Rob Kitchin, and Gill Valentine, eds. *Key Thinkers on Space and Place*. Sage 2004.

Huggan, Graham, and Winfried Siemerling. "U.S./Canadian Writers' Perspectives on the Multiculturalism Debate: A Round-Table Discussion at Harvard University." *Canadian Literature*. N° 164 (Spring 2000): 82-111.

Huggan, Graham. "Derailing the 'trans'? Postcolonial Studies and the Negative Effects of Speed." Antor, *Inter- und Transkulturelle Studien* 55-61.

---. "Postcolonial Studies and the Anxiety of Interdisciplinarity." *Postcolonial Studies*. Vol.5, N°3 (2002): 245-275.

---. "Postcolonialism, Globalization, and the Rise of (Trans)Cultural Studies." Davis et al. 27-36.

Hulan, Renée, ed. *Native North America: Critical and Cultural Perspectives*. Toronto: ECW Press, 1999.

Huntington, Samuel P. *The Clash of Civilizations and the Remaking of World Order*. New York: Simon & Schuster, 1996.

Hutcheon, Linda, and Marion Richmond, eds. *Other Solitudes: Canadian Multicultural Fictions*. Oxford: Oxford UP, 1990.

Hutcheon, Linda. "A Crypto-Ethnic Confession." *The Anthology of Italian-Canadian Writing*. Ed. J. Pivato. Toronto: Guernica Editions, 1998. 314-323. *Centre for Language and Literature*. Athabasca University. Homepage. 14 Apr. 2008. http://www.athabascau.ca/cll/writers/hutcheon_essay.html

---. *A Poetics of Postmodernism: History, Theory, Fiction*. London: Routledge, 1988.

---. Introduction. Hutcheon and Richmond 1-16.

---. "Multicultural Furor: The Reception of *Other Solitudes*." Siemerling and Schwenk 10-17.

---. *The Canadian Postmodern: A Study of Contemporary English-Canadian Fiction*. Toronto: Oxford UP, 1988.

Imbert. Patrick, ed. *Consensual Disagreement: Canada and the Americas*. University of Ottawa. Gatineau: Gauvin Press, 2005.

Irvine, Lorna Marie. "Pluralism, Diversity, Heterogeneity: Continuing the Debate." Hinz (*Mosaic* Special Issue) 141-153.

Itani, Frances. *Deafening*. New York: Grove Press, 2003. (U.S. Edition)

Jaenen, Cornelius J. Introduction. "Ethnic Studies: An Integral Part of Canadian Studies." *Identities: The Impact of Ethnicity on Canadian Society*. Ed. Wsevolod Isajiw. Canadian Ethnic Studies Association. Vol. V. Toronto: Peter Martin Associeates Ltd., 1977. xi-xvii.

Jaggi, Maya. Interview with M. Ondaatje. "Michael Ondaatje with Maya Jaggi." *Writing Across Worlds: Contemporary Writers Talk*. Ed. Susheila Nasta. London: Routledge, 2004. 250-265.

Jameson, Fredric. *Postmodernism, Or, the Cultural Logic of Late Capitalism*. 1991. Repr. London: Verso, 2008.

Johansen, Emily. "'Streets Are the Dwelling Place of the Collective': Public Space and Cosmopolitan Citizenship in Dionne Brand's *What We All Long For*." *Canadian Literature*. N° 196 (Spring 2008): 48-62.

Johnston, Basil. "The Wampum Belt Tells Us . . ." The Dominion Institute. *Our Story*. 69-101.

Johnston, Wayne. *The Colony of Unrequited Dreams*. 1998. Toronto: Vintage Canada, 1999.

---. *The Custodian of Paradise*. Toronto: Random, 2006.

---. *The Navigator of New York*. Toronto: Vintage Canada, 2003.

Kalogeras, Yiorgos, Eleftheria Arapoglou, and Linda Manney, eds. *Transcultural Localisms: Responding to Ethnicity in a Globalized World*. Heidelberg: Winter, 2006.

Kalogeras, Yiorgos et al. Introduction. ibid. vii-xiv.

Kamboureli, Smaro, and Roy Miki, eds. *Trans.Can.Lit. Resituating the Study of Canadian Literature*. Waterloo (ON): Wilfrid Laurier UP, 2007.

Kamboureli, Smaro. Introduction. ibid. *Making a Difference* 1-16.

---. *Making a Difference: Canadian Multicultural Literature*. Toronto: Oxford UP, 1996.

---. Preface. Kamboureli and Miki vii-xv.

---. Preface and Acknowledgements. ibid. *Scandalous Bodies* vii-xii.

---. *Scandalous Bodies: Diasporic Literature in English Canada*. Don Mills (ON): OxfordUP, 2000.

Karmasin, Matthias, and Carsten Winter, eds. *Kultur als Kommunikationswissenschaft: Projekte, Probleme und Perspektiven*. Wiesbaden: Westdeutscher Verlag, 2003.

Kertzer, Jonathan. *Worrying the Nation: Imagining a National Literature in English Canada*. Toronto: UoT Press, 1998.

King, Thomas. *A Short History of Indians in Canada: Stories*. 2005. Toronto: Harper Perennial, 2006.

---. "Coyote and the Enemy Aliens." The Dominion Institute. *Our Story*. 155-174.

---. *Green Grass, Running Water*. 1993. Toronto: Harper Perennial, 1999.

---. "Godzilla vs. Post-Colonial." Sugars 183-190.

---. *The Truth About Stories: A Native Narrative*. CBC Massey Lectures. Toronto: Anansi Press, 2003.

Klinck, Carl F., gen. ed. *Literary History of Canada: Canadian Literature in English*. Toronto: UoT Press, 1965.

---. *Literary History of Canada: Canadian Literature in English*. 1976. 2nd ed. Vol. 1. Toronto: UoT Press, 1977.

Klinck, Carl F. "Introduction to Volumes I and II." Klinck, *Literary History of Canada*, Vol.I vii-xiii.

Klooss, Wolfgang, ed. *Across the Lines: Intertextuality and Transcultural Communication in the New Literatures in English*. Cross/Cultures – Readings in the Post/Colonial Literature in English 32. Amsterdam: Rodopi, 1998.

---. "Forms of Identity Construction in English-Canadian Historical (Meta) Fiction." *Canada 2000: Identity and Transformation*. Ed. Klaus-Dieter Ertler and Martin Löschnigg. Frankfurt: Lang, 2000. 81-94.

---. "From Colonial Madness to Postcolonial Ex-Centricity: A Story about Stories of Identity Construction in Canadian Historiographic (Meta-)Fiction." Engler and Müller 53-79.

---. *Narratives of Exploration and Discovery: Essays in Honour of Konrad Gross*. Trier: WVT, 2005.

Kofman, Eleonore, and Elizabeth Lebas. "Introduction: Lost in Transposition – Time, Space and the City." *Writings on Cities*. By Henri LeFebvre. Selected, translated and introduced by Eleonore Kofman and Elizabeth Lebas. Oxford: Blackwell, 1996.

Kogawa, Joy. *Obasan*. 1981. Toronto: Penguin, 1983.

Koval, Ramona. Interview with M.Ondaatje. "Michael Ondaatje on *Divisadero*." *ABC National Radio*. 20 May 2007, Book Show, Presenter Ramona Koval, Producer Rhiannon Brown. Transcript. 7 Mar. 2009. http://www.abc.net.au/rn/bookshow/stories/2007/1925576.htm

Kraidy, Marwan M. *Hybridity, Or the Cultural Logic of Globalization*. Philadelphia: Temple University Press, 2005.

Kröller, Eva-Maria, ed. *Cambridge Companion to Canadian Literature*. Cambridge: Cambridge UP, 2004.

Kröller, Eva Maria. Introduction. ibid. 1-21.

Kroetsch, Robert. *Badlands*. 1975. Toronto: General Publ., 1982.

---. "Disunity as Unity: A Canadian Strategy." *Canadian Story and History: 1885-1985*. Eds. Colin Nicholson and Peter Easingwood. Papers presented at the Tenth Annual Conference of The British Association for Canadian Studies. Edinburgh: Centre of Canadian Studies, Edinburgh University, 1985. 1-11.

---. *The Studhorse Man*. 1969. Markham (ON): Paperjacks, 1980.Kuester, Martin. Framing Truths: Parodic Structures in Contemporary English-Canadian Historical Novels. Toronto: UoT Press, 1992.

Kuester, Martin. "'A Mythic Act of Possession': Constructing the North American Frontier(s) in Guy Vanderhaeghe's *The Englishman's Boy*." *New Worlds: Discovering and Constructing the Unknown in Anglophone Literature*. Eds. Martin Kuester, Gabriele Christ, and Rudolf Beck. Schriften der Philosophischen Fakultäten der Universität Augsburg 59. Munich: Vögel, 2000. 277-92.

Kulyk Keefer, Janice. "From Dialogue to Polylogue. Canadian Transcultural Writing During the Deluge." Easingwood et al. 59-70.

---. "From Mosaic to Kaleidoscope. Out of the Multicultural Past Comes a Vision of a Transcultural Future." *Books in Canada* (Sept. 1991): 13-16.

---. "Writing, Reading, Teaching Transcultural in Canada." Braun and Klooss 180-197.

Kyser, Kristina. Interview with G.E.Clarke. "George and Ruth: An Interview with George Elliott Clarke about Writing and Ethics." *University of Toronto Quarterly: A Canadian Journal of the Humanities*. 76:3 (2007 Summer): 861-73.

Lassotta, Carmen. "Dionne Brand." Author Profile. *Northwest Passages: Canadian Literature Online*. 16 Dec. 2007. http://www.nwpassages.com/bios/brand.asp

Latouche, Daniel. "Le viceversaisme ou l'envers de l'esthétisme." *Vice Versa*. N° 28 (Spring 1990): 44.

Lechner, Frank J., and John Boli. *The Globalization Reader*. 2000. 2nd ed. Malden: Blackwell, 2006.

Lecker, Robert. Making It Real: The Canonization of English-Canadian Literature. Concord: Anansi, 1995.

LeFebvre, Henri. *The Production of Space*. 1974. Trans. Oxford: Blackwell, 1991.

Linton, Patricia. "Narrative Geography in Guy Vanderhaeghe's *The Englishman's Boy*." *American Review of Canadian Studies*. 31:4 (2001): 611-21.

---. "Subaltern Identity in Guy Vanderhaeghe's *The Last Crossing*." *STAR*. (Scotland's Transatlantic Relations) Project Archive. April 2004. 2003 Symbiosis Conference: 'Across the Great Divide': Web Publications. 30 Aug. 2008. http://www.star.ac.uk/star-publications/2003-symbiosis-conference-'across-the-great-divide'-web-publications.aspx

Literature Online (LION). Datenbankservice der Universitätsbibliothek Wien. http://bibliothek.univie.ac.at/eressourcen.html

Little Mosque on the Prairie. TV Series. By Zarqa Nawaz. Produced by Westwind Pictures. Broadcasted by CBC. Premier 9 Jan. 2007. 4th Season: 28 Sept. 2009.

Löffler, Sigrid. "Ein Hybrid-Roman." Review. *Deutschlandradio*. Online. 7 Mar. 2009. http://www.dradio.de/dkultur/sendungen/kritik/660911

Lösch, Klaus. "Begriff und Phänomen der Transdifferenz: Zur Infragestellung binärer Differenzkonstrukte." Allolio-Näcke et al. 26-51.

Löschnigg, Martin. "Creating Lives: Narrative and the Problem of Individual Identity in Canadian Novels of the 1990s." *Canada 2000: Identity and Transformation*. Ed. Klaus-Dieter Ertler and Martin Löschnigg. Frankfurt: Lang, 2000. 95-107.

---."Historical Perspectives on Migrant Communities in the Contemporary Canadian Novel: The Case of Rudy Wiebe's *Sweeter than All the World* (2001)." Ertler and Löschnigg, *Canada in the Sign* 183-194.

Loomba, Ania. *Colonialism/Postcolonialism*. 2nd ed. London and New York: Routledge, 2005.

Lorrigio, Francesco. "Multiculturalism and Literary Criticism: Comparisons and Possibilities." Hinz (Mosaic special issue) 187-198.

Lucking, David. *The Serpent's Part: Narrating the Self in Canadian Literature*. Bern: Peter Lang, 2003.

Lüsebrink, Hans-Jürgen. "Globalisation et transculturalité – les années soixante et leur redécouverte (inter)médiatique au Québec." Ertler and Löschnigg, *Canada in the Sign* 195-206.

Luft, Joanna. "Elizete and Verlia Go to Toronto: Carribean Immigrant Sensibilities at 'Home' and Overseas in Dionne Brand's *In Another Place, Not Here*." *Essays in Canadian Writing*. 77 (Fall 2002): 26-49.

Lukács, Georg. *The Historical Novel*. 1937. Reprint. trans. Harmondsworth: Penguin Books, 1976.

Lutz, Andrea. "Canada." Eckstein 302-327.

Macey, David. "Modernity." *The Penguin Dictionary of Critical Theory*. 2000. ibid. London: Penguin, 2001. 259-260.

---. "White, Hayden V." *The Penguin Dictionary of Critical Theory*. 2000. ibid. London: Penguin, 2001. 396-397.

MacDonald, Ann Marie. *Fall On Your Knees*. 1996. Toronto: Vintage Canada, 1997.

MacDonald, Gayle. "The battle of the small-town, high-stakes, big-network sitcoms just got a whole lot hotter, with two pivotal writers deciding to abandon CTV's Corner for CBC's Prairie." 6 Mar. 2007. *Westwind Pictures*. Homepage. 20 Dec. 2008. http://home.westwindpictures.com/_shows/littlemosque/mar0607.html

MacGillivray, Alex. *A Brief History of Globalization: The Untold Story of Our Incredible Shrinking Planet*. London: Robinson, 2006.

MacLeod, Alexander. "History versus Geography in Wayne Johnston's *The Colony of Unrequited Dreams*." *Canadian Literature*. 189 (2006): 69-83.

MacLeod, Alistair. *No Great Mischief*. 1999. London: Vintage, 2001.

MacLulich, T.D. *Between Europe and America: The Canadian Tradition in Fiction*. Oakville: ECW Press, 1988.

---. "Romances of the New World." ibid. 37-60.

MacMechan, Archibald. *Headwaters of Canadian Literature*. 1924. Introduction by M.G. Parks. Toronto: McClelland and Stewart, 1974.

"Madeleine Thien: Author Bio." *Hachette Book Group*. Homepage. 25 Feb. 2009. http://www.hachettebookgroupusa.com/authors/12/2487/index.html

Maes-Jelinek, Hena. "Postcolonial Criticism at the Crossroads: Subjective Questionings of an Old-Timer." Davis, et al. 1-19.

Mandel, Eli. "Northrop Frye and the Canadian Literary Tradition." *Centre and Labyrinth: Essays in Honour of Northrop Frye*. Toronto: UoT Press, 1983. 284-297.

Maracle, Brian. "The First Words." The Dominion Institute. *Our Story*. 11-31.

Maracle, Lee. "Goodbye, Snauq." The Dominion Institute. *Our Story*. 201-219.

Marchessault, Jovette. "The Moon of the Dancing Suns." The Dominion Institute. *Our Story*. 125-153.

Marlatt, Daphne. *Ana Historic*. 1988. Concord (ON): Anansi, 1997.

"Massey Report." *The Canadian Encyclopedia*. 7 Mar. 2008. http://www.thecanadianencyclopedia.com/index.cfm?PgNm=TCE&Params=A1ARTA0001225

Massey, Doreen, and Pat M. Jess, eds. *A Place in the World? Places, Cultures and Globalization*. Oxford: Oxford UP, 1996.

Massey, Doreen. "A Global Sense of Place." *Marxism Today*. (June 1991): 24-29.Maufort, Marc, and Franca Bellarsi, eds. *Reconfigurations: Canadian Literatures and Postcolonial Identities*. Bruxelles: Peter Lang, 2002.

---. *For Space*. London: Sage, 2005.

Mavjee, Maya. Interview with D.Brand. "Opening the Door: An Interview with Dionne Brand." *Read Magazine*. 25 Feb. 2009. http://www.randomhouse.ca/readmag/page28.htm

McCallum, Pamela, and Christian Olbey. "Written In The Scars: History, Genre, and Materiality in Dionne Brand's *In Another Place, Not Here*." *Essays on Canadian Writing*. Issue 68 (Summer 1999): 159-183. *Literature Online*. 17 Jan. 2009. http://gateway.proquest.com/openurl?ctx_ver=Z39.88-2003&xri:pqil:res_ver=0.2&res_id=xri:lion&rft_id=xri:lion:ft:mla:R03421170:0

McChesney, Robert Waterman, and Edward S. Herman. *The Global Media*. London: Cassell, 1997.

McCourt, Edward A. "The Canadian Historical Novel." *Dalhousie Review*. 26 (1946): 30-36.

Melchart, Astrid. "The Healing Potential of the Spoken Word In the Native American Storytelling Tradition." Diploma Thesis. Leopold-Franzens-Universität Innsbruck, 2005.

Merrifield, Andy. *Henri LeFebvre: A Critical Introduction*. London: Routledge, 2006.

Methot, Suzanne. "Dionne Brand: She's A Wanderer." *Quill & Quire*. April 1999. 19 Jan. 2009. http://www.quillandquire.com/authors/profile.cfm?article_id=1351

Meyer, Birgit, and Peter Geschiere, eds. *Globalization and Identity: Dialectics of Flow and Closure*. Oxford: Blackwell, 1999.

Middleton, Peter, and Tim Woods. *Literatures of Memory: History, Time and Space in Postwar Writing*. Manchester: Manchester UP, 2000.

Miki, Roy. "'Inside the Black Egg': Cultural Practise, Citizenship, and Belonging in a Globalized Canadian Nation." *Mosaic*. Vol. 38, N°3 (Sept. 2005): 1-19.

Mistry, Rohinton. *A Fine Balance*. 1995. London: Faber & Faber, 1996.

---. *Such A Long Journey*. 1991. London: Faber & Faber, 1992.

Moisan, Clément, and Renate Hildebrand. *Ces Étrangers du Dedans: Histoire de l'écriture migrante au Québec (1937-1997)*. Québec: Nota bene, 2001.

Moses, Daniel David, and Terry Goldie. "Preface: Two Voices." *An Anthology of Canadian Native Literature in English*. Ed. Moses and Goldie. Oxford: Oxford UP, 1992. xii-xxii.

Moss, Laura, ed. *Is Canada Postcolonial? Unsettling Canadian Literature*. Waterloo: Wilfrid Laurier UP, 2003.

Mouat, Jeremy. Interview with G.Vanderhaeghe. "Prairie Storyteller: An Interview with Guy Vanderhaeghe." *Aurora Online*. 2003. 1 May 2009. http://aurora.icaap.org/2003Interviews/Vanderhaeghe.html

Moya, Paula M.L., and Micael R. Hames-García, eds. *Reclaiming Identity: Realist Theory and the Predicament of Postmodernism*. Berkeley: U of California P, 2000.

Moya, Paula M.L. "Introduction: Reclaiming Identity." Moya and Hames-García 1-26.

Moynagh, Maureen. "Uses of cultural memory." Review of Austin Clarke's *Pigtails 'n Breadfruit. Rituals of Slave Food: A Barbadian Memoir*, and Dionne Brand's *At the Full and Change of the Moon." Canadian Literature*. Autumn 2001: 193-195. *Literature Online*. 12 Feb. 2009.
http://gateway.proquest.com/openurl?ctx_ver=Z39.882003&xri:pqil:res_ver=0.2&res_id=xri:lion&rft_id=xri:lion:ft:abell:R01612232:0

Mudge, Alan. Interview with Madeleine Thien. "Conversations: Madeleine Thien, author of *Certainty*." *Waterbridge Review*. 25 Feb. 2009. http://www.waterbridgereview.org/062007/cnv_thien.php.

Munro, Alice. *The View from Castle Rock*. New York: Knopf, 2006.

Nabokov, Peter. "Native Views of History." *The Cambridge History of the Native Peoples of the Americas*. Ed. B.G. Trigger and W.E. Washburn. Vol. 1, Part 1. Cambridge: Cambridge UP, 1996. 1-59.

"Native People, Government Policy." *The Canadian Encyclopedia*. 19 May 2009. http://www.thecanadianencyclopedia.com/index.cfm?PgNm=TCE&Params=A1SEC824931

Nelles, Henry Vivian. *A Little History of Canada*. Don Mills (ON): Oxford UP, 2005.

Nepveu, Pierre. "Qu'est-ce que la transculture?" *Paragraphes* 2. Autrement, Le Québec: Conferences 1988-1989. Montréal: Département d'Études Francaises, UdM: 1989. 15-31.

Neumann, Birgit. *Erinnerung–Identität–Narration: Gattungstypologie und Funktionen kanadischer "Fictions of Memory."* Berlin: Walter de Gruyter, 2005.

---. "Literatur als Medium (der Inszenierung) kolleltiver Erinnerungen und Identitäten." Erll. Gymnich, und Nünning 49-78.

---. "Literatur, Erinnerung, Identität." Erll, und Nünning, *Gedächtniskonzepte* 149-178.

---. "Narrative Constructions of Cultural Memory and Identity: Theoretical Approaches and Fictional Explorations in Guy Vanderhaeghe's *The Englishman's Boy*." *Focus on Canada: European Perspectives. Regard vers le Canada: Perspectives canadiennes*. Ed. Elke Nowak. Canadian Studies in Europe Vol. 3. Brno: Masaryk University / European Network for Canadian Studies, 2003. 189-210.

New, W.H., gen. ed. *Literary History of Canada: Canadian Literature in English*. 2nd ed. Vol. 4. Toronto: UoT Press, 1990.

New, W.H. *Borderlands: How We Talk About Canada*. Vancouver: UBC Press, 1998.

---. "Editorial: Learning to Listen." *Native Writers and Canadian Writing*. Ed. W.H. New. *Canadian Literature* Special Issue. Vancouver: UBC Press, 1990. 4-8.

Nischik, Reingard M., ed. *History of Literature in Canada: English-Canadian and French-Canadian*. Rochester: Camden House, 2008.

"North-West Territories, 1870-1905," *The Canadian Encyclopedia*. 8 May 2009. http://www.thecanadianencyclopedia.com/index.cfm?PgNm=TCE&Params=A1ARTA0005805

Nünning, Ansgar. "Literarische Geschichtsdarstellung: Theoretische Grundlagen, fiktionale Privilegien, Gattungstypologie und Funktionen." *Erinnern und Erzählen. Der Spanische Bürgerkrieg in der deutschen und spanischen Literatur und in den Bildmedien*. Ed. Bettina Bannasch and Christiane Holm. Tübingen: Gunter Narr Verlag, 2005. 35-58.

---. "Where Historiographic Metafiction and Narratology meet: Towards an Applied Cultural Narratology." *Style*. 38:3 (Fall 2004): 352-375. 28 Sept. 2008. http://findarticles.com/p/articles/mi_m2342/is_3_38/ai_n27846938/

O'Grady, Carrie. "Sweeping all before." Review. Saturday, 17 Dec. 2005. *The Guardian*. 15 Apr. 2009. http://books.guardian.co.uk/reviews/generalfiction/0,6121,1669097,00.html?84%3A+Book+reviews

O'Grady, Jean, and David Staines, eds. *Northrop Frye on Canada: Collected Works of Northrop Frye*. Vol. 12. Toronto: U of Toronto P, 2003.

Olbey, Christian. Interview with D. Brand. "Dionne Brand in Conversation." *Ariel*. 33.2 (April 2002): 87-102.

Oliva, Peter. *The City of Yes*. 1999. Toronto: McClelland & Stewart, 2001.

Ondaatje, Michael. *Anil's Ghost*. 2000. Toronto: Vintage Canada, 2001.

---. *Divisadero*. New York: Knopf, 2007.

---. *In the Skin of a Lion*. 1987. Toronto: Vintage Canada, 1996.

---. *Running in the Family*. 1982. Toronto: McClelland & Stewart, 1993.

---. *The Collected Works of Billy the Kid: Left-Handed Poems*. Toronto: Anansi, 1970.

---. *The English Patient*. 1992. Basingstoke: Picador, 1993.

Onega, Susana. *Telling Histories: Narrativizing History, Historicizing Literature*. Costerus New Series 96. Amsterdam: Rodopi, 1995.

Oonk, Gijsbert. "Book review." Review of Tomlinson, *Globalization and Cuture*, and Meyer and Geschiere, *Globalization and Identity*. Journal of World History 13.2 (2002): 532-537. Accessed via Project Muse at the Austrian National Library. 1 Oct. 2008. http://muse.jhu.edu/journals/journal_of_world_history/v013/13.2oonk.html

Ortiz, Fernando. *Cuban Counterpoint: Tobacco and Sugar*. 1940. Trans. Harriet de Onís. Introd. to the Duke University Press Ed. by Fernando Coronil. Durham: DukeUP, 1995.

O'Shea Bonner, Margaret. Interview with Jane Urquhart. "Finding Your Place in the Story: An Interview with Jane Urquhart." Interview. *The New Quarterly*. 88 (Fall 2003): 72-90.

Pache, Walter. "'The Fiction Makes Us Real': Aspects of Postmodernism in Canada." *Gaining Ground: European Critics on Canadian Literature*. Eds. Robert Kroetsch, and Reingard M. Nischik. Edmonton: NeWest Press, 1985. 64-78.

Padolsky, Enoch. "Ethnicity and Race: Canadian Minority Writing at the Crossroads." Verduyn 19-36.

Patriquin, Martin. "Canada's Renown for Tolerance Is Breaking Down." *Maclean's*. October 22, 2007. 10 Jan. 2009. http://www.thecanadianencyclopedia.com/index.cfm?PgNm=TCE&Params=M1ARTM0013162.

"Paul Ricoeur." *Stanford Encyclopedia of Philosophy*. 10 May 2008. http://plato.stanford.edu/entries/ricoeur/#3.4

Pearlman, Mickey, ed. *Canadian Women Writing Fiction*. Jackson: UP of Mississippi, 1993.

Pearsall, Judy, ed. *The Concise Oxford Dictionary*. 10th ed. Oxford: Oxford UP, 1999.

Petrone, Penny. Introduction. Native Literature in Canada: From the Oral Tradition to the Present. ibid. Oxford: Oxford UP, 1990. 1-8.

Pieterse, Jan Nederveen. *Globalization and Culture: Global Mélange*. Lanham: Rowman and Littlefield Publishers, 2004.

Pound, Ezra. *The Cantos of Ezra Pound*. 1930-1969. New York: New Directions Books, 1995.

Pratt, Mary Louise. *Imperial Eyes: Travel Writing and Transculturation*. London: Routledge, 1992.

Qitsualik, Rachel A. "Skraeling." The Dominion Institute. *Our Story*. 33-66.

Rabaté, Jean-Michel. *Jacques Lacan: Psychoanalysis and the Subject of Literature*. Basingstoke: Palgrave, 2001.

Redekop, Magdalene. "Canadian Literary Criticism and the Idea of a National Literature." Kröller 263-275.

Renzi, Alessandra. "Identity and Transculture in *Vice Versa*." *Coll. Antropol*. 28. Suppl.1 (2004): 109-113.

"Residential Schools." *The Canadian Encyclopedia*. 19 May 2009. http://www.thecanadianencyclopedia.com/index.cfm?PgNm=TCE&Params=A1ARTA0011547

Ridington, Robin. "Happy Trails to You: Contexted Discourse and Indian Removals in Thomas King's *Truth and Bright Water*." *Canadian Literature*. No 167 (Winter 2000): 89-107.

Rieuwerts, Sigrid, and Bernhard Reitz, eds. *Anglistentag 1999 Mainz: Proceedings*. Trier: WVT, 2000.

Rimstead, Roxanne. Introduction. "Double Take: The Uses of Cultural Memory." Introduction. *Essays on Canadian Writing*. Special Issue on Cultural Memory and Social Identity. N°80 (Fall 2003): 1-14.

Robertson, Roland, and Kathleen E. White, eds. *Globalization: Critical Concepts in Sociology*. 6 vols. Vol IV. Culture and Identity. London: Routledge, 2003.

Robertson, Roland. *Globalization: Social Theory and Global Culture*. London: Sage Publications, 1992.

Rosenthal, Caroline. "English-Canadian Literary Theory and Literary Criticism." Nischik 291-309.

Rossington, Michael, and Anne Whitehead, eds. *Theories of Memory: A Reader*. Edinburgh: Edinburgh UP, 2007.

---. Introduction. ibid. 1-16.

Sandiford, Robert Edison. "The Continuing Saga of George and Rue." Review. *Antigonish Review*. N° 147. 23 Apr. 2009. http://www.antigonishreview.com/bi-147/147-review-robert-edison-sandiford.html

Sassen, Saskia. *Globalization and Its Discontents*. New York: New Press, 1998.

---. *The Global City*: New York, London, Tokyo. Princeton: Princeton UP, 1991.

Schiefer, Nancy. "Urquhart overcolours Map." Review. *The London Free Press*. 17 Sept. 2005. 15 Apr. 2009. http://www.lfpress.com/cgi-bin/publish.cgi?p=105293&x=articles&s=musique

Schmidt, Patrick. "Zwischen Medien und Topoi: Die *Lieux de mémoire* und die Medialität des kulturellen Gedächtnisses." Erll and Nünning, *Medien des kollektiven Gedächtnisses* 25-43.

Schulze-Engler, Frank. "From Postcolonial to Preglobal. Transnational Culture and the Resurgent Project of Modernity." Davis, et al. 49-64.

---. "Literature in the Global Ecumene of Modernity: Amitav Ghosh's *The Circle of Reason* and *In an Antique Land*." Antor and Stierstorfer 373-390.

---. "Theoretical Perspectives: From Postcolonialism to Transcultural World Literature." Eckstein 20-28.

---. "Transnationale Kultur als Herausforderung für die Literaturwissenschaft." *Zeitschrift für Anglistik und Amerikanistik*. 50.1. (2002): 65-79.

---. „Von ‚Inter' zu ‚Trans': Gesellschaftliche, kulturelle und literarische Übergänge." Antor, *Inter- und Transkulturelle Studien* 41 53.

---. "What's the Difference? Notes towards a Dialogue between Transdifference and Transculturality." *Journal for the Study of British Cultures*. Vol. 13/2 (2006): 123-132.

Schwenk, Katrin. Introduction. "Thinking about 'Pure Pluralism'." Siemerling and Schwenk 1-9.

Scott, Sir Walter. *Waverley, Or 'Tis Sixty Years Since*. 1814. Oxford: Clarendon Press, 1981.

Siemerling, Winfried, and Katrin Schwenk, eds. *Cultural Difference and the Literary Text: Pluralism and the Limits of Authenticity in North American Literatures*. Iowa City: Uo Iowa Press, 1996.

Siemerling, Winfried. ed. *Writing Ethnicity: Cross-Cultural Consciousness in Canadian and Québécois Literature*. Toronto: ECW Press, 1996.

Siemerling, Winfried. "Genealogies of Difference." ibid., *New North American Studies* 116-154.

---. "Native Writing, Orality, and Anti-imperial Translation: Thomas King and Gerald Vizenor." ibid., *New North American Studies* 59-115.

---. "Rereading the Nation: Cultural Difference, *Transculture*, and Literary History in Canada and Quebec." *Literature and the Nation*. *REAL* 14. Ed. Thomas Brook. Tübingen: Gunter Narr Verlag, 1998. 183-204.

---. *The New North American Studies: Culture, Writing, and the Politics of Re/cognition*. London: Routledge, 2005.

---. "Trans-Scan: Globalization, Literary Hemispheric Studies, Citizenship as Project." Kamboureli and Miki 129-140.

Simon, Sherry, et al. eds. *Fictions de l'identitaire au Québec*. Montréal: XYZ, 1991.

Simonds, Merilyn. *The Holding*. 2004. Toronto: McClelland & Stewart, 2005.

Skidmore, James. "Urquhart's Fairytale: The German Cultural Imaginary in *The Stone Carvers*." *Refractions of Germany in Canadian Literature and Culture*. Ed. Heinz Antor, et al. Berlin: De Gruyer, 2003. 319-330.

Slemon, Stephen. "Climbing Mount Everest: Postcolonialism in the Culture of Ascent."

Smith 51-73.

Smith, Rowland. Introduction. ibid. 1-10.

Sollors, Werner, ed. *Theories of Ethnicity*. New York: NYUP, 1996.

Sparling, Don. "History and Identity – The Case of Historical Fiction." *Exploring Canadian Identities*. Eds. Anna Branach-Kallas, Ewa Welnic and Jakub Wójcik. Toru´n: Wydawnictwo Uniwersytetu Mikolaja Kopernika, 2002. 251-260.

Stachniak, Eva. *The Garden of Venus*. London: Harper Collins, 2005.

Staines, David, ed. *The Canadian Imagination: Dimensions of a Literary Culture*. Cambridge: Harvard, 1977.

Staines, David. "Canadian Literature at the Millennium." *Canada And the Millennium – Proceedings of the 2nd Canadian Studies Conference in Central Europe: A Selection*. Ed. Anna Jakabfi. Budapest: Loránd Eötvös University and the Hungarian Canadianists' Association, 1999. 32-44.

---. "The Pillars of Canadian Non-Fiction." Ertler and Löschnigg, *Inventing Canada* 17-32.

Steenman-Marcusse, Conny. *Re-Writing Pioneer Women in Anglo-Canadian Literature*. Amsterdam-Atlanta: Rodopi, 2001.

---, ed. *The Rhetoric of Canadian Writing*. Amsterdam: Rodopi, 2002.

Stenson, Fred. *Lightening*. Vancouver: Douglas & McIntyre, 2003.

---. *The Trade*. Vancouver: Douglas & McIntyre, 2000.

Sugars, Cynthia. "Original Sin, or, The Last of the First Ancestors: Michael Crummey's *River Thieves*." *English Studies in Canada*. 31:4 (2005 Dec): 147-75.Soja, Edward W. *Postmodern Geographies: The Reassertion of Space in Critical Social Theory*. London: Verso, 1989.

---. "The Hands of Chance and Change." Review. *Books in Canada. The Canadian Review of Books*. Online. 2 July 2008. http://www.booksincanada.com/article_view.asp?id=4558

---, ed. *Unhomely States: Theorizing English-Canadian Postcolonialism*. Peterborough: Broadview Press, 2004.

Swan, Susan. *The Biggest Woman of the World*. Toronto: Lester & Orpen Dennys , 1983.

Tassinari, Lamberto. "La Reprise." *Vice Versa*. N° 48 (Jan-Fév 1995): 1.

---. "Le pouvoir et ses phantasms: La nostalgie du pouvoir et ses représentations dans les media et le corps policier au Québec." *Vice Versa*. N° 22-23 (1988): 4-5.

---. "Why this Triangular Vice Versa?" *Vice Versa*. N° 49 (1995): 1.

Taylor, Charles. *Multiculturalism: Examining the Politics of Recognition*. Ed. and Introd. by Amy Gutman. Princeton: Princeton UP, 1994.

Taylor, Drew Hayden. "A Blurry Image on the Six O'Clock News." The Dominion Institute. *Our Story*. 221-243.

"Tecumseh." *The Canadian Encyclopedia*. 24 May 2009. http://www.thecanadianencyclopedia.com/index.cfm?PgNm=TCE&Params=A1ARTA0007898

Teelucksingh, Jerome. "Carribean Rebels: Examining Dionne Brand's At the Full and Change of the Moon." Revisiting Slave Narratives – Les avatars contemporains des récits d'esclaves. Texts collected by Judith Misrahi-Barak. Coll. "Les Carnets du Cerpac" n°2. Université Montpellier III. Montpellier: Centre d'Études et de Recherches sur les Pays du Commonwealth, 2005.

The Canadian Encyclopedia. Online. www.thecanadianencyclopedia.com

The Dominion Institute. "About." *The Dominion Institute – Memory/Democracy/Identity*. 22 May 2009. http://www.dominion.ca/about.htm

The Dominion Institute, ed. *Our Story: Aboriginal Voices on Canada's Past*. 2004. Collection of Stories. Toronto: Anchor Canada, 2005.Smith, Rowland, ed. Postcolonizing the Commonwealth: Studies in Literature and Culture. Waterloo (ON): Wilfrid Laurier UP, 2000.

Thien, Madeleine. *Certainty*. 2006. Faber & Faber: London, 2007.

Tomlinson, John. *Globalization and Culture*. Chicago: UoChicago Press, 1999.

Tough, David. "Trudeau through the Looking Glass." Review. *The Underhill Review: A Forum of History, Ideas, and Culture*. Fall 2008. 23 Apr. 2009. http://www.carleton.ca/underhillreview/08/fall/reviews/tough.htm

Tunkel, Nora. "Deconstructing the Multicultural Myth – Transcultural Imaginaries in Madeleine Thien's *Certainty*." Ertler and Löschnigg, *Inventing Canada* 113-126.

---. "Historical Fiction in the Light of Globalization – Transnationalism, Transculturalism and Identities." *Transcultural Perspectives on Canada / Perspectives transculturelles sur le Canada*. Ed. Klaus-Dieter Ertler and Paulina Mickiewicz. Canadian Studies in Europe Vol.7. Brno: CEACS / Masaryk University, 2007. 157-174.

---. "Mapping the Glass Labyrinths of the Past – Re/Constructing Identities in Jane Urquhart's *A Map of Glass*." *Space and Gender: Spaces of Difference in Canadian Women's Fiction*. Ed. Doris Eibl and Caroline Rosenthal. Innsbruck: University of Innsbruck Press, 2009.

Uglow, Nathan. "Waverley, Or Tis Sixty Years Since." 18 June 2002. *The Literary Encyclopedia*. 24 Aug. 2008. http://www.litencyc.com/php/sworks.php?rec=true&UID=9046.

Umar, Yusuf K., ed. *George Grant and the Future of Canada*. With a Foreword by Barry Cooper. Calgary: UoCalgary Press, 1992.

Urquhart, Jane. *A Map of Glass*. London: Bloomsbury, 2005. (U.K. Edition)

---. *Away*. 1993. New York: Penguin, 1995.

---. *The Stone Carvers*. 2001. London: Bloomsbury, 2001. (U.K. Edition)

---. *The Underpainter*. 1997. London: Bloomsbury, 1998. (U.K. Edition)

Vanderhaeghe, Guy. *The Englishman's Boy*. 1996. Toronto: McClelland&Stewart, 1997.

---. *The Last Crossing*. New York: Grove Press, 2002. (U.S. Edition)

Van Schendel, Nicolas. "Nationalité, langue, et transculture." *Vice Versa*. N° 27 (Déc 1989): 22-25.

Van Toorn, Penny. "Aboriginal Writing." Kröller 22-48.

Vassanji, M.G. *The Book of Secrets*. 1994. Toronto: McClelland&Stewart, 1997.

Vautier, Marie. *New World Myth: Postmodernism and Postcolonialism in Canadian Fiction*. Montreal: McGill-Queen's UP, 1998.

---. "Religion, Postcolonial Side-by-sideness, and *la transculture*." Moss 268-281.

Verduyn, Christl, ed. *Literary Pluralities*. Peterborough (ON): Broadview Press, 1998.

Wadell, Elizabeth. "*Divisadero* by Michael Ondaatje." Review. *The Quarterly Conversations: "Good lit crit for good readers."* Issue 8 (Summer 2007). 7 Mar. 2009. http://quarterlyconversation.com/divisadero-by-michael-ondaatje-review.

Wainwright, J.A. "Trudeau: Long March & Shining Path." Review. *Antigonish Review*. #151. 23 Apr. 2009. http://www.antigonishreview.com/bi-151/151-review-ja-wainwright.html

Weisenmiller, Mark. Interview with Michael Ondaatje. "We live in an Age of Migration." *Full Moon Fever: Sublime Reflections*. Tampa, Florida, US, Aug 23, 2007. 7 Mar. 2009. http://fullmoonfever.wordpress.com/2007/10/18/we-live-in-an-age-of-migration-interview-with-michael-ondaatje/

Wells, Paul, Benoit Aubin, and Martin Patriquin. "Election 2007 Changes Quebec's Political Landscape." *Maclean's*. 9 April 2007. 10 Jan. 2009. http://www.thecanadianencyclopedia.com/index.cfm?PgNm=TCE&Params=M1ARTM001 3047

Welsch, Wolfgang. "Transculturality – The Puzzling Form of Cultures Today." Featherstone and Lash 194-213. *Prof. Dr. Wolfgang Welsch*. Homepage. "Online Texts." 19 Dec. 2006. http://www2.uni-jena.de/welsch

Wesseling, Elisabeth. *Writing History as a Prophet: Postmodernist Innovations of the Historical Novel*. Amsterdam: J.Benjamins Publishing Company, 1991.

Westwind Pictures. Official homepage. 20 Dec. 2008. www.westwindpictures.com.

"Whoop-Up." *The Canadian Encyclopedia*. 5 May 2009. http://www.thecanadianencyclopedia.com/index.cfm?PgNm=TCE&Params=A1ARTA0008 573

Wiebe, Rudy. *A Discovery of Stranger*. 1994. Toronto: Vintage Canada, 1995.

---. *Sweeter Than All the World*. Toronto: Knopf, 2001.

---. *The Blue Mountains of China*. 1970. Toronto: McClelland&Stewart, 1975.

---. *The Scorched-Wood People*. Toronto: McClelland&Stewart, 1977.

---. *The Temptations of Big Bear*. 1973. Toronto: McClelland&Stewart, 1995.

Wilson, Rob, and Wimal Dissanayake, eds. *Global/Local: Cultural Production and the Transnational Imaginary*. Durham: Duke University Press, 1996.

---. Introduction. "Tracking the Global/Local." 1-18.

Woodcock, George. "Away From Lost Worlds." ibid. 1-11.

---. *Odysseus Ever Returning: Essays on Canadian Writers and Writing*. Introduction by W.H. New. Toronto: McClelland and Stewart, 1970.

---. "Views of Canadian Criticism." ibid. 130-143.

Wylie, Hal. "The Cosmopolitan Condé, or Unscrambling the Worlds." *World Literature Today*. Vol. 67, Issue 4 (Autumn 1993): 763-769. *Literature Online*. 5 Feb. 2009. http://search.ebscohost.com/login.aspx?direct=true&db=hlh&AN=9408022443&site=ehost-live">The cosmopolitan Conde, or unscrambling the worlds

Wyile, Herb, Jennifer Andrews, and Robert Viau. "Introduction: Past Matters/Choses du passé." *Studies in Canadian Literature / Études en Littérature Canadienne*. Vol 27.1. (2002): 5-14.

Wyile, Herb. "Dances with Wolvers: Choreographing History in *The Englishman's Boy*." *Essays on Canadian Writing*. N° 67 (Spring 1999): 23-52.

---. "Doing the Honourable Thing: Guy Vanderhaeghe's *The Last Crossing*." *Canadian Literature*. 185 (Summer 2005): 59-74. *Literature Online*. 28 Oct. 2007. http://gateway.proquest.com/openurl/openurl?ctx_ver=Z39.88-2003&xri:pqil:res_ver=0.2&r es_id=xri:lion&rft_id=xri:lion:rec:mla:R03824738

---. Interview with G.E. Clarke. "We Have to Recover their Bodies." ibid., *Speaking in the Past Tense* 133-164.

---. Interview with Guy Vanderhaeghe. "Making History." ibid., *Speaking in the Past Tense* 25-51.

---. Interview with Jane Urquhart. "Confessions of a Historical Geographer." ibid., *Speaking in the Past Tense* 79-103.

---. Introduction. ibid., *Speaking in the Past Tense* 1-24.

---. "Making a Mess of Things: Postcolonialism, Canadian Literature, and the Ethical Turn." *University of Toronto Quarterly*. Vol. 76, N° 3 (Summer 2007): 821-837.

---. "Ransom Revisited: The Aesthetic of Regionalism in a Globalized Age." *Canadian Review of American Studies / Revue canadienne d'études américaines*. Vol. 28, N°2 (1998): 99-117.

---. "Regionalism, Postcolonialism, and (Canadian) Writing: A Comparative Approach for Postnational Times." *Essays on Canadian Writing*. N°63 (Spring 1998): 139-161.

---. *Speaking in the Past Tense: Canadian Novelists on Writing Historical Fiction*. Waterloo (ON): WLU, 2007.

---. *Speculative Fictions: Contemporary Canadian Novelists and the Writing of History*. Montreal and Kingston: McGill-Queen's University Press, 2002.

Yaeger, Patricia, ed. *The Geography of Identity*. Ann Arbor: UoMichigan Press, 1996.

---. Introduction. "Narrating Space." ibid. 1-38.

Zacharasiewicz, Waldemar. "Rereading Frye." Review of O'Grady and Staines, *Northrop Frye on Canada*. *Canadian Literature*. N° 189 (Summer 2006): 168-169.

Zimmermann, Jutta. *Metafiktion im Anglokanadischen Roman der Gegenwart*. Trier: WVT, 1996.

---. "The New Sentimentalism in Recent Canadian Fiction." *Zeitschrift für Kanada-Studien*. 25. Jahrgang, Nr. 2, Bd. 47 (2005): 87-102.

Index

Author

Nora Tunkel received her M.Phil. in English and American Studies and Romance Studies from the University of Vienna in 2005. She has worked as a research assistant, tutor, and assistant conference organizer at the Center for Canadian Studies in Vienna. From 2006 to 2008 she was a member of the Steering Committee of the Graduate Students' Forum of the German Association for Canadian Studies (GKS). She is the co-editor of *Apropos Canada / Á propos du Canada. Fünf Jahre Graduiertenkonferenzen* (2010). Between 2008 and 2010 she completed an inter- and transdisciplinary training program dealing with the role of science for a future-oriented and visionary society at the "Fakultät für Interdisziplinäre Forschung und Fortbildung" (IFF / University of Klagenfurt).